Phaedo and *Euthyphro*

The *Phaedo*:
A Platonic Labyrinth

and

"On Plato's *Euthyphro*"

Ronna Burger

ST. AUGUSTINE'S PRESS
South Bend, Indiana
2025

St. Augustine's Press, South Bend, Indiana 46680
© 2024 by Ronna Burger
First paperback edition © 1999 by Ronna Burger
First edition © 1984 by Yale University Press
"On Plato's *Euthyphro*"—Über Platons *Euthyphron* (Reihe "Themen," Bd. 100)
© 2015 Carl Friedrich von Siemens Stiftung, München

1 2 3 4 5 6   29 28 27 26 25 24

ISBN 978-158731-670-8 (paperback)
ISBN 978-158731-671-5 (ebook)

Library of Congress Cataloging-in-Publication Data

Author: Burger, Ronna, 1947–
Title: The Phaedo: A Platonic labyrinth and On Plato's Euthyphro.
Description: New and expanded edition. | South Bend, Indiana :
    St. Augustine's Press, 2024. |
    Includes bibliographical references and indexes. |
    Originally published: New Haven : Yale University Press, c. 1984.
Identifiers: LCCN 2024938058 | ISBN 978-158731-670-8 (paperback)
    ISBN 978-158731-671-5 (ebook)
Subjects: Plato. Phaedo. | Plato. Euthyphro. | Philosophy, Ancient.
Classification: LCC B379.B87 2024
LC record available at https://lccn.loc.gov/2024938058

∞ This paper meets the minimum requirements of the ANSI Sciences
Permanence of Paper for Printed Materials, ANSI Z39.48–1984.

The typefaces used in this book are Monotype Ehrhardt and Palatino.
Images:
    Theseus in the Labyrinth, Bayerische Staatsbibliothek, München
    (Clm. 14731, Fol. 82 v.)
    Menelaus and Proteus, *Emblems of Achilles Bocchius*, Plate 61
    ©The Trustees of the British Museum

Interior design by Susan P. Johnson

Published by
St. Augustine's Press
www.staugustine.net

Printed and bound by CPI Group (UK) Ltd, Croydon, CR0 4YY

εἰς μνήμην
Seth Benardete (1930–2001)

For Robert Berman

Contents

Note to the Reader

The Phaedo: A Platonic Labyrinth, first published by Yale University Press in 1984, is reprinted here largely unaltered. That study follows the underlying argument of the dialogue as it advances a critique of the doctrines of Platonism while disclosing their motivation. My interpretation has not changed significantly, but my treatment would differ now partly in response to a new body of scholarship, which appeared after my book was written, that adopts an approach akin to mine (see p. xxxii, n. 4 below).

The Preface to this volume is a revision and expansion of the one that appeared in the paperback edition of the book by St. Augustine's Press in 1999. "The Death of Socrates and the Post-Socratic Schools" is intended as a free-standing essay that reconsiders the dialogue through a double lens. It explores, first, Socrates' intellectual autobiography and the one moment in the dialogue when he recalls the political conditions of his current situation, illustrating what a true cause is by the decisions he made in response to his trial and conviction. That in turn leads to a reflection on Plato's concern with the fate of philosophy, more precisely, political philosophy, after the death of Socrates.

"On Plato's *Euthyphro*," which completes this volume, was originally published by The Carl Friedrich von Siemens Stiftung in 2015.

Acknowledgments

My enduring recognition of the special debts acknowledged in the original edition of this work is indicated by the memorial inscription and dedication in this volume. Seth Benardete, with whom I first studied the *Phaedo* over forty years ago, is still present as a silent voice in my internal dialogue. The manuscript for my book on the *Phaedo* was written while on a fellowship in Germany in 1979–1980 with my husband, Robert Berman. The pleasures of "living together" (συζῆν), over all the years since then, include the conversations that enliven every day, by which my ideas have been clarified, extended, and enriched.

The role of Plato as a guide, not only in my studies but in my understanding of life, has grown through "sharing speeches and thoughts" with friends, in particular with graduate students who have kept the excitement of discovery fresh for decades. I am fortunate to hold the Catherine & Henry J. Gaisman Chair at Tulane, which has provided the conditions to pursue writing, teaching, and programming in mutually enhancing ways. I am grateful to Heinrich Meier for the opportunity to present my study of the *Euthyphro* in a public lecture in 2010 at The Carl Friedrich von Siemens Stiftung in Munich and for our discussions of it. I owe thanks to the Stiftung for publishing the essay based on that lecture, with Wiebke Meier's German translation ("Themen," Bd. 100) and for granting permission to reprint it now.

I am indebted to Susan Johnson for her skillful preparation of the manuscript. I want to acknowledge, in memory, Bruce Fingerhut, who produced the previous version of this study, and now his son Benjamin, who is supporting this new edition and carrying on the work of St. Augustine's Press. The Bayerische Staatsbibliothek granted permission to reprint the cover image, CUM MINOTHAURO PUGNAT THESEUS [IN] LABORINTO (1175–1200), and the British Museum to reprint the engraving by Giulio Bonasone of Menelaus wrestling with Proteus (1555), used as frontispiece to the *Euthyphro*.

New Orleans, Summer 2024

Preface

The Death of Socrates and the Post-Socratic Schools

> The philosophy that answers to this description [of the true philosopher] was handed down to us by the Greeks from Plato and Aristotle only. Both have given us an account of philosophy, but not without giving us also an account of the ways to it and of the ways to re-establish it when it becomes confused or extinct.
>
> —Alfarabi, *The Attainment of Happiness*, §63[1]

I. *Remembering the Trial of Socrates: The Extended Center of the Phaedo*

Plato's Socrates as *the* exemplar of the philosopher and the philosophic life comes to light nowhere more vividly than in the inspiring depiction of his death day. He spends the hours conversing with his young companions, providing a model for them to follow in accepting the end of his life. Of course, Plato includes some signs of the limits of the philosopher's seemingly perfect equanimity. And Socrates' attempt to persuade his companions to overcome their confused condition of resentment and pity, fear and sorrow at the imminent loss of their teacher and friend does not—could not—simply succeed. Yet his effort to redirect their concerns to preserving "the life of the *logos*" is not a failure. Plato, in any case, through his portrayal of Socrates on this last day, rescues for posterity confidence in *logos*—not perhaps the argument for immortality of the soul, but the possibility and worth of ongoing philosophic inquiry.

That Platonic portrayal is accomplished by embedding speeches in the context of deeds. Despite the young men's understandable objections to the arguments, they are encouraged, if mystified, by the composure Socrates exhibits. At his trial Socrates rejected fear of death on the grounds of our ignorance of what, if anything, comes after life as we know it. Now he goes further: for the lover of wisdom, at least, death should be most welcome. After all, the "genuine philosopher" would believe that his lifelong desire for knowledge of the beings could be fulfilled only with the release of his soul from the prison of the body. But the flawed arguments that follow, supposedly to provide support for that claim, expose problems that end up threatening trust in reason itself. In the course of confronting that danger, Socrates offers a report of the theoretical stumbling blocks he himself encountered as he began his own quest for knowledge. He was able to save reason in the face of those obstacles and disappointments thanks to his discovery of a new way of philosophizing, "taking refuge in speeches." He carried out this Socratic turn through examination of the opinions of his fellow citizens and others, above all opinions about the just, the beautiful, and the good. That practice, however, has led to a crisis now at its culmination, for Socrates and perhaps for the future of philosophy. The arguments devoted to the question of immortality cover over, almost completely, the real sign of that crisis at the end of Socrates' life: the imprisonment, not of his soul in his body, but of himself by the city, as he awaits legal execution. The significance of that reality Socrates will address at only one moment in the conversation, just before introducing the account of his distinctive philosophic turn. His reflection at that point implicitly recalls the conversation he conducted in the prison cell days before with his old friend Crito.

On that occasion Socrates engages in a deliberation about his predicament by constructing an imaginary dialogue with the personified laws of Athens: if, he warns himself, he were to run away to a nearby, well-governed city like Thebes or Megara, he would be looked upon as a corrupter of the laws, which would only confirm the jurors in the conviction that their verdict was correct, since a corrupter of the laws might well be thought a corrupter of thoughtless youth (53b). The historical Socrates did not try to save his life by running off to Thebes or Megara. But the Socrates of the Platonic dialogues, with his indictment and trial in mind, figures out a way to send philosophy off to safety outside Athens. He provides the narrator of the *Theaetetus* with a version of Socratic philosophy to carry to Megara. And he entrusts his final conversation to the narrator of the *Phaedo*, who transports it to Phlius, home of a community associated with the Pythagoreans of Thebes.

This suggestion situates the *Phaedo* within the Platonic corpus by placing it, on the one hand, at the conclusion of the sequence of seven dialogues leading up to and following Socrates' trial,[2] on the other, in the set of four dialogues in which a Socratic conversation is reconstructed years after the original occasion by a narrator other than Socrates himself.[3] The links that bind the *Phaedo* to those two groups of dialogues are forged at that one moment when Socrates explicitly comments on the political circumstances of his present situation, looking back to his trial and conviction: he would not be in prison now but in Megara or Boeotia (Theban territory), led by an opinion of what is best, had he not had other reasons for deciding to abide by the verdict of the Athenian jury (99a). This statement proves to be the displaced center of Plato's labyrinth.[4]

The position from which it is displaced is the quantitative center of the *Phaedo*, the turning point that sets the argument in a new direction as it moves from the first to the second half of the dialogue. At that point, Phaedo reports, after all the attempted proofs of immortality had failed, everyone present was filled with distrust, not just in their preceding efforts, but in the power of argument altogether (88c). Echecrates, who is listening to the report, interrupts to express his own despair and beg Phaedo to tell him, "by Zeus!," how Socrates rescued the *logos*. It was indeed wondrous, Phaedo responds, the way Socrates recalled them all from their flight, encouraging him, in particular, not to mourn for the death of Socrates but for the death of the *logos* if it could not be brought back to life. Socrates armed them by identifying the monster they were facing in the labyrinth of their arguments: the experience of "misology." Like the condition of misanthropy, when an overly idealistic standard of human nature leads finally to cynical disillusionment with human beings, an innocent trust in the power of *logos* unguided by an art of speeches is apt to meet with repeated disappointment, which could result in the bitter condition of misology.[5] There is no greater evil, Socrates warns, than this hatred of speech, by which we would deprive ourselves of the only way to seek truth and knowledge of the beings (89d–90d).[6] This warning is indeed a pivotal moment in the dialogue, but it is only a starting point; its task of redirection is not completed until Socrates outlines an art of speeches that should avert the peril of misology, which he will apply in one last reconsideration of what it means for the soul to be deathless.

Socrates seems to be carrying out a strategic plan: he aroused the dissatisfaction of his interlocutors, as Simmias and Cebes confirm, in response to the original series of arguments for the immortality of the soul in order to diminish—if not overcome—it with an art of speeches that would allow the investigation to continue.[7] Phaedo's report of Socrates' *technē* of *logoi* will induce Echecrates to interrupt once again at that point to express his admiration, "by Zeus!," for the wondrous clarity now brought to the discussion, even (or especially?!) for one having little sense (*smikron noun*, 102a). The two moments at which the narrative exchange disrupts the flow of the reported conversation, reaffirming in the present the experience of the original occasion, together form a frame: what that frame encloses is the extended center of the *Phaedo*, which effects the turnaround of the dialogue's underlying argument through a dynamism of its own, as it moves from the despair of misology to the safety of the Socratic art of speeches.

At the center of this extended center (95e), Phaedo tells us that Socrates fell into a deep silence. He had taken up Simmias' objection to the preceding arguments for immortality and turned to Cebes, but after being absorbed in thought for some time, he broadens and deepens the still unanswered problem before them. It requires, Socrates explains, a consideration of the cause of coming to be and passing away as a whole and he offers to report his own past experience in pursuing that kind of knowledge. Socrates will recount two different stages of that youthful pursuit, with distinct obstacles that led him to relinquish the endeavor of his predecessors, and he will offer two different descriptions of the new path he discovered, each meant to address the particular difficulties he encountered.

Socrates begins his personal story with what looks like the starting point of philosophy as such—a wondrous eagerness for the wisdom called "inquiry into nature." He thought it would be splendid to know the causes of each thing, why it comes to be or perishes and—as if it were the same sort of question—why, or through what, it is. How do animals grow, how do the senses, memory, and opinion produce knowledge, and how again are these things destroyed (96a–b)? The young Socrates was already interested in life and cognition—functions of the human soul. But assuming that subject to be part of a greater whole, his curiosity extended to the conditions of heaven and earth, only in the end to find himself so "blinded" that he lost all confidence in what he previously believed he knew. This is a productive blindness, it seems, that amounted to or resulted in a certain knowledge of ignorance along with a discovery about his own nature—his lack of fitness for the sort of investigation in which he had been engaged.

It sounds as if Socrates must have been stopped short by problems he discovered in his original, seemingly common-sense opinions concerning the matter or mechanisms of natural processes, such as how someone grows and becomes great from small. Instead, looking back on those opinions, he sketches a series of apparent contradictions he came to see in the logic of great and small, culminating in a puzzle about mathematical operations: What is the subject that becomes two when one and one are brought together? And how could that operation be the cause of two coming to be when the same result could just as well be produced by the contrary cause, dividing one in half? What might sound like worry about a sophistic charge of inconsistency was evidently enough for Socrates to abandon the investigation of nature altogether.[8] He does not pause in his report to consider now how different the dyad of one whole with its internal division might be from the dyad of independent one's added together, though that is the core of the question of body and soul, life and death, that their entire conversation is exploring.[9] Instead, he maintains that the allegedly self-contradictory explanation of two led him to realize he no longer knew how one, or in fact how anything at all comes to be, passes away or is.[10] Feeling compelled to give up on such causal analysis of nature, he turned to "mixing up" at random some other way of his own (97b).

Before offering any further description, Socrates introduces a second stage of his search for knowledge of nature. This new development attracted him with the promise of some kind of rational necessity, though it comes to his awareness by a chance encounter: One day he happened to hear someone reading from a book by Anaxagoras, identifying mind as that which orders the whole and is the cause of all things (97c).[11] That claim indicates what would be required for the natural universe to be truly a "cosmos," a rationally ordered whole of parts.[12] Socrates draws his own inference from the Anaxagorean thesis: if mind orders all things, it must do so looking to the good as an end. Mind infused with longing for its own good might sound like a formula for philosophic *erōs*. But on the view Socrates attributes to Anaxagoras, mind is in possession of a knowledge of the good that enables it to perform its function of establishing order. The work of mind, Socrates assumes, is not just the formation of an intelligible pattern, but the arrangement of a whole in light of what is best for each and good for all in common (98b). Fulfilling that twofold standard would require a divine mind to solve for the natural universe what looks like an insurmountable problem for a political community and its individual members. Enticed, in any case, by his own interpretation, Socrates found the teaching of Anaxagoras most pleasing (*kata noun*), literally "in accordance with mind": a universe governed by a cosmic mind looking to the good is suspiciously satisfying to the human mind.[13] Socrates pinned his last hopes for knowledge of nature on the conception of teleological cosmology that he imposed on Anaxagoras. But the pre-Socratic, while invoking mind as the cause of order in the whole, offered nothing but material, mechanistic accounts of natural processes, which Socrates had already found, in their very logic, reasons for rejecting.

Socrates now presents different grounds for a critique of such accounts when he explains his disappointment in teleological cosmology by drawing upon an analogy with his own action in the present state of affairs: Anaxagoras' failure to demonstrate the work of mind looking to the good in the mechanical operations of nature would be equivalent to maintaining that Socrates does everything by mind, then trying to explain why he is now sitting in prison by describing the structure and movement of his bones and sinews, or offering, as the causes of the conversation they are holding, voice and air and hearing, and never mentioning the true causes (98c–e). We have arrived here at the fulcrum of the dialogue: the clarification Socrates is about to provide of those true causes lies at the center of his intellectual autobiography, which began in turn midway through the extended center of the *Phaedo*.[14]

At the heart of his narrative about how Socratic philosophy came to be, Socrates inserts a reflection on how his current situation has come to be. Supposedly only to illustrate what a true cause is, he elaborates for the first time what has led to this conversation taking place in the Athenian prison in the hours before he will drink the hemlock and fulfill the sentence of the city's court. He defended himself at the outset against a potential accusation of impiety for violating a divine prohibition against suicide, while his interlocutors put him on trial for his injustice in willingly abandoning them and his imprudence in leaving behind gods who are good masters (61e–63b). No one asks Socrates about the series of decisions he has been making in the course of the six conversations leading up to this last: to pick up the indictment, to attend the trial and conduct it in a certain spirit, to remain in prison after the trial when it would have been feasible to escape, and finally, to defy the prison authority who warned him in the morning that talking all day would heat him up and make it harder for the hemlock to work effectively (63d–e). He now offers one final analysis of the motivating reasons for the actions he has taken.

Socrates makes two statements, separated by a counterfactual: since it seemed better to the Athenians to condemn him, it seemed better to him to sit where he now finds himself and more just to undergo the penalty they commanded. For "by the dog," Socrates adds, he believes his bones and sinews would have been in Megara or Boeotia long ago, transported by an opinion of the best if he hadn't thought it more just and more noble or beautiful, instead of fleeing and running away, to undergo the penalty ordered by the city (99a). According to his initial statement, Socrates' decision is a response to the judgment of Athens, and to that extent what he found better was determined by, or at least consistent with, the standard of the just. In his restatement, Socrates articulates the alternatives over which he has been deliberating—fleeing or remaining; and the standard in light of which he decided to act includes, not only the authority of the city's law, but also a desire to leave behind a model of the beautiful or noble. His immediate opinion held the preservation of life to be the desired end, powerful enough to have moved his bones and sinews in its service.[15] Describing his rejection of that option in favor of the more just and more beautiful, Socrates makes his decision sound like a matter of moral self-sacrifice. He does not clarify what the good is to which his mind must have been directed while taking into account the more just and beautiful under the circumstances. He does not elaborate the process of deliberation that would have been required, for which he was prepared by a lifetime of investigation. Weighing in the end his choice and action, Socrates arrived at a considered opinion, at least, of his true self-interest.[16] Plato leaves that for his reader to uncover more fully.

Having introduced the analysis of his own action as a model for his critique of Anaxagoras, Socrates returns to spell out its implications. A causal account would have to recognize that he could not be sitting in prison as he is without the mechanical operation of his bones and sinews, or conversing with his companions without the mechanical operation of voice and air and sounds; these are only the conditions, however, that make possible the work of what is really the cause—the choice he came to make after deliberation about what would be best. For a parallel account of the natural world, material-mechanistic operations should not be rejected, but would have to be understood as necessary conditions for the causal role of mind ordering all things in the cosmos looking to the good. Of course, this is a standard Socrates himself imposed, while an immanent critique would accuse Anaxagoras of failing to show mind at work in any way at all. Socrates concludes his assessment, however, with a charge against all the cosmologists, who are blamed for ignoring the role of "the good and the necessary" in binding together (99c): only a teleological analysis, he implies, of mind looking to the good, is capable of accounting for a whole of parts.[17] Socrates does not insist on the impossibility of such a cosmological counterpart to his own action—that would be an inconsistent claim to knowledge of the whole—but only his inability to discover it himself or learn it from another.

Looking back on this disillusionment, which brought his journey to a stand-still, Socrates explains how, with the winds failing, he had to row for himself, on a "second sailing in search of the cause" (99d).[18] The misgivings that led to this ostensible lowering of his goal call to mind the skepticism Simmias expressed when he prepared for his objection to the first round of arguments: despite the great difficulty, if not impossibility, of knowing anything certain about the matters they had been discussing, it would be a sign of real weakness to avoid testing everything in an effort to discover the way things are or learn from another; but if that fails, one must sail through the dangers of life on a raft of the human account that seems least refutable, unless a more safe journey on some divine account is available (85c–d). Simmias does not explicate what he means by a "divine *logos*," which seems to count for him as the best option. The doctrine of recollection, which inspired such great trust in himself and Cebes, might have come to mind; but Simmias considered it an hypothesis accepted on sufficient and correct grounds, by comparison with the more refutable doctrine of the soul as a harmony (91e–92a). At this point, Simmias has not yet heard Socrates' report of his disappointed hope for an account of divine mind ordering the whole cosmos, which sounds as if it would have to be revealed through a divine *logos*. Perhaps he will think of the concluding myth Socrates offers him as a divine *logos*, which could go beyond the limits of the last argument.[19] The doubts Simmias raises, in any case, might sound disturbingly close to those Socrates experienced in his search for knowledge of nature; but Socrates proves able to save reason precisely by abandoning illusory ideals about its capacity. The "raft" he is about to introduce as the vehicle of his second sailing aims to provide the safety that renders hope for a more secure divine account unnecessary, and thus prevents the despair that would follow if that hope is not fulfilled.

Socrates probed the nature of such despair in his warning about misology, resulting from an unrealistic expectation about the power of argument. That threat loomed in the promise of a teleological cosmology, with its requirement for knowledge of the good that guides mind's ordering of the beings in the universe as a whole. But the collapse of that promise did not throw Socrates into a state of bitter disillusionment; instead, it led him to realize the mistaken assumptions of the project he was pursuing, and with that the need for and the possibility of a second sailing. He offers an extended analogy now to illustrate the danger he came to understand and the way he found to avoid it. Just as one risks blinding one's eyes trying to look directly at the sun in an eclipse, rather than turning to a reflected image, one risks blinding one's soul trying to grasp things of concern (*pragmata*) through the senses without an analogous precaution (99d–e). The objects we see with our eyes are naturally visible in the light of the sun, but staring at the sun itself is blinding, above all in the darkness of an eclipse, when one might be tempted to gaze at it directly, unaware of its harmful power.[20] If analogous, truth as the medium in which the mind knows and the intelligible beings are known would be a product of the good, but trying to apprehend the good directly blinds the soul, above all when unaware of its hidden effect. Socrates speaks now, however, of being blinded by trying to look directly at the *pragmata*, in the midst of explaining why he abandoned investigation of the beings: his image of the eclipsed sun implicitly raises the question of the relation between the good and the beings.

Socrates' description of the harmful and self-defeating effort to grasp things through the senses sounds like the frustrated hope of the genuine philosophers, who resent the body as the impediment to their longing for the soul's direct access to the beings themselves (65c–67b). But that very longing indicates the real problem the Socratic second sailing is designed to address. The attempt to apprehend reality directly, unaware of our susceptibility to the blinding light of the good, leads to mistaking the *pragmata* for the beings: the obfuscating filter is not sense perception, but the occluded good of our partial or mistaken self-interest, which shines through the things of concern and darkens our understanding, especially if we are unmindful of its impact.

To avoid the danger of being blinded by the eclipsed sun, we need to recognize as far as possible its nature and power; hence, as Socrates concludes his image, we need an indirect way to see the sun, by looking at its image in water or some reflected surface and inferring what it is like from that.[21] To avoid the danger of blinding our soul, we must find an analogous path to understanding the nature of the good and its effect on our discernment of the beings. Socrates found such a path by taking refuge in *logoi* and seeking in that medium the truth of the beings (99e). The truth of the beings is not revealed to the human mind in the noetic light of the openly shining good; our access is filtered through the whole realm of opinion, individual and collective, colored by the hidden good of our attachments, our hopes and concerns. The way to the truth of the beings requires becoming aware of our opinions, their implications and limitations, which is possible only through examination in speeches or arguments.

Socrates has been relying on an extended image to illustrate his turn to *logoi*, but he qualifies its status finally with the comment that investigating in speeches is no more a reliance on images than examining deeds (*erga*) would be. Perhaps neither should be understood as images of the beings. But if Socrates means they both together serve that purpose, each a potential corrective of the other, that relation is artfully exemplified by the Platonic dialogue. The intertwining of speeches and deeds is exhibited more dramatically in the *Phaedo*, perhaps, than any other dialogue: Socrates restored confidence in human reason, Phaedo stresses, not only by his words but also by his conduct in the face of death and the fear it naturally inspires (58e–59a, 88e–89a). Of course, it is Plato's written image that represents this relation of speeches and deeds; but that pair shows up again applied to the dialogue itself, as its underlying argument unfolds through an action of its own, and our interpretation must uncover the *logos* of the whole through that *ergon*.

Socrates offers the account of his second sailing to explain why he had to turn away from investigation of nature and reject, in particular, the expectation he formed based on his construal of Anaxagorean mind. He clarified the letdown of that expectation by an analogy with his own action confronting death, determined by mind looking to the good—or at least an opinion of what is best. That action encapsulates the whole meaning of his life, yet Socrates brings it up almost as an aside, for the merely instrumental purpose of illustrating, by contrast, the unfulfilled prospect of mind looking to the good in ordering the cosmos. The breakdown of the analogy has far-reaching consequences. While human action, governed as it is by deliberation and choice, is a natural fit for teleological treatment, our ignorance of any counterpart in the natural universe means that human life cannot be understood by appeal to first principles of a homogenous whole.[22] The Socratic turn to *logoi*, in that case, might be expected to consist in a restriction to "the human things" in place of the investigation of nature as a whole.[23] Yet Plato's Socrates does not speak that way. In fact, his recognition of the special character of the human things provides the key to a new conception of the whole: the particular domain of political philosophy, carved out by the Socratic turn, furnishes the evidence for an understanding of being as a plurality of intelligible kinds.

Only because of this comprehensive consequence can the Socratic turn to *logoi* serve as the medium for examination of "the truth of the beings."

Socrates goes on to elucidate the procedure constitutive of that examination by recommending a hypothetical method of reasoning and the "safe answer" it puts to work with the hypothesis of the "ideas."[24] If this Socratic art of speeches provides the way to preserve trust in reason, it does so through a radical reconstruction of the ideas: the separate beings accessible only to a soul released from the body after death are now reinterpreted as the first hypothesis for a *technē* of *logoi*. Of course, Socrates leaves much to be clarified when he refers to these ideas as simply the things he is always babbling about (cf. 76d), and Cebes grants the hypothetical ideas with no questions, encouraged by Socrates' assurance that with this premise they will be able to "display the cause" and "discover the soul as deathless" (100b). Socrates introduces the *idea* here as a safe, albeit uninformative answer to why any particular becomes and is what it is. It sounds as if it should stamp the seal of a conclusion on any investigation. In fact, it shows up in Plato's representations of Socratic conversation as essentially interrogative—the more so, the more deeply understood. What is knowledge? What is the holy? What is virtue? What is justice? What is courage? What is moderation? What is law? What is friendship? What is love? If, in addressing those questions, the examination of opinion considers particular instances that "participate" in the idea, it is for the sake of discovering an adequate definition of the idea itself.[25] Far from providing a safe answer, what we might call this "zetetic form" is the starting point that sets philosophic inquiry in motion and the challenge that incites its continuation.

At the moment, Socrates illustrates the hypothesis of the ideas by returning to the question of the cause of two with advice for Cebes, describing the fear he should feel before the "monster" of self-contradiction. While Cebes understandably laughs at this threat, he accepts Socrates' demand that he must cling to the safe answer in the face of it. He is to shout out loud that he knows no cause of anything becoming two other than its participation in the dyad and to dismiss all wise causes—the source of the puzzles that compelled Socrates to abandon his investigation of nature. Cebes should leave all such refined causal accounts, like two coming to be from the addition of two units or the division of one into two, to "those who are wiser" (101a–c). The *technē* of *logoi* not only serves to save philosophy from any sophistic charge of self-contradiction; it also enables "the wiser" to proceed with the causal accounts required for mathematics and the investigation of nature. Socrates will soon find a way to bring back for his own purposes a refined cause of how something comes to be and perishes, but only insofar as it is derived from the safety of the admittedly "simple, artless, and perhaps foolish" cause (100d). The extension of that safe answer enables Socrates to construct the one last argument he promised for a deathless soul (100b): just as the *idea* of life necessarily excludes death, if soul is essentially that which brings life to the body, it too will never admit the opposite, but at the approach of death must either withdraw or perish (105c–e). The principle of non-contradiction establishes the "immortality" of the soul, as long as it exists.[26] Socrates must have applied that principle in coming to his own decision about facing death: given the defining identity of his life of examination, when the opposite approached through the verdict of the court, he realized he could not remain Socrates and give up philosophy, but must either withdraw or perish.

Preparing for the account of his second sailing, Socrates had presented two stages of his thwarted quest for knowledge of nature, two different kinds of resulting blindness (96c, 99e–100a), and with that, two motivations for his turn to *logoi*. After outlining his initial doubts about knowing how any being comes to be or is, Socrates referred to the discovery of a path of his own; his abrupt introduction of Anaxagoras at that point, with no obvious connection to what preceded, prepares in advance for the question of the relation between the beings and the good. That question underlies the two stages in Socrates' explanation of the path on which he embarked, in reverse order of the problems he had to address. His image of the blinding light of the eclipsed sun conveys the need for a new way of proceeding given the unfulfilled task of a teleological cosmology. His account of a hypothetical method of reasoning explicitly addresses the number problem, or the disputatious exploitation of it on the charge of opposite causes producing the same effect.[27] But how is the safe answer to that problem provided by the ideas related to the safety offered by Socrates' second sailing against the danger of being blinded by the occluded good? The hypothetical method is supposed to illustrate the art of speeches that should preserve trust in human reason. But the *technē* of *logoi*, as the very formula suggests, cannot itself explain and defend the goodness of human reason; it does not reflect on the quest for knowledge and its driving force, the impediments and the satisfactions. It is silent about the experiences of wonder and perplexity, knowledge of ignorance, dialogic interaction and the relation of opinions to souls. The speeches of the *Phaedo* do not explicitly yoke the *technē* of *logoi* to the human good, in particular, to the philosopher's *erōs* for wisdom. But the action of the dialogue does exhibit that link: whatever its limits may be, Socrates' appeal to an art of speeches accomplishes his goal on the occasion of avoiding despair and restoring faith in their investigation. Echecrates at the end is as eager for Phaedo to go on with the conversation as Socrates' companions were on the original occasion, and Plato's reader in observing that transformation.

Restoring confidence in reason was a need Socrates felt, surely for his companions, but perhaps also for himself, confronting the situation at the end of his life and the decisions required. He did confess his worry that he might be speaking on this occasion, not as a lover of wisdom but a lover of victory, above all in an effort of self-persuasion (91a–b). Socrates' initial opinion of the best, he admitted, would have moved his bones and sinews to preserve life had he not had a way of protecting his soul from the blindness produced by that immediate interest. Investigation in *logoi* furnished that protection: Socrates could come to understand the depth and breadth of his true self-interest only by examining in speeches the complexity and inner structure of the good he was seeking. If self-preservation is desirable, what is the self that should be preserved?[28] What is it exactly that makes life worth living? How is the meaning of one's own life connected with what one leaves behind for the future? What is the relation of the human good to the just and the beautiful?

Socrates' search for an understanding of his true self-interest had to go through the city and the realm of opinions, in particular about the beautiful and the just. It is striking, though, that with his present audience Socrates only hints at the questions he had to think through in order to reject the option of exile in defiance of the Athenian court. In some way he seems less open with this inner circle than he was with the whole jury of citizens when he told them that a life without philosophy is not worth living (*Apology* 38a). Yet, while he holds back now from spelling out in full the true causal account of his present situation, he does, even if only for a brief moment, bring to light the circumstances under which he is acting and that is enough to correct for the impression the *Phaedo* might have otherwise supplied. Socrates did not seek death on the basis of a proof or a wager about the immortality of the soul; he is not one of the genuine philosophers, who long for death as a purification of the soul from the contamination of the body (64b–67b).[29] At the center of the dialogue, we get a glimpse of the real deliberation that brought Socrates to this last day in prison. The choice he came to make involved reflection on the relation of the just, the beautiful, and the good, and with that, on the philosopher's relation to the city, more specifically, his own relation to Athens. Socrates' account of that choice looks as if it is just a digression within an objective report on his youthful intellectual development. In fact, it is through the lens of this reflection on his current situation that Socrates must be looking back on the obstacles he discovered in pre-Socratic philosophy and the turn he took to overcome them.

II. *Plato's Non-Socratic Narrations and the Schools of Philosophy*

Socrates' explanation of how he came to understand the good in the decisions he made at the end of his life exemplifies his turn to *logoi* and his discovery of political philosophy. But that discovery seems to have brought about a paradoxical consequence: the conversation Socrates conducts as he sits in prison awaiting death exhibits a strikingly apolitical image of the philosopher. Conveying that image requires the cooperation Socrates elicits from the narrator of the *Phaedo*, who transmits the conversation of the philosopher's death day. Socrates is even more involved in working together with the narrator of the *Theaetetus*, repeatedly rehearsing during his last weeks the first conversation that sets in motion the sequence of his trial and execution. Socrates, who refrained his whole life from writing, is concerned at the end, in Plato's portrayal, with the problem of passing on his legacy.

Besides these two reported conversations set at the end of Socrates' life, two other dialogues in the Platonic corpus present Socratic conversations as ascribed to non-Socratic narrators, more precisely, through a complicated chain of narrative reiterations, in the course of which the figure of Socrates becomes an increasingly distant echo. These two, the *Parmenides* and the *Symposium*, prove to be those dialogues that, together with Socrates' autobiography in the *Phaedo*, make the coming to be of Socratic philosophy an explicit theme. In the one, we hear at third hand of a very young Socrates—his earliest appearance in Plato's fictional world—meeting up with the venerable Parmenides, who offers his criticisms of Socrates' newly discovered "theory of ideas." In the other, we hear one version of a second-hand report, which in turn contains Socrates' own recollection of his early encounter with the mentor he conjures—a wise woman and seer, Diotima—who initiated him into the erotica.

However divergent Diotima's teaching on *erōs* may be from Parmenides' critique of the ideas, both instructors target in common the defect they perceive in Socrates: in his neglect of or disdain for the ugly and defective in contrast with the beautiful and perfect, they see a youthful vulnerability to the power of human opinions.[30] Whatever Plato's Parmenides and Socrates' Diotima might have had in mind, Socrates clearly did not gain from them an understanding of philosophy's task as an attempt to turn away from human opinion; on the contrary, from the critique each one issued he must have inferred the need to examine opinion in order not to be determined by it unawares. The second sailing Socrates came to pursue, by investigating the truth of the beings in *logoi*, is rooted in that realization.

While Plato never speaks in any dialogue in his own name, he adds another layer of distance or absence by rendering Socratic conversation through the eyes of his non-Socratic narrators. By choosing this narrative form for the dialogues that present the stages of Socrates' education, Plato stands back behind the story of Socrates on the way to becoming who he is.[31] Plato separates himself once again from his narrators' accounts of Socrates before his death, faced with the problem of how Socratic philosophy can live on, detached from the life of the man. Whatever the dramatic date and context might be, the Socrates of the dramatic dialogues is in a sense a timeless one; what we see, in contrast, through the eyes of the narrators Plato depicts is a pre-Socratic Socrates, or a post-Socratic one.[32] If the four dialogues that reflect these narrators' perspectives could be understood to compose a whole, it would be governed by a double set of paired principles—motion and rest, *erōs* and death—that belong to philosophy as such; but the Socrates who appears within that comprehensive whole is one who has not yet made or fully appreciated his characteristic philosophic turn, or one who appears no longer committed to it. There is, however, a difference between this "not yet" and "no longer."

In his encounter with Parmenides and his reported education by Diotima, a youthful Socrates has still to discover, or at least to realize the import of his distinctive philosophic identity.[33] In the conversations he conducts at the end of his life, to be preserved after he is gone, he deliberately covers it over. The philosopher, as Socrates portrays him—to the delight of the mathematician Theodorus—lives in leisure and perfect freedom, in contrast with the rhetorician enslaved by the necessities of the lawcourt; an utter stranger in the market and other public places, the philosopher dwells in the city in body alone, while his thought, disdaining all petty human concerns, is borne everywhere, beneath the earth, "geometrizing" on the surface of the earth, and "astronomizing" above the heavens (*Theaetetus* 173e).[34] These words take on a different tone, of course, for the reader who remembers that this is the conversation from which Socrates departs to receive the city's indictment against him (210d), and he is recounting it sometime after that, including, presumably, after his trial, while sitting in prison awaiting execution.[35] The philosopher, as Socrates introduces him to the young men in the *Phaedo*, is indifferent to the city but a bitter enemy of the body, held back from his longing to free himself through death only by a divine prohibition (61e–62c). Imagining an accusation against himself for violating that prohibition, Socrates appeals to "some necessity a god has now sent upon us" (62c): a theological-political problem is lurking in Socrates' attributing or extending to a god the real necessity imposed by the verdict of the Athenian court.[36] An attempt to correct the misleading implications of the images constructed by the narrators of the *Theaetetus* and *Phaedo* might direct us to the portrait Socrates paints of himself at his trial—spending his days in the streets of Athens, questioning the citizens and refuting them, practicing his service to the god, which is the greatest good to the city (*Apology* 29d–30a). But that is a self-presentation under very particular circumstances in need of its own corrections.

Lying on the horizon of the Platonic corpus as a whole is always this paradox: Socrates, so unique an individual that he can be compared to no other human being, real or fictional, is at the same time *the* paradigm of the philosopher as such.[37] What is to become of philosophy after this exemplary individual is gone? There is surely no guarantee that one great thinker at a particular moment in history will be followed directly by another—the sequence of Socrates, Plato, and Aristotle looks like a miracle! The traces of a philosopher's living thought must be preserved and passed on by a school or plurality of schools, each bound to carve off some partial aspect of the original.[38] In the *Theaetetus*, the transmission of Socrates' conversation with the young mathematician is ascribed to an author known as the founder of the Megarian school, reported to a fellow member.[39] In the *Phaedo*, Socrates' last conversation is transmitted by a narrator who will establish his own school, reported to the founder of a Pythagorean community, a fitting audience for Socrates' conversation with two young Thebans who belong to the Pythagorean tradition.[40] In choosing the narrators of these conversations, Plato's Socrates is portrayed facing in advance the problem of his own necessary but perhaps impossible replacement.

The schools that are indispensable for the preservation and transmission of a tradition can accomplish that task, it seems, only by turning the dynamic of genuine thinking into doctrines. Plato's art of writing shows itself nowhere more brilliantly than in the way he exhibits and overcomes that problem. The argument of the *Theaetetus* involves a critique of the presuppositions and implications of the Megarian doctrines, in particular, the denial of potentiality. The *Phaedo*, even more manifestly, is a critique of the apparent contradictions among "Pythagorean" doctrines, especially the idea of the soul as a harmony, at least as Simmias interprets it, with the notion of the soul's transmigration.[41] Plato presents through representatives of the post-Socratic schools conversations that undermine the tenets of those schools.

That strategy is thematic in the *Sophist*, set on the day after Socrates' conversation with Theaetetus. Introduced on that occasion to a Stranger from Elea, Socrates expresses fear that he may be a punitive god in disguise, come to punish him for some "weakness in speeches" (*Sophist* 216a–b; cf. *Theaetetus* 196d–197a). Socrates is assured that the Stranger is no god, just "a very philosophic man," but the philosopher, Socrates knows, is as hard to recognize as the gods: his hidden being must be uncovered from the phantom images in which he appears, above all, as sophist and statesman. Assigning the investigation of that problem to the Stranger, Socrates seems to anticipate that it will amount to a trial of Socratic philosophy. The Stranger does indeed employ a new, technical form of analysis, the method of division, which might appear to claim superiority to Socrates' seemingly informal mode of conversation. To accomplish his task of separating the philosopher from the sophist, however, the Stranger will be compelled to commit an act of intellectual parricide and argue against his Parmenidean heritage. He prepares for that development when he completes his initial set of divisions with one that uses the method to show its own limits while vindicating the distinctive Socratic practice.[42] Like the narrators of the *Theaetetus* and the *Phaedo*, Plato's Eleatic Stranger is one more representative—in this case with self-awareness—of a school whose teachings come under scrutiny as a satisfactory replacement of Socratic philosophy.

The perpetuation of a tradition after its founding faces a special challenge in the case of Socrates' discovery of political philosophy, represented in Plato's dialogues: while pre-Socratic philosophy—ontology or cosmology—preceded this Socratic discovery, the post-Socratic schools are depicted reverting in some way to that starting point.[43] With the sects that emerge after the death of Socrates, the understanding of political philosophy as the "eccentric core" of philosophy goes underground.[44] The philosopher appears as the theoretical man in the *Theaetetus*, the ascetic in the *Phaedo*; and Plato's reader is challenged to find the Socratic political philosopher amidst those appearances. Images of the "pure" philosopher—detached from the city, resentful of the body, practicing a technical method of analysis—cover over Socrates' effort to call philosophy down from the heavens and introduce her into the homes and the cities. Whatever the case may be for the actual historical schools, in Plato's hands their apolitical portrait of the philosopher serves in part a rhetorical purpose—a response to the crisis brought about by the trial of Socrates and its ongoing consequences. In the middle of his last conversation, Socrates warned his companions of the great evil of misology, which amounts to the self-destruction of philosophy from within. But there is also a misology writ large, we might say, exhibited in the city that found Socrates' examination of opinion so threatening it condemned him to death. Socrates, in his death-day conversation, struggles to save philosophy from internal self-destruction; Plato, through his art of writing, portrays that effort and draws his reader into it, while aiming at the same time to protect philosophy from the potential, lethal misology of the city.[45]

Plato's depiction of the post-Socratic schools, their doctrines and traditions, suggests what ancient philosophy would have become if we did not have in the Platonic dialogue the enactment of Socratic philosophy through the representation of the living Socrates. The realism of that representation shows the limits of Socrates' urging Phaedo and the others not to mourn for his death.[46] But Socrates does offer a horizon for experiencing or understanding that loss when he advises mourning instead for the death of the *logos* if they fail to keep it alive: he identifies the meaning of his life with the life of the *logos*. If that counts as the philosopher's paradoxical practice of dying and being dead, it is accomplished, finally, by Plato's writing.[47] No Plato without Socrates, no fulfillment of Socrates' life and death without Plato: the Platonic Socrates is a true indeterminate dyad.

Plato's dialogues preserve the life of the *logos* by their recovery of Socratic political philosophy, which requires the rediscovery of Socrates the individual. That rediscovery is possible because Plato's Socrates discloses himself enough to make us aware of what he has hidden—his sudden reflection, for example, on the political conditions of his situation at the center of the *Phaedo*. Surely Socrates' collision with the city has brought a painful recognition of the need to be circumspect; but Plato indicates, beyond that pressure, the intrinsic and essential grounds for the need to uncover the being of the philosopher behind his appearances. If the philosopher is a hunter—hence so hard to tell apart from the sophist—it is because the beings he seeks to know do not offer themselves openly to him; he has to camouflage himself, and come upon his prey in a crafty way, without being sure what he will track down.[48] The problem is acute when it is the philosopher himself who is the ultimate object of the search. It is as necessary to find an indirect path as it is in the case of the blinding light of the eclipsed good. When Socratic philosophy leaves the Athenian prison in the form of Plato's narrated dialogues, it does so just as Socrates worries he would have had to do—wrapped in a leather skin or whatever disguise runaways don to change their own figure (*Crito* 53d).[49]

---

1   Alfarabi, *The Attainment of Happiness*, in *Philosophy of Plato and Aristotle*, 49. See n. 43 below.

2   The sequence is: *Theaetetus, Euthyphro, Sophist, Statesman, Apology, Crito, Phaedo*. A quartet of the utmost practical urgency for Socrates—from the indictment and trial to his imprisonment and death—is linked to a theoretical trilogy, beginning with the question "What is knowledge?," and proceeding to the pair of dialogues on sophist and statesman, which together indirectly raise the question, "Who or what is the philosopher?"

Given their content and the relations among them, these seven dialogues constitute an exclusive set. But that calls for an explanation of Socrates' claim in the *Cratylus* that he had just spoken earlier with Euthyphro, as if his "inspired" examination of language were continuing a conversation with the seer (396d). The *Euthydemus*, as Gwenda-lin Grewal's reading shows, is another dialogue that belongs on the horizon of Socrates' death (see *Thinking of Death in Plato's Euthydemus*, especially 1–6).

Even among the core seven dialogues, there are issues with the ordering Plato has chosen. The dramatic form of the *Theaetetus* introduces complications about its place in the series (see nn. 3 and 35 below). And the position of the *Euthyphro* is a puzzle: the action of the dialogue—Socrates' meeting with the "seer" at the Stoa of the King where he picks up the indictment—should lead directly to the Athenian courtroom; but the argument of the dialogue, with its inquiry, "What is the holy?," places it in the framework of the trilogy, intervening between the *Theaetetus* and the *Sophist*.

3   The four are: *Parmenides, Symposium, Theaetetus, Phaedo*. Although the *Theaetetus* has a place in this set for a number of reasons, it is really a unique case: as we learn from the opening of the dialogue, the conversation Socrates had with the mathematicians Theaetetus and Theodorus before his trial, he rehearses repeatedly after that with Euclides, who visits regularly from Megara in the time leading to Socrates' death. Writing up the conversation, Euclides turns Socrates' narration into dramatic form, which he has his slave boy read aloud many years later. With this dialogue, Leo Strauss remarks, Plato "permits us a glimpse into his workshop by making us the witnesses of the transformation of a narrated dialogue into a performed one" (*The City and Man*, 58–59). Cf. n. 35 below.

PREFACE

4   On the structure of the center of the dialogue, see n. 14 below.

    Several illuminating interpretations that have appeared in the decades since the original version of this book was written shed light on the autobiography Socrates presents in the center of the *Phaedo* and the work as a whole. Among studies that share a common approach to the reading of a Platonic dialogue, those I have found especially fruitful include the following (see the publication information in the Bibliography): Peter Ahrensdorf, *The Death of Socrates and the Life of Philosophy: An Interpretation of Plato's Phaedo*; Jesse Bailey, *Logos and Psyche in the Phaedo*; Seth Benardete, "On Plato's *Phaedo*," in *The Argument of the Action*; David Bolotin, "The Life of Philosophy and the Immortality of the Soul: An Introduction to Plato's *Phaedo*"; Eva Brann, Peter Kalkavage, and Eric Salem, Plato's *Phaedo*, with Translation, Introduction and Glossary; Jacob Howland, *The Paradox of Political Philosophy*; Laurence Lampert, *How Socrates Became Socrates: A Study of Plato's Phaedo, Parmenides, and Symposium*; M. Ross Romero, *Without the Least Tremor: The Sacrifice of Socrates in Plato's Phaedo*; Dustin Sebell, *The Socratic Turn: Knowledge of Good and Evil in an Age of Science*; Paul Stern, *Socratic Rationalism and Political Philosophy: An Interpretation of Plato's Phaedo*; and David White, *Myth and Metaphysics in Plato's Phaedo*.

5   The Eleatic Stranger in Plato's *Sophist* sees this experience as an effect of the sophist's art of imitation, which he analyzes on the model of the painter's art. An artist might make visual images that deceive the foolish young who stand at a distance from the beings, so they come to think he is most competent to do anything, as long as they don't draw closer to the objects of imitation. In the parallel, though not identical case, the sophist enchants those who stand at a distance from the truth of things (*pragmata*) with verbal images that seem to be truly spoken while the speaker appears wisest in everything; but as the young mature, inevitable disappointments in life could incline them to overturn completely the beliefs they once held (234b–c). It is not just "the sophist" in some narrow sense, but all moral education of the young that faces such a challenge, when later experience can lead, not necessarily to discovery of the truth, but only to the inversion of an earlier idealism.

    Aristotle brings this problem to light when he begins his account of pleasure in Book 10 of the *Nicomachean Ethics* with the view that pleasure is altogether base—a view held by some persuaded of it, but others who think it salutary to combat the natural attraction of pleasure. This is not a helpful strategy, Aristotle argues, since speeches will inevitably be compared with deeds and if someone who blames all pleasure is ever seen aiming at it, it will undermine whatever germ of truth there is in the view he puts forward. The problem of misology lurks in Aristotle's warning at the beginning of the *Ethics* about the importance of a proper expectation for the inquiry, since too high a demand is bound to lead to disappointment, which could threaten confidence in the capacity of reason to address questions about human life in any meaningful way (1094b12–19).

6   One can suffer "no greater evil" than hatred of *logoi*, Socrates warns Phaedo, if we blame arguments themselves that do not satisfy our expectations instead of recognizing how we ourselves may be falling short (89d). Svetozar Minkov raises the question how this is related to the point Socrates makes earlier to Cebes, about the soul of the true philosopher calculating that "the greatest and most extreme evil" lies in the experience of intense pleasure or pain, which binds the soul to the body and prevents departing to Hades in purity (83c–d). Are the two claims more closely connected than it might appear? Or is the message to Phaedo a correction of the true philosophers' understanding of the greatest evil?

7   Socrates' strategy depends in part on not explicitly addressing the question, "What
     is the soul?," relying instead on various assumptions needed in the sequence of argu-
     ments. While (or perhaps because) soul looms so large for Plato, it is always treated,
     Michael Davis observes, "as instrumental to an inquiry into something else," in the
     Republic justice, in the *Phaedrus* love, and in the *Phaedo* fear of death (*The Soul of the
     Greeks*, 19). As the action of the *Phaedo* unfolds through Socrates' evolving confronta-
     tion with the fear of death, the conception of the human soul changes with it.
8   The stumbling block here, Robert Berman proposes, involves the problem of mathe-
     matical physics: Socrates' inability to explain how two comes to be results from erro-
     neously imposing on arithmetic operations the categories of efficient cause, which
     then leads him to give up altogether the search for such causes in nature. Cf. "the true
     perplexity" Maimonides ponders in an astronomical theory that furnishes an accurate
     mathematical account of the motions of the stars but only on assumptions that violate
     the principles of Aristotelian physics (*The Guide of the Perplexed* 2.24, 325–36).
9   The difficulty Socrates faced in explaining the composition of two out of two units is
     exemplified by the puzzle he poses to Hippias about themselves conversing together:
     how could *each* of them be one, but not *both* that which each is, since *both* are two (*Hip-
     pias Major* 301d–302b)? See Jacob Klein's account of this "arithmological structure"
     in its application to the ideas, in *Greek Mathematics and the Origin of Algebra*, especially
     81–82, 89–91.
        Seth Benardete differentiates two formal structures: a "conjunctive two," as a pair
     of independent subjects that each retains its own identity, in contrast with a "disjunc-
     tive two," as an "indeterminate dyad" of elements integrally connected in one whole,
     each defined solely by its relation to the other. He finds the distinction first illustrated
     in the *Phaedo* by Socrates' twofold description of the mixture of pleasure and pain he
     experiences after the shackles are removed from his leg (60b–c). The two structures
     then underlie the dialogue as a whole, where the opening arguments consider soul and
     body in their separability, as a conjunctive two, while the soul in the final argument,
     which cannot admit death, belongs to the disjunctive two of an ensouled body. See
     "On Plato's *Phaedo*," 282–283, 286.
10   Socrates finally arrives at the question of how *one* comes to be or is, having started
     with the problems he encountered in relations *of the great and small* (96b). Are we to
     think of the two principles that, according to Aristotle, exhibit the Pythagorean back-
     ground of Plato's ontology—the unlimited or indeterminate as a dyad of the great
     and the small and the limit in the form of the one (*Metaphysics* Book 1.6, 987b24–27,
     988a11–14)? The two stages, then, of Socrates' youthful quest for knowledge would
     target two issues of pre-Socratic thought and the Platonic response: Pythagorean num-
     ber theory in relation to ideas and Anaxagorean mind in relation to the good. It's strik-
     ing that they are taken up together in the *Philebus*: on the good, see especially 20c–d,
     60c; on great and small in the class of the unlimited, 24c–25c, 42b; on the idea-monads
     and arithmetic number, 14d–15c, 56c–57d.
11   What Socrates describes in the *Phaedo* as his own contingent development, Aristotle
     traces, in Book 1 of the *Metaphysics*, as the necessary progression of thought itself: the
     starting point with material cause leads naturally to the need for some source of mo-
     tion, but when those two together are "found inadequate to generate the nature of
     things," the truth itself made it necessary to look for another cause, in order to account
     for goodness and beauty in being and becoming (984b9–13). A more complicated route
     leads eventually to Plato's neo-Pythagorean, neo-Socratic conception of the forms

(987b1–15). Michael Davis reflects on this account in "Philosophy and the Question of Being in Aristotle's *Metaphysics* A." On Aristotle's critique of Anaxagoras in this context, see my essay, "Eros and Mind: Aristotle on Philosophic Friendship and the Cosmos of Life," 8, n. 21, n. 30.

Dustin Sebell follows Socrates' trajectory through a careful examination of the problems he encountered, first in failing to see the primacy of form while seeking the material-efficient causes of natural science, then in considering the failed promise of teleology to account for the nature of the beings. Noting the unexpected turn Socrates makes to Anaxagoras after sketching his disappointment with natural science without fully explaining it, Sebell raises the question whether and how the treatment of teleology might cast light on the grounds for that original disappointment (*The Socratic Turn: Knowledge of Good and Evil in an Age of Science*, 47ff.).

12 The Anaxagorean thesis extends to the natural universe the principle of "logographic necessity" as the standard for a beautifully composed written work (*Phaedrus* 264b–c).

13 In the course of the *Philebus* debate whether pleasure or mind is the good, Socrates assigns pleasure, as well as pain, to the class of the unlimited. When he then asks—playfully, as he claims—to what class mind should be assigned without impiety, he offers his own "easy" answer: all the wise agree in claiming mind is king for us on heaven and earth, which is really a matter of magnifying themselves (28a–c).

14 The concentric centers of the *Phaedo* have this structure:

88c	95c	99a	102a
Socrates' warning against misology narrative interruption (center of the dialogue)	Socrates' autobiography (center of extended center)	The true causes of Socrates' situation (center of Socrates' autobiography)	Socrates' *technē* of *logoi* narrative interruption (conclusion of extended center)

15 This immediate opinion of the best displays the same life-preserving impulse that Socrates claims his *daimonion* fostered up until the day of his trial (*Apology* 40a–c). Socrates rejected that opinion insofar as it required exile, which, the "laws" in the *Crito* argue, would have prevented him from continuing the kind of life he believed worth living (52e–53e). Socrates' decision to accept the city's death sentence is in fact an affirmation of the goodness of life—of his life—not an embrace of death. The tragic Antigone represents an essential contrast, encapsulated in her devotion to burial and attachment to Hades. Cf. Evanthia Speliotis, "Enlightened Piety in Sophocles' *Antigone*," 3–26.

16 Socrates' reasoning at the end of his life reveals the good to be, as Benardete puts it, a "complex of three things whose unity is as puzzling as its fragmentation" (*Socrates' Second Sailing: On Plato's Republic*, 4).

The deliberation that must have led Socrates to his final decision would be the work of *phronēsis* or prudence, the kind of thoughtfulness in action that he identified as the "only genuine coinage" of virtue, in contrast with the ordinary understanding of courage or moderation, which simply exchanges one kind of fear or one kind of desire for another (69a–c). But that cannot be what the genuine philosophers have in mind when they blame the body as the obstacle to the soul's grasping the beings through *phronēsis* (65a–b, 66a), always frustrating their *erōs* for *phronēsis* (68a–b). This might appear to support the common view that Plato, unlike Aristotle, does not sharply differentiate theoretical and practical wisdom; but the use of *phronēsis* as some kind of intellectual intuition, which could be an object of *erōs*, looks rather like one sign among others of an implicit critique of the genuine philosophers. It is corrected when Socrates introduces his final myth stressing the need to become as *phronimos* as possible by the proper care for the soul (107d), and when Phaedo concludes his whole narration identifying Socrates as the most *phronimos* and most just of his time.

17 Aristotle's *Metaphysics* is devoted to an investigation of being as such, seeking an account of the first causes of being *qua* being (4.1). It is when ontology is replaced by cosmology, in *Metaphysics Lambda*, that the argument concerns not simply the attributes of beings as such, but the cosmos as an ordered whole, unified by a highest good (12.7). Aristotle illustrates the relation of the good and the cosmos through the image of an army, with the question whether its good lies in the order of the whole or in the leader: in both, he answers, but more in the leader, since he does not depend on the order of the whole but it depends on him (12.10, 1075a11–19).

18 Plato's Eleatic Stranger develops an extensive critique of law by contrast with the flexibility and precision of decisions by the wise statesman; but as the discussion unfolds, its critique of what might be thought best leads to the conclusion that rule by law is a necessary "second sailing" (*Statesman* 300c).

Aristotle uses Socrates' formula in his investigation of virtue once he acknowledges the great difficulty—perhaps impossibility—of hitting the mean directly and recommends instead resorting to the "second sailing" of avoiding the worse extreme (1109a34–35). Of course, Plato's Socrates embarks on his second sailing by taking "refuge in *logoi*," while Aristotle seems to imply his critique by using that expression in mocking the many, who "believe they are philosophizing" merely by listening to speeches without performing the requisite deeds—like a sick person who believes he will become healthy merely by receiving a doctor's prescription (1105b12–16). See my comments in Aristotle's *Dialogue with Socrates: On the Nicomachean Ethics*, 52, 61–62.

19 Arguing against Simmias' interpretation of soul as a harmony determined by bodily elements, Socrates will appeal to the "divine poet" Homer (94d–e), whose verses depict Odysseus' internal struggle for self-control (*Odyssey* 20.17–18). Socrates cites the same Homeric passage in Book 3 of the *Republic* to illustrate beneficial poetry that encourages endurance in the face of challenges (390d); but in Book 4, he uses these verses to support his account of a tripartite soul, supposedly illustrating in this case the calculative part rebuking the spirited (441b–c). Cf. my analysis in "The Thumotic Soul," 158–60.

20 The image of the sun in the *Phaedo* invites comparison with the *Republic*, where Socrates presents the sun as the "offspring" of the good, "the counterpart in the visible region to the good in the intelligible region" (508a–509a). His analogy there of the soul grasping the intelligible beings in the medium of the truth produced by the good, like the eye seeing the visible beings in the light produced by the sun, conveys a conception of knowledge like that of the *Phaedo*'s genuine philosophers, imagining the condition of the pure soul after death. The possibility of such knowledge is represented in the cave image of *Republic* 7, when Socrates depicts the experience of someone who manages to escape from the city's world of shadows: adjusting to the light outside, he would advance from looking at images to gazing directly at the natural beings, and finally at the sun itself (515e–516c). Of course, this series of images—from the sun to the divided line to the cave—is colored by the purpose it is meant to serve, justifying rule in the best city by a philosopher-king on the basis of his extraordinary knowledge. Plato offers the hint of a correction by his allusion to Socrates, not outside the cave contemplating the sun, but *inside*, standing with a prisoner watching the passing artifacts that cast the shadows on the wall and asking "What is it?" (515d).

21 Maimonides employs a similar image in the Introduction to Part 1 of *The Guide of the Perplexed*, speaking of the incomplete disclosure of the "great secrets." After describing the intermittent lightning flash of the truth that illuminates the dark night to varying degrees for different prophets, he ends with a condition of darkness brightened only by a polished stone that reflects light, even if just to flash before being hidden again, like the flaming sword that guards the way back into the Garden of Eden after the expulsion (4b). The impossibility of an unmediated revelation and the necessity of an indirect path guides Maimonides' reading of Moses' exchange with God preparing for a second giving of the Law (*Guide* 1.54). God warns Moses, "Thou canst not see My face, for man shall not see Me and live," but He does grant him the privilege of seeing His back as He withdraws (Ex. 33:20, 33:23). Cf. Maimonides' analysis of the biblical terms, "face" and "back" (*Guide* 1.37 and 38).

Maimonides' different treatment of this issue in *Eight Chapters* sounds like the genuine philosophers of the *Phaedo*: while the other prophets see God through many veils, or a few, Moses has only one diaphanous veil, which the Sages likened to a transparent glass (*sefaqlaria*). This last veil is "the unseparated human intellect," that is, the condition of embodiment (ch. 7, 80–83). In the last chapter of this work, Maimonides explicitly compares the inadequacy of our intellects to perceive God in His perfection with "the inadequacy of the light of our vision to perceive the light of the sun" (ch. 8, 95). But in this context, he does not propose the possibility of turning to a reflective light from a "polished stone," the equivalent in *The Guide of the Perplexed* to the Socratic second sailing.

In Aristotle's striking simile: "As the eyes of bats are to the blaze of day, so is the mind in our soul to the things that are by nature most evident of all" (*Metaphysics* α, 993b9–10). Joseph Albo adopts the image in the *Book of Roots* (2.29)—"By reason of the intensity of the sun's light the eyes of the bat are dimmed, so that it cannot look at the sun, nor enjoy its light as the other animals do"—but only to contrast that condition with the eagle, "which, by reason of its intense power of vision, takes pleasure in light and flies high by reason of its desire to get near to it." Cf. Strauss, "Maimonides' Statement on Political Science," 169.

22 Socrates' turn to the study of the human things was based, as Strauss puts it, "not upon disregard of the divine or natural things, but upon a new approach to the understanding of all things." The special character of the human things leads to the insight that "to be" is "to be something," hence "the being of a thing or the nature of a thing, is primarily its What, its 'shape' or 'form' or 'character,' as distinguished in particular from that out of which it has come into being" (*Natural Right and History*, 122–23). Socrates' philosophic "founding" lies in a recognition of the political things as a class by themselves, but this entails an understanding of the whole characterized by distinct classes or kinds of beings accessible to thought, the condition Strauss calls "noetic heterogeneity" ("The Origins of Political Science and the Problem of Socrates: Six Public Lectures," 163).

23 In Cicero's famous words, Socrates was "the first to call philosophy down from the heavens and set her in the cities of men and bring her also into their homes and compel her to ask questions about life and death and things good and evil" (*Tusculan Disputations* 5.4.10). Xenophon tells us Socrates was "always speaking about the human things"—silently raising the question what Socrates was doing when he was not speaking (*Memorabilia* 1.1.16). The Socrates Aristotle describes, busying himself with ethical matters and neglecting nature as a whole (*Metaphysics* 987b1–4), looks as if he

belongs in an independent Aristotelian discipline, "some kind of political science" (*Nicomachean Ethics* Book 1, 1094a27–b28) or "philosophy concerning the human things" (Book 10, 1181b15). But through his investigation of ethical matters, Aristotle adds, Socrates discovered the importance of definitions, and that general discovery became the source of Plato's "ideas" (*Metaphysics* 987b5–14).

24 In the *Republic* Socrates moves from the sun as image of the good to the stages of cognition in the divided line, in which the two upper segments are characterized by two different modes of hypothetical reasoning: while the lower is illustrated by mathematical deduction, from an assumed hypothesis to consistent consequences, the highest level is supposed to be an ascent to a non-hypothetical first principle (Book 6, 510b–511c, Book 7, 533a–534c). The *Phaedo* account, in contrast, speaks only of reaching, through hypothetical reasoning "something sufficient" (101d–e). "The sufficient," which must be adequate for someone or some purpose, can be identified as one criterion for the good, "the complete or perfect" as another (*Philebus* 20d, 60c, cf. Aristotle *Nicomachean Ethics* Book 1.7, 1097a34–35, b7–16). The Socratic conversations represented in Plato's dialogues conclude not with the complete or perfect but at best with something sufficient for the interlocutor, while Socrates appreciates any progress he achieves in knowledge of ignorance. In the *Phaedo*, Cebes expresses satisfaction with the conclusion of the final argument, and Simmias goes along with it, though he maintains his general distrust of human reason, which prompts Socrates to urge that their first hypotheses would have to be examined more fully until going through them sufficiently, following the argument as fully as possible for a human being (107b).

25 "The variety of expositions of the nature of the Ideas," Stanley Rosen observes, "and the fact that these expositions are more poetic and mythical than analytical or ontological, supports the inference that Socrates (and indeed Plato) has no fully elaborated conception of the Ideas as separate entities. This does not alter his conviction that the Ideas are the 'strongest' (100a4) or 'most steadfast' (100d8) hypothesis in the following sense. They account for the presence within the flux of genesis of identifiable unities or beings of a definite look. It does not however follow that, in making beings intelligible, the Ideas are themselves fully intelligible" ("Socrates' Hypothesis," 47).

26 Socrates prepares for this conclusion with a model of natural phenomena (103c–105c). Not only does the *eidos* "the hot," as a safe causal answer, never admit its opposite, but also the more refined cause, fire, always characterized by heat, will never accept the opposite idea; so if anything cold approaches, fire cannot remain what it is and become cold, but must either withdraw or perish, and likewise snow, if anything hot approaches. On that model, the soul, which always brings life to the body, when hemlock approaches bringing death cannot remain soul and become dead but must either withdraw or perish. It would be a contradiction for soul, understood as cause of life, to be dead, but its being "deathless" does not entail being imperishable.

27 Socrates advises Cebes to follow the hypothetical method in order to avoid "mixing things up" as the disputatious do (*ouk an phuroio hōsper hoi antilogikoi*), engaging in dialogue about the starting point and consequences at the same time (101e). In response to the contradiction he found in mechanical causal accounts, Socrates had already turned to a procedure he "mixes up at random" (*eikē phurō*, 97b). Did his procedure too require correction by the hypothetical method he now outlines? Or is Socratic inquiry intrinsically resistant to the systematization of a *technē*? It is certainly amusing to hear Socrates describe the black horse of the soul, in the *Phaedrus* chariot image, as snub-nosed and put together at random (*eikē sumpephorēmenos*, 253d–e)!

28 In two books, according to Alfarabi—the *Protest of Socrates Against the Athenians* and the *Phaedo*—Plato investigated under what conditions one ought to prefer death to life. Realizing that there is no difference between living like a beast or being dead and transformed into that beast—"no difference between a man who acts like a fish, and a fish with a shape like that of a man"—"he saw that the time and life of whoever does not investigate are not those of a human being, and that he should not mind dying and preferring death to life as Socrates did" (*The Philosophy of Plato*, 63–64).

29 It is through an analysis of the art of purification that Plato connects the *Sophist* with the *Phaedo* as well as the *Theaetetus* to capture the distinctive character of Socratic philosophy. In the most elaborate division of his search for the sophist, the Eleatic Stranger contrasts his method of separating like from like with an art of purification that separates better from worse, which sounds like a version of Socrates' midwifery (*Sophist* 226d–231b). In an unexpected split between purification of ensouled bodies, inside vs. outside, and soul-less ones, the Stranger comments on all the trivial arts in that last class, such as "*kosmetikē,*" the art of beautification. Noting their many ridiculous names, he is led to observe that his own "*methodos* of the speeches" has no more concern with sponge-bathing than *pharmakon*-drinking: with this apparently casual example the Stranger suddenly invokes the death scene of the *Phaedo* and indicates the inability of his own method to evaluate the worth of life and death.

From the death of Socrates, embedded in the purification of bodies, the Stranger turns to the soul and proposes an analogy: the two bodily conditions of disease and ugliness correspond to the psychic states of inner conflict and ignorance. Perfect health of soul would be, as Theaetetus understands it, moral virtue, perfect beauty omniscience. In the absence of such perfection, bodily purification by medicine or gymnastics has its psychic counterpart in punitive justice or instruction. The Stranger finds one last cut in the instructive art by separating a single form of ignorance from all others: thinking one knows what one does not really know. Those purified of this condition of *doxosophia* grow gentle toward others, the Stranger observes, but angry with themselves; Socrates, in his self-portrait as midwife, remarked that such individuals are ready to bite him (*Theaetetus* 151c–d)! The Stranger compares the soul-purifier to the doctor who holds that the body cannot benefit from food until any impediments are removed: the treatment of ignorance as ugliness of soul, which was supposed to be the task of a psychic gymnastics, has shifted into psychic medicine. But the Stranger concludes by identifying anyone who remains unrefuted as uneducated and ugly in just the way one who is to be happy should be most pure and beautiful (230e). After indicating the limits of his own method, the Stranger's "cosmetics" proposes a beautified Socratic art of purification, which cures *doxosophia* as both disease and ugliness, while replacing the health of moral virtue and the beauty of omniscience by knowledge of ignorance.

30 Socrates, Parmenides maintains, is reluctant to admit separate ideas of hair, mud, and dirt, though he is confident about the beautiful, the just, and the good, because he dishonors such things, being young and still looking toward the opinions of human beings, philosophy not yet having taken hold of him (*Parmenides* 130e). How, Diotima presses Socrates, could he possibly accept the common opinion that Eros is a great god, when by his own account *erōs* is a desire for the good and beautiful things and must lack what it desires (*Symposium* 201e–202d)?

31 Benardete highlights three stages of Socrates' philosophic education: from his discovery of the ideas, described in the *Phaedo*, through his encounter with Parmenides,

who leaves him with the problem of the separation between divine and human knowledge, to the way out of the impasse that Diotima provides with her notion of the in-between ("On Plato's *Symposium*," 178–79). In "Plato's *Parmenides*: A Sketch," Benardete observes that only the *Parmenides* represents Socrates without the framing he himself gives to his younger self. In the *Phaedo* Socrates explains "his turn away from teleological cosmology, and in the *Symposium* he recapitulates his instruction into the mysteries of *erōs*," but the *Parmenides* provides a symbolic link between Anaxagorean mind and the erotic soul (230).

While Socrates' accounts looking back on his youth in his *Phaedo* autobiography and on the teaching of Diotima in the *Symposium* are colored by their dramatic context, "the only complete account of Socrates' education," Alex Priou argues, is the *Parmenides*. That dialogue, along with Socrates' statement at the outset of the *Sophist* and *Statesman*, make up "the Eleatic bookends to his philosophic life." See *Becoming Socrates: Political Philosophy in Plato's Parmenides*, 9–15, 208–9n21.

In *How Philosophy Became Socratic*, Laurence Lampert traces the stages in Socrates' discovery of political philosophy by considering Plato's dramatic ordering of the *Protagoras*, *Charmides*, and *Republic*. In *How Socrates Became Socrates*, Lampert examines the sequence of *Phaedo*, *Parmenides*, and *Symposium* to follow the development of Socrates' understanding of fundamental philosophic questions of being and knowing. While he contrasts the *Parmenides*' portrayal of the young Socrates with the autobiographical accounts in the *Phaedo* and *Symposium*, Lampert recognizes the common form of these dialogues as non-Socratic narrations and its essential connection with the coming to be of Socrates' way of philosophizing. See especially the Introduction, 1–5.

Socrates' own account of his intellectual development in the *Phaedo* is "somewhat sparing," as Sebell puts it, about what he learned from his later conversations with Diotima and Parmenides, while it barely touches on the "Delphic mission" Socrates describes in the *Apology*. But Sebell sets out to demonstrate the comprehensive character of the *Phaedo* account, which would make it necessary to understand the others in light of Socrates' autobiography on his death day. See *The Socratic Turn: Knowledge of Good and Evil in an Age of Science*, 21.

Catherine Zuckert analyzes the phases of the young Socrates' education indicated by his three "retrospective statements": in the *Phaedo* Socrates looks all the way back to report on how he came to the notion of the ideas he presents in his encounter with Parmenides and in the *Symposium* he describes what he learned about *erōs* that enabled him to address Parmenides' criticisms; finally, he provides "his one public explanation of how he became the distinctive kind of philosopher he is" in the *Apology*, where he traces his investigations to the command of the Delphi oracle (*Plato's Philosophers: The Coherence of the Dialogues*, 180–82). In that context, Socrates blames the long-standing prejudice he faces on Aristophanes' comic portrait of him as an investigator of the things in the heavens and beneath the earth (*Apology* 18a–19d): he does not explicitly give credit to the comic poet for a well-intentioned warning, which might supply a crucial moment in his philosophic education. Cf. n. 33 below.

32 The "first sailing" of Socrates' pre-Socratism, Michael Davis argues, illustrates the necessity of beginning in error, reproduced in the first series of arguments in the *Phaedo* ("Socrates' Pre-Socratism: Some Remarks on the Structure of Plato's *Phaedo*," 559–77). The post-Socratic Socrates, who appears in the reports of Phaedo and Euclides, is replaced, one might say, by the alternative figures Plato represents leading a conversation, especially the Eleatic Stranger and the Athenian Stranger.

33 Strauss concludes his study of Aristophanes with the observation that "it is certainly impossible to say whether the Xenophontic-Platonic Socrates owes his being as much to poetry as does the Aristophanean Socrates." But Strauss adds, "It is almost equally difficult to say" whether it is necessary to trace their "profound differences" to "a profound change in Socrates himself: to his conversion from a youthful contempt for the political or moral, things, for the human things or human beings, to a mature concern with them" (*Socrates and Aristophanes*, 314). Plato provides a critical response to Aristophanes' portrait of Socrates when, in the *Philebus*, he has Socrates illustrate the mixture of psychological pleasures and pains with a complex account of envy and laughter in the soul of the comic poet. Cf. Derek Duplessie, "Socrates' Analysis of Comedy in Plato's *Philebus*."

34 The contemplative philosopher at the conclusion of the *Nicomachean Ethics* looks like Aristotle's version of such a portrait in speech, which must be reconsidered in light of its relation to the "deed" of the inquiry leading up to it. See my analysis in *Aristotle's Dialogue with Socrates*, especially 110, 205, 227n4, 258n1.

35 Commenting on the *Theaetetus*, Benardete remarks: "Plato has imagined what the transmission of Socrates' teaching would have been like had his illness at the time of Socrates' death been fatal (*Phaedo* 59b10), and Socrates had had to rely on Euclides for getting out his message. The extreme skepticism of the Megarian school, with its reliance on nothing but *logos*, would have received its imprimatur in Euclides' *Theaetetus*. The solution to such a radical skepticism that we now find in the *Sophist* and the *Statesman* would have been missing." See "Plato's *Theaetetus*: On the Way of the *Logos*," 298.

   In *Defending Socrates: Political Philosophy Before the Tribunal of Science*, Priou investigates the unique form of the *Theaetetus* as a key to Plato's trilogy as a whole (see especially, "Overture"). The tragic understanding of Socrates that might emerge from the original conversation in fact reflects the limited perspective of Theodorus and Theaetetus. It should be corrected by re-interpreting the dialogue with an eye to Euclides' reconstruction of Socrates' account of that conversation, conveyed sometime after his encounter with the Eleatic Stranger. From that perspective, the *Theaetetus* conveys Socrates' response to the *Sophist* and *Statesman* and could thus make a claim to replace the missing but anticipated fourth dialogue, *The Philosopher*, which would complete the set.

36 Socrates had just remarked in passing that he would die on this day by the command of the Athenians (61b). The divine being to whom Socrates appeals seems to be his own internal, idiosyncratic *daimonion*: as he assures his supporters after receiving the death sentence, that prophetic voice, which usually held him back from an action that would be harmful, did not oppose him coming to the court or conducting the speech as he did (*Apology* 40a–b). Socrates must justify his decision again in the face of Crito's accusation that his stubborn refusal to escape from prison is not the conduct of a just, good, and manly man (*Crito* 45c–e). After seeking to defend himself through the voice of the personified laws of Athens, Socrates concludes by urging Crito to accept this decision as the way the god leads.

37 Plato's Alcibiades, appearing at the end of the *Symposium*, offers a vivid depiction of the utter incomparability of Socrates (221c–d). Yet, as Hegel recognizes, Socrates becomes a figure of world historical importance (*Lectures on the History of Philosophy*, 384) and Nietzsche could understandably see in him "the vortex and turning point of so-called world history" (*Birth of Tragedy*, 15). Richard Velkley discusses Hegel's understanding of Socrates' daimonic voice as a "turning-inward of consciousness" in

"On Possessed Individualism: Hegel, Socrates' Daimon, and the Modern State," especially 593–99. In Robert Berman's account, Socrates embodies the category of individuality as "virtuosity": "for all his radical singularity," Socrates "was responsible for introducing a new principle into the world." He is "the unique one who more than any other of the same best exemplifies what it is to be a philosopher." See "Ways of Being Singular: The Logic of Individuality," 124.

38 In "The History of Philosophy and the Intention of the Philosopher: Reflections on Leo Strauss," Heinrich Meier thinks through the need for and the cost of the "institutionalizing [of philosophy] in schools in order to carry it further in instruction with the aid of a growing body of doctrines." The motivation lies, in part, in the attempt to make philosophy politically respectable, but Meier asks whether "the danger of descent into a second cave" begins precisely with the success of that effort. He goes on to examine Strauss's way of seeking the intention of the philosopher behind the "petrification of philosophy in the history of its teachings and systems." See *Leo Strauss and the Theologico-Political Problem*, 61–65. Cf. Meier's essay, "Why Leo Strauss? Four Answers and One Consideration Concerning the Uses and Disadvantages of the School for the Philosophical Life," especially 202–5.

39 According to Diogenes Laertius, Euclides "applied himself to the writings of Parmenides, and his followers were called Megarians after him, then Eristics, and at a later date, Dialecticians" (*Lives of Eminent Philosophers*, 2.10.106). Plutarch mentions Terpsion, the recipient of Phaedo's report, in connection with the Megarian School (*De Genio Socratis* 518a).

40 After the death of Socrates, Phaedo is said to have founded an Elean school of philosophy. Originally, Diogenes Laertius relates, he "was a native of Elis, of noble family, who on the fall of that city was taken captive and forcibly consigned to a house of ill-fame. But he would close the door and so contrive to join Socrates' circle, and in the end Socrates induced Alcibiades or Crito with their friends to ransom him; from that time onwards he studied philosophy, as becoming for a free man" (*Lives of Eminent Philosophers*, 2.9.105). In the *Phaedo*, he meets up in Phlius—the legendary ancestral home of Pythagoras—with Echecrates, whom Diogenes Laertius mentions as the last of the Pythagoreans in that community (*Lives of Eminent Philosophers*, 8.1.45).

In *De finibus* (5.29.87), Cicero's character identifies "the whole importance of philosophy" with "the attainment of happiness," and asks whether the systems of the philosophers can achieve that, as they profess to do: Or "Why did Plato travel through Egypt to learn arithmetic and astronomy from barbarian priests? Why did he later visit Archytas at Tarentum, or the other Pythagoreans, Echecrates, Timaeus and Arion, at Locri, intending to append to his picture of Socrates an account of the Pythagorean system and to extend his studies into those branches which Socrates repudiated?"

41 Aristotle reports as the teaching of the Megarian school the assertion that "a thing 'can' act only when it is acting, and when it is not acting it 'cannot' act," and he proceeds to spell out the absurdities this entails (*Metaphysics* Book 9.3, 1047b28–32). Euclides' transformation of Socrates' narration of the past conversation into the dramatic representation of a present one is a literary sign, one might say, of this denial of potentiality. The issue is introduced in the opening exchange of the dialogue, when Euclides describes to Terpsion how, having just seen Theaetetus being carried back from battle barely alive, he recalled with amazement how "prophetic" Socrates had been about the young man's nature when he met up with him shortly before his own death (*Theaetetus* 142c–d).

Aristotle makes fun of the idea, found in "the Pythagorean myths," of transmigration—as if a particular kind of soul could enter into any body (*De Anima* Book 1.3, 407b14–26) and then goes on to examine and criticize the conception, which many find persuasive, of the soul as a harmony (Book 1.4, 407b27–408a29).

42 See *Sophist* 241d–242b, 258c–e. When the Stranger requests Theaetetus' sympathy not to consider him "mad" in carrying out this action against his intellectual father, he calls to mind Socrates' observation, at the outset of the dialogue, about the being of the philosopher hidden behind his appearances as sophist or statesman while sometimes giving the impression of being altogether mad (216d–e). On the Stranger's implicit self-critique and vindication of Socratic philosophy, see n. 29 above.

43 At the conclusion of *The Attainment of Happiness*, as Alfarabi prepares to go on to Parts II and III of his *Philosophy of Plato and Aristotle*, he implies a distinction between philosophy as such and the particular form represented by Platonic philosophy. The clue comes with the difference between two statements he puts forward about the ancient heritage—the second cited in the epigraph for this essay. According to his first claim, "The superior science and the one with the most perfect authority," whose purpose is "supreme happiness and the final perfection to be achieved by man," is said to have been passed on from the Chaldeans to the Egyptians and from there to the Greeks, then transmitted to the Syrians and the Arabs. "The Greeks who possessed this science used to call it *true wisdom* and the *highest wisdom*. They called the acquisition of it *science*, and the scientific state of mind *philosophy* (by which they meant the quest and the love for the highest wisdom)" (§53, p. 43). Alfarabi's second claim comes after a complex discussion of the knowledge and capacities that would characterize the "true philosopher." Once "true philosophy" has been separated from its defective and mutilated forms, Alfarabi concludes: "The philosophy that answers to this description was handed down to us by the Greeks from Plato and Aristotle only. Both have given us an account of philosophy, but not without giving us also an account of the ways to it and of the ways to re-establish it when it becomes confused or extinct" (§63, p. 49). What Alfarabi is presumably trying to reestablish is implied in the *Philosophy of Plato* by one feature in particular, which captures our whole reading of the *Phaedo*: the remarkable silence in his account of that dialogue, and indeed of the whole Platonic corpus, about the ideas or the immortality of the soul. On the significance of this absence—whether meant as a sign of Plato's intention or Alfarabi's disclosure of his own view, protected by his role as commentator, or both—see Leo Strauss, "Farabi's Plato," especially pp. 364, 371, 375–76.

44 In his 1974 Memorial Speech for Leo Strauss, Benardete identifies "the political-theological issue as the philosophical issue, since the problem of the human good is grounded in the city, and the problem of being in god." And he concludes, "Political philosophy was therefore the eccentric core of philosophy, and the problem of Socrates the problem of philosophy itself" (375). In his review of Strauss's *City and Man* (362), Benardete repeats that formula, which seemed a fitting title for our edited collection, *The Eccentric Core: The Thought of Seth Benardete* (St. Augustine's Press, 2018).

45 That effort, Strauss observes, "was achieved by Plato with a resounding success," and his accomplishment in the Greek city was done for Rome by Cicero, for the Islamic world by Farabi and for Judaism by Maimonides. See "Restatement on Xenophon's *Hiero*," 126–27.

46 Despite all Socrates' efforts, Mary Nichols notes, he "cannot remove the sting of death, which Plato captures in the tears of Socrates' companions at the end of the dialogue."

See *Socrates on Friendship and Community: Reflections on Plato's Symposium, Phaedrus, and Lysis*, 196.

47 Socrates' interpretation of "death" as the philosopher's "practice of dying and being dead" exemplifies the characteristic procedure by which the Platonic dialogue, in the course of exploring a concrete phenomenon, uncovers its significance as a way of understanding philosophy. This extension or deepening of meaning is not a rejection of the ordinary sense—of *erōs* or courage or justice, among others, but perhaps above all, of death in all its reality as the end of life. Consider, in contrast, Socrates' replacement of Homer's Hades, the underworld home of the ghosts of the dead, transformed by a pun into *aïdēs*, the invisible sphere where the mind should encounter the ideas. That kind of philosophic reconstruction is illustrated by Maimonides' attempt to replace the literal meaning of "the world-to-come" by an inner meaning, as the actualization of intellect. Cf. Seth Appelbaum, "The World-to-Come in Maimonides' *Introduction to Pereq Heleq*," 253–66.

48 See *Sophist* 219e, 221d–223b; cf. *Theaetetus* 197d–198a, *Lysis* 206a–b, *Symposium* 203d, *Phaedrus* 253c, *Euthydemus* 290b–c, *Republic* Book 4, 432b–c, *Philebus* 20d, 65a, *Laws* Book 7, 823b–824c. Aristotle's set of examples of friends engaging with one another in the activity they find most worthwhile culminates with "hunting or philosophizing together" (*Nicomachean Ethics* Book 9, 1172a5).

49 The personified laws imagine Socrates arriving in disorderly Thessaly, where Crito's friends would hear the laughable story of his escape from prison in disguise, clothed in a leather hide (*diphthera*, *Crito* 53d). Steven Berg called my attention to the function of that animal skin as writing material: from ancient times, according to Herodotus, the Ionians called a papyrus roll (*bublos*) a *diphthera*, because for lack of papyrus they used to use sheep or goat skins on which to write (*Histories* 5.58).

Aulus Gellius tells a story of Euclides, living during a time of such great enmity between Athens and Megara that a decree prohibited any Megarian from coming to Athens on pain of death. Euclides, "after the enactment of that measure, at nightfall, as darkness was coming on, clad in a woman's long tunic, wrapped in a parti-coloured mantle, and with veiled head, used to walk from his home in Megara to Athens, to visit Socrates, in order that he might at least for some part of the night share in the master's teaching and discourse. And just before dawn he went back again, a distance of somewhat over twenty miles, disguised in that same garb" (*Attic Nights* 7.10).

A complex, thought-provoking variant on the theme, and a key to Plato's art of writing, is the tale Alfarabi tells in the introduction to his *Summary of Plato's Laws*, about the kind of disguise and the particular practice of irony that allowed a pious ascetic to escape from the city ruled by an unjust sovereign, who had issued a command to search for and arrest him. See *Alfarabi: The Political Writings*, trans. Charles Butterworth, 2:130.

The Phaedo: A Platonic Labyrinth

> Das Sein—wir haben keine andere
> Vorstellung davon als Leben—Wie
> kann also etwas Totes 'sein'?

> —Friedrich Nietzsche
> *Aus dem Nachlaß der Achtzigerjahre*

Acknowledgments (1984)

The opportunity to write the original draft of this book was provided by a fellowship in 1979–1980 at Tübingen University, for which I express appreciation to the Alexander von Humboldt Foundation, and in particular to Professor H.J. Kramer. Maureen MacGrogan of Yale University Press offered valuable suggestions and encouragement in seeing the manuscript through the early stages of preparation for publication; at later stages the manuscript benefited from the editorial comments of Jean van Altena. Many improvements in the final product are due to the thoughtful recommendations of Michael Davis. I am grateful to Robert Berman for innumerable discussions inspired by the *Phaedo* but ranging far beyond it.

This project began with Seth Benardete, with whom I read and studied the *Phaedo* in 1978–1979, and has been sustained since then by our correspondence and conversations. Having shared in this turn to the *logos*, I find it difficult to determine the limits of what this work owes him.

Introduction

The doctrines of "Platonism," as typically understood throughout the
Western philosophical tradition, do not always seem to be substantiated
by, and often seem to conflict with, the evidence of the Platonic dialogues.
The various strategies pursued in the attempt to account for this discrep-
ancy are distinguished by the different consequences they draw from a
common recognition of the peculiar character of the dialogue as a literary
form.[1] The admittedly elusive and perplexing character of the dialogue,
however, has not often put into doubt the presumably clear and obvious
character of the doctrines assumed to be Platonic. This lack of skepticism
would indeed be inexplicable were there no evidence at all in the dialogues
for these purported teachings: those dialogues, or passages therefrom, that
most readily appear to provide such evidence have long enjoyed, for just
that reason, a privileged status. This is illustrated, perhaps more explicitly
than in any other case, by the reception, interpretation, and evaluation of
Plato's *Phaedo*.

   Agreement on the status of the *Phaedo* as a *locus classicus* of the Platonic
teaching has been shared by contemporary scholars no less than by ancient
commentators, beginning with Aristotle. And despite centuries of debate
about the success or failure of its execution, there has been little dispute
about the intention of the dialogue: the *Phaedo* is meant to be an exposition and defense of "the twin pillars" of Platonic philosophy, the theory
of ideas and the immortality of the soul.[2] On the basis of this double
theme, the *Phaedo* has been accorded the distinction—sometimes thought
to be a dubious honor—of having inaugurated Western metaphysics, in
its double form of *Metaphysica generalis* and *Metaphysica specialis*.[3] Even
when these metaphysical themes are not taken to be the primary objective
of the dialogue, they are not disclaimed but are only considered to be subordinate, for example, to the Socratic teaching concerning the supreme
importance of man's "tendance of his soul."[4] That the *Phaedo* is Plato's

"tribute of admiration to his beloved friend and master" may be hard to deny,[5] although there has been much controversy over the issue of the accuracy of its representation of the historical Socrates.[6] This controversy, however, concerns only the extent to which Socrates is portrayed as the originator of the doctrines assumed to be Platonic—namely the theory of ideas, and the immortality of the soul.

It is, more precisely, the mutual interdependence of these two doctrines that is thought to constitute the theme of the *Phaedo*. The immutable and eternal ideas, which exist apart from the sphere of ever changing phenomena, furnish the objects of pure reason when it operates unhampered by perception and bodily desire. To apprehend and thus realize its kinship with the ideas, the soul must be freed from reliance on the senses and attachment to the passions, released from its corporeal prison. Since death is nothing but this separation of the soul from the body, it is to be sought after and welcomed by the lover of wisdom: the result of the philosopher's success in "the practice of dying and being dead" is fulfillment of the desire for communion of the pure soul with the pure beings. Such "pure intellectualism divorced from life" would indeed seem to have as its aim "the eternal preservation of the soul in the cold storage of eternally frozen absolute Forms."[7]

This account of the "Platonism" of the *Phaedo* is surely not conjured up out of thin air: it is more or less the understanding of the speeches of Socrates displayed by his interlocutors. But should one assume that Plato, in fabricating this image of Socratic conversation, intends to present to his readers no more, and no less, than Socrates appears to address to his interlocutors? To make this assumption would be to ignore the very character of the dialogue as a dialogue, which more often than not displays the intellectual limitations of the characters it represents. If Socrates is indeed the Platonic spokesman, it is only to the extent that he speaks over the heads of his interlocutors, whose very partial understanding of his speeches affects the direction in which the conversation develops. Plato's address to his readers cannot be assumed to be identical, then, with Socrates' address to his interlocutors. Since Plato speaks nowhere in his own name, no particular position presented in the dialogue can be directly identified as *the* Platonic teaching.[8]

The distance between the Platonic dialogue as an imitation and the Socratic conversation it imitates is signified in the following way: everything contingent in spontaneous speech is transformed, by the written work, into a necessity. Certainly, if the dialogue is to have the appearance of a live conversation, it must represent the arbitrary and superfluous factors that characterize any particular encounter; but what appears accidental—if we forget we are reading—belongs in the representation only if it has some significance which is not arbitrary or superfluous. Whatever role chance plays in the object of imitation, teleology reigns supreme in the work as imitation. This issue is made thematic by the Platonic dialogue in which Socrates criticizes the dangers of the written word—and thus indicates, of course, the obstacles that Platonic writing seeks to overcome.[9] In that context, Socrates offers this criterion of a properly constructed written work: it must be organized like a living animal, with every joint and member designed to serve a particular purpose in the whole. It must be governed by "logographic necessity."[10]

To the extent that the Platonic dialogue fulfills this criterion—and it is hard to imagine any written work that does so more adequately—no argument can be immediately isolated from its context; its significance, particularly if it is or appears to be unsound, can be grasped only by taking into account its function in the whole. The discovery of the definitive purpose served in the dialogue by an unsound argument or an undefended position suggests its intentional status; but in that case, the very charges typically directed against Plato—which make him seem, at least on occasion, like a rather primitive or careless thinker—would be precisely the critical issues deliberately raised by the dialogue itself. At the same time, what is of genuine philosophical import in the dialogue, if it is indeed governed by the principle of logographic necessity, is not immediately self-evident; or rather, if that principle is strictly heeded, nothing that appears in the dialogue—including the title, the setting, the explicit opinions and implicit interests of the interlocutors, the images and examples together with the arguments—is without philosophical import. It is the failure to give sufficient consideration to this character of the dialogue as a dialogue that is exemplified in the prevailing account of the Platonism of the *Phaedo*, and it is the attempt to overcome that failure that motivates the present study.

Such an attempt must be guided by the recognition that every dialogue represents speeches in the context of deeds.[11] It adjusts the argument, consequently, to the circumstances, and that adjustment challenges, at the same time as it must direct, our interpretation. Of course, the hermeneutic principle that may be a necessary condition for reading the dialogue is not a sufficient condition to guarantee the result of its application:[12] to construe it as an automatic "method" for interpretation would be self-con-

3

tradictory. The dialogues do indeed furnish explicit methodological analyses of the proper way to think and speak; but since these speeches, like any others, are embedded in a drama, they cannot simply be extracted from the various contexts in which they appear. In fact, the analysis in one dialogue often seems not only to conflict with that in another, but even to be put into question, rather than confirmed, by the very discussion in which it appears. It is precisely this tension, however, between the theoretical proposals for procedure and the practice exemplified by the conversation that serves as a clue to the intended limitations of each.

It is necessary to recognize the Platonic dialogue as a representation of *conversation* in order to avoid mistaking it for a treatise. But it is necessary to recognize it as a *representation* of conversation in order to discover the carefully constructed plan in accordance with which it is organized. The structure of the dialogue, just for that reason, provides one, if not the, guide for interpretation. The so-called "digression," for example, that often appears in the very center of a dialogue, seems to be—and in a spontaneous conversation would be—an interruption of the subject under discussion; but in the Platonic representation, this deliberate "digression" typically uncovers what is conspicuously absent from the discussion, and hence reorients our understanding and evaluation of it. A spontaneous conversation, furthermore, may just happen to be conducted by particular individuals in a particular situation; but the Platonic representation connects by design a certain topic of discussion with certain types of individuals who conduct it. The opinions expressed in the discussion must be examined, consequently, in the light of the characters and motivations of those who express them. Only through this examination can the reader distance himself from the limited understanding that Socrates' interlocutors may have of his aims, and of his success or failure in fulfilling them. Those aims may be partly disclosed by his intermittent reflections on the status of the arguments, particularly his confessions of ignorance. Socrates' ability to speak in a way that conceals what he means from the person whom he is addressing arouses resentment in those who suspect they are its victims; but the audience that should benefit from this practice in the dialogue is Plato's reader.

This potential benefit, however, is not necessarily actualized by every reader; for the Platonic dialogue, being itself an imitation of Socratic irony, addresses different meanings to different audiences through the same words. Nor is this merely ornamental: the multiplicity of meaning that is the condition for Platonic irony is the very material out of which the dialogue is fabricated. The germ out of which each dialogue unfolds is a connection between some concrete phenomenon, or more than one, and an abstract notion. Such a connection—between, say, the experience of a mixture of pleasure and pain, the death of a living animal, and the analytic and synthetic processes of thought—looks necessary by the end of the dialogue but rather arbitrary at the beginning. It is forged by linking through some common ground the ordinary understanding of a term with a philosophic reconstruction of it. This is exemplified in the *Phaedo* by the way in which Socrates appeals to the ordinary understanding of "death" or "immortality," while deriving, from reflection on the unrecognized presuppositions and implications of that ordinary understanding, his own philosophic reconstruction of it. These double meanings are linked, in turn, to a twofold determination of *psychē*.[13] Indeed, the double meaning of soul is brought to our attention especially by death, or more precisely, by Plato's representation of Socrates dying. Our inability to comprehend how thought or awareness can be affected by the cessation of certain mechanistic processes in the body leads us to an understanding of soul that affirms its independence from the body, precisely when we are compelled to confront just the opposite. The transition, inspired by this paradox, from one implicit sense of soul to another explicit one determines the structure of the *Phaedo*. And that structure, as we shall see, governs the relation between the arguments of the dialogue and its dramatic action.

The inseparability of argument and action, which is displayed by every Platonic dialogue, would seem nowhere more unavoidable than on the occasion represented in the *Phaedo*, which portrays Socrates between dawn and sunset on the last day of his life.[14] No one, Socrates remarks, could accuse him now of idly chattering about matters of no immediate concern to him. Yet, as Socrates also warns his companions, it is in precisely this situation, with the powerful emotions it evokes, that it is especially necessary for them to judge the soundness of their reasoning by separating it from its particular context. Since the arguments, however, are indeed motivated by the immediate, perhaps distorting, interests of Socrates or his companions, it is only by taking those interests into account that Plato's reader can accomplish the required separation of the *logos*.[15] To pursue this task of interpretation is to engage in what Socrates calls "the practice of dying and being dead," which he describes as a kind· of "purification."

The separation of argument from action, which becomes an explicit theme in the dialogue, is reflected at the same time in its form of presentation. For there is in fact no Platonic dramatization of the death of

Socrates, but only of Phaedo's retelling of that event at some time after and at some distance from Socrates' last hours in the Athenian prison. The conversation Socrates conducts on the day of his death is thus transformed from a deed into a speech conducted by Phaedo in a Pythagorean community and addressed to a man associated with the Pythagoreans. The Pythagoreans, Aristotle argues, differ from Plato only in denying any separation between the first principles—which they identify with numbers rather than "ideas"—and the things said to be their imitations;[16] the Pythagorean teaching on reincarnation, on the other hand, presupposes the separability of the soul from the body.[17] The attempt to reinterpret the meaning of "separation," and in so doing to reverse the Pythagorean position, is, one might say, the fundamental intention of the *Phaedo*.

The clue to this intention is provided by the first word of the dialogue—*autos*. The very expression that will be used to designate the "*idea*," that which is "itself by itself," refers at the outset to the individual and identifies the self with the living being, without implying any separation of soul from body: "Yourself, Phaedo, were you present with Socrates on that day when he drank the poison in prison or did you hear of it from another?" While Phaedo seeks to relive his own experience, having been present himself at the event of Socrates' death, Plato, he announces, was sick that day: the fabricator of the *logos* is not himself present at the conversation he represents. With Phaedo's attempt to recreate in his audience the emotions of pity and fear that he and the others suffered, the *Phaedo* would seem to be *the* Platonic tragedy. But if it is the separation of the *logos* from such emotions that is indicated by Plato's reported absence, the kind of "purification" identified with such separation would be accomplished by the dialogue itself.

It is not only the Pythagorean setting of Phaedo's report that explains the centrality of the theme of purification but, at the same time, the ceremony that provides the context for the conversation he narrates. It takes place in the interval between Socrates' trial and death brought about by an Athenian ritual of abstention from public execution. While the guilt from which the Athenian *dēmos* seeks purification, as this ritual suggests, is its condemnation of Socrates, Socrates himself begins the conversation by acknowledging the need to purify himself before dying. Throughout his life, Socrates explains, a dream repeatedly came to him, in different shapes but invariably conveying the same command, to "make music and work at it"—to practice, that is, the arts over which the Muses preside.[18] Having always interpreted the dream as encouragement to continue what

6

he was already doing, practicing philosophy as "the greatest music," Socrates suspects now, after his trial and before his death, that he may be guilty of having neglected to produce "demotic music." He expresses concern about the insufficiency of his attempt to make himself understood by the nonphilosophers who have convicted him. Purification from this guilt would require a combination of demotic music with the greatest music. And this is precisely what is accomplished by Plato's *Phaedo*: the arguments that appear unsound insofar as they appeal to the ordinary understanding of "death" or "immortality" are open to a very different interpretation based on the philosophical reconstruction of those terms.

That the parallel guilt of Socrates and Athens should provide the context for the last of the Platonic dialogues centering on Socrates' trial and death is hardly accidental. At his public trial on the charges of injustice and impiety, Socrates insists on his unwillingness to run away from the practice of philosophy, the post where he has stationed himself or has been stationed by his commander;[19] at his self-imposed trial before the laws of Athens, which Socrates conducts in his private conversation with Crito, he insists on his unwillingness to run away from the prison to which he has been committed by the Athenian jury.[20] Socrates is compelled, consequently, to run away from life, and for this he is put on trial once more in this final conversation. Although his apparent eagerness for death would seem to be a violation of the divine prohibition against suicide, as Socrates himself admits, he absolves himself of this responsibility by interpreting his conviction as "some kind of necessity" imposed upon him by a god. The potential charge of impiety is replaced, therefore, by an accusation against the imprudence Socrates displays in wanting to run away from his good masters the gods and another accusation against the injustice he displays in wanting to run away from his present companions. Socrates' defense against these charges consists in an *apologia* for "the practice of dying and being dead," which he delivers as a description of, partly in the voice of, those whom he calls the "genuine philosophers." In this speech, Socrates constructs the "idea" of the class of philosophers, which is as alien to himself as the philosophers' understanding of the "ideas" is to his own.

Like these genuine philosophers, the young men to whom Socrates addresses his defense understand the practice of dying to consist in the separation of the soul from the body: they warn Socrates that his defense will be acceptable to them only if it can be shown that after death the soul does indeed have "some kind of power and *phronēsis*."[21] It is, presumably, the attempt to provide this justification of his defense that guides the first series of arguments in the dialogue. Socrates thus pursues the purification he sought to compensate for his neglect of demotic music; for his account of the fate of the soul after death is, he admits at one point, an "incantation" designed to charm the child in us who is overcome with fright at the thought of death. Socrates thus tries, or seems to try, to satisfy the challenge issued by his interlocutors, whose understanding of the practice of dying is motivated by the fear of annihilation and the correlative hope for immortality. But precisely by calling attention to that motivation, Socrates transforms the meaning of the practice of dying; he brings to light his own understanding of it as a separation of *logos* from just that attachment to the self that the hope for immortality betrays.

The necessity of this transformation is exhibited at the very center of the dialogue, when Phaedo, after describing the failure of the first series of arguments to prove the immortality of the soul, interrupts his account to report the exchange he shared with Socrates. Warning Phaedo not to cut off his hair on the morrow in mourning for Socrates, but to cut it immediately if they cannot revive the *logos*, Socrates establishes an alliance with Phaedo against the most threatening danger facing them, which is not the fear of death, but the loss of trust in argumentation altogether. This experience of "misology," which Socrates considers the greatest evil, is the inevitable result of a misconception of wisdom as direct contact of the pure soul with the "beings themselves." For, Socrates explains, just as the eyes are blinded by the attempt to observe the sun directly in an eclipse, the soul is blinded by the attempt to investigate the beings directly in the *pragmata*, the many, variously qualified things that come to be and pass away.[22] While Socrates' conduct may provide the most effective weapon against the fear of death, the only defense against misology that is capable of protecting the soul from blinding itself is an art of argumentation. This *technē* of *logoi* Socrates identifies as a "second sailing":[23] it abandons the attempt to investigate the beings themselves in order to investigate their truth through *logoi* and is illustrated by the turn from the first to the second half of the dialogue.

The division of the *Phaedo* into two halves, separated by this central interlude, exhibits the tension between concern with the self and concern with the argument for its own sake, between the fear of death together with the hope for immortality and the fear of misology together with a *technē* of *logoi*. This tension is reflected not only in the transformed understanding of what it is to think and to know, but at the same time in the transformed meanings of *psychē*, death, and immortality. The series of

8

arguments in the first half of the dialogue assumes the identification of soul with mind, medium of cognition; it defines death as the separation of soul from body and takes that separation to be the necessary condition for knowledge. But this series of arguments turns out to be as incapable of accounting for life as it is of demonstrating the continued existence of the soul after death. In the second half of the dialogue, consequently, the psychological analysis of knowledge is replaced—in part for psychological reasons—by a logical one. Not despite, therefore, but precisely because it illustrates the Socratic *technē* of *logoi*, the final argument ignores the understanding of soul as mind. It attempts, rather, to account for what the first half of the dialogue left inexplicable by identifying soul as that which "brings forward life to the body it occupies" and defining death as the destruction of that vital principle. It establishes only that it would be a contradiction to speak of soul, whenever it exists, as dead; but this conclusion appears to contradict the fundamental presupposition of the first series of arguments—that the soul is most pure and in contact with the pure beings only when it is "dead," separated from the body.

The model for this structural and thematic division of the dialogue is provided by Socrates' seemingly arbitrary remarks at the outset of the conversation, just after being released from his fetters—the deed that is mirrored, according to the imagery of the dialogue, in the final deed of release from the chains binding Socrates to life. The pleasure Socrates experiences once the chains are removed from his leg only retrospectively uncovers the pain that must have preceded it; Socrates, filled with wonder, offers a double account of this union of apparent opposites. According to his own explanation, neither pleasure nor pain "wishes" to be present in a man at the same time as the other, yet whenever a man pursues one he gets the other as well, as if the two were joined in one head. An Aesopian *mythos*, on the other hand, might claim that the god, seeing the two at war and wishing to reconcile them but unable to do so, fastened their two heads together so that one always follows upon the other. This double account is a model in miniature of both the form and the content of the dialogue as a whole: while it is derived from the tension between *logos*, or what Socrates considers the greatest music, and *mythos*, or demotic music, it reflects at the same time the tension between the philosopher's desire for release of the soul from the body and the divine will responsible for imprisoning the soul in the body.

Socrates' twofold account of the relation between pleasure and pain— an original unit that human desire attempts to separate into two or an original dyad that divine will attempts to put together—presents opposite causes of the same result; it exhibits precisely that perplexity—the coming to be of two by the addition of two ones or by the division of one into two—that made Socrates, according to the intellectual autobiography he offers, recognize the danger of self-contradiction lurking behind all mechanistic explanation of how something comes into being. He discovered a protection against that danger by applying his *technē* of *logos* to the question of cause—the cause, that is, of something being *what* it is. That anything which is to be two, for example, must participate in the dyad is the "safe but foolish" answer to the question of the cause of the doubleness of pleasure and pain, and consequently of the twofold structure of the dialogue modeled on that account.

Participation in the dyad, then, is the cause of the dialogue being *what* it is; it does not inform us whether it comes into being by the addition of two originally separate units or by the division in two of an original unity. But the necessity of there being two opposing parts is the same necessity that compels Socrates to explain his second sailing only after showing the deficiencies of a first sailing.[24] The way in which the second half of the dialogue serves as a corrective for the first is manifest in the internal structure of each, for which Socrates' remarks on the relation of pleasure and pain furnish the model. The opposites that are united in the first half of the dialogue, when Socrates invites his interlocutors to "investigate and mythologize" about his imminent journey abroad, are separated in the second half of the dialogue: the pure argument, which considers the immortality of the soul only as an illustration of the danger of self-contradiction, is followed by a pure *mythos*, which illustrates the danger of neglecting "care for the soul" by describing the souls of the dead, assigned to their proper dwelling places within the great body of the earth. The separability of the soul from the body is established in the first half of the dialogue only through an inseparable mixture of *logos* and *mythos*; the inseparability of the soul from the body is established in the second half of the dialogue only by the separation of *logos* from *mythos*. The tension between the "mythological" interpretation of purification as the separation of the soul from body and the "dialogic" interpretation as the separation of *logos* from the soul united with the body is reflected in Socrates' last words, acknowledging his debt to Asclepius, the god of healing, son of Apollo, the god of purification. At the moment when he seems to give thanks for his own release from the long disease of life, Socrates expresses gratitude for a concurrent recovery of a different sort: Plato, who has

Phaedo tell us that he was sick on the day of Socrates' death, is in fact very much present—not indeed "himself," but in and through the dialogue "itself by itself." The practice of dying as Socrates understands it is accomplished by the *logos* as a written product, separated from the living Socrates whose image it represents. The desired purification, not of the soul from the body but of the *logos* from the soul united with the body, is produced not by the *pharmakon*—poison and remedy—that brings Socrates release from life, but by the *pharmakon* of the Platonic dialogue.[25]

Chapter One: The Prologue

[57a1–58a5] The title of the *Phaedo* does not inform us about the subject of the conversation it represents but indicates only the proper name of the narrator, who simply reports a discussion in which he was almost entirely an observer. Phaedo plays a role only in the dramatic prologue, the concluding statement, and a brief interlude in the exact center of the dialogue; yet he perhaps justifiably provides its title, for the long speech he delivers takes the place of a Platonic dramatization of the last day of Socrates' life.[1]

Although a substantial period of time must have elapsed between Socrates' death and Phaedo's report (cf. 57a–b), Phaedo promises to try to -satisfy Echecrates' request to hear as precisely and clearly as possible everything that was said and done (cf. 58d). At only three points in the course of the report does Phaedo's narrative omniscience falter. That Plato was absent because of illness Phaedo believes but does not know for certain (59b). He expresses the same uncertainty in reporting the transition between Socrates' account of his own philosophic procedure and its application to the final argument on immortality.[2] Of this crucial transition, in which the interlocutors establish their agreement on the relation between the ideas and the things said to get their names from them (102a–b), Phaedo provides only a minimal summary, in indirect discourse, which stands out from the direct discourse through which he claims to present an imitation of the original conversation in its entirety. When he returns to his narration after this moment of uncertainty, Phaedo relates the objection of the one person who recognizes the apparent contradiction between Socrates' first and last arguments; but the name of the speaker responsible for this observation—it turns out to be a fundamental problem of the entire discussion—Phaedo, unfortunately, cannot remember (103a).

While these lapses in Phaedo's memory might seem to reflect the accidental character of spontaneous speech, they prove to be a sign of the artfulness of the Platonic dialogue, for they point to the way in which this representation of Socrates' last conversation is determined by the perspective of its narrator. The clues to that perspective are provided not only in the opening prologue, which dramatizes Phaedo's exchange with Echecrates, but also in Phaedo's presentation of the brief exchange he shared with Socrates on that last day. In the course of this central interlude, Phaedo enters into an alliance with Socrates for the sake of preserving the *logos*, which is under attack. Their discussion seems to be a mere interruption of the attempt to demonstrate the immortality of the soul, which Socrates' interlocutors take to be the goal of their conversation. But the subsequent return to that topic in the second half of the dialogue is influenced in important ways by the apparently digressive discussion devoted to the subject of *logos* itself that Socrates shares with Phaedo in the intervening interlude.

The relation between Phaedo's role as narrator and the theme of the conversation he reports is implicitly introduced by the first word of the dialogue. When asked if he "himself" (*autos*) was present at Socrates' death, or whether he only heard of it from another, Phaedo replies "myself" (*autos*). The dialogue, traditionally understood as the Platonic account of the separability of the soul from the body, begins by referring to the self as an inseparable unity of soul and body.[3] But Phaedo's claim to have been present "in the flesh" is almost immediately contrasted with his remark that Plato was not present. On this very rare occasion in the dialogues when Plato allows his own name to appear,[4] he does so only to mark his absence from Socrates' death. Whatever historical significance this may bear, its function as a dramatic element is to call attention to the narrative form of the dialogue, which creates a separation between the experience of being present at Socrates' death and the *logos* in which that event is represented. As a transformation of deed into speech, the narrative form is *the* exemplification of what Socrates will present as the crucial turn in his own philosophic development: insisting that speeches are no more images of the beings than deeds are, he will defend the necessity of turning away from the attempt to observe the beings themselves in order to investigate their truth in *logoi* (99d–100a).

Such a turn would seem to be especially necessitated by the deeds of this particular occasion—the most emotional represented in the Platonic dialogues.[5] Everyone but Socrates—and he too was forced in the end to cover his face—is incapable of restraining himself from intermittent laughing and weeping. Apollodorus is only the most extreme,[6] but Phaedo admits that he himself was stirred up, as well as the others (cf. 117c–d). Yet the distance that could accompany the narration of a past event is just what Phaedo wants to overcome; he hopes to recreate the original experience as closely as possible and seems to succeed, for Echecrates is overcome by the same emotions at the same moments as the participants present on the occasion. He does not take Phaedo's report as a special opportunity of attending to the *logos* separated from its emotional context, but only as a compromising alternative to the more desirable opportunity of being an eyewitness to the deed itself. One should not assume that the exchange between Phaedo and Echecrates is intended as a model to be imitated by the reader of the dialogue; it may be dramatized by Plato, rather, as a warning of what is to be overcome.

It is only at the conclusion of their preliminary conversation that Echecrates restricts his request to hear not about *how* Socrates died, but about the *logoi* that were spoken (59c). Yet he immediately indicates the importance of hearing Phaedo's *logos*, when he reveals what it would be like to know only the deed: since no stranger has come for a long time from Athens to Phlius,[7] the Phliasians know only that Socrates drank the poison and died. They have indeed been informed about the trial; yet Echecrates, like the interlocutors present with Socrates in the Athenian prison, shows no interest in discussing its implications but is curious only about the length of time intervening between Socrates' condemnation and death. In the explanation of this lapse of time that Phaedo offers, however, he illuminates, without being aware of doing so, the connection between Socrates' death and its political context.[8]

[58a6–59b2] It just so happens, Phaedo explains, that Socrates' trial took place on the very day after the Athenians sent their sacred ship on its mission to Delos, and no public execution is allowed to occur until the ship returns. In this yearly ritual, the Athenians purify the city before Apollo, the god of purification, while acknowledging the heroism of the legendary founder of Athens. For it is the very ship in which Theseus once went to Crete, the Athenians claim, that the priest of Apollo crowns every year. The identity that the Athenians ascribe to the ship itself, however, seems to belong to nothing but the *logos* in which that ascription is made; for what else is it that remains the same over time as each plank of the ship is worn away and replaced by another? The ship of Theseus thus introduces what will prove to be a crucial question of the dialogue:[9] if the material components of the human body are constantly being worn away and replaced by others (cf. 87d–e), what is it that accounts for the identity of the individual over even one life span, let alone beyond that?

Through the *logos* that proclaims the identity of their sacred ship, the Athenians associate their yearly mission to Delos with the journey in which Theseus sailed to Crete with "those two times seven" companions and saved them as well as himself. He thus liberated the Athenians from the tribute imposed by King Minos of Crete, who demanded that every ninth year a mission of seven young men and seven young women be sacrificed to the Minotaur. It was on the third of these sacrificial voyages, according to legend, that Theseus determined to kill the Minotaur. He took with him five young women, seven young men, and two additional young men with girlish faces but manly spirits who were to dress and walk like women. He owed his success, however, not only to this clever ruse, but also to his good fortune in meeting Ariadne, the daughter of Minos; for, falling in love with Theseus, she gave him a ball of thread that allowed him, after killing the Minotaur, to find his way back through the twisted labyrinth in safety.

Because of the public ceremony recalling this legend, Phaedo repeats, Socrates passed a long time in prison between his trial and his death. But Echecrates does not ask about Socrates' response to this delay; he is eager to hear only about what took place at his death, and in particular whether the authorities allowed his friends to be present or compelled him to die alone. Since he is at leisure, Phaedo admits, he will attempt to relate the whole story; for he finds it the greatest of all pleasures to remember Socrates, in either speaking of him or listening. And when Echecrates affirms that Phaedo will have listeners who share that feeling, perhaps Plato's readers are meant, at least in this respect, to be included among them.

In contrast, however, with being reminded of Socrates, which produces the greatest of pleasures, being present at his death, Phaedo confesses, produced in him a strange and wondrous mixture of pleasure and pain. He did not feel the pity one might expect to feel at the death of a friend, he tells Echecrates, since Socrates seemed happy in his manner and speeches, dying fearlessly and nobly; nor, on the other hand, did he feel pleasure as he usually would when occupied with philosophic speeches. In construing philosophy as pure pleasure, Phaedo shows no awareness of the possibility of a painful gap between its ambition and its achievement; in construing pity as pure pain, he is unaware of the possibility of pleasure in one's distance from the sufferer. If he could not pity Socrates because he seemed to be going into Hades "with some kind of divine lot," he might have felt envy at this selfish escape;[10] this is suggested in fact by his portrayal of the other participants in the conversation, who express pity only in combination with resentment of Socrates for abandoning them (cf. 63a–b). Phaedo unwittingly points to the necessity of a complicated mixture, in which neither pleasure nor pain is free from the presence of the other, despite his naive account of each as naturally separate, combined only on this unique occasion.

[59b3–59c7] Judging by the behavior Phaedo ascribes to them, the others who were present at Socrates' death experienced the same strange mixture of emotions. Prompted by Echecrates' question of who these men were, Phaedo offers a list: first three (Apollodorus, Critoboulos, and Critoboulos' father), then four native Athenians (Hermogenes, Epigenes, Aeschines, and Antisthenes), two additional Athenians (Ctesippus and Menexenus), then three non-Athenians (Simmias and Cebes of Thebes and Phaedonides), and finally two others (Eucleides and Terpsion of Megara).[11] Phaedo lists five strangers, seven native Athenians, and two additional Athenians, young men of manly spirit.[12] The group present with Socrates on the day of his death, which takes place just after completion of the public ritual celebrating the mythical voyage of Theseus, matches the group of nine youths and five maidens present with Theseus on that voyage.[13] But while the Athenians present with Socrates might have been flattered by their identification with those nine youths, it is to the group of strangers identified with the maidens that the two active participants in the conversation belong. While explicitly mentioning the names of three others who were absent,[14] the non-Athenian Phaedo leaves his own name out of the list of those present at Socrates' death. Yet he points to his own role in the Platonic drama by reporting his exchange with Socrates at the center of the conversation: gathering Phaedo's long hair at the back of his neck, advising him to cut it not in mourning for Socrates' imminent death, but only in mourning for the *logos* if they cannot save it (89b), Socrates singles out Phaedo to play the role, it seems, of Ariadne, an ally necessary for the success of his mission. The Minotaur that they must together confront is the childish fear of death that threatens to overcome all manliness (cf. 77d–e).

The miraculous convergence of the historical celebration of a mythical event with the situation of the conversation he is about to relate, Phaedo judges to be "some kind of chance or fate" (*tuchē tis*). Phaedo is an unwitting vehicle for the Platonic logographic necessity[15] that represents

17

Socrates' last conversation as a reenactment in *logos* of Theseus' victory over the Minotaur, dramatically embedded in the context of the Athenian reenactment of the same heroic myth. The sense of guilt from which the Athenians seek purification is revealed by the law that prohibits public execution during the period of the sailing of the sacred ship. The ritual pretense of the city that it has no involvement with killing is the purification of the pollution it experiences from just that involvement. The convergence of the mission to Delos and the trial of Socrates is hardly, then, a matter of chance, as Phaedo believes, but is rather the sign identifying the condemnation of Socrates as the immediate source of guilt that the Athenians feel compelled to expiate.

Nor is it accidental that, on the day when the sacred ship has returned and his sentence is to be carried out, Socrates begins the conversation with an account of his own act of purification. The suspected guilt for which Socrates seeks purification, as he will explain, is his lifelong neglect of producing "music for the *dēmos*" (cf. 60e–61b). Because of Socrates, Athens bears the weight of guilt for the possibly unjust execution of a citizen, indeed the citizen who may have been the god's gift to the city;[16] because of Athens, Socrates bears the weight of guilt for his exclusive concern with philosophy as "the greatest music," and consequent neglect of "demotic music." To purify itself, Athens delays the execution of Socrates long enough to send out the sacred mission; to purify himself, Socrates takes advantage of that delay to make up for what he may have neglected throughout his life. Yet precisely because of its ceremony of purification, Athens is able to carry out the act through which its guilt would have been incurred: having performed a mere ritual,[17] the Athenians hand over the cup of hemlock to Socrates, thus effecting the form of an "involuntary suicide."[18] Perhaps in the same way, the demotic music that Socrates will claim to have produced during his days in prison is no more than a mere ritual, which does not preclude his persistence, to his final hour, in the lifelong pursuit for which this purification was required.

The city's concealment of the execution under the guise of a self-inflicted death is appropriately reflected in the attitude of Socrates' companions, who accuse him of being eager to abandon both his friends and his good masters the gods (cf. 63a). Having refused the opportunity to escape from the Athenian prison, having conducted his trial as if he hoped to provoke the sentence of death, having allowed the case to come before the court in the first place,[19] Socrates must begin his final conversation with a defense of what seems to be an act of running away from life. But rather than defend himself by forcing responsibility back upon the city, he saves himself and Athens by seeing in his trial and conviction the sign of divine necessity (cf. 62c). He thus appears to imitate the Athenians, who seek divine sanction for a political act of execution. Only their mutual appeal to Apollo, the god of purification and music, provides the common ground for the reconciliation of Socratic philosophy and Athenian law; it is a reconciliation, of course, that takes place only on the level of ritual and thus seems to confirm, rather than resolve, the conflict it brings to light.

What Phaedo interprets as a mark of chance emerges—through the logographic necessity of the Platonic dialogue, at least—as an account of the "causes" of Socrates' death: the will of the gods coincides perfectly with the decision of the Athenian *dēmos*, and both coincide with Socrates' own desire, which he will defend by identifying philosophy as "the practice of dying and being dead." This practice will itself be described as a kind of purification: it entails liberation from the illusions that accompany submission to pleasure and pain. Since, however, the confrontation of philosophy and death produced in Phaedo, as he explained, only a strange and wondrous mixture of pleasure and pain, it is not at all evident what reasons motivate Socrates to choose Phaedo as his ally.

Socrates requires this alliance, as he suggests in his exchange with Phaedo, because he can overcome the Minotaur that consists in the fear of death only by discovering a safe thread leading through the twisted passages of the *logos* in which that monster hides. And that very effort is itself threatened by another danger: Socrates will have to overcome the many-headed monster of misology, which consists in distrust not just of the present argument for the immortality of the soul, but of the power of *logos* in general (cf. 89c–d). The fear of death, which motivates the desire for a demonstration of the immortality of the soul, can be subdued only by being transformed into the fear of misology, which would motivate the desire for an art of argumentation capable of defending its own trustworthiness. And while the analysis of this *technē* of *logoi* may appear, to Socrates' companions, subordinate to the goal of demonstrating the immortality of the soul, the overturning of that appearance is precisely the challenge presented by the dialogue to its reader.

[59c8–59d8] Phaedo began his exchange with Echecrates by referring to the conduct of Socrates' trial; he concludes by describing the days following the trial, when the young men met each day at dawn and made the same journey Socrates once made from the Athenian court to the prison. Despite this reminder of the political context, however, Phaedo and the others speak as though Socrates' death were entirely willful, or simply a natural phenomenon. Despite the one moment, moreover, when Socrates admits that the causes of his present situation are the judgment of the Athenian *dēmos* and his own acceptance of it (98e), he seems to adapt himself all too readily to the perspective of his interlocutors. In constructing a model of "the best city in speech," Socrates identifies the city, the domain of political authority and opinion, as the prison in which the philosopher is interned and from which he longs to escape;[20] in attempting to demonstrate the immortality of the soul, he identifies that prison no longer with the city, but with the body (cf. 82d–83c).

In adopting a perspective that seems to conceal the political context of his death, Socrates acts as if he knew that this conversation would be transported beyond the Athenian prison in which it takes place. At his public trial, he argued that, if his only alternative were to give up philosophy, and thus lead a life not worth living, death would be preferable.[21] In his private conversation with Crito, he implied that philosophy could not be carried on in a lawless regime, or even in a regime totally governed by law:[22] for Socrates, philosophy—that is, political philosophy—requires Athens. To the nearby and well-governed cities like Thebes or Megara, Socrates says he could not escape, for he would be received as an enemy, bringing with him the reputation of philosophy as a destroyer of the laws, hence of thoughtless young men.[23] But if the historical Socrates could not make this journey,[24] the Socrates of the Platonic dialogues, in the days following his condemnation, shows how philosophy can be exported to safety outside Athens: in the *Theaetetus*, Socratic philosophy is carried to Megara,[25] and in the *Phaedo*, to Phlius, the Pythagorean community associated with Thebes.[26]

The dramatic prologue of the *Phaedo* sheds light not only on the themes of the dialogue but also on its structure, articulated by the opening and closing frames as well as by the central interlude in which Phaedo plays a part. The outermost frame of the dramatic prologue, alluding to Socrates' trial as the background of his death, encloses an internal frame, linking the Athenian mission to Delos, as a ritual enactment of the legend of Theseus, with the Socratic mission, as a philosophically reconstructed enactment of that legend. At the center of this double frame stands Phaedo's account of the strange mixture of pleasure and pain he experienced at Socrates' death; at the center of the conversation he is about to

20

narrate stands his exchange with Socrates on the necessity of achieving liberation from pleasure and pain by directing attention to the *logos* itself. The Platonic prologue representing the exchange between Phaedo and Echecrates is a mirror that seems to present an inverted image of the whole of which it is a part.

Chapter Two: *Logos* and *Mythos*

[59d8–60a9] Phaedo refers to the many conversations Socrates conducted in the Athenian prison prior to this last one, but the Platonic dialogues present only the one in which Socrates, speaking in the voice of the personified laws of Athens, rejects the entreaty of his old friend Crito to escape. Crito comes to the prison immediately upon receiving a report concerning the arrival of the ship from Delos, since this means that Socrates will have to drink the poison on the following day. But Socrates seems assured that his life will not come to an end on the morrow; for during the time that Crito has been watching him asleep and marveling at his apparent calmness in the face of death, Socrates has been dreaming of a beautiful woman in white, who informs him that "on the third day you would come to fertile Phthia." Socrates' dream conflates the words of Homer's Achilles, who refuses Odysseus' entreaty to return and fight for the common cause, with the figure of the goddess Thetis, who warns her son Achilles, unsuccessfully, against acting in a way that will result in his death.[1] It thus implies that Socrates' death is the fulfillment of his own wish, against the command of his superiors, to return to his homeland, and at the same time, the result of a decision to die nobly rather than go on living disgracefully.

But Socrates' interpretation of his dream, with its denial of the rumor reported by Crito, is not confirmed by the series of Platonic dialogues in which it is presented. For Phaedo does not announce when it is that the young men receive the report of the arrival of the sacred ship; he explains only that, on the following morning, they gathered together as early as possible at the prison but were compelled to wait outside by the jailer—the same man, perhaps, who let Crito in before dawn after receiving a small favor from him.[2] The first direct speech that makes the past into the present is the jailer's announcement that "the Eleven are releasing Socrates from his chains and giving directions on how he is to die";[3] it is the "servant of the Eleven" who enters at sunset to announce the time to drink the poison, which should release Socrates from the chains binding him to life. When his visitors enter, they find Socrates just released, with Xanthippe and their child sitting beside him.[4] Phaedo has promised to narrate all the deeds and speeches, but he cannot, of course, recognize the logographic necessity that binds them in the Platonic dialogue: he gives no interpretation of the fact that Socrates must at first have been lying down, although he remarks that as soon as Xanthippe left, Socrates sat up (60b), and that, finally, with the introduction of the issue of the philosopher's desire for death, Socrates put his feet on the ground (61c) and remained in that position until the end of the day, after drinking the poison.[5] Like Socrates' reclining position, Xanthippe's presence belongs to the dramatic action that frames the *logos* but remains apart from it: she departs before the conversation begins and presumably returns with the women of the family when it is ended. With what appears to be a selfless grief, Xanthippe laments the last occasion on which Socrates will be able to speak with his companions. But when she cries out[6]—according to Phaedo, the way women always do—Socrates looks up at Crito in the first of a series of increasingly intense glares. Just as Socrates will address a request to Crito in his last words, he addresses to Crito, in his first words, the request that Xanthippe be taken home. She departs wailing and beating her breast in her sorrow, while perhaps finding some relief in the very deed of expressing it:[7] she enacts her own version of the strange mixture of pleasure and pain that Phaedo first ascribed to himself and now reports as the theme of Socrates' first reflections.

[60b1–60c7] Whereas Phaedo marveled at his experience of a unique combination, Socrates' wonder is aroused at the thought of an inseparable union by nature between what men call pleasant and what is thought to be its opposite, the painful.[8] The pain that must have been present when his leg was fettered Socrates can recognize only in contrast with the pleasure he subsequently experiences once the chain is removed: his experience of pleasure is nothing but the absence of a pain that was determined by objective causes but did not appear in experience as such. In his interpretation, Socrates attempts to correct Phaedo's misunderstanding of pleasure and pain as autonomous and indifferent to each other: though neither " wishes" to come to be present in a man at the same time as the other, if someone pursues one and gets it, he is almost always compelled to take the other with it.[9] It is as if the so-called pleasant and the painful were joined together in "one head," so that neither term is independent, and each—or at least one of them—is nothing but the absence of the other.[10] Now if Aesop had thought about this experience, Socrates imagines, he would have put together the following *mythos*: the god, wishing to reconcile pleasure and pain, which were at war with each other, but finding himself unable to do so, instead fastened them together in "two heads," so that whenever one comes to be present, the other always follows it later.

In accordance with this Aesopian story, the chains that imprison the soul in the body make life a present experience of pain, which will be followed by the release of the soul at death as a subsequent experience of pleasure. In accordance with Socrates' original account, on the other hand, to construe the union of soul with body as painful would require an inference made retrospectively if and when the soul were released from the body, and the pleasure of that release, in turn, would be nothing but recognition of the absence of a prior union. While it seeks to explain why pleasure follows on the withdrawal of pain, the Aesopian *mythos* presupposes that each is nonproblematic in itself. The Socratic account, in contrast, which considers how strangely these apparent opposites are related by "nature," points to the problematic character of each in itself. The Aesopian *mythos* thus assumes what the Socratic account makes into a problem: What is the so-called pleasant or the painful? It is because it implicitly raises this question—at least once it is contrasted with the *mythos*—that Socrates' account can be labeled a *logos*. It nevertheless preserves a mythological element. For its description of pleasure and pain "wishing" not to come to be present together is, we would say, a personification: it is the projection onto the feelings themselves of the human will to separate them.

By supplementing his own description of the attempted division of an original unit with an Aesopian *mythos* about the attempted unification of an original dyad, Socrates provides a double account of how pleasure and pain come to be two. If, on the other hand, the attempt to unify pleasure and pain were really successful, they would together become one, or if the attempt to separate them were really successful, each would become one with no relation to the other. Addition and division thus constitute not only opposite causes of how two comes to be, but the same opposite causes of how one comes to be. This was just the perplexity, Socrates later reports, that compelled him to abandon any claim to know the "refined cause" of how something comes to be and to replace it with a safe hypothesis: the cause of anything being two is its participation in the dyad, of anything being one its participation in the monad (cf. 96e–97b, 101c). Still, despite their problematic status, the operations of addition and division are informative in a way that cannot be replaced by the noncontradictory "cause" of *what* it is to be two or one. Despite its problematic status, therefore, the juxtaposition of a Socratic *logos* about pleasure and pain with an Aesopian *mythos* is informative: it identifies separation as an effort based on the desire of a man, unification as an effort based on the will of the god. The union of soul with body, which will be identified with life (cf. 103c–d), must be explained, accordingly, through a *mythos* about divine will, while their separation, which will be identified with death (64c), must be explained through a *logos* about human desire. That these two models for the relation of opposites should be determined by the opposition of human desire and divine will is hardly accidental, for Socrates will soon be called upon to defend his apparent desire for death, when he himself admits that life is a god-given responsibility (cf. 61c–63c).

[60c8–61e9] In the transition leading to this issue of the divine prohibition against suicide, Socrates justifies the necessity of his juxtaposition of *logos* and *mythos*. He does so in response to the first question raised by Cebes, who is surprised—he swears by Zeus—at how fittingly Socrates' mention of an Aesopian *mythos* reminds him of rumors he has heard about Socrates' recent poetic productions. He had been questioned by the poet Evenus about the meaning of Socrates' sudden turn to writing poetry, Cebes explains, only two days earlier—the very day, perhaps, on which Crito questioned Socrates about his apparently sudden appeal to the laws of Athens as the highest authority. But this possible coincidence is even more fitting than Cebes could realize. For his turn to poetry was motivated, Socrates acknowledges, by a suspicion of having neglected to fulfill the command of certain dreams—that is, of one dream that came to him throughout his life in various shapes but always saying the same thing. The identity of the Athenians' sacred ship, despite its constantly changing components, was nothing but the *logos* that declared it one and the same; the identity of Socrates' dream, despite its constantly changing appearances, is determined by one and the same *logos* it commands—to "make music and work at it."[11] Socrates felt compelled to test this dream in these last days, he explains to Cebes, just as he felt compelled, he explained to the Athenian jury, to test the oracle of Apollo that declared no man wiser than he was. As a result of that lifelong testing, Socrates discovered his unique significance: he arrived at his understanding that the greatest human wisdom is knowledge of ignorance.[12] On that basis, Socrates could

26

interpret his recurrent dream simply as encouragement to continue his practice of philosophy, which he takes to be "the greatest music";[13] only his trial and the festival of the god that has delayed his death make him suspect his possible guilt in having neglected demotic music—poetry, that is, that would communicate with the *dēmos*.

Believing it safer, Socrates claims, to purify himself before departing, he has spent his days in prison composing a hymn to the god whose festival it is—the same who proclaimed him the wisest of men—and, since he considers himself no mythmaker—though he seems to have no trouble inventing a tale to conclude this conversation—Socrates claims to have taken over the *mythoi* of Aesop and set them to verse. Socrates suggests the double source of his possible guilt in describing this work of ritual purification, which combines a display of piety to the god with moral fables comprehensible to children. But even if the poetic work Socrates claims to have produced were not merely a fiction in the Platonic dialogue, it is questionable whether such demotic music would be capable of combination with "the greatest music"; perhaps, then, only Plato's *Phaedo*—in part a hymn to Apollo, the god of purification, in part an elaborate *mythos* about the human soul—could sufficiently purify Socrates from his suspected guilt without abandoning the pursuit that causes it. That this issue should be raised by Socrates' mention of an Aesopian *mythos* is, in any case, no contingency, as Cebes believes, but one more instance of Platonic logographic necessity; for the tension between the philosopher's desire to practice the greatest music and the divine command to produce demotic music reflects precisely the tension between the human desire to pursue pleasure in separation from pain and the god's will to unite them, or the human desire to seek death as the separation of the soul from the body and the god's will to unite them.

Socrates asks Cebes to bid farewell to Evenus, the poet and sophist,[14] bearing the message to follow after him, if he is indeed a philosopher, as quickly as possible; only in that way could he correct his commitment to demotic music, just as Socrates had to correct his commitment to philosophy. Evenus is advised to pursue what will soon be called "the practice of dying," but he is to do so, Socrates adds, without taking his own life, which is said to be forbidden.[15] The tension within this double message shows up in the split between the responses of Socrates' two interlocutors: while Simmias is surprised by Socrates' recommendation that Evenus follow after him, Cebes is puzzled by the claim that it is not lawful to take one's own life, though the philosopher wishes to follow after one who is dying. Socrates, in turn, claims to be surprised that Simmias and Cebes, who have heard the teachings of the Pythagorean Philolaus, nevertheless know nothing definite about the prohibition against suicide.[16] He himself is willing to say what he knows from hearsay, Socrates admits, since it seems fitting on this particular occasion to "investigate and mythologize" about his journey abroad: this double enterprise may be necessitated, Socrates implies, by the double content of his message to Evenus.

[62a1–62c5] Socrates begins, understandably enough, by warning Cebes that he must strive eagerly if he is to grasp this paradoxical law:[17]

> Perhaps, however, it will appear wondrous to you, if this alone of all others is simple and, unlike other things, it never happens to man that for some and at some times it is better to be dead than alive; but for whom (or for what) it is better to be dead, it is perhaps wondrous to you if, for those men, it is not holy to benefit themselves but necessary to wait for some other benefactor.[18]

Socrates himself experienced wonder at the conjunction of pleasure and pain when the chain was removed from his leg; of the two models he presented for this relation of opposites, one was based on the human desire for separation of an original unit, the other on the divine will to unify an original dyad. Socrates now expects his interlocutors to undergo a corresponding experience of wonder at the opposition between the divine command against suicide and the possible superiority of death to life. If the divine command were indeed the only law without exception, it might seem to entail the universal superiority of life over death[19]—if, at least, the gods know and support the good for man. Precisely because it is a prohibition, on the other hand, the law against suicide presupposes the possibility of the human desire for death. But this admission in itself is a puzzling one: there seems to be no standpoint from which one could make the judgment that it is better to be dead, since it is a judgment that can only be made by one who is alive, and it is for himself, presumably, that he determines what is preferable.[20] Socrates thus indicates a tension within the divine prohibition and within the human desire for death, as well as between them.

The two clauses through which Socrates describes this structure of opposition, however, are only apparently parallel. For while the first is entirely conditional—it will appear wondrous *if* the divine prohibition is universal and entails the universal superiority of life over death[21]—the second clause is introduced with an unconditional claim—since there is someone for whom or something for which death is better, it may appear wondrous *if* the pursuit of that benefit were forbidden. The asymmetry of the two clauses is indicated, moreover, by the distinction between future and present: the universal goodness of life, construed as a consequence of the "simplicity" of the divine prohibition against suicide, *will* perhaps appear wondrous, and this prediction is fulfilled at the moment Socrates begins the second clause, with its admission of the possible superiority of death. But the one unconditional claim asserted by Socrates could be accepted, without contradicting that which precedes or follows, only if those for whom or that for which it is better to be dead is not a man: Socrates is about to argue that it may be better if one is a philosopher—not for the man himself, however, but only for his soul.[22] The kind of "death" that is preferable, consequently, may not be the physiological phenomenon that constitutes the ordinary understanding of the word.[23]

Socrates' paradoxical formulation does indeed so arouse Cebes' wonder that he utters an oath, slipping into his native dialect—"Let Zeus know!"—while smiling gently. That the prohibition that simultaneously implies and denies the possible superiority of death to life would fill even Zeus with wonder makes Cebes smile for the first time,[24] just as Simmias is about to smile for the first time in acknowledging that the many would make fun of the philosopher's desire for death (64b). A surprising alliance is thus implied between the gods and the many, with their natural desire for life, over against the philosopher, with his strange desire for death. But this conflict as a rule is confirmed by its one exception: Socrates' apparent readiness for death is to be satisfied only through the cooperation of the Athenian *dēmos*, who believe death to be the greatest evil, while their decision is in turn interpreted by Socrates as a sign of "some necessity sent by a god" (cf. 62c).

Since his statement, Socrates admits, must appear irrational (*alogos*), to consider what sense it may have, he must initiate his interlocutors into a secret *logos*, which describes both the desire for liberation from life and the source of restraint against it. It is as if we men are on some kind of guard duty or in some kind of prison and are not allowed to set ourselves free or run away. With this secret *logos*, Socrates transforms the political significance of his discussion with Crito concerning his responsibility not to run away from the Athenian prison;[25] at the same time, he transforms the significance of his defense before the Athenian jury concerning his responsibility not to run away from the post where he believed the god stationed him, engaging in the activity of examination, any more than he ran away from the post in battle where his Athenian commanders stationed him.[26] But the "great secret" Socrates now divulges, which presents life itself as the true prison or the true guard duty, puts those prior claims into question: If the highest responsibility were the obligation not to run away from the prison of life, Socrates would have had to run away from the Athenian prison, as Crito entreated, or if it were the obligation not to run away from the guard duty of life, Socrates would have had to run away from the duty of philosophy, no less than from a post in battle, as he admitted to his Athenian judges.

The secret *logos*, which Socrates finds "weighty and not easy to see through," says either that life is an imprisonment, without revealing the guilt for which we are incarcerated, or that we are ourselves guardians, without revealing that for which we are responsible, nor why we are compelled to maintain this position.[27] The intentional exploitation of this ambiguity is indicated by its exemplification of the conflicting assumptions of the dialogue as a whole: while the sense of imprisonment suggests the desire of the soul for contact with the beings themselves, which would require its separability from the body, the image of the guard post suggests the responsibility of the soul for animating the body, which requires its inseparability. To clarify the secret *logos*, with its ambiguous assumptions concerning the relation between soul and body, Socrates turns to the "well-spoken" claim that the gods are our guardians and we men their chattel.[28] That the gods, however, might not have the best human interests in mind in their support of human life is suggested by the illustration Socrates offers to Cebes: if one of your chattel should kill itself before you indicated that you wished it to die, you would be angry and would punish it, if you could.

[62c6–63d2] Socrates absolves himself from this potential accusation simply by asserting his recognition of the divine necessity now sent upon him. He is saved from having to defend himself only because Cebes is troubled, not so much by the impiety of suicide, as by the foolishness—if the god is indeed our guardian and we his possession—of the desire for death. While a foolish man, Cebes argues, might thoughtlessly desire to run away from a good master, the most prudent (*phronimos*) man would never think he could take better care of himself when free but would wish to be always with one who is better than himself;[29] but in that case, it is the wise who ought to be troubled by dying and only the foolish who would rejoice. Cebes' earnestness seemed to please Socrates, Phaedo believes, although he casts doubt on that interpretation when he reports that Socrates, for the second time, stared upward at his companions. Just because of the threat posed by Cebes' discovery of an apparent contradiction, Socrates praises him for his relentless pursuit of the *logos* and his unwillingness to be convinced by anyone apart from it. What Cebes points to, however, in his insistence on the prudence of submission to good masters, is the situation of himself and his friends, who every day since the trial, have come to be in the presence of Socrates. Indeed, Simmias immediately takes up the argument as a direct accusation against Socrates' willingness to abandon not only his good masters the gods, but his friends as well.

Socrates managed to avoid, in his public trial, any attempt to defend himself against the charge of not believing in the gods of the city,[30] although that very avoidance is of course suspicious. He manages now to avoid any attempt to defend himself against the apparently justifiable charge of impiety; for that charge, although it has been suggested by the conflict between the philosopher's desire for death and the divine prohibition against suicide, has been replaced by Cebes' attack on Socrates' foolishness and Simmias' attack on his injustice. Although Socrates immediately responds to Simmias' demand for a defense of his conduct, he directs his response to Cebes' accusation: by admitting that he would be wrong in not grieving at death only if he did not believe that he was going to other wise and good gods and to men better than those here, Socrates displays more concern with defending his prudence than his justice.

He seems, indeed, to go out of his way to insult his companions by declaring his hope of traveling to the company of better men, especially since, Socrates adds, he is not willing to insist on this claim, as he would about the gods—as much as he would insist on any such matters. He is confident that, in going to Hades, he goes to good and wise gods, for Hades is nothing but the name of the good and wise god (cf. 80d, 81a).[31] Socrates is willing to insist, as he later makes clear, only on a nonfalsifiable *logos*.[32] But the defense of this kind of confidence, which Socrates will provide through his analysis of a *technē* that guarantees the safety of *logos*, is not identical with the defense his interlocutors now demand, although Simmias believes it would be a benefit to all in common:[33] the benefit Socrates bestows by providing his companions with a defense he himself does not require itself constitutes the *apologia* of his prudence and his justice.

[63d3–63e7] But the *apologia* that Socrates hopes to make more persuasive than the one he offered the Athenian jury is momentarily delayed.

For Socrates is aware that Crito has been attempting to interrupt for quite a while and now gives him a chance to speak. Crito has been eager to issue the warning, on behalf of the man who is to administer the poison, that Socrates must converse (*dialegesthai*) as little as possible to avoid getting heated up, which would interfere with the effects of the hemlock. The war of opposites, which Socrates described in his account of the relation between pleasure and pain and will analyze in his final argument,[34] is reflected in the dramatic deeds of the dialogue: the activity of conversing, which brings forth heat and thus prolongs life, is engaged from the outset in a battle against the poison, which brings forth cold, and with it death. But conversing has in fact a double function: if, in its physiological effect, it chains the soul to the body, it is at the same time the means of separating the *logos* from the soul united with the body. Socrates allows Crito to interrupt only after he has committed himself to delivering a defense and is therefore compelled to continue: he demonstrates his allegiance to life and *logos* in the interval between announcing and carrying out his defense of philosophy as the practice of dying.

The series of leave-takings,[35] which ends when Socrates bids farewell (*chairein*) to the servant of the Eleven who announces the time to drink the hemlock (116d), begins when Socrates now commands Crito to bid farewell to the man who warns him of the opposition between the effect of conversing and that of the poison. Just as Socrates displayed his willingness, at his public trial, to obey every law of the city but not the command to cease the practice of philosophy,[36] he refuses now, on the day of his execution, to heed the warning to converse as little as possible. Let twice as much of the poison be prepared, or even three times if necessary, Socrates boasts, calling to mind the proverb, "Twice and even thrice the beautiful things!"[37]

Chapter Three: The Practice of Dying

[63e8–64c9] Prepared to defend his justice and prudence in not grieving at the approach of death, Socrates addresses Simmias and Cebes as his "judges." He refused to assign that name to the Athenians who condemned him of injustice and impiety, assigning it only to those who acquitted him.[1] Yet Socrates has just expressed his hope of offering a more persuasive speech now than the one he offered to the judges at his trial (63b). Was Socrates, then, unable to persuade those who acquitted him that death was, at this point, preferable? He wishes now, in any case, to give a *logos* explaining why it appears to him likely that a man who really spent his life in philosophy would be confident in dying and hopeful of finding the greatest goods "there" when he has died. Socrates is silent about the nature of these goods to be received after death, which seems to be a place as well as a time; nor does he confirm whether such hope for the future is identical with the philosopher's confidence in dying based on the life he has led.

That identity is implicitly put into question by the premise with which Socrates begins his defense. If it is true that those who happen to grasp philosophy correctly practice nothing but dying and being dead, it would surely be strange if they were troubled in the achievement of what they eagerly pursued throughout their lives. It is no wonder that, as Socrates claims, others are unaware of this. To die and to be dead would seem to be one thing that could never be a habitual practice. The formulation sounds as strange as does that of its practitioners, those who "correctly grasp philosophy," as if it were an object that could be possessed once and for all. It is clear, in any case, that Socrates intends to respond to the attack against his acceptance of death, understood simply as the termination of life, by reinterpreting death as the goal of a lifelong practice of dying. But whatever death turns out to mean, if this practice of dying is a progressive activity that ceases with death in the ordinary sense, its practitioners might well lament the moment that puts an end to their lifelong pursuit;[2] the man who "really spent his life in philosophy" might well regret its termination, which is not necessarily its fulfillment.

In spite of himself, Simmias is forced to laugh, for Socrates' assertion is actually in perfect accordance with the opinion of the many, who agree quite disdainfully that "the philosophizers" do desire death and indeed deserve it.[3] They would speak the truth, Socrates admits, but without realizing what they say, since they do not know what kind of death it is that the "true philosophers" desire and deserve. Socrates reproaches the ignorance of the many on the basis of the very ambiguity he himself exploits; for if the practice of being dead implies something other than the ordinary understanding of death as a physiological phenomenon, why would it necessarily exclude the fear based on that ordinary understanding? To clarify what kind of death it is that the philosophers desire, they must "bid farewell" to the many, Socrates recommends, and speak only among themselves; yet the account that follows betrays a harmony between the opinion of the many and that of the true philosophers, which Socrates indicates only by implying his own distance from both.[4]

It is striking, then, that Socrates calls them "the true philosophers," or a little later "the genuine philosophers." He gives them a name that reflects perfectly their own self-understanding. Each identifies himself with the pure soul, which will reach its goal when it is released from the body at death and reunited with "the true" (66b). Given this interpretation of truth, "true lover of wisdom" looks like a contradiction in terms. Yet it is in accordance with this self-understanding that the true philosophers construct their understanding of the "pure beings" to which the pure soul is thought to be akin. If the union of these assumed kindred were realized, the soul of the philosopher would be indistinguishable from its object of knowledge. In fact, if each true philosopher actualized his nature as a pure soul, none could be differentiated from any other: Socrates does not arbitrarily refer to them in the plural. The traditional reading of the *Phaedo* takes the following account to be a genuine formulation of the Socratic-Platonic view of the "ideas" and the way they are known; it naturally turns Socrates, therefore, into one more indistinguishable member of the class of genuine philosophers. But Socrates fails to breed true to this *genos*. If he shares with the genuine philosophers in the practice of dying and being dead, he will eventually disclose his own unique interpretation of it.

Socrates begins his account of this practice with a presumably self-evident question: "Do we believe that death (*to thanatos*) is something?" And

Simmias enthusiastically affirms this before inquiring about what it is he affirms.[5] He does not consider the possibility of a distinction between death and dying, nor the association of death with nonbeing,[6] and he seems to have already forgotten Socrates' immediately preceding reference to the different kind of death desired by the philosopher. Socrates himself, however, now proceeds to offer three formulations of what death is:

> Is it anything other than the release of the soul from the body? And is this "being dead" (*to tethnanai*), on the one hand, the body itself by itself becoming separate, released from the soul, on the other, the soul itself by itself being separate, having been released from the body? Is death anything other than this? (64c4–9)

If "death," according to Simmias, is some one thing, "being dead," Socrates now suggests, is a state that represents two different results of the event of dying. While the body only becomes separate, the soul is separate; from the perspective of the body, its union with the soul is primary, whereas from the perspective of the soul, its separation from the body is primary. There is, consequently, no single subject that undergoes death. Socrates suppresses the fact that it is a man who dies. At the moment that he defines death as a separation, he performs a separation. It is not a physiological change but the Socratic *logos* that divides the living animal into body and soul.

In accomplishing this separation, Socrates at the same time points to the hidden union between the many and the true philosophers. Just as the philosophers seek the separation of the pure soul from the body, the many—who want to "die of pleasure"[7]—seek the separation of pure body from soul. The hedonist, who pursues nothing but pleasure, resenting the soul as an impediment to the fulfillment of his desire, and the ascetic, who flees from pleasure, resenting the body as an impediment to the fulfillment of his desire, exhibit the same union of opposites that Socrates initially described in his account of pleasure and pain themselves. In disclosing this relation between hedonism and asceticism mistaken for philosophy, Socrates stands back from both at once.

[64d1–66a10] He indicates this distance by beginning with a description of the effort of the "philosophic man" to flee from the body, without offering any explanation of the purpose of that attempt. Nor does Socrates need any argument to obtain Simmias' agreement that such a man "could not take seriously" the so-called pleasures such as eating and drinking and the *aphrodisia*; that he would not "honor" the other cares of the body "except as necessary"; that he "more than most men" would separate the soul from communion with the body. However much Socrates adopts a perspective that is not his own, he speaks only the truth. His boldest claim is to assert that the philosopher, more than most men, does not assign the highest priority to the pleasures and adornments of the body.

Only after describing this attempted flight from the body does Socrates identify its goal—the acquisition of *phronēsis*. This goal, he implies, is derived from the desire for purification of the soul, since *phronēsis*, as understood by the true philosophers, is precisely the condition of the soul in its separation from the body.[8] Only, they believe, when the soul has "bid farewell" to the body[9]—for the senses together with the passions are identified as mere affections of the body—can it "reach out and grasp the being."[10] The acquisition of *phronēsis* is described as a matter of "grasping," "reaching out," "seizing," "possessing," or "hitting." This unacknowledged metaphoric language, in which the allegedly purest state of the soul is depicted in terms of the sense of touch,[11] betrays the same union of opposites implicitly ascribed to asceticism and hedonism. It expresses the understanding of *phronēsis* as nothing but a paradoxically noncorporeal contact with noncorporeal entities, whose necessary counterpart is the abstraction of a pure soul. For if one were to admit that perception and the passions belong to the soul itself, even its release from the body could not serve as a sufficient condition for the acquisition of *phronēsis*. Motivated by this goal, the soul of the philosopher dishonors the body and flees from it to be alone by itself; while presumably aiming at contact with "the beings," the soul in fact desires to be only with itself as a separate being.

Socrates draws attention to this implication by turning, with an apparent abruptness, from considering soul itself by itself to ask Simmias, "Do we say that the just itself is something or nothing?" When Simmias shows no more hesitation than he did in agreeing that we believe death is something, Socrates supplements his question about the just with one about the beautiful and good. He does not raise the question of how, if each is "itself by itself," there could be any relation between them, and if there is not, how it is possible to formulate *what* each is. Socrates first inquires whether such things are ever seen with the eyes or grasped by any of the senses, through the body, before he adds to his list size, health, and strength,[12] which seem to be necessarily related to our perception of bodies as characterized by a particular size, state of health, or degree of strength. Socrates' apparently superfluous reference to these characteristics tacitly invites us to step back and reconsider the cases of the just, beautiful, and good. In fact, Socrates observes, his account concerns "all the others, in a word (*heni logō*), the being (*ousia*), what each in fact is."[13] But the figure of speech he uses indicates, if read literally, that this being is "in *logos*," its unity "in one *logos*."

At the moment, however, Socrates avoids confronting the questions implicitly raised by his account. He can do so because he speaks here from the perspective of the true philosophers, who conceive of the pure beings simply in opposition to objects of perception, just as they conceive of the pure soul simply in opposition to the body. The being, however, that the true philosophers understand as the object of a nonaesthetic vision by the passive soul becomes, in Socrates' account of his own way of reasoning, the object of a hypothesis, laid down as the necessary foundation for investigating "the truth of the beings" through *logoi* (cf. 100b–d, 101c). Socrates presents this procedure, moreover, as an escape from the danger of the soul blinding itself by attempting to investigate the beings directly in the *pragmata*—in the many, variously qualified things that come to be and pass away (cf. 99d–100a). But it is precisely that danger which is represented by the true philosophers' understanding of *phronēsis* as direct contact of the soul with "the *pragmata* themselves" (cf. 66e).

Socrates seems to include himself for the first time when he refers to "whoever among us most precisely prepared himself to think about (*dianoēthenai*) what he investigates." If anyone were to "hit upon the being," Socrates acknowledges with qualification, "it would be accomplished most purely by one who approached each with thought (*dianoia*) alone, as much as possible," without introducing the senses into his calculation. In elaborating this account, Socrates preserves the true philosophers' insistence on the necessity of investigation independent of perception, but, at the same time, he replaces soul as the agent of that activity by thought itself.[14] He admits, furthermore, the separation of thought from the senses only "as much as possible" and speaks not of automatically grasping the beings, but of a twice-removed striving—"trying to hunt the beings."[15] He expresses not resentment against the body as *the* insurmountable obstacle, but only recognition that it does not in itself lead to the goal, which is no longer identified as a condition of the separate soul, but as *phronēsis* in conjunction with truth.

[66b1–67b6] Socrates does not, however, explore his own interpretation of this somewhat cryptic account. Instead he offers to clarify the opinion of the "genuine philosophers" by imitating the speeches they might exchange—without explaining why they would have any desire for communication, given their understanding of *phronēsis*. As long as our soul is mixed up with the evil of the body, the genuine philosophers complain,[16] we can never acquire sufficiently what we desire, namely "the true"; and "the true," as Socrates has them surmise at the end of their speech, is perhaps that, released from the body after death, being pure, "we shall through ourselves know all the pure."[17] Their claim to be led to this insight by some kind of "short-cut" may be a sign of their awareness of its inexplicability: apparently conversing while alive, "in the body," how could they justify the truth of the claim that the body prevents all possible access to the truth?

But it is the body, they are convinced, that produces loves, desires, fears, and illusions; it demands money for its needs and is *the* cause of wars and factions. The genuine philosophers seem to have misdirected their anger and resentment. They are eager to cast blame on the body not only for the distractions of the senses and the passions, but also for political opinions and economic conditions. They have mistaken all internal dissension within the soul for dissension between the pure soul and the alien body. Because it interrupts any rare moment of leisure, the genuine philosophers conclude, the body makes it almost impossible to think at all. Reducing every obstacle to a corporeal one, while identifying the self with the soul, the genuine philosophers absolve themselves of all responsibility for their inability to obtain the *phronēsis* they desire. But this is precisely a sign of the condition Socrates will later attack as the greatest evil: to maintain a false standard of absolute wisdom, while refusing to acknowledge one's own deficiency, results in that resentment against *logos* through which one deprives oneself of the very possibility of seeking truth and knowledge of the beings (cf. 90c–d).

If *phronēsis* were indeed what the genuine philosophers believe, either it could not be acquired at all or it could be acquired only after death. The genuine philosophers can claim, therefore, only to be as close as possible to knowledge by keeping as themselves purified as possible from the contamination of the body "until the god releases us." Yet the value of this preparation is unintelligible, for if death itself is a release of the soul from the body, it must automatically lead to the goal consisting of union of "the pure with the pure." When Socrates concludes his imitation by attributing these opinions to all "correct lovers of learning,"[18] he ironically casts judgment on their position: between a lifetime of deception guaranteed by communion with the body and an afterlife of wisdom guaranteed by separation of the soul, why should learning be necessary, and how could it be possible at all?

[67b7–68c4] If there is any truth in this speech, Socrates reflects with restraint:

> there is much hope that one, arriving where I am traveling, there if any-where, would sufficiently acquire that which has been the object of much concern for us in this life, so that the journey now imposed on me is begun with good hope, and for any other man who believes he has prepared his thought (*dianoia*) as if having been purified. (67b–c)

The genuine philosophers long to possess "there," that for the sake of which Socrates has lived "here"; but whether their hope for a purified soul that could be in communion with the pure beings after death is identical with "preparation of *dianoia*" remains in question. Purification not of the soul but of thought itself requires, as Socrates discloses in the course of the con-versation, separation not from the body alone but from the self and its pas-sions, including the fear of death and correlative hope for immortality.

Socrates believes that he has prepared his thought *as if* having been purified, and he referred previously to that knowledge of the beings that is "most purely" pursued by one who attempts to hunt each with thought alone (65e–66a); but he now claims that purification [*katharsis*] was "long ago in the *logos*" said to consist in the separation of the soul from the body, "habituating itself to collect itself together from everywhere in the body."[19] *Katharsis* is an activity of "collection" and "division"; but the very terms that could describe the practice of "dialectics"[20]—which might indeed constitute the "preparation of *dianoia*"—are now applied to the soul, in its attempt to release itself from the body "as from a prison," and to be alone by itself, both now and hereafter. Is this *katharsis*, Socrates asks, what we call "death"? Death, which was first defined as a separation of likes, of soul from body as well as of body from soul, is now redefined as a purification—that is, a separation of better from worse.[21] By emphasiz-ing, however, that the question concerns what we *call* "death," Socrates indicates his exploitation of its ambiguous meaning: the name that refers, on the one hand, to a physiological phenomenon, the destruction, namely, of the living being, has been applied, on the other hand, to the way of in-vestigation practiced by the philosopher throughout his life.

Just that ambiguity underlies Socrates' repetition of the claim with which he began his defense: for the man who prepared himself by living

39

as closely as possible to being dead, it would be laughable to fear death when it comes.[22] For if one's life were determined by the *erōs* of *phronēsis*, Socrates asks, would it not be irrational to fear what is acknowledged as the condition for its attainment? In order to explore this apparent absurdity, Socrates reminds his interlocutors of familiar stories: when "human loves"—boys or wives or sons—have died, many have willingly gone to Hades, led by the hope of seeing and being with the beloved there. But, given the ambiguous meaning of death defined as the separation of the soul from the body, the lover's wish for communion in Hades—the invisible place[23]—would not arise simply with the termination of the life of his beloved, with whom he was once united but from whom he is now painfully separated; it points, rather, to the truth of *erōs* that always moved him—the unfulfilled longing for simultaneous contemplation and possession of the pure soul of his beloved. The lover somehow recognizes the body as the obstacle to the fulfillment of his desire, without perhaps understanding what it would mean to see and be with a pure soul. Socrates has discovered an illuminating model for the lover of *phronēsis*, who should not grieve when he dies, clinging to the hope that he will meet nowhere else but in Hades the object of his desire. Yet if he, like the human lover, construes *erōs* as a merely provisional route toward a goal, which could be overcome with the arrival at that goal, he would misunderstand its nature: the genuine philosophers misunderstood the nature of philosophy.

Now Socrates, of all men, might be thought the least susceptible to such a misunderstanding; yet his ability and willingness to defend philosophy as the practice of dying and being dead do seem to depend upon having lost or abandoned his lifelong "art of erotics."[24] But whereas the genuine philosophers' longing for death is based on a resentment of life that is unconditional, it is Socrates' awareness of his particular—political—circumstances that allows him to construe as a benefit his imminent release from the city, from the body, from life itself.[25] When Socrates concludes that a man who is troubled at the approach of death cannot be a lover of wisdom, he affirms the common ground he shares with the genuine philosophers. But he reveals its internal articulation when he adds that such a man must be a lover of the body, hence necessarily of money or honor or both;[26] for while Socrates would understand these desires as conflicting motives within the soul,[27] the genuine philosophers deny the possibility of any internal dissension, just as they misunderstand the nature of *erōs*. They would want to oppose, then, to the lover of the body a "lover of soul," but the latter is precisely the formula for one who clings to life at all costs.[28] It is, therefore, the appropriate, if paradoxical, label for those whose longing for death is motivated by hope for the survival of the separate soul in contact with the beings themselves. That this hope is not the ground for Socrates' practice of dying and for his steadfast conduct in the face of death becomes the implicit argument of the final phase of his defense.

[68c5–69c3] Simmias readily agrees—before any examination—that what is called courage is most characteristic of the philosopher, while superiority over the desires, which the many call moderation, is characteristic only of him. But since most men consider death to be the greatest of evils, Socrates reasons, those who face it bravely must do so through fear of even greater evils, they are courageous, although it is irrational (*alogon*), through fear and cowardice. And those among the many who are moderate refrain from present pleasures only because they fear being deprived of others: they are moderate, although it is said to be impossible, through incontinence. Socrates does not give a parallel account of courage resulting from fear and moderation resulting from desire but condemns both for coming into being through fear, either of greater pains or of deprivation of pleasures: demotic virtue, he suggests, is a flight from the reality of pain rather than a positive search for pleasure.[29] To bring out its irrationality, Socrates must juxtapose the speech of the many, which implies that the cause of any courageous action is courage itself, of any moderate action moderation itself, with the practice of the many, in which each purported virtue comes into being through its opposite. Demotic virtue, determined entirely by pleasure and pain,[30] furnishes one more model for the structure of opposition that Socrates first exemplified in describing the relation of pleasure and pain themselves; it exhibits precisely the perplexity that compelled Socrates, according to the report he will give of his own philosophic development, to abandon all investigation of the beings in order to preserve the safety of *logos*.[31]

As for his own conduct in the face of death, Socrates may display justice and prudence but apparently neither courage—since he claims not to count death among the greatest evils—nor moderation—since he claims to have no desire for the pleasures he will be leaving behind.[32] The possible autonomy of courage and moderation is indeed rendered problematic by Socrates' concluding account of "true virtue together with *phronēsis*."[33] He introduces this account through the metaphor of monetary transaction: the correct exchange for acquiring virtue cannot be that practiced by the many, in which pleasure is exchanged against pleasure, pain against pain, and fear against fear,[34] greater against less, as if they were coins; but the only correct coin for which and with which all these are to be bought and sold is *phronēsis*.[35] This image, which has understandably puzzled readers of the dialogue,[36] is in fact a most appropriate form to mirror the content it expresses: the structure of monetary exchange is reflected, first in the structure of metaphoric exchange, with money standing in the place of *phronēsis*, while the latter is itself thereby described as belonging to a context of exchange. The acquisition of money may be the immediate end for which goods are sold, but its proper function would be abused if taken to be solely an end in itself, and not rather a medium for the exchange of goods. The proper function of *phronēsis*, accordingly, is abused when construed—as by the genuine philosophers—to be solely an end in itself, separated from the exchange of the passions with one another. For the latter, apart from *phronēsis*, is in reality, Socrates maintains, a slavish sort of virtue, neither healthy nor true, a kind of shadow-painting determined by the shifting appearances of pleasures, pains, and fears.[37]

The true virtue, Socrates concludes, is in reality some kind of purification (*katharsis tis*) from this illusion, as are moderation and justice and courage, and *phronēsis* itself some kind of purgation (*katharmos tis*). Socrates seems to distinguish between the purified state constituted by true virtue and the purgation by *phronēsis* through which that state is achieved; he maintains his original obscurity about the status of *phronēsis*, which was presented as both the means by which virtue is to be acquired and a part of true virtue—that which makes it possible to speak of virtue as a whole.[38] He puts into question, in any case, the genuine philosophers' understanding of *phronēsis* as nothing but a goal to be awaited after death, when the pure soul would be united with the pure beings. That goal could not be identified with the *phronēsis* Socrates now displays through his conduct in the face of death—the *phronēsis* that this entire speech is intended to defend.

[69c3–69e5] Socrates began his defense by discovering, in the demotic opinion that the philosophers do indeed desire and deserve death, the truth of philosophy as the practice of dying. He concludes by uncovering the hidden meaning in the dark language of the mysteries, contrasting the uninitiated and unpurified who will lie in the mud in Hades with the initiated and purified who will dwell with the gods.[39] Appealing to the formula

of initiation—"The thyrsus-bearers are many but the Bacchae are few"—
Socrates surmises that the latter must be those who have correctly philosophized. He adopts the distinction within the mysteries between the
many and the few only to imply a distinction between the philosophers,
who are few, and the pious, who are many. That distinction is not made
explicit until the myth Socrates addresses to Simmias at the end of the
dialogue, to persuade him that "we must do our best to acquire virtue and
phronēsis in life" (114c), which serves as a counterpart to the speech
Socrates now addresses to Simmias in order to defend the *phronēsis* of his
acceptance of death. Just as the first half of the dialogue consists in an inseparable mixture of "investigating and mythologizing," while the second
half accomplishes their separation, Socrates' opening defense presents
the philosopher through the mask of the pious ascetic, while the final myth
explicitly separates them. For it contrasts the initiates who will dwell
among the gods with those "sufficiently purified by philosophy" (114b–c).
This sufficient purification consists, as Socrates will show, in the turn to
a *technē* of *logoi* that is designed to guarantee consistency in reasoning: it
replaces the genuine philosophers' understanding of *phronēsis* as direct
contact of the pure soul with the pure beings.

To become one of those who have perfectly philosophized, Socrates
admits at the end of his defense speech, he has striven throughout his
life, though he may not have done so correctly. But it is only on this last
day that he could acknowledge his eagerness "to have philosophized correctly"; to understand philosophy as a completed action seems to be a
contradiction in terms. Socrates corrects it, however, at the moment he
expresses it. For when he concludes that he may know shortly, if god is
willing, whether or not he has striven correctly, what he confirms is his
present knowledge of ignorance. In light of that admission, the belief he
first expressed and now repeats—that he will find good masters "there
no less than here"—must be intended less as a prediction of the unknown
future than as a judgment of the present: "here" in the Athenian prison,
Socrates' immediate master is the servant of the Eleven, representative
of the Athenian *dēmos*, and among the circle of his friends, Plato is absent.
Socrates' speech is in fact a test of his judgment, for he completes it by
repeating his hope that, in comparison with his public defense, this one
will prove more persuasive—not necessarily more true. Socrates could
hardly be more overt in acknowledging the status of his defense, without
altogether defeating the rhetorical purpose he ascribes to it. That rhetorical purpose is necessitated by interlocutors who are moved by their own

fear of death, together with pity at the imprudence, and anger at the injustice, of Socrates' acceptance of his own death. Precisely by representing these motivating grounds, the Platonic dialogue attempts to protect its reader from the persuasion Socrates claims to want to induce in his companions.

Chapter Four: Genesis

[69e6–70c3] Socrates' defense apparently satisfies Simmias, who is silent at its conclusion, but Cebes immediately speaks up with an objection: however persuasively Socrates may have spoken of the philosopher's desire for the acquisition of *phronēsis* after death, he has simply presupposed the continued existence of the soul. Yet men are filled with distrust, for they fear that, upon leaving the body, the soul is no longer "anywhere" but is corrupted and destroyed when the man dies, dissipating like breath or smoke.[1] There would be good grounds for the great and beautiful hope Socrates expresses only if it could be shown that after death the soul is gathered together "somewhere," itself by itself, freed from all the evils Socrates has just described. Cebes makes a reasonable criticism of the preceding speech; but he does not make the reasonable assumption that Socrates is equally aware of the problem and consequently, must have intentionally invited this distrust in the great and beautiful hope that his defense appears to offer.

Cebes has been preoccupied, perhaps, with the thought of what it will be like to look upon the corpse of Socrates, pure body itself, after the sudden disappearance of whatever made it alive. If *psychē* is anything more than the name for this quality of the body, then it too after death must be "somewhere," itself by itself. To be, Cebes assumes, means to be in some place;[2] but that is the unique characteristic of a body, and the soul, which is only a subtle form of body, like breath or smoke, must be especially subject to destruction. Cebes speaks as if the issue ought to be the object of a physicist's investigation. Yet he betrays the self-interest that motivates his question by limiting it to the fate of the human soul. He earns Socrates' praise for speaking the truth when he guesses that no little encouragement or persuasion would be needed to show that the soul of the dying man exists and has some power (*dunamis*) and *phronēsis*. Cebes does not specify what this power is that, in addition to *phronēsis*, remains after death. If he did, he would confront the contradiction that turns out to haunt the series of arguments that follows; for the power besides *phronēsis* that would ordinarily be thought to belong to soul is its function as the cause of life.[3] It is no wonder that, despite his criticism of Socrates' defense speech, Cebes neglects as much as Socrates did to raise the question, "What is soul?"[4]

Socrates responds to Cebes' challenge by asking what they should do. He inquires, more literally, "What shall we make?" and clarifies the question by asking if Cebes wishes to "mythologize" about what is likely.[5] He could not now at any rate, Socrates insists, be accused even by a comic poet of chattering at leisure and making *logoi* that are of no concern to him. It was the accusation of a comic poet, according to Plato's *Apology of Socrates*, that inspired the long-standing prejudice against Socrates. The source of his condemnation by the Athenian *dēmos* was Aristophanes' portrayal of Socrates as an investigator of "things beneath the earth and above the heavens."[6] But this image, Socrates complains at his trial, makes him appear indistinguishable from Anaxagoras, and Socrates denies its truth, albeit with qualification: no one present ever heard him *speak* of such things.[7] He seems willing now, however, to confirm it; he will conclude the argument that follows, at least, with an allusion to the Anaxagorean cosmology.

That he was indeed attracted to the Anaxagorean project, Socrates will admit in the course of his intellectual autobiography. But he will disclose at the same time the disappointment that compelled him to find a replacement for Anaxagoras' teaching, and he now foreshadows that correction. For even if the forthcoming argument looks like an assimilation of Socratic to Anaxagorean philosophy, Socrates justifies it by the urgency of his concerns at the moment; and it is this very admission of his self-interest, Socrates indicates, that distinguishes him from Anaxagoras. It denies, at the same time, the Aristophanic charge against him as an "idle babbler,"[8] whose concern with things in the heavens and beneath the earth makes him blind to "the human things" right at his feet. Socrates' allusion to that Aristophanic charge brings to mind not only his public trial, but also his self-accusation this final day for his guilt in separating the greatest music from demotic music:[9] his reminder of Aristophanes does not by accident stand between his invitation to mythologize and his subsequent recommendation, that "it is necessary to investigate." Socrates introduces the first argument, which sets the pattern for the first half of the dialogue, as an inseparable mixture of *mythos* and *logos*, like pleasure and pain joined "in one head."

This opening argument is, perhaps, the most perplexing in the entire dialogue. In contrast with the subsequent arguments, which are more evidently determined by the unresolved problems preceding them, this first argument is the one Socrates seems to choose most freely. Yet it turns out to be surreptitiously determined by the beliefs of the genuine philosophers; and while Socrates is supposedly trying to defend those beliefs, he will in fact attempt to disclose their incoherence. That attempt, however, has no effect whatsoever on those to whom the argument is addressed. We are therefore deprived of the clues customarily provided by the responses of Socrates' interlocutors, since they do not say a word in response to this first argument, either immediately after its conclusion or as the conversation develops. There is, however, one individual—whom Phaedo cannot identify—who does not simply ignore the first argument: he objects that its fundamental assumption seems to be contradicted by that of the last argument, which brings the discussion full circle, back to its beginning. But it is not evident why Socrates is compelled to wait to provide the clarification he offers in response to that objection: he seems purposely to delay precisely the considerations that might have helped overcome the obscurities in the present speech.

This speech turns out to be an analysis of the logic of becoming, but it never specifies unambiguously what it is that undergoes *genesis*. While this first argument looks, at least to begin with, as if it is meant to be a Socratic "physics," it is paradoxically silent about body. This is especially surprising following immediately after the speech of the genuine philosophers, who never cease speaking of the body, even if only as the obstacle to the attainment of *phronēsis*. But in fact the first argument only carries out the radical consequences of the genuine philosophers' suppression of the body: it identifies the soul with the living being, while inconsistently construing it as the neutral subject that can be alive or dead. Of course, with its silence about the body, the first argument must ignore the original definition of death as the separation of soul from body. The change from being alive to being dead becomes, therefore, nothing but a change of place. Thus the suppressed body returns in the guise of soul, whose only motion is locomotion.

Just because of the opposition that the anonymous interlocutor observes, the last argument brings to light what is conspicuously absent in the first. The *genesis* described in the last argument, accordingly, is the transformation of the living body into the corpse, the former distinguished from the latter by its "participation" in the *eidos* of life. The last argument thus reveals the silence of the first, not only about the body, but at the same time and with equally perplexing implications, about beings that are not subject to becoming: it is the one argument in the dialogue that never mentions the "ideas" in any form. It thus avoids simultaneously the question of how soul is related, on the one hand, to the body, on the other, to the objects of knowledge, although these two relations emerge together as the fundamental problem of the dialogue.

[70c4–70d9] Socrates did warn Cebes before plunging into this argument that it would be some kind of "mythological investigation." That mixture is exemplified when Socrates reformulates Cebes' question as to whether the soul is somewhere after death. Let us investigate it in this way, whether the souls of men who have died are in Hades or not. As a starting point for this inquiry Socrates recalls "some kind of ancient *logos*": they are there after arriving from here and then come back here again, being born from the dead. Whatever kind of *logos* it may be, this ancient tale describes a journey from this world to another and back again, without mentioning what it is that makes this journey—though it is presumably the souls[10]—and without explaining what "the dead" are from which these travelers return to life again.

If this is true, Socrates ostensibly repeats, that the living are born again from those who have died, then, he reasons, "our souls would be there."[11] Yet Socrates has transformed the antecedent of the argument, replacing "the souls born from the dead" with "the living born again from those who have died," as well as its consequent, replacing "the souls of men who have died" with "our souls." Making use of this transformation without explaining it, Socrates defends his reasoning: if our souls did not continue to exist, they could not be born again, so it would be "sufficient witness" that they exist if it could really be made evident that the living come to be from nothing but, and from nowhere else than, the dead; otherwise, he admits, some other *logos* would be needed (cf. 76e, 106d). This generation of the living from the dead would mean, in accordance with the original definition of death, the coming to be united of separate soul and body; but Socrates conceals, as much as the ancient tale did, the role of the body, hence the relation between the soul born again and the living generated from the dead.

In presenting the strategy of the argument, Socrates anticipates its systematic confusion of two alternatives: either the soul is an enduring subject that undergoes a *genesis* from one place to another, from Hades to the body and back again, or there is a *genesis* of one thing, the living, into another, the dead, and back again but with no enduring subject that persists through the change. The dead, in any case—from nowhere else but whence the living come to be—seem to be identified with Hades itself, the invisible place (80d, 81a) appropriate for the separate soul that is invisible but somewhere. Yet in sliding from the first consideration about the souls of the dead to the subsequent one about our souls, Socrates transforms the meaning of being "in Hades": it seems to be no longer the place of the soul after death but rather a characterization of soul as such, whenever it is, or perhaps, as Socrates suggested in the previous speech, whenever it is engaged in a particular mode of investigation.[12] Socrates may be interested only in demonstrating that our invisible souls are; but in adjusting this aim to meet Cebes' challenge, he treats the being of the soul simply as the condition for the possibility of coming back to life again.

The demonstration would be carried out most easily, Socrates advises, if considered with regard not only to men, but also to plants, animals, and everything that comes into being. Socrates does appear to display his Aristophanic image, conspicuously distant from the concern with "the human things" that might be considered his essential contribution to the philosophic tradition.[13] He seems to prepare his audience for the later account he will offer of his own philosophic development, beginning with the pre-Socratic investigation of nature and never turning to "the human things" in particular. Despite this initial appearance, however, the argument Socrates is about to conduct in fact examines not the nature of plants and animals, but the structure of any *logos* about becoming.

[70d9–71a11] Concerning everything that has *genesis*, Socrates begins, let us see if each necessarily comes into being from its opposite if, that is, there happens to be one. After offering as examples the beautiful and the ugly, or just and unjust, and "thousands of others"—opposites that do not seem to "have *genesis*" at all[14]—Socrates claims to repeat the original question. Only now, instead of asking whether everything that comes into being does so from its opposite, he asks whether everything that is an opposite necessarily comes to be from "nowhere else" than its own opposite.[15] Socrates does not insist, then, that all opposites do come into being, nor that everything that comes into being has an opposite, but only that any opposite that comes into being must do so from its opposite. Although he does not clarify the meaning of this "from," he preserves the general assumption of the argument by implying that one opposite is the place from whence the other emerges.

The restricted scope of the principle is confirmed, in any case, by Socrates' illustration of it on the model of comparatives: when something comes to be greater, it must first have been smaller, and if it later becomes smaller, it must first have been greater. Socrates does not argue that something that is small must necessarily become greater, or something great smaller, but only that something that does become greater or smaller must have previously been less so. The "now" in which something is said to have become greater is the same "now" that determines its having been smaller. To determine, as in Socrates' further examples, that something has become stronger, quicker, or better is simultaneously to determine that it must have been weaker, slower, or worse. A prior condition is not what it is until a posterior condition makes it so—like the painful revealed to be such only by comparison with the so-called pleasant that follows from it (cf. 60b).

The coming to be of a present "more" is by definition from a past "less," the coming to be of a present "less" by definition from a past "more": the principle is based on the necessity not of *phusis*, but of *logos*. Yet what is it exactly that does thereby come to be from its opposite? Socrates will attempt to clarify this principle only when it later emerges as an apparent contradiction of the final argument based on the principle of mutual exclusion of opposites. The generation of opposites from each other refers, Socrates will then explain, not to the opposite qualities themselves, which would lead to a violation of the law of noncontradiction, nor to the coming to be and passing away of a subject as such, which may not have an opposite, but rather, to the *pragmata*—like "Socrates greater" and "Socrates smaller"—each of which is the inseparably bonded union of a subject with one or two opposite qualities (cf. 102d–103b).[16] It is precisely this distinction between opposite *pragmata* and opposites themselves, however, that Socrates seems intentionally to suppress in the present argument. He has established the mutual generation of opposites, furthermore, only on the model of comparative states, without explaining whether or how this model can be applied to the generation of the living and the dead from each other, which is presumably the intention of the argument.

[71a12–71b11] Socrates claims nevertheless to have established sufficiently that all things come to be in this way, opposite *pragmata* from their opposites. And since Cebes does not dispute it, Socrates proceeds to inquire whether there are between each member of a pair of opposites two *geneseis*, mediating processes from each to the other.[17] Before giving Cebes a chance to answer, Socrates offers the example of increase, the *genesis* from a smaller *pragma* to a greater, and decrease, the *genesis* from a greater *pragma* to a smaller. But since the standard in relation to which something becomes greater or smaller is not necessarily its own prior state, it could come to be one or the other of these opposites without either increasing or decreasing.[18] Simmias, Socrates later insists, comes to be greater when compared with Socrates who is smaller, smaller when compared to Phaedo who is greater (102b–e). The relational qualities Socrates chooses as examples thus put into question, rather than confirm, the necessary connection between opposite states and the *geneseis* mediating them. Perhaps dying, Socrates implies, cannot be connected with being dead, or being alive with having come to be so. Even to grant the connection, in any case, between one opposite state and the *genesis* leading to it does not entail a connection between that *genesis* and its opposite: even if something does become greater by increasing, it is not by definition true that it must have been previously decreasing, or conversely. It would be a mistake—which Socrates seems to have invited—to interpret his reference to two mediating *geneseis* as a claim about a continual cycle of alteration.

Whether or not we have names to designate these processes, Socrates inquires, is it not necessary indeed that there be "everywhere" a *genesis* from one opposite to the other? Cebes is certain of this, without asking Socrates to clarify what the subject is of these *geneseis*. But while increase and decrease, Socrates' first example, or cooling and heating, his last example, refer by definition to the becoming greater or smaller, cooler or hotter, of one subject, Socrates' central example, the *geneseis* of separation and combination, does not seem to fit this pattern. For, strictly speaking, at least two units would be required for combination, while one unit would be the subject of separation (cf. 96e, 97b): if dying is a separation, it is the living being as a whole that undergoes that *genesis*, and if coming to life is, by analogy, a combination, two separate entities would undergo that *genesis*. This central example thus points to the unspecified alternative at stake in the argument from the outset. For combination and separation seem to be the *geneseis* through which the living and the dead would come to be from each other, with no identical subject enduring through the cycle, rather than *geneseis* mediating between the states of being alive and being dead, which would characterize the soul as one enduring subject.[19]

51

[71c1–71e3] Socrates has spoken only of cases in which the coming to be of one opposite is by definition the passing away of the other. Since, however, the scope of this model may be too restricted for its intended application,[20] Socrates begins his attempt to supplement it by proposing an analogy. Is there something, he asks, that is the opposite of being alive, just as being asleep is the opposite of being awake? Cebes responds, "Being dead," as quickly as Simmias responded to Socrates' original question, whether we believe that death is something (64c). He does not stop to consider the possibility that there may be no opposite state applicable to a thing characterized as "being alive"; whether life has an opposite is still an open question, apparently, in the final argument (105d). Nor does Cebes consider the possibility that the only opposite of "living" is simply the negation, "not-living."[21] Of course in that case, the claim that one comes to be from the other might appear to be a claim that something comes into being from nothing, and it is the intention of this argument to preclude just such a possibility.

If being alive and being dead are opposites, Socrates reasons—without confirming this condition—they must come to be from each other and have two *geneseis* mediating between them. But while dying appears to be a *genesis* from one opposite state to another, Socrates has not shown that there is an existing subject that is dead after having come to be so. Being born, on the other hand, is not by definition the *genesis* from one opposite state to another, and Socrates has not identified a subject that exists before coming to be alive. He could have done so, one might think, by emphasizing the difference between conception and birth. Such a proposal calls attention, of course, to what the entire argument seeks to avoid, namely the origin of a living animal through sexual reproduction. It points, at the same time, to the lack of symmetry between birth and death. For what would be parallel, in the case of dying, to the interval between conception and birth? In fact, however, the distinction between conception and birth only pushes the problem back a step and leaves the origin of a living animal as problematic as its destruction. For it does not solve the mystery of what soul is and how it is related to the body.

Socrates attempts to cover over these difficulties by relying on his proposed analogy. It is indeed a powerful one,[22] since sleep, at least a deep, unconscious sleep, may be the closest experience we have of what death is. But Socrates must now conceal what the poets have long recognized when they imagine death as the long sleep from which we do not awaken. Being awake, Socrates proceeds, comes to be from its opposite, being asleep, just as the latter does from the former; and they are necessarily mediated by the *geneseis* of falling asleep, which, by definition, means being no longer awake, and reawakening, which, by definition, means being no longer asleep.[23] Now Socrates wants Cebes to apply this model to "the other," the pair, namely, life and death. Since, however, these are opposites that do not seem to "have *genesis*" at all, Socrates does not ask about their necessary generation from each other but instead repeats their former agreement on the opposition between being alive and being dead. The analogy with the living animal that undergoes the cycle of being awake and being asleep should indicate that the soul undergoes the cycle of being alive and being dead. But rather than ask about the *geneseis* mediating between these opposite states of one subject, Socrates transforms the question into one about the generation of one subject from its opposite.

What is it, he inquires, that comes to be from the living? Had Cebes thought about our most common human experience, he might have chosen this point to challenge the assumptions of the argument. He might have asked Socrates why they do not simply acknowledge that it is the living who come to be from the living, and that it is not the individual but the species that endures through the *genesis*.[24] But Cebes feels compelled by the argument to answer, "The dead." In response to Socrates' complementary question, "And what from the dead?," he betrays his sense of this compulsion: "It is necessary to agree that it is the living." As if to emphasize its inappropriateness as a demonstration of the existence of the human soul after death, Socrates repeats only half the conclusion, while acknowledging its unlimited application: "Then from the dead, the living—both things and persons—come to be." With Cebes' unenthusiastic admission that it appears so, Socrates draws the consequence he first presented as its necessary condition: "Then our souls are in Hades." Cebes admits, with the same reluctance, that it seems so. For if he sees no way to attack the argument, he must certainly feel dissatisfied: Socrates' conclusion in the present tense seems to describe not the fate of the soul after death, but the nature of the soul that is always "in the invisible."

[71e4–72a10] Socrates reaches this conclusion without having established the actuality of two mediating *geneseis*. He now returns to that consideration with the claim that one of these processes can be accepted: "For dying is surely evident, isn't it?" Since the existence of the soul as dead is precisely what is in question, hence the *genesis* defined as a transition to that state, Socrates unexpectedly refers to the evidence of dying rather than of being born. What would have to be evident, however, is not birth as such, but a process through which something comes to be alive after first being dead. This *genesis* can be affirmed, therefore, only if the opposite *genesis* of coming to be dead is simply assumed. And even then it requires a hypothesis that is more a construction than discovery, as Socrates indicates by his question—the same one with which he began the argument (70b)—"What shall we make?" "Must we not deliver back in turn (*antapodōsomen*) the opposite *genesis*," Socrates inquires, "or shall nature be lame?"[25] Inspired by Socrates' model of reawakening (*anegeiresthai*) as the opposite of falling asleep, Cebes is willing to give back to dying its opposite *genesis*, "coming back to life again" (*anabiōskesthai*). He does not ask why nature must be symmetrical, nor why that requires the return to life as the opposite of dying in the cycle of one identical subject. Their agreement, Socrates soon confirms, was made "not unjustly." It projects the notion of human justice, Socrates implies, onto natural *genesis*. The translation of birth into coming back to life is thus shown to be motivated by the desire to construe it as a just punishment, the penalty for the crime of attachment to life.[26]

Socrates confirms the hypothetical status of their agreement—*if* there is coming back to life—while asking whether it would not constitute the *genesis* from the dead into the living. But he conspicuously avoids the question of what "the dead" are when he concludes that, in this way too, it can be agreed that the living come to be from the dead, no less than the dead from the living. Had he admitted that the latter has been simply assumed, along with the assumed self-evidence of the *genesis* of dying, he could not claim, as he does, to have established a "sufficient witness" that "the souls of the dead are somewhere from whence they come back again." Socrates has not forgotten his own warning that the argument would require mythologizing as well as investigating. For the being of the souls of the dead "somewhere" seems to be an opposite that follows upon their existence in the body while living, like pleasure and pain joined in two heads, according to a *mythos*, such that one always follows upon the other. The being, on the other hand, of *our* souls in Hades, the invisible place, must represent that "practice of dying," which attempts to separate soul from body while alive, like pleasure and pain joined in one head, according to the Socratic account, such that the pursuit of one is almost always accompanied by the other. The two alternative conclusions in the first argument thus echo the competing interpretations of Socrates' initial defense, construing purification as the fate of the soul after death, on the one hand, and as a mode of investigation not reducible to perception, on the other (cf. 70c–d). Of course, the first argument, since it has never even raised the question of what soul is, could hardly make these alternative interpretations explicit. It thus appears, to Cebes at least, to neglect his question about whether the soul possesses *phronēsis* after death, and hence to be radically incomplete.[27]

[72a11–72e2] Cebes is willing to admit only that it looks to him as if their conclusion follows from previous agreements. But since they have only hypothetically posited the *genesis* of coming back to life, Socrates engages in one last effort to defend the justice—not necessarily the truth—of the agreements on which that hypothesis was based. If *genesis* did not always proceed in a circle,[28] Socrates reasons, from opposite to opposite and back again, then finally everything would have the same figure (*schēma*), would suffer the same condition (*pathos*), and would cease coming into being at all.[29] Socrates does not say why this consequence must be rejected. He intends, presumably, only to present an argument for the conditional necessity of a cyclical structure of becoming: it guarantees the impossibility of *genesis* exhausting itself in a linear development toward one state that would preclude all determinacy.[30] Socrates claims to be surprised when Cebes does not understand what he means; although he seems to have compressed into a single statement his reflection on the fundamental principles of pre-Socratic thought, Socrates assures Cebes that it is nothing difficult!

If, he explains, there were only falling asleep and no waking up, the myth of Endymion would be nonsense, the youth who falls asleep forever would appear "nowhere." To be, Socrates implies, is to be something, and that is, in the language of this argument, to be somewhere: Socrates preserves the contradictory character of an argument that never mentions the body yet identifies something being *what* it is with its being in some place. Now Socrates is presumably trying to prove that an irreversible process in a closed system leads eventually to a standstill in which no particular condition can be differentiated from its opposite. He seems to argue only that Endymion would be indistinguishable from everything in the same state unless some one of the things that fall asleep were to wake up again; he does not explicitly insist that everything that falls asleep, including Endymion, must necessarily wake up again. Yet, an eternally sleeping Endymion would have to be alive, but without motion, without desire or thought. Endymion seems to illustrate the genuine philosophers' paradoxical wish for an eternally existing soul that is transformed into a being and is therefore no longer a soul.

In the same way, Socrates continues, if all things were mixed together and nothing separated, there would quickly come to be that chaos—*homou panta chrēmata*—that Anaxagoras describes as the original state of the cosmos.[31] It is only, according to the Anaxagorean cosmology, with the appearance of mind (*nous*), which initiates motion, and hence separation, that the determinacy of things is rendered possible.[32] In making his cosmic *nous* responsible for motion and discrimination, Anaxagoras indicates the twofold function of soul, though without acknowledging the dependence of *nous* on soul. Socrates himself, then, has just performed a combination guided by "mind": he has not by accident put together the eternally sleeping Endymion and the cosmic chaos of all things mixed together, which are linked by the absence of soul. This juxtaposition is meant, furthermore, to illustrate the end state of an irreversible process: Socrates implicitly reproaches Anaxagoras for not recognizing that combination is itself a process that presupposes a prior state of separation,[33] and that, if mind is the cause of one *genesis*, it must be no less the cause of the other. In fact, as Socrates will argue in his later criticism of Anaxagoras, the operation of mind should be guided by the good; but it is the good and binding that truly hold all things together (99c). Yet, if the ordering of mind were unobstructed, and the goal of Anaxagorean teleology realized, Socrates seems now to suggest, it would have the same results as the mindless state of original chaos. For a closed system that progresses in only one of two opposite directions with no recycling must inevitably come to a standstill in which no further discrimination of one thing from another is possible.

Socrates has laid the groundwork for the final application of the principle of opposite *geneseis*. If all living things were to die, he inquires, and the dead were to remain in that condition without coming back to life, isn't it most necessary that in the end all things would be dead and nothing alive? To defend this necessity, Socrates asks what would happen if the living were generated from "the others." He presumably means anything other than the dead but tacitly points to the alternative that has been suppressed throughout the argument: that from which the living are generated are "the other living."[34] But Socrates must want Cebes to discover this alternative himself. If the living were to die, he repeats, and not be regenerated from the dead, is there any way out of the conclusion that everything would in the end be swallowed up in death? Cebes sees no way out: he is unwilling to accept what appears to be the only alternative, namely, that the living could come to be, in the strict sense, from nothing.[35] That the continuation of *genesis* could be guaranteed by an infinite source, he simply assumes to be impossible.[36]

But why does Cebes believe this is the only alternative? Why does he not suggest that the function Socrates assigns to coming back to life could be fulfilled by the generation of the living from the living? Having submitted so thoroughly to the premises of the argument and to its seemingly inexorable logic, Cebes has become blind to the most evident facts of experience; having assimilated, perhaps without realizing it, the genuine philosophers' disdain for the body, he has completely forgotten about sexual reproduction, the process through which life rejuvenates itself.[37] Socrates did preface the argument by recommending the consideration of plants, animals, and all things that have *genesis*; but the principle that all opposites are generated from opposites has led to a suppression of the essential characteristic of living things, which are as a species self-reproducing. In the absence of that consideration, Cebes has been forced to affirm coming back to life as the opposite of dying, to preclude the possibility of everything ending up dead.

But is this to be regarded as a reductio ad absurdum because it contradicts our experience? It would seem possible at any moment simply to claim that the source of *genesis* hasn't been used up yet. Of course, it has been assumed all along that something cannot come from nothing, hence that *genesis* has no beginning, and an infinite stretch of time behind the present moment would guarantee that the end state would already have been realized. Socrates seems, however, to have conflated a cosmological argument for the eternity of becoming with an argument about the conditions for intelligibility in *logos*. For he has emphasized another way in which it would be absurd to speak of everything ending up dead. Since coming to be is always coming to be something, if everything were to have the same *schēma* or *pathos*, it would be impossible to speak of anything becoming or being *what* it is. "Death" is significant, then, only as the opposite of life and would be meaningless in the absence of that opposition. But Socrates has only mentioned opposite determinations like life and death, the just and the unjust, the beautiful and the ugly, without articulating their status: his pre-Socratic argument, which eliminates coming to be in the strict sense—that is, from nothing—at the same time reduces being to eternal becoming.[38] Socrates intends to show, perhaps—although none of his interlocutors grasp this intention—that a coherent account of the *genesis* of opposite *pragmata* from each other depends upon the postulation of "opposites themselves," which are ungenerated and indestructible."[39]

Socrates offers this first argument about the coming to be and passing away of a living being as his response to Cebes' challenge about the existence of the soul after death. The entire discussion that follows thus appears to be a digression until the final argument, called forth by another challenge from Cebes, which Socrates interprets as a demand for an analysis of the cause of coming to be and passing away as a whole (95e). Socrates will respond to an attack against the apparent contradiction between these arguments by distinguishing the mutually exclusive opposites themselves that are the subject of the last from the mutually generating opposite *pragmata* that are the subject of the first. He seems to contend that the two arguments that frame the entire series are complementary. But that contention conceals the fact that their presuppositions and conclusions are incompatible: while the argument on the cycle of opposites presumably demonstrates the existence of the soul as alternately living and dead, that is precisely what will be denied by the final argument.

Socrates nevertheless concludes the first argument, as he will the last (107a), with the same expression of certainty:

> For it is, as it seems to me, Cebes, in this way above all, and we are not deceived in agreeing on these things, but there really is coming back to life, and from the dead the living come to be, and the souls of the dead are.[40] (72d–e)

Socrates completes both arguments by affirming the existence of the soul after death "really" (*tō onti*), literally "in being."[41] But the movement of the dialogue is an attempt to put any such claim into question. This is made explicit in the central interlude, which begins by describing the danger of resentment of *logos* and ends by introducing, as the only escape from that danger, the necessity of a turn from investigation of the beings to investigation through *logoi*. Perhaps it is only if reconstructed in accordance with this turn that the present conclusion ought to be affirmed: at the moment the dialogue is taken up by its reader, Socrates comes back to life—although not, as he agreed to demonstrate, "somewhere," not "in being" but "in *logos*."

Chapter Five: *Anamnēsis*

[72e3–74a8] Cebes joins in immediately after the conclusion of Socrates' first argument but without saying a word about it. Instead, he reveals his dissatisfaction by simply introducing another argument; this one too, he believes will show that "the soul seems to be something immortal." Perhaps Cebes realizes, despite his reference to another way of proving immortality, that Socrates never mentioned the word in the first argument.[1] If being born is nothing but coming back to life, Socrates has just argued, then our souls must exist somewhere after death from whence they come back again. If, Cebes now adds, there is truth in Socrates' customary claim that our learning is nothing but recollection, then we must have learned in some prior time what we now only recall, and that would be possible only if the soul were somewhere before coming into being in the human form (*eidos*).[2] That all birth is nothing but coming back to life revives Cebes' dormant memory that all learning is nothing but recollection: the denial that life comes into being in the strict sense—that something comes to be from nothing—brings to mind the denial that knowledge comes into being in the strict sense, from absolute ignorance.

Cebes introduces an argument that reproduces in its formal structure the argument he has just heard from Socrates. But Socrates' argument gave no indication of what the soul is, or what it does, either in Hades or "here." It unfolded the consequences of the genuine philosophers' belief in the separability of the soul from the place it happens to inhabit; but it ignored their understanding of *phronēsis* as the condition of the soul when released from the body and in contact with the pure beings to which it is akin. Cebes now intends to make up for that limitation. But while he might think that the teaching of the genuine philosophers is supported by the following argument, it is in fact completely undermined by it. Whereas they speak of death, or the separation of soul from body, as the condition for the acquisition of *phronēsis*, the recollection argument supposedly accounts for the possibility of learning throughout life, when the soul is united with the body, and particularly as a result of perception.

This is not the only difficulty of which Cebes is unaware. He seems to believe that recollection is awakened by both perception and Socratic questioning; but he is not concerned about how to understand the relation between these. He takes the recollection doctrine to be the perfect assimilation of Socratic inquiry and the genuine philosophers' notion of *phronēsis*, without recognizing the problematic assumptions he holds about each, let alone the fundamental incompatibility between them. Nevertheless—or rather, precisely because of this limited understanding—the recollection argument will turn out to be the only one in the entire conversation that both Cebes and Simmias wholeheartedly endorse. It is, therefore, *the* tool that Socrates shamelessly exploits: he need only appeal to the recollection thesis, and his interlocutors will immediately give up any opinions they believe conflict with it. Socrates takes advantage of their acceptance, despite the fact that it is based upon unexamined, and even preposterous, assumptions about the soul, knowledge, and the objects of knowledge. In fact, Socrates even uses their acceptance of the argument to undercut the very assumptions on which it is based.

As soon as Cebes mentions the doctrine of recollection, Simmias interrupts to ask for the demonstrations that will remind him of it: he wants an enactment in deed of the theory about learning of which Cebes speaks. The sign, Cebes reminds him, that the learner possesses in himself knowledge and correct *logos*—he does not say whether these are identical—is his ability to answer for himself when questioned beautifully by another, an ability most clearly illustrated by the use of mathematical constructions.[3] This very reminder Cebes considers "most beautiful"; yet he certainly does not ask any questions through which Simmias could discover the truth for himself but simply expects him to trust a doctrine he had heard before. Socrates naturally expresses concern, therefore, with Simmias' possible distrust of the proposition that so-called learning is really recollection. And Simmias, not despite, but because of, denying his distrust, justifies that concern: he admits that he already begins to remember, hence to be persuaded—not to learn.

Dissatisfied, apparently, with Cebes' enactment of recollection, Socrates takes over. But he does not bolster our confidence in the thesis when he seeks Simmias' agreement that, if anyone remembers anything, he must have previously known it. For knowing is here presented as the condition for remembering, when remembering is supposed to explain how knowledge comes into being. Socrates cannot, in any case, have a precise sense of "knowing" in mind when he refers to it as a condition for remembering: Simmias has just remembered a doctrine he previously heard, without necessarily having understood it. Socrates nevertheless uses the word for scientific knowledge (*epistēmē*). But he does not clarify its meaning when he seeks Simmias' further agreement that, if someone has seen or heard or perceived something in any way and recognizes not only that but also some other thing of which the knowledge is not the same, he must recollect the other thing that he has in mind. Socrates does not say only that the recollected object is other, but also that the knowledge of it is other, distinguished, presumably, from the perception that awakens it; he had originally claimed only that recollection requires knowledge that is prior. This difficulty turns out to haunt the entire argument, which is precisely an attempt to translate knowledge other than, but related to, perception into another time of acquiring it.

Although knowledge of a man, Socrates explains, is other than knowledge of a lyre, whenever a lover sees the lyre or cloak or any possession of his beloved, the perception of it awakens in his thought the form (*eidos*) of the boy to whom it belongs. The term that we expect should designate the noetic "form" awakened by perception, refers in fact to the body of the beloved imagined by his lover at the sight of something that belongs to him. It is *erōs* or desire, Socrates implies, that forges the link between a present perception and an absent object of thought.[4] The lover's idealization of his beloved spreads from the *eidos* of the boy to all his possessions. He projects what is really his own longing for the boy onto the objects that awaken that longing, and his unawareness of that projection is the condition for his idealization. Socrates does not say why this should be the primary model for the recollection thesis. But it brings to mind his earlier account of the lover of *phronēsis*, based on the model of the human lover who would willingly follow his beloved to Hades in the hope of seeing and being with his pure soul (68a). It is no accident, then, that Socrates' apparently arbitrary examples of the lyre and the cloak, which point beyond themselves to the beloved, happen to be precisely what Simmias and Cebes will choose as images of the body, which points beyond itself to the soul (85e–86b, 87b–e).

Like the lover's recollection of his beloved, Socrates proceeds, the thought of Cebes is often awakened by the sight of Simmias; and thousands of other cases, Simmias swears by Zeus, thinking perhaps of countless other inseparable pairs of young men. This experience occurs mostly, Socrates admits, when the object has been forgotten through time or inattention. But the required "otherness" of the reminder and that of which it is a reminder is not dependent on temporal distance necessarily: recollection of a man can arise from seeing a picture of a lyre or horse, recollection of Cebes from seeing a picture of Simmias, or finally, recollection of Simmias himself from his own picture. In the cases preceding the last, the link between the present perception and the thought it awakens depends upon subjective associations in the observer; only in the last case does it seem to belong necessarily to the image itself. Of course, one would "know" the image only if one knows Simmias, and just for that reason, it is unclear how it could satisfy the condition that knowledge of what is recollected be other than knowledge of what causes the recollection.[5] In fact Socrates slides almost imperceptibly from speaking of the otherness of a present perception and absent object of thought to speaking of their likeness or unlikeness.

He seems to go out of his way to observe that recollection can be aroused by a reminder that is unlike that to which it points, as well as by that which is like it. But he concludes that only the latter case entails consideration of the adequacy of the likeness that serves as a reminder. Socrates thus confirms that his last example was the crucial one. In looking at the picture of Simmias, one is indeed reminded of what is missing: the image falls short of that which it imitates by the absence of soul. If it were not for that absence, there would simply be two "Simmiases";[6] what distinguishes the portrait from that which it represents is life. Socrates speaks only of our awareness of the defectiveness of the image. But the example he chooses suggests just the opposite—that it is possible, namely, for an image to arouse resentment of the defectiveness of that which it represents:[7] in contemplating the perfection of the portrait, one would recognize the mortality of the living being.[8] What might indeed be aroused by this contemplation is the contradictory longing for an eternally existing soul, as untouched by life as a portrait is.

[74a9–74d8] Socrates invites Simmias to investigate whether any such defectiveness is at stake when we perceive equal pieces of wood or stone but speak of something other, "the equal itself." The argument, Socrates will shortly inform Simmias, is concerned just as much with any other "itself by itself" as it is with "the equal itself." Why, then, is this example given such prominence? If a present perception serves as a reminder,

Socrates has just explained, because of its likeness to an absent object of thought, it may also be thought to fall short of it. The one is to be measured against the standard of the other; its aim is to be "equal" to that standard. Of course, the closer the image comes to being a perfect image, the more it approaches identity with that of which it is an image, thus annihilating itself as an image. Now Socrates might seem to have avoided this problem by translating identity into equality, a qualitative determination into a quantitative one. In fact he points to the problematic status of the notion of equality, which presupposes the simultaneous identity and difference of that which it relates. Since equality seems to require at least two relata, how can there be "the equal itself"?

But Socrates is not dogmatic. Shall we say, he asks Simmias, that this equal itself is something or nothing? Just as he first affirmed our belief that death is something before considering what it is (64c), Simmias now enthusiastically asserts, with an oath by Zeus, that we say the equal itself is something, before affirmatively responding to Socrates' subsequent question as to whether we know what it is.[9] Socrates proceeds to test that response, therefore, by asking whether it is from seeing equal pieces of wood or stone that we derive knowledge of the equal itself that is other— if, that is, it does appear other to Simmias. But since Socrates does not explain what it would mean for the equal itself to appear (*phainesthai*) at all, he gives Simmias no chance to answer. He proceeds instead to describe the way equal pieces of wood or stone, while being the same, sometimes appear equal to one but not to another.[10] He does not deny that phenomena that appear equal to each other can truly be so; for it is sufficient, apparently, to agree that they appear and really are equal in some, but not every, respect, in order to distinguish them from "the equals themselves" (*tauta ta isa*), which never appear unequal, like equality, which never appears to be inequality.[11]

Simmias, who was confident of knowing what the equal itself is, does not seem disturbed at its sudden replacement by the plural, equals themselves, nor with the problem of their relation to equality. He does not question whether that "other" to which he claims equal pieces of wood or stone point is to be understood as the characteristic, equality, or as a paradigmatic instance of what is thus characterized, the equals themselves. These equals themselves, which never appear unequal, are the product resulting from an operation of abstraction. To determine that the sticks and stones are equal requires an act of counting or measuring; if one then "takes away" all the other qualities that characterize the phenomena, all that is left is the mathematical determination in regard to which they are equal, their number or magnitude.[12] Yet, once the sticks and stones have been stripped of every characteristic that makes each one distinct, once they have been turned into the pure members of the class of equals themselves, how can any one be distinguished from another? How can there be a plurality of, say, one inches or ones?

As soon as the members of the class of equals themselves are produced, they threaten to collapse into the unintelligibly singular equal itself. This operation of successive abstraction thus results in another version of the perplexity involved in the thought of a perfect image, which would be indistinguishable from what it represents. Simmias could be differentiated from his portrait by the presence of soul. But the problem underlying the series of arguments in the first half of the dialogue is whether soul itself measures up to the standard of the beings, with which it should display its kinship after death, when it is freed from the contamination of the body. If, however, it were to become "equal" to its desired object of knowledge, the pure soul would become a being "itself by itself" indistinguishable from any other and would cease to be soul.

It is no accident that Socrates prepared for the discussion of the equal itself by first offering the example of Simmias and his portrait; but Simmias himself is entirely unaware of the questions implicitly raised by that move. And Socrates simply takes advantage of his passivity when he asks whether the equal itself is the same as "those equals," without specifying whether he refers to equal phenomena or the so-called equals themselves. When Simmias replies inappropriately, but following Socrates' lead, that they never *appear* the same to him, Socrates repeats the question he at first suppressed—whether our knowledge of "that equal" is conceived and grasped from "those equals." Simmias agrees immediately to the derivative status of our knowledge of the equal itself, without inquiring whether it is from perceptible phenomena or from a mathematical model that such knowledge is said to be derived.[13]

Without resolving this ambiguity, Socrates inquires further about the way equal pieces of wood and "the equals of which we were just speaking" appear to us equal. Do they fall short of being like the equal itself or nothing? Socrates suggests the possibility, once again, that there is no unique being "itself by itself" of which members of the class of equals are an inferior likeness. For what is paradigmatically equal could only be the members designated as "the equals themselves,"[14] and their superiority would be nothing but their abstraction from every other aspect of equal phenomena. "The equal itself," on the other hand, is the formula Socrates is about to generalize when he refers to "the what it is" that we posit as the object of investigation in questioning and answering. Socrates suppressed recognition of the act of counting or measurement required for the designation of phenomena as equal; he only hints at the activity that is required for positing in *logos* the being of the equal itself.

[74d9–75d6] Simmias is convinced, in any case—without needing any argument—that the others fall far short of the equal itself. Socrates proceeds, therefore, to describe the experience of someone who supposes that what he sees "wishes" to be like some other of the beings but is unable to and must remain inferior. Isn't this just what we have suffered, Socrates inquires, with regard to the equals and the equal itself? Despite Simmias' certainty, this is not at all the experience they have undergone. Socrates and Simmias have not perceived any phenomena that could be judged to be an inferior instance of equality; they have been simply constructing an account in speech. Simmias is utterly unaware of the effects on that account of their own speaking.

Socrates, meanwhile, has emphasized the *pathos* suffered by one who perceives things in this way: the characterization of phenomena as willing to be like a perfect paradigm of the determinations ascribed to them is a *pathos* undergone by the person who makes that ascription. And the paradigm to which he refers must, as Socrates will soon reveal, belong in some way to the soul itself: to perceive phenomena as inferior to their perfect model betrays resentment of the inferior condition of the embodied soul, suffering from forgetfulness of knowledge that is rightly its own (cf. 76e). *Erōs* does indeed seem to be the appropriate, if concealed, model for the recollection thesis, which has proven to be an account of the unwitting projection of the will onto that which is thought to be independent.[15] It is no accident that Socrates first describes this experience before arguing for the necessity of prior knowledge of the standard to which perceptible phenomena are allegedly referred.

Before we began to see or hear or perceive in any other way, Socrates will soon conclude, we must have somewhere grasped knowledge of "the equal itself, what it is," to which we refer the equals perceived through the senses, recognizing that they eagerly desire to be like it but are inferior. Before he reaches that conclusion, however, Socrates seeks Simmias' agreement that the deficiency of phenomena striving to be like the equal is brought to mind by nothing but sight or touch or some other of the senses. Simmias does not ask why prior knowledge of the noetic standard is required if the phenomena display their own defectiveness to the senses, all of which, he agrees, can be treated alike for the purpose of the argument. He does not notice Socrates' sudden omission of hearing from his list of the senses; but hearing is the condition of speech, and that is precisely what links the perceptible phenomena with the "much-babbled about" names that Socrates, like the poets, is constantly drumming into our ears (cf. 65b, 76d, 100b). It is, moreover, through hearing, not through sight or any other sense, that Simmias is being "reminded" of the recollection thesis; Simmias' self-forgetfulness calls our attention to the conspicuously absent consideration in the argument of speech or *logos*.

Socrates has good reasons, in any case, for gaining Simmias' assent to the claim that we possess knowledge of the equal itself before using our senses, which we employ from the moment of birth; for only then can he deduce that such knowledge must have been acquired "as it seems" before we were born. We must, in that case, have acquired before birth and known at the moment of birth, not only the equal itself and the greater and smaller,[16] but all such, for the present *logos*, Socrates now acknowledges, is concerned no more with the equal than with the beautiful and the good and the just and the holy.[17] Yet just when he seems to have admitted the existence of a "second world" of noetic beings beyond that of perceptible phenomena, Socrates suddenly articulates his own understanding of the "itself by itself," which puts such an interpretation into question. That which "it seems" we must have come to know before birth is, according to Socrates' present formulation, nothing but that which we stamp with the seal of "the what it is,"[18] through questioning in questions and answering in answers.[19] What the recollection thesis identifies as the object of a passive "noetic vision" by the pure soul, Socrates understands as the product of, and condition for, the activity of inquiry. Yet he does transform the question, "What is it?," the distinguishing mark of Socratic inquiry,[20] from the interrogative to the indicative mode: the context of the recollection thesis calls for the replacement of a true question with what seems to be an illusory answer.[21]

[75d7–76d6] Had Socrates established the necessity of acquiring knowledge of the beings themselves prior to the use of our senses, he could presumably have concluded that the soul must exist with *phronēsis* before birth, and that all subsequent learning is really recollection. But one further condition has yet to be guaranteed, for the fact that we acquired knowledge before birth still leaves open an alternative: either we were born with it and know throughout our lives, or we lost it at birth and later regain it through the use of our senses. Only in the latter case would it be possible to account for so-called learning as really the recovery of knowledge that is our own. Even if it assumes an original acquisition of knowledge, then, the recollection doctrine still has to account for its loss: forgetting turns out to be as difficult to explain as learning. Now for the genuine philosophers, entrance into the body at birth is the sufficient condition for the self-forgetfulness of soul, hence its release from the body at death is the necessary condition for its self-recovery. But the recollection doctrine faces the dilemma of having to affirm the former while denying the latter.

To defend the doctrine, Socrates must reassign all names in accordance with the truth of *genesis* and the falsehood of being: to know is simply to have acquired knowledge, to forget is to lose it, and there is no name for ignorance. The recollection argument thus translates into epistemological terms the argument on the cycle of opposites, which describes the coming to be and passing away of the living and the dead without ever defining what life or death is. But insofar as both arguments reflect the assumptions of the genuine philosophers, their juxtaposition leads to this striking result: being born (awakening) is parallel to forgetting, being alive (awake) to being ignorant, dying (falling asleep) to remembering, and being dead (asleep) to knowing. Yet the recollection thesis, while it depends upon this parallel sequence, nevertheless requires that the means by which the soul recovers its own knowledge is not dying but perception, not separation from, but union with, the body.

Socrates wove together two alternative conclusions in the first argument: either our souls are always in Hades, or the souls of the dead must be there if they are to come back to life again. He has now offered Simmias two parallel alternatives: either we are always knowing, or we forget as the condition for recovering knowledge. In order to help Simmias with his justifiable perplexity over which to choose, Socrates finally offers a definition of knowledge independent of its *genesis*: to know is to be able to give a *logos*.[22] Given the alternatives Socrates has offered, Simmias feels compelled to conclude that, if and when men do come to know, they must recollect what they once learned; for without examining what it means to give a *logos*, he is certain that not all men can do this—indeed, he fears that by the following day, no man alive will be able to do so (cf. 77e). Simmias affirms, however unwittingly, that Socrates has just given a *logos* of learning as recollection, which is not itself the result of recollection: surely no object of perception has awakened it. Yet Simmias betrays the grounds for the persuasiveness of the thesis, despite its apparent lack of justification: if learning were in fact nothing but recovery of knowledge that is one's own, every man should be capable of this self-actualization.[23] The argument on recollection—which replaces the required analysis of "giving a *logos*" with an assumption about the inherent possession of knowledge by the separate soul—is Socrates' response to the fear and anger his interlocutors expressed at his willingness to abandon them.

It is no wonder that, until confronted with the question of whether all men can give a *logos*, Simmias could not choose between the claims that either we are born with knowledge or we later recollect knowledge we had previously. For the choice Socrates offers of mutually exclusive alternatives in fact implicitly distinguishes between our capacity for knowing and its actualization through learning. Simmias confirms this, without realizing it, when he objects to Socrates' conclusion that our knowledge of the itself by itself must have been acquired before birth; perhaps, he suggests, we might acquire this knowledge at the moment of birth, for that time still remains. Socrates compels Simmias to agree that he is saying nothing in suggesting that we gain and lose this knowledge simultaneously. But Simmias should not have given in as easily as he does, for his claim points to the nonmythological core of the recollection thesis: learning is intelligible only as the actualization of a potential that belongs to man as such.[24]

[76d7–77a5] Socrates confirms this implication by his formulation of the conclusion of the argument. For the affirmation of the existence of the soul before birth depends not only on an undefended hypothesis about the existence of the beings themselves, but also on the claim that we refer and liken all our perceptions to these, discovering that they were previously and are now our own: the beings must belong, somehow, to the soul itself. Socrates refers to the beautiful and the good and every such being (*ousia*):[25] he implicitly raises the question of whether it is possible to perceive something as good in the same way as it is possible to perceive something as beautiful. Socrates describes the *ousia*, moreover, simply as that which we are always babbling about: he recalls his earlier description of the being itself by itself as that which we stamp with the seal of "the what it is" in questioning and answering. The *ousia* may indeed have some necessary relation to the soul; it is, however, not the object of a passive noetic vision before birth but is, rather, posited in *logos* for the sake of *logos*.

Some other *logos* would be needed, Socrates admitted in the first argument, to demonstrate the being of the soul after death, unless it could
be established that the living are born only from the dead (70d, cf. 106d).
Some other *logos* would be needed, he now admits to Simmias, to demonstrate that our soul is before we are born, unless it is established that the
beings are. The limitation of Simmias' understanding of the beings is precisely the condition for deducing the prior existence of the soul. What the
recollection argument has in fact shown is the common illusion that stands
behind each. The unrecognized projection responsible for the perception
of phenomena as "willing" to be like the beings is the *genesis* of the "itself
by itself"; and the motivation for that idealization, Socrates has implied,
is its application to the soul, turned into a permanent being itself by itself.

Socrates confirms this common ground by concluding the argument
with a return to, but reinterpretation of, equality: Is it not equally necessary, he asks, that the beings are, and that our souls are before we are born,
and if these are not, neither is that? The "equal necessity" of which
Socrates speaks is no quantitative measure; it designates, rather, the relation between two *logoi*, neither of which has been proven necessary in itself, but each of which implies the other. Simmias, on the other hand, sees
only the "same necessity"; he must assume that each assertion itself, and
only derivatively the relation between them, has been sufficiently demonstrated. For he finds nothing so clear as the existence of the beautiful, the
good, and all the others of which Socrates speaks, and the existence of the
soul before birth must be guaranteed by its likeness with these. The *logos*,
Simmias judges, "has taken refuge in the beautiful": Socrates' later insistence on the necessity of "taking refuge in *logoi*" is motivated precisely
by the kind of illusory confidence Simmias displays here in the possibility
of acquiring knowledge of the beings themselves (cf. 99e).

[77a6–77d5] To Simmias' enthusiastic affirmation, Socrates makes no
response, except to ask about Cebes, for he too must be persuaded. Although Simmias considers Cebes "the most obstinate of men in distrusting *logoi*," he is confident that they have been equally convinced by the
argument but also share the same dissatisfaction: the demonstration of
the existence of the soul apart from the body before birth only intensifies
their real fear as to whether and how it exists after death. The symmetry
of logical possibility, which would make the claims of existence before
birth and after death mutually supportive, does not converge with a symmetry of emotional concern, which is directed solely to the question of

our survival. Only if the recollection argument had shown that the soul is ungenerated, would it have offered hope that it is also imperishable.[26] But nothing has been shown, Simmias protests, to prevent the soul, once set free from the body, from coming to an end and suffering corruption.[27] Cebes too finds the demonstration only half accomplished unless it can be shown that the soul is after death as well as before birth: he joins Simmias not only in endorsing the recollection argument, but also in ignoring the argument on the cycle of opposites, which concluded with the claim that the souls of the dead continue to exist.

Socrates, however, assures both his interlocutors at once that the complete demonstration has been supplied, albeit only implicitly: the recollection argument, with its demonstration of the preexistence of the soul, must be "put together" with the argument on the cycle of opposites, with its demonstration that "all the living (every living being) come(s) to be from the dead." Yet this complete demonstration would have been furnished by the first argument alone, had it succeeded in establishing, as it was presumably intended to, that the living come to be from the dead no less than the dead from the living.[28] Socrates wants to take from that argument, however, only what seems to be another claim to the preexistence of the soul; he thus indicates simultaneously the superfluous status of the recollection argument and the questionable validity of the first argument, which simply assumed the *genesis* of the dead from the living in order to prove the opposite *genesis* of the living from the dead. Socrates confirms this difficulty in elaborating the required combination: if the soul is agreed to exist before birth, and if in coming to life, it necessarily comes to be from nothing and nowhere but death and being dead, how could it not exist after dying, since it must come back to life again? Socrates argued originally only that coming back to life must be possible for at least one thing, unless everything were to end up dead; he now claims to have shown that every living being that dies must necessarily come back to life again.

The conjunction Socrates proposes would suffice only if it could overcome the qualified status of the conclusions derived in the first two arguments from hypotheses that remain undefended. But the strategy Socrates outlines does not itself defend the hypothesis of the existence of the beings, agreed on in the recollection argument, any more than the hypothesis of coming back to life, agreed on in the argument on the cycle of opposites. Just as problematic is the assumption that the soul construed merely as the subject of the cycle of living and dying could be "put together" with the soul construed as the possessor of *phronēsis*. While Socrates reduces his interlocutors' dissatisfaction to their fear (77d), he seems to betray his awareness of their justification through his willingness to conduct a third argument, either as a supplement or a replacement for the required combination of the first two.[29] If it were to succeed in its task, the ensuing argument would have to defend the unexamined hypotheses of the first two arguments and, at the same time, overcome the tension brought to light by their proposed combination: it would have to explain how the single nature of soul accounts for its double function, animating the body as source of life and in contact with the beings as medium of cognition.[30] Socrates has yet to present an account of the soul that would allow the philosophers' desire for death to be reconciled with the divine prohibition against suicide.

Chapter Six: Likeness

[77d5–78b1] Simmias and Cebes wish to continue the *logos*, Socrates charges, only because of their childish fear that the soul may be dispersed in departing from the body, especially, he adds in ridicule, if the man happens to die in a high wind. Cebes, who first stated the common distrust that the soul may be nothing more than breath or smoke, now laughs—betraying a momentary relief from fear[1]—at Socrates' mockery of just that understanding. Realizing that he can overcome his distrust only through self-persuasion, Cebes must separate himself from the fear attributed to him: he projects his internal dissension onto an autonomous and alien being by transforming Socrates' accusation of "childish fear" into "the child in us" who fears. The tension between Socrates' adjective and Cebes' noun points to the question of whether "the soul in us" is anything other than a reification of the quality of "ensouled" body: it was only, indeed, by projecting all internal dissension onto the body as alien that the genuine philosophers could postulate the separability of the soul as an autonomous being.

To free the child in us from that hobgoblin, the fear of death, it is necessary, Socrates advises, to sing daily incantations. But Cebes betrays his resentment of being abandoned by the one man able to do this, just as Simmias, when Socrates defined knowledge as the ability to give a *logos*, betrayed his resentment of being abandoned by the one man able to do so (76b). Cebes, who attacked Socrates for his imprudence in running away from the care of the gods, considers Socrates indispensable for persuasion; Simmias, who attacked Socrates for his injustice in running away from his present companions, considers Socrates indispensable for the *logos*. While Simmias is impressed with Socrates' unique powers of argumentation, Cebes is impressed with his unique powers of enchantment. Perhaps it is not despite, but because of, that division that Socrates addresses the speeches that seem most enchanting to Simmias, those that seem most argumentative to Cebes—with the apparent exception, that is, of the present one. For while Socrates responded to Simmias' reproach by appealing to the universal capacity for recollection, he now responds to Cebes by recommending that, in quest of a good enchanter, he ought to search among all the Hellenes and the barbarians too, sparing neither money nor toil, and also among themselves, for perhaps he would find none more capable of such enchantment.[2] Socrates indicates, with this recommendation, the status of the argument that follows. Yet, at its conclusion, he in fact encourages Simmias and Cebes to share with the others their objections, which result precisely from the failure of their attempted self-persuasion. Socrates must hope, then, to accomplish just the opposite of what he allegedly recommends, for he leads his interlocutors to participate in their own persuasion only in order to awaken critical distrust.

The argument that is, at least by its conclusion, most evidently "mythological," thus proves to be most capable of stimulating reasoning. The mixture of opposites that underlies the series of arguments in the first half of the dialogue is thus emphasized by the argument in which that series culminates. The third argument is a culmination, at the same time, of the unfolding implications of the initial definition of death as a separation of soul from body. That separation is here manifestly a performance in *logos*: the soul, which is agreed to be "like" one principle, is separated from the body insofar as it is "like" the opposite principle. Yet the recollection argument has just established that a reminder that awakens an object of thought because of its likeness to it may, for just that reason, fall short of it. *Psychē* and body, Socrates will disclose, in their mere likeness to opposite principles, fall short of them. And the deficiency of each implies that their separability from each other is always a matter of degree. This continuum amounts, in turn, to a hierarchy of kinds of souls: each is "like" the kind of life it leads, determined by the degree of its attachment to corporeal needs and related desires. When Socrates finally translates this likeness into identity, he turns the argument into an Aesopian fable: each soul *becomes* in another life what it is like in this life, given its habits, its hopes, and its fears. The argument thus transforms what looks at first like a physiological analysis of the nature of soul into a psychological one.

That transformation is anticipated by the outline Socrates provides for the strategy of the argument. He begins with a question: For what sort of thing is it fitting to suffer the *pathos* of dispersion, and for what sort is it not fitting? But he inserts at the center of this apparently ontological dichotomy a very different consideration: For what sort of thing would we fear suffering this *pathos*? After determining these matters, he inquires, must we not investigate, as the basis for our hopes and fears about our soul, to which class it belongs? Yet the very order of this proposed outline casts doubt on the possibility of discovering an objective division of the dispersible and the indispersible that could be applied to the nature of the soul independently of our hopes and our fears.

[78c1–79c1] It is fitting, Socrates proceeds, "by nature"—since nature is not lame—for that which has been compounded and is composite to suffer decomposition in the same way that it was put together. If, on the other hand, there is something that happens to be uncompounded, that alone, if anything, would not fittingly suffer decomposition.[3] And it is most likely, he adds, that the uncompounded are always the same and unvarying, while the compounded vary from one time to another and are never the same. But Socrates can claim for this no more than likelihood, for he has not shown, on the one hand, that there is in fact something incomposite; and, on the other hand, while that which is composite might undergo the change of decomposition, he has offered no defense for the more radical claim that it *never* remains the same as itself.

To support this merely probable division, Socrates suggests that they return to those things under consideration in the preceding argument, namely the being itself (*autē hē ousia*) of whose being we give a *logos* in questioning and answering. Socrates does not, at this moment, explain what it means to give a *logos* of the being of the being itself.[4] He has acknowledged only that it is "the *what* it is" that we stamp with the seal of being in questioning and answering (cf. 75d); and when he now attempts to confirm the self-identity of something like the equal itself or the beautiful itself, he identifies "the being" (*to on*) with "each itself, *what* it is." None of these could undergo any alteration, Cebes agrees, being entirely monoeidetic.[5] But how could we ever know or state "what it is" if each has no relation to any other nor any internal articulation? Cebes is not troubled by this question; nor does he ask how, if each being is indeed "itself by itself," it could account, as Socrates proceeds to suggest, for the predication of the quality that it is to other things.

Nor does Socrates resolve this problem when he simply contrasts the monoeidetic *ousia* with "the many"—men or horses or cloaks—that bear the names of equal, beautiful, and all such. Not only do these "many" represent a plurality of instances in which beauty or equality are predicated, but each is in itself a plurality of the various qualities ascribed simultaneously to it. Socrates qualifies his claim, however, that they would be constantly other than themselves and each other and "so to speak" never the same; for this complete lack of identity seems to contradict our speech, in which we assign one name to each. Yet Socrates indicates the misleading character of our speech by avoiding the expected dichotomy between a phenomenal plurality of men, horses, or cloaks, and the *ousia* of each from which it would presumably gain its name. The monoeidetic form that never admits variance belongs only to the qualities equal, beautiful, and such, which we predicate of the many things, while no monoeidetic form "man," "horse," or "cloak" is postulated as the source of unity for the *pragmata*, each of which is always a "beautiful and large man," or horse, and so on.

Socrates proceeds to contrast the invisibility of that which is grasped only by reason through calculation with the tactility and visibility of the many, which are never the same (cf. 65e–66a): he is conspicuously silent about audibility. He emphasizes, moreover, the derivative status of the invisible as a mere absence of visibility. In making this the principle of his division, he betrays its subjective determination: the noetic objects are unseen by whom or what? With the apparently redundant description of the noetic objects as "not to be seen" (*ouk horata*) and "invisible" (*aeidē*),[6] Socrates slips in a double pun: he points to the paradoxical designation of the invisible *eidē* by a word that means the visible looks of things and then links it with the paradoxical "invisible place" to which the soul is said to journey after death.[7] Hades, Socrates now suggests, is the invisible structure of the visible. He thus clarifies the alternative presented only obscurely in the first argument—that our souls are always "there." It is for the sake of demonstrating that conclusion, Socrates reminds us, that he offers his present account of the monoeidetic beings.

Socrates invites Cebes to join him, if he wishes, in laying down two forms (*eidē*) of the beings—the invisible and the visible—although it is precisely as "the beings" that the members of one of the classes have been uniquely characterized. They lay down, further, that the invisible are always the same, the visible never the same, without defending the necessary connection between visibility and constant alteration, invisibility and self-identity. Socrates does not, in any case, present their division as a discovery of the nature of things, but as a hypothesis Cebes may wish to posit with him, an instrument useful for the purposes of the argument. Socrates points to that purpose when he asks whether "we" are anything other than, on the one hand, body, on the other, soul; but his reference to the subject constituted by this dyad presupposes that "we" are indeed something other, namely living animals. Socrates may have been justified in asserting only that this unified subject is characterized as, on the one hand, corporeal, on the other, psychic, qualities "like and akin," as he is about to establish, to the visible and the invisible laid down as two *eidē*.

In agreeing, not simply that the body is visible, but only that everyone would consider it more like the visible, Cebes unwittingly points to the invisible source of motion in the living body: what is most completely visible is the corpse.[8] Socrates does not ask the parallel question, to which *eidos* the soul is more like, but rather whether it is visible or invisible. And Cebes shows how hard it is to relinquish the identification of being with visibility when he agrees only that the soul is invisible to men at least; it might be, as the genuine philosophers would maintain, visible "itself by itself" when freed from imprisonment in the body. This is sufficient, in any case, for Socrates to draw the moderate conclusion that the soul, because it cannot be seen by human vision, is more like the invisible than the body is, and the body more like the visible. Since it is the living animal that constitutes this continuum of more or less, only death would reveal the kinship and likeness of the soul with the invisible, the body with the visible.

[79c2–80b7] By contrasting the monoeidetic noetic object and the multiform perceptible *pragmata*, Socrates was able to characterize the invisible as always self-identical and the visible as always changing. He did not defend the assumption that everything invisible is necessarily self-identical and everything visible always changing. Agreement on the mere likeness of the soul to the invisible and of the body to the visible is not sufficient, then, to ascribe to each the properties connected with the two principles. But Socrates does not make the expected attempt to characterize the soul in contrast to the body; he attempts, rather, to establish opposing characterizations of the soul itself, determined by its independence from, or dependence on, the body. We have been saying for a long time, he reminds his interlocutors, that whenever the soul makes use of the body, that is, the senses, for investigation, it is dragged down to those things that are never the same, where it wanders about, confused and dizzy, like a drunkard. The soul seems to have no nature of its own but only to assimilate itself to its object. For when, on the other hand, it investigates alone by itself, departing into the pure and everlasting and deathless to which it is akin, it has rest from its wanderings and remains always the same and unchanging, since it is in contact with such.

Isn't it this condition (*pathēma*) of the soul, Socrates asks, that is called *phronēsis*?[9] He recalls with this question the genuine philosophers' longing to escape from the dizziness of inquiry through the senses in the hope of acquiring *phronēsis* by the separate soul after death. But Socrates' evaluation of this hope will be made clear only when he presents his own interpretation of that mode of inquiry through which he seeks escape from dizziness and blindness by taking "refuge in *logoi*" (cf. 99d–100a). Now, however, it is on the basis of his appeal to *phronēsis* as a condition of the soul that Socrates raises the question he should have asked originally—to which *eidos* the soul is more alike and akin. For Socrates' description of *phronēsis* saves Cebes from having to ask about the necessary connection between invisibility and self-identity in order for him to agree that the soul is as a whole and completely more like that which is always the same than like that which is not. And while they should have contrasted with this the characterization of the soul when it is not in possession of *phronēsis*, they conclude by agreeing that the body must be more like "the other."

To grant the likeness of the soul to the invisible and unchanging, does not, of course, satisfy the challenge for a demonstration of its immortality and indestructibility. Socrates therefore supplements the proposed division with the distinction between the divine, which is by nature fit to rule and lead, and the human, fit to obey and serve.[10] To which should the soul and body be likened, Socrates asks, if, when they are joined together, nature commands one to rule and be master, the other to be ruled and enslaved? Cebes ignores Socrates' reference to the "command" of nature, which implies the recalcitrance of body as well as of soul to their assigned roles as ruler and ruled; he is confident that the body is like the mortal, soul like the divine. While Cebes must assume the identity of the divine and the immortal, hence of the mortal and the human, he does not seem to realize that his agreement on the likeness of the soul to the divine thus commits him to acknowledge the mortality of man as such.

Without making this consequence explicit, Socrates reaches the desired conclusion of the argument: the soul is most like the divine and immortal and noetic and monoeidetic and indissoluble and that which is always the same, while the body is most like the human and mortal and polyeidetic and nonnoetic and dissoluble and that which is never the same.[11] Not only has the division of the invisible and visible, which provided the premise for the argument, disappeared altogether, but the original claim that the soul is more like one *eidos* than the body is, and the body more like the other, has been transformed into the more radical conclusion that each is most like one of two opposing classes characterized by a presumably inseparable set of qualities. Through its function in ruling over the body, the soul is like the divine and immortal; through its possession of *phronēsis* it is like the noetic and monoeidetic, hence like what is always the same and unchanging. But the indissolubility of the soul—the crucial question at stake—would follow only from its being incomposite, which Socrates has not established, and he has argued only that, *if* there were something incomposite, it would most likely be that which is always the same and unchanging.

[80b8–82b9] Having analyzed the relation between body and soul as a continuum governed by greater or lesser degrees of likeness to opposite principles, Socrates draws the consequence that it would be fitting for the body to be dissolved quickly at death, and for the soul to be completely indissoluble, or nearly so. It is precisely the consequences of this "nearly so" that provoke Cebes' dissatisfaction with the argument (cf. 87d–88b), just as the consequences of the mere invisibility of the soul provoke Simmias' (cf. 85e–86d). Not only does Socrates reach a conclusion that confirms the fears of his interlocutors, but he draws out its painful implications in seemingly unnecessary detail. When a man dies, he observes, even the visible part of him, which we call the corpse, does not undergo decomposition at once. The Egyptians, in fact, can preserve the body for an incalculable amount of time,[12] and certain parts of the body, because they continue to "lie in the visible," are "so to speak, deathless." Having referred to the *athanaton* as that which the soul is most like (80b) or that toward which it moves when it inquires alone by itself (79d), Socrates now uses it for the first time as a quality, not of the soul however, as Cebes and Simmias might expect, but of the bones and sinews![13]

The invisible soul, on the other hand, departs to another place that is like itself, noble and pure and invisible. This natural *telos* of the pure soul is Hades, the name given by the poets to an invisible place in which the dead "live," and at the same time to the god who rules there.[14] It is a name that may inspire fear of one's fate after death, but only while overcoming the more fundamental fear of nonbeing.[15] Hades combines the obscurities about place in the first argument with those about time in the second. For it is the combination of a paradoxical place that is not seen and a paradoxical time in which nothing changes: its nonmythological equivalent are the unseen and unchanging "ideas." To this dwelling, Socrates concludes, his own soul is about to journey, if god is willing, drawn by the attraction of likes. The desire for communion with Hades, the good and wise god,[16] transformed by a pun into the principle of the invisible, proves Socrates' prudence in his willingness to face death. Socrates' reconstruction of the creation of the poets thus provides precisely the reconciliation he seeks: Hades overcomes the tension between the greatest music and demotic music, between the desire for death and the divine prohibition against suicide.

Could the soul characterized by its kinship with this invisible place, the good and wise god, be immediately dispersed, Socrates asks, and destroyed when released from the body, as the many fear? But he answers his own question without any claim about the physiology of the soul as such. For apparently not every soul leads a life in accordance with its "likeness to the invisible," but only the one that is pure because it avoided association with the body and gathered itself into itself alone. But this is precisely to engage in "correct philosophizing" and to practice really being dead, or wouldn't it, Socrates inquires, be the practice of death? It is no accident that this question reminds *us*, if not Cebes, of the ambiguity of Socrates' initial defense. For what his interlocutors may take to be the fate of the soul after death is Socrates' description of a mode of investigation carried on throughout life: *whenever* the soul engages in this activity, it departs into what is like itself, the invisible, divine, immortal, and *phronimos*.

Whenever, throughout life, the soul practices dying in this way, it is freed from its wanderings and folly and fears and savage desires and all other human evils; but unless the latter belong to the body, as the genuine philosophers might insist, the desire for purification from these *pathē* is the desire of the soul to escape from itself, to become like the noetic and monoeidetic. If it were freed from all these evils, it would dwell, according to Socrates' formulation, with the divine; it would dwell, as the initiates say, through all time with the gods (81a). That these might not be the same "place," appropriate for the same soul, Socrates suggests in the myth he recites at the end of the conversation (cf. 111 b–e, 114b–c); that myth, with this subtle correction, assumes in the second half of the dialogue the place and function of the present discussion as the conclusion of the first half.

But Socrates is concerned now only to distinguish the purified soul from the one that departs defiled and impure. Because of its constant intercourse with the body, the impure soul is bewitched by the body's desires and pleasures and thus becomes penetrated in its nature by "the somatoeidetic"; it is not the body itself, then, but the somatoeidetic nature of the soul in its chosen attachment to the body that constitutes the hindrance to purification. Such a soul is compelled to believe that nothing is true except what can be touched or seen—Socrates does not say "heard— or drunk or eaten or used for "the *aphrodisia*," while it would fear and hate and avoid what is dark and invisible to the eyes but intelligible and comprehensible to philosophy. Just as the attraction of likes draws the purified soul to its invisible dwelling, the natural gravity of the visible, which is burdensome and heavy and earthly, drags the unpurified soul back into the visible place. What is said to be an account of the fate of the soul after death, Socrates makes as clear as possible, is nothing but a description of what constitutes its purity or impurity in life.

"As it is said," Socrates qualifies his account, the spectres (*eidōla*) of those souls weighed down by their attachment to the visible come to be visible, as *phantasmata* seen rolling around monuments and tombs. If Cebes wishes to believe that the purified soul will dwell with the gods, he must believe at the same time that the impure will become ghosts.[17] But the latter must, in fact, be all human beings, whose souls have been entombed in visible bodies.[18] Each soul, "as is likely" (*hōsper eikos*)—or more appropriately, as a likeness—should be bound into a character corresponding to its practice in life: the gluttonous, violent, and drunk into asses and other beasts, the unjust and tyrants and robbers into wolves and hawks and kites. Socrates turns finally to those who practice by nature and habit, without philosophy, the demotic and political virtues called moderation and justice.[19] By contrasting such habitual practice with philosophy, he silently raises the question, once again, of what it means to engage in the practice of dying. Those who pursue it, in any case, do not belong in this fable; for it is the practitioners of the demotic virtues, Socrates insists, who go to the best "place" and are happiest. When Cebes expresses surprise, Socrates explains: these souls enter into the political and gentle *genos* of bees or wasps or ants—Cebes does not stop to wonder about the inclusion of that gentle species at the center of Socrates' list!—or they return again to the human *genos* as moderate men. When Cebes admits all this is "likely," he must recognize by now that the argument on likeness has become an exemplification of image making.

[82b10–84b8] Every human life can be characterized, apparently, through the image of a beast; for the soul that departs pure does not return to human life at all. In ascribing this fate to the "lover of learning," Socrates recalls his imitation of the speech of the "correct lovers of learning" (67b), who were characterized by their opposition to the lover of the body, that is, of money or honor or both (68c). Unlike the many who refrain from bodily pleasures only because they fear poverty or dishonor, Socrates now repeats, the correct philosophizers do so only for the sake of entering the *genos* of the gods. In turning their backs on the body, they "bid farewell" (*chairein*) to other men as being ignorant[20] and turn instead to follow philosophy wherever it leads, believing it to be deliverance and purification. For when possessed by philosophy, the lover of learning realizes that his soul is welded to the body, compelled to investigate the beings not in themselves, but through the body as if through prison bars. Condemning the body as the obstacle to his desire for direct contact with the beings, he never imagines that this very desire may be the true source of the systematic illusion he resents. Only philosophy, therefore, sees what is most terrible about the situation—namely, that it comes about through desire, so that the prisoner himself is responsible for his own incarceration.

In the course of constructing a model of "the best city in speech," Socrates depicts a cave, in which we human beings are imprisoned, as an image of the *polis*, in which we are compelled by laws and political opinion systematically to mistake images for reality.[21] In the course of defending philosophy as the practice of dying, on the last day of his life, Socrates identifies the prison no longer with the city but with the body. While an unnamed liberator leads the prisoner out of the cave of the *polis* by force,[22] a personified philosophy attempts to lead the soul of the lover of learning by gentle encouragement and exhortation. The philosopher who escapes to the sunlight and no longer wishes to return is compelled by those who educated him for the best city to go back into the cave; but if he reentered any city other than the best in speech and tried to inform the other prisoners of their situation, he would be killed.[23] The soul of the philosopher who longs to escape from the cave of the body, Socrates implied in his remarks on the divine prohibition against suicide, is compelled to remain imprisoned by the gods (62b). Yet his own imminent departure is justified, Socrates insisted, by some kind of divine necessity.

Socrates' description of the attempted liberation of the soul from the body preserves, however, the ambiguity of his original account of the practice of dying. For philosophy does not encourage the lover of learning to terminate his life, but only to withdraw from investigation using the senses,[24] which is full of deception. It exhorts the soul to collect itself within itself, to trust nothing but itself and the itself by itself of the beings, which it grasps by intellection itself by itself. Socrates' personified philosophy assimilates to the object of knowledge the act of intellection and identifies the soul with the latter; it never attempts to account for the possibility of this perfect union of two independent entities. Yet the soul of the "true philosopher," who sees in this exhortation a mirror of his own desire, considers it a deliverance not to be resisted. He attempts, therefore, to withdraw his soul from pleasures and desires and pains and fears, realizing that the greatest evil resulting from them is the compulsion to believe falsely that their cause is most clear and true. Only, however, if one did not understand that these *pathē* belong to the soul, so that its deliverance must be from itself, would he agree, as Cebes does, that the causes of intense pleasure and pain are "mostly the visible things."

In suffering the illusions produced by submission to the *pathē*, the soul puts itself in bondage to the body. For every pleasure and pain, like a nail, Socrates explains, welds it to the corporeal, so that it takes as true whatever the body says to be so, adopting its manner and nurture because of sharing its opinions and gratifications. If the soul becomes somatoeidetic in this submission, the body, as Socrates describes it, becomes capable of opinion and speech. The embodied soul, which is indistinguishable from the ensouled body, is by definition unable to depart in purity to Hades, the invisible place; it has by definition no communion with the divine and pure and monoeidetic. It falls back quickly, Socrates adds, into another body, like a seed sown: he supplements the description of the nature of the impure soul, characterized by its attachment to the corporeal, with an image of the cause of its coming into being.[25] Socrates' description of the practice of dying was open to a double interpretation: the separation of soul from body, construed in the ordinary sense as the termination of life, meant in its reconstructed sense a mode of investigation pursued throughout life. The union of soul with body that he now describes is open to the same double interpretation: what is apparently meant to explain the physiological origin of the living being is in fact the description of a mode of conduct in life.

Whereas Socrates first identified the motivation of the lover of learning as a desire to enter the *genos* of the gods, now, after describing philosophy's attempted liberation, he identifies the motivation for accepting this deliverance as a desire for communion with the divine and pure and monoeidetic, which may not be identical with the gods.[26] The soul of the philosophic man, Socrates concludes, since it does not "calculate" as the many do (cf. 69a–b), would not think it right that philosophy should set it free so that it would then only enslave itself again to pleasure and pain. It would not want to reweave itself back together with the body, engaging in a labor like that of Penelope, who took apart each night the web she wove each day.[27] It is Cebes' understanding of this metaphor that must inspire the image he will shortly offer of the soul as a weaver, fabricating the body with which it clothes itself (cf. 87b–e). But Socrates will soon clarify his concern for the separation not of the soul from the body, but of the argument from all the fears and hopes that distort it. In his image of Penelope, then, Socrates must be thinking of the way in which *logos* or the greatest music is constantly being rewoven with, after having been separated from, *mythos* or demotic music. And there is no better reflection of that process than the present argument.

Socrates' own understanding of his image, however, is not shared by the soul of the philosopher he describes to Cebes, any more than it would have been by the genuine philosophers he described to Simmias. The same illusion that motivates their desire for purification motivates the belief of the soul to which Socrates now refers—that it must follow calculation (*logismos*) as long as it lives and thus arrive, when it dies, at what is akin to itself, freed from human evils. Socrates admits that the soul is released from human evils only when *it* dies (cf. 77d). But what is this soul that dies? Always abiding in *logismos* and thus actualizing its kinship with the monoeidetic, it seems to be no longer a soul, but a being itself by itself. Of course, to identify this being with one's true self, as the genuine philosophers do, is to be entirely determined by the fear of annihilation and the hope of avoiding it, hence to be enslaved to, rather than liberated from, human evils. If that liberation is what it means to be dead, perhaps Socrates alone is capable of dying.

Simmias and Cebes could not possibly refute the conclusion Socrates addresses to both of them—that such a soul would hardly fear being torn apart at its release from the body, scattered by the winds; having been purified of all *pathē*, it could not experience such a fear even if it were, after death, "no longer anything anywhere." Socrates ends this third argument, as he indicated in his original outline for it, by determining not what kind of being is naturally subject to dispersion, but what kind of soul is naturally inclined to fear dispersion. His condemnation of the foolishness of this fear is entirely independent of any proof of the immortality of the soul. Socrates thus completes the initial series of arguments, in the same way that he completed his opening defense (69d e) and will complete his final myth (114d–e), with an appeal to the necessity of overcoming that attachment to the self manifest in the fear of death.[28] But this is a self-overcoming, as Socrates understands it, by and within the soul, not by a pure soul of the body, and its basis is not the hope of eternal existence after death but confidence in a particular mode of inquiry and in the way of life devoted to it.

Chapter Seven: Images of the Soul

[84c1–85b9] The third argument, introduced as a magic charm to assuage the childish fear of death, concludes with Socrates' description of what the soul passes into when it dies. With this disturbing conclusion, a long silence descends upon the entire company for the first time.[1] Socrates himself seemed to be absorbed in the prior *logos*, Phaedo reports; he cannot, of course, report the content of this internal conversation, in which Socrates must have reflected on the unexamined assumptions underlying the preceding discussion.[2] For Socrates admits, when he observes Simmias and Cebes conversing together, that there are many grounds for suspicion and accusation if anyone cares to work through the speeches sufficiently. But Simmias and Cebes, even in their dialogue with each other, do not seem to constitute the same self-sufficient whole as Socrates does in dialogue with himself. For they had been urging each other all along, as Simmias admits, to ask Socrates their questions; and while Socrates has been concerned, as he soon discloses, with the preceding series of arguments as a whole, Simmias and Cebes neglect the first argument entirely, as well as its recommended synthesis with the second, and raise their objections against the third argument alone. Socrates, therefore, invites himself along when he encourages them to continue the discussion; he seems to enter the second half of the conversation with more willingness than he displayed in the first half, which began with the compulsory *apologia* of his acceptance of death and continued with the compulsory defense of the presuppositions of that *apologia*.

They refrained from raising their objections, Simmias explains, in fear of displeasing Socrates in his present misfortune. Simmias and Cebes pity him for the failure of the prior arguments, which they must construe as Socrates' attempt to convince himself that death is not to be feared (cf. 91b). Yet the need that compels them to speak indicates that their pity is a veil covering unacknowledged anger: they resent Socrates' willingness to pursue his own self-interest while leaving them to rely on themselves.

Socrates, however, only reasserts his conviction that death is no misfortune. But he recognizes how difficult it would be to make this belief persuasive to others, since he cannot persuade even Simmias, who fears that Socrates must be more fretful in his present circumstances than he was throughout his life. With that remark, Phaedo reports, Socrates for the first time smiled gently. Since it is questionable whether he ever intended merely to persuade his interlocutors, it is not surprising that Socrates betrays, with his gentle smile, that now familiar mixture of pleasure and pain.[3] When he insists that he in fact sings for joy in anticipation of his imminent release, Socrates tries to overcome the pity expressed by his companions; in doing so, he necessarily reinforces the resentment mixed with that pity. Socrates' present response thus echoes his initial defense, directed toward demonstrating the prudence of his desire for death, rather than his justice in running away from life (cf. 69d–e).

Simmias and Cebes do not recognize that they are listening to Socrates' "swan song." Perhaps they believe, like most men, that the swans sing for sorrow on their last day; but such a belief, Socrates charges, is just a projection of our own, uniquely human, fear of death. Men read in the natural sounds of the birds their own *pathē*; they neglect to "calculate" that no bird sings when it is hungry or cold or suffering from pain. The mixture of pain with the pleasure of expressing it may be as uniquely human as the fear of death. The swans, at any rate, sing most and best when about to die, in their joy at departing to the god of purification and prophecy, whose servants they are. Socrates has this privileged understanding of the swans, he assures his companions, because he is a fellow servant of the same god. He has already informed them, indeed, of the hymn to Apollo he composed during these last days, as a ritual of purification (61a–b); of course the offering to Apollo that Plato chooses to represent is, rather, the swan song of the *Phaedo*.[4] With this song, Socrates departs from life no more sorrowful than the swans, blessed with the gift of prophecy from the same master. At his public trial before the Athenian jury, Apollo's Delphic oracle provided Socrates' one link with the gods of the city, hence the only recognized support for his defense against the charge of impiety.[5] But it is with an ironic prophetic utterance that Socrates sanctions his claim to knowledge of what awaits him after death—that ultimate limit of human knowledge[6]—by appealing to the god who proclaimed him the wisest of men only because he had knowledge of his own ignorance.

Immediately after identifying himself as a servant of the *despotēs* Apollo, Socrates remembers his servitude to his present masters here: Simmias and Cebes should not hesitate to ask whatever they wish—as long as the Eleven do not prevent it. In contrast to his companions, Socrates has not forgotten that this conversation is circumscribed by the power of the city, manifest from the first moment, when Echecrates asks Phaedo whether the authorities allowed Socrates to speak with his friends or compelled him to die alone (58c), to the last moment, when the servant of the Eleven announces the hour for Socrates to drink the hemlock (116c–d). When called upon by the Athenian jury to propose a penalty he considers fitting for himself, Socrates insists that he has no reasons to think of death as a great evil, but he has good reasons to think that of imprisonment, when one is compelled to live like a slave to those in power.[7] For imposing on him, however indirectly, just that punishment, Socrates should feel resentment of the Athenian *dēmos*. Yet just as Socrates turned the tables when he put the Athenian *dēmos* on trial in place of himself, so, on the day of his execution, he transforms them into unwilling benefactors. The authorities of the city have not compelled him to die alone, and Socrates therefore begins the second half of the conversation after paying respect to them; he reminds us, of course, that it was only because he refused to obey the warning issued by the man in charge of administering the poison that the entire conversation has taken place at all.

[85b10–85d10] Encouraged by Socrates to speak, Simmias nevertheless begins with a defense of his boldness in continuing the inquiry. Although it is impossible or very difficult, Simmias believes, to know anything about these matters clearly in this life, anyone who wouldn't persevere in testing them until he was completely worn out would be a weakling. Simmias sees two alternatives, which turn, significantly, into three: either one must learn or somehow discover the truth; or, if that is impossible, one must take the best and most irrefutable human *logos* as a raft on which to sail through the dangers of life, unless one is able to sail on a more stable vessel, some kind of divine *logos*. Simmias believes that Socrates shares this opinion with him, and in some sense he does: having discovered the impossibility of obtaining clear knowledge of the beings, Socrates found himself, he later explains, compelled to proceed on a second sailing, on the safer vessel provided by the most irrefutable *logos* (cf. 99d–100a). But the procedure Simmias recommends, which could result equally in extreme dogmatism or skepticism, looks rather like a parody of the Socratic enterprise. For the safety Socrates identifies precisely with irrefutability in *logos*—for which he will present definitive criteria—is in Simmias' opinion only a means toward the goal of security in guiding one's life. Simmias does not clarify, moreover, how the divine *logos* that he thinks best provides this security would be distinguished from the most probable human *logos*; he does not define what makes the latter irrefutable, nor whether the former is identical with, or superior to, that discovery of the truth he considers difficult or impossible. While, on the other hand, it is knowledge of the beings themselves that Socrates considers impossible, it is precisely their truth that he claims to investigate by means of his second sailing through *logoi*.

[85e1–86d6] Socrates consequently accepts Simmias' dissatisfaction but questions the way in which the preceding arguments appear insufficient to him. Having ignored the first argument and uncritically embraced the second, Simmias is disturbed only by the third: the invisibility of the soul, upon which Socrates based its likeness to the divine and noetic and unchanging, does not seem sufficient to prove its immortality and indestructibility, nor even its independence from the corporeal. Socrates substituted for an analysis of the nature of the soul a description of its mere likeness to the invisible objects of thought; Simmias now attempts to attack that description on the basis of a mere likeness. A harmony, like the soul Socrates has described, may be invisible and incorporeal and altogether beautiful and divine in the harmonized lyre.[8] But the lyre itself and its strings are bodies and somatoeidetic and composite and earthly and akin to the mortal; and if someone were to shatter the lyre or cut and break its strings, the harmony would perish with the instrument. Yet, according to Socrates' argument, one would have to maintain that the harmony continues to exist somewhere, that the wood and strings must decay before the harmony suffers destruction.

Simmias presents an analogy for the relation of soul to body, whose traditional support is both a condition for, and a result of, its persuasiveness, as Echecrates is about to confirm (cf. 88c–d).[9] His image is in fact so convincing that Simmias quickly forgets its status as an image, transforming it into an analysis of the physiology of the soul. If the body is an instrument strung and held together by wet and cold and hot and dry, the soul must be a harmony of these elements when mixed beautifully and in due measure;[10] but if the body is too relaxed or too tightly strung by diseases or other ills, then the soul, no matter how divine, will necessarily perish. Simmias turns soul into a mere quality, which could not come into being apart from, and would necessarily perish with the destruction of, the living body. He offers this proposal in the belief that Socrates too must consider the soul to be something of this sort. That belief is, in fact, never explicitly refuted; for Socrates never directly attacks the image as such but only shows Simmias' interpretation of it to be incapable of accounting for the soul as a medium of cognition, which Simmias himself has enthusiastically endorsed (cf. 76e–77a).

Socrates tacitly suggests that Simmias' interpretation of harmony, as a likeness of soul, is not the only possible one.[11] For Simmias has not in fact distinguished between the silent instrument, the audible harmony produced when the instrument is being played, and an autonomous "noetic" harmony of mathematical proportions;[12] yet the latter would not be affected in any way by the destruction of the instrument and consequent cessation of the harmony produced in sound. In presenting his Pythagorean account of soul as a harmony, with no separation of the noetic from the aesthetic, Simmias unwittingly reveals the fundamental problem of the Pythagorean account of reality as a whole.[13] But while the separation of noetic harmony might seem to imply the separation of an "idea of soul" from its embodied instances, that is precisely what Socrates implicitly rejects. He indicates instead the proper interpretation of the noetic level when he refutes Simmias' objection on the basis of the demand for maintaining harmony of *logoi* (cf. 92c). Simmias' image thus suggests, through Socrates' implicit interpretation, that the invisible, incorporeal, beautiful, and divine harmony is that produced through a *technē* of *logoi*,[14] separable from the embodied soul, which is itself one with the ensouled body.

But Simmias, who is satisfied with his analysis of the soul as a harmony of corporeal elements, draws its unwelcome consequence: it must be the soul that is the first to be destroyed in what is called "death."[15] What is called "death," Socrates first argued, is the release and separation of the soul from the body, and that is in fact the practice of the philosophers (67d). Simmias has now anticipated, however, the redefinition of death as nothing but the destruction of the soul, which Socrates will construe as the point of Cebes' objection (cf. 91d, 95d). Simmias "seems to have grasped the *logos* in no trifling way," Socrates admits and, at the same time, Phaedo reports, stared, wide-eyed, straight ahead and smiled.[16] Phaedo, in his own habitual way, interprets Socrates' gaze as nothing but his customary gesture (cf. 117b); yet his interpretation may be no less questionable than his initial interpretation of the customary separation of pure pleasure and pain (59a), which was put into doubt by Socrates' subsequent analysis of their necessary union. For if Socrates' smile betrays his pleasure at Simmias' discovery of the limitation of the prior argument, perhaps the stare that accompanies it marks a moment of fear, either real or pretended: Simmias' objection has, at least momentarily, for everyone but Socrates, completely shaken confidence in the power of *logos* (cf. 88c–d).

[86d7–88b3] Socrates admits that he himself is at a loss in confronting Simmias' challenge and calls upon anyone else more prepared to do so. Without waiting for a volunteer, however, he recommends that, before addressing Simmias' objection, they first listen to Cebes' and then either agree with them if they seem to be "in harmony" or, if not, continue to plead for the *logos*. Socrates cannot apparently accept or refute the separate objection of Simmias or Cebes but can only accept a harmony or reject a contradiction that might obtain between them (cf. 95a). He will refute Simmias' objection in regard to those presuppositions—concerning the derivative status of soul from body—with which Cebes disagrees (cf. 87a); and he will respond to Cebes' objection, in turn, on the basis of an analysis of the meaning of harmony in *logoi*, which is the unstated implication of the image Simmias has offered. While this strategy might seem to be a refuge in despair, it in fact illustrates just that procedure Socrates will describe in the account of his philosophic development as a turn from investigation of the beings to investigation of their truth through *logoi* (cf. 99d–100a).

Encouraged to report his own disturbance before the battle to defend the *logos* can begin, Cebes objects that the argument seems still to be open to the original attack (cf. 77c): although it has been cleverly and sufficiently demonstrated that our soul existed before entering the human form, no demonstration has established that it will exist somewhere after we have died. This is just the question Socrates claims to have taken up in the argument on the cycle of opposites that he conducted with Cebes, whereas the preexistence of the soul, which Simmias denied through his image, is the question Socrates took up with him in the argument on recollection. It was Cebes, however, who introduced that argument in order to persuade Simmias of something he himself accepted; he now addresses his objection to Simmias in order to persuade him of his error in suggesting that the soul is weaker and less enduring than the body. But Cebes thus launches what he believes to be a more fundamental attack on Socrates' argument: even granting the superiority of soul to body will not guarantee its indestructibility.

Why, Cebes has the personified *logos* ask, should he distrust the claim that, if the weaker part still exists after a man dies, the stronger part must necessarily be preserved? Like Simmias, Cebes can express his distrust only through a likeness; yet, unlike Simmias, he is not misled into ignoring its status as an image, perhaps because it seems to be such a preposterous one.[17] To say, Cebes argues, that the soul lives on after death because it is stronger than the body, which does not perish immediately, would be like saying that an old man who had died did not perish but must be safe and sound somewhere if the cloak that he wove and wore was still safe and had not perished, since a man must last longer than a cloak. And yet, although the weaver is not weaker than the cloaks he produces, he must nevertheless have woven and worn many cloaks throughout his life, so that even if he outlasted many of them, he might perish before the last one. Cebes proceeds to spell out the analogy that is meant to explain the physiology of the living organism. The soul is always weaving anew the body, which is constantly changing and being destroyed.[18] But eventually the soul exhausts itself in this toil and, however many deaths it has survived, in one of them, it is finally destroyed. Now the last garment it was wearing, the final condition of the body, survives it; but once the soul has been destroyed, the body displays its natural weakness and decays.

Cebes thus transforms the notion of the soul enduring through a cycle of many lives, which Socrates introduced in the first argument, into an analysis of the constant passing away and reproduction of the body by the soul within what we consider one life span.[19] But he is willing to concede—since the structure of the argument is no different—that the soul might endure through a repeated cycle of births and deaths as ordinarily understood; for even this concession would not prove that the soul could not be altogether destroyed in one of its deaths. Cebes thus reproaches Simmias for his denial of the possible survival of the soul beyond the destruction of the body; and if "immortality" means the capacity to endure through what we call death, Cebes is willing to grant it. But he does so only to render more explicit the common fear he shares with Simmias: if death is redefined as the destruction of the soul, which finally occurs in one particular dissolution of the body, Socrates has not yet proven that the soul is incapable of meeting that fate.

Simmias and Cebes think they have brought to light Socrates' failure to demonstrate that the soul cannot be destroyed at death. Simmias attempts to do so through an apparently reasonable image that reduces soul to nothing but a quality resulting from the mixture of elements of the body. Cebes' more laughable image, on the other hand, reduces body to nothing but a product of the soul, though it does not explain why the soul requires this protection or adornment. It is now clear why Socrates insisted on combining their two objections before responding to either. For one amounts to the claim that there is in truth only body, the other that there is only soul; their juxtaposition thus results in the separation of soul from body that Socrates first presented as the definition of death. But while their combined objections perform this separation in *logos*, each one alone is an attempt to account for soul as a principle of life. What they have unwittingly brought to light is the true problem underlying the first series of arguments: not only have they failed to demonstrate immortality, for which we have no evidence, but in assuming the identification of soul with mind, they have also failed to account for life itself.

Now Simmias' image of the derivative status of soul, as Socrates will shortly argue, simply contradicts his acceptance of the identification of soul with mind. Cebes' image, on the other hand, because it makes body derivative from soul, raises this question: Why, if soul is mind, should it take on its ministerial role in producing the body, especially since that toil is the cause of its own destruction? Cebes must have been convinced by now of Socrates' prudence in wanting to run away from his present masters, the gods. But wouldn't it be better, then, not to be born at all? If it were, the genuine philosophers' desire would be reasonable, even if it is not fulfilled. Of course in that case, the recollection thesis, which requires perception as the condition for learning, would have to be rejected; and this Cebes is no more willing to do than Simmias. Yet, while the recollection thesis thus presupposes the necessity of life, it cannot explain its possibility. In his response to Cebes, which occupies the second half the dialogue, Socrates attempts to meet his objection by accepting and unfolding its implications. He must replace the recollection thesis with an account of thinking and knowledge that does not depend on the identification of soul as mind. Life remains inexplicable, Socrates acknowledges, unless it is simply assumed to belong to the essence of soul.

The question raised by Cebes' image thus points to the transformation that will be accomplished by the second half of the dialogue. But as Cebes himself understands it, his objection only shows the necessity of completing what he thinks the first series of arguments was meant to accomplish: Socrates has yet to demonstrate, Cebes insists, that the soul is altogether immortal and imperishable (*pantapasin athanaton te kai anōlethron*). And in the absence of that demonstration, Cebes concludes, anyone who feels confident about death displays his utter foolishness. But Cebes thus betrays his lack of understanding of Socrates' confidence in the face of death, which has nothing to do with an illusory belief about the character of the soul as a natural phenomenon. Socrates would presumably show no more fear in his present circumstances even if he in fact accepted the account of the relation between soul and body that Cebes has just presented.[20] Both Cebes and Simmias recognize Socrates' failure to demonstrate that the soul cannot perish or be destroyed, and is in that sense immortal. But neither entertains the possibility that this is the fulfillment, rather than the failure, of his intention.[21] Socrates himself, however, has spoken nowhere of the imperishability of the soul, and he referred to the *athanaton* only as a principle to which the soul may be likened insofar as it engages in a particular mode of inquiry. He made it painfully clear that he has never characterized the soul as deathless by ascribing that quality, however loosely construed, only to the bones and sinews (80d). His interlocutors seem to be proud of having discovered objections that take Socrates by surprise. But Socrates must have smiled for the first time precisely because they have grasped—even if they don't realize it—the intended implications of the first series of arguments.

Chapter Eight: Misology

[88c1–89c13] The objections raised by Simmias and Cebes launch a double attack on the argument in which the first half of the dialogue culminates. Simmias objects to the consequences derived in the third argument from the mere invisibility of the soul; his image of the soul as a harmony of corporeal elements requires a reconsideration of the argument on recollection that Socrates addressed to him. Cebes objects to the consequences derived in the third argument from the mere superiority of the soul to the body; his image of soul as source of *genesis* and destruction requires a reconsideration of the argument on the cyclical *genesis* of opposites that Socrates addressed to him. Their objections thus disclose—even if unwittingly—the relations among the preceding arguments,[1] as well as the deficiencies from which they suffer, at least insofar as they are meant to demonstrate the unceasing existence of the soul. It should be a benefit, then, when this double attack throws the entire company into confusion and despair. But they suffered a loss of confidence, Phaedo recounts, not simply in a demonstration of the immortality of the soul, but in regard to all future inquiry.

Simmias' and Cebes' twofold attack on the argument creates an experience of pain in everyone present. But they do not think of their pain as merely an indication of their own fears and hopes; they take it to be, rather, sufficient evidence of the truth of what Simmias and Cebes propose. The painful, Socrates' listeners believe, is a sign of the true; they were perfectly willing, after all, to accept the antihedonism of the genuine philosophers, for whom philosophy is identical with asceticism. Socrates saw far ahead when he indicated, in his opening remarks, the need for an examination of pleasure and pain and their relation to each other. In the absence of that examination, all those present with Socrates interpret their own disappointment to mean either that they are worthless judges or that the *pragmata* themselves are untrustworthy. It is precisely such an experience that

Socrates is about to identify as the source of the hatred of *logos* that he considers the greatest evil. The failure of the *logos* to serve as a satisfactory weapon against the fear of death calls attention to its own need to be rescued from an even greater danger.

This danger is manifest in the effect that emanates from the original participants and spreads to the frame conversation: Echecrates interrupts Phaedo's report for the first time, and thus marks the beginning of the central interlude that divides the dialogue into two halves. Echecrates sympathizes with the response Phaedo describes; for he too thought the arguments seemed entirely persuasive, yet now they have suddenly fallen into distrust. What is so disturbing to Echecrates, however, is not simply the apparent defeat of Socrates' arguments, but his realization of what he would have to give up if he were to accept Simmias' image of the soul as a harmony. For although that doctrine, as Echecrates now recalls, always had, and continues to have, a marvelous hold on him,[2] he had not recognized that it implied the denial of immortality. And while he believes that he must now begin all over again, he too fears that after this no *logos* can be trusted. Whether the reader of the dialogue should share this despair depends, of course, on whether he too seeks only persuasion to confirm comforting beliefs. Motivated by this desire, Echecrates is eager to hear how Socrates defended the *logos*, and whether he was as disturbed as the others, just as he asked to hear, in the opening exchange, what Socrates said and how he died (58c): he betrays the incomplete separation of deed and speech, *pathos* and *logos*, and thus appropriately introduces the interlude in which Socrates attempts most explicitly to accomplish that separation.

Yet Phaedo describes that attempt, paradoxically, by expressing his admiration not for the argument itself, but for the pleasant, gentle, respectful way in which Socrates listened to the young men. Phaedo was impressed with Socrates' quick recognition of how they were affected by the speeches, with his skill in curing them, and with his ability, like a brave general, to call his men back from cowardly flight.[3] When Echecrates asks, finally, how he accomplished this, Phaedo reports not the *logos* Socrates presented, but the deed he performed and its emotional effect. While he was sitting on a low couch at Socrates' feet, Phaedo recounts, Socrates stroked his long hair and held it tightly at the back of his neck—as if imitating his intention of cutting it off the next day as a traditional sign of mourning. Socrates will warn Crito, at the conclusion of the conversation, not to be concerned with his burial, since the corpse will be something entirely other than "this Socrates" with whom they are conversing (115c).

He now warns Phaedo not to cut off his hair on the morrow in mourning for him, but to cut it off today, as Socrates would his own, if the *logos* dies and cannot be brought back to life.[4] Socrates admits that he is neither the corpse nor the argument; in doing so, he betrays his awareness that "he" will indeed be absent on the morrow, and thus indicates the urgent necessity of his alliance with Phaedo for the preservation of the *logos*.

Faced with the challenge of confronting the joint attack of Simmias and Cebes, however, Phaedo protests, "Even Heracles is said to be no match for two." And he insists, understandably enough, when Socrates offers to come to his aid as Iolaus serving Heracles, that the relation must be the other way around. Engaged in the battle to cut off the nine heads of the Hydra, Heracles was met by two new heads for each one slaughtered, while being attacked at the same time from another direction by a large crab emerging from the sea. Only by calling Iolaus to his aid was Heracles able to burn away the heads, while burying under a rock the central one that was immortal.[5] In the mythical context first established by the dramatic frame of the dialogue, Socrates/Theseus engaged in a heroic mission to overcome the Minotaur that consists in the fear of death. But the labyrinth of *logoi* in which that monster lies has become itself a more forbidding monster, a Hydra whose multiple heads each double to meet any attack against it. The initial problem of the relation between body and soul, for example, turned into a more complicated problem of the relation between two functions of soul. And even if any one of the heads of this Hydra were slaughtered, its immortal one is that distrust of *logos* itself that is always a potential threat, not only at this particular moment of despair. To confront this monster, Socrates/Heracles must transform the fear of death, and of his death in particular, into the fear of the death of the *logos*. He addresses for that purpose not Simmias and Cebes, but his potential ally Phaedo and speaks no longer of the soul, but of men; not about purification, but about a *technē* of *logoi*; not about the practice of dying and being dead, but about the difficulty of maintaining love of men and love of *logos*.

[89d1–90d8] Socrates takes Phaedo as his ally in the mission of subordinating concern for himself to concern for the *logos* itself. But in analyzing the threat against the latter, Socrates begins by articulating not the correlative distinction between hatred of men and hatred of *logos*, but rather their common root. Misology, Socrates explains, is like the misanthropy that comes into being when someone with intense trust but no art believes a man to be altogether true and healthy and trustworthy but soon finds him to be wicked and untrustworthy; and when one undergoes this experience again and again, particularly among those nearest and dearest, one ends up hating everyone. Socrates describes the experience he himself might have undergone in pursuing his examination of the Delphic oracle, approaching everyone reputed to be wise and discovering nothing but pretense.[6] He must have avoided misanthropy because of not beginning with complete trust in the soundness and truth of those he examined: his knowledge of human nature must have warned him that the majority of men lie between the extremes of the perfectly good and the perfectly bad (cf. 113a, d–e).

Socrates' observation on the mediocrity of most human beings does not seem very startling. What is startling is that Phaedo does not understand it. It is unusual, Socrates must explain, to find a very large or very small man or dog, or anything quick or slow, beautiful or ugly, black or white. But while this explanation is enough to satisfy Phaedo, Socrates does not support it by articulating the distinction between the "opposites themselves" that represent those extremes and the *pragmata*, the many things that are always more or less characterized by such qualities.[7] Socrates speaks loosely when he says that, even in a contest for wickedness, the extreme would be most rare; strictly speaking, perfect wickedness, no less than perfect virtue, in human character would be, in principle, impossible.[8] But Phaedo considers the absence of these extremes only "likely"; we know he believes, after all, that, with the exception of this unique occasion, every experience of pleasure or pain is always an unadulterated instance of each, with no mixture of them (59a). If Phaedo thinks this true even of pleasure and pain, there must be no limits to the array of separate beings he imagines. Phaedo is a genuine philosopher, and, in choosing him to preserve the conversation, Socrates seems intentionally to have invited misunderstanding. But in representing this strange alliance, Plato must have had another end in mind: the portrayal of Phaedo's crucial misunderstanding is the necessary condition for illuminating the character of the Socratic turn that is its correction.

Socrates introduces his account of misanthropy and elaborates the illusion that produces it only, presumably, as a model for misology: when someone, without possessing a *technē* of *logoi*, has complete trust in the truth of an argument and later believes it to be false, and undergoes this experience time after time, he must end in distrusting and hating all *logoi*. This is precisely the case among those who pass their time in disputation and come to believe that they are the wisest of men because they alone have discovered that there is nothing sound or firm in any *logoi*, nor in any *pragmata* whatsoever. Socrates seems again to describe his own experience, identifying himself as the wisest of all men because he knows that he knows nothing.[9] He looks like the disputatious (*antilogikoi*), who spend their time in refuting arguments without finding anything to take the place of what is rejected; but whereas the disputatious discover the untrustworthy character of all *logoi*, as well as of *pragmata*, Socrates discovers only knowledge of his own ignorance, without abandoning trust in the soundness of *logos* itself. Precisely that knowledge of human nature that saved Socrates from misanthropy must save him at the same time from misology, for only by recognizing his own deficiency can he escape from blaming his ignorance on *logos* itself.

Misological, like misanthropical, resentment arises from hope based on an illusory standard, followed by inevitable disappointment, directed not against oneself and one's own illusions, but projected onto something alien. But while this analysis of the *pathē* uncovers the common structure of misology and misanthropy, the very possibility of escape from this double danger requires recognition of the tension between them. For *logos* does not share with human nature the character of always being somewhere between the extremes of truth and falsehood. The man who suddenly appears to be base and false may indeed be so, at least in part; but the *logos* that is first considered sound and true and then suddenly appears to be base and false may only appear to be so. Recognition, however, of the criteria that determine the soundness of *logos* would require a *technē*, which Socrates has yet to introduce; its analysis will bring to light the distinction between "opposites themselves" and the *pragmata* characterized by their participation in the opposites (cf. 103b), which explains the necessity of the continuum of degrees displayed by human character. It is such a *technē*, then, that at the same time prevents misanthropical resentment arising from illusory standards of human character and the misological projection of our own deficiency onto the *logos* itself.

The experience of misology, Socrates concludes, is the greatest evil that can befall a man; he recalls his claim, at the conclusion of the preceding series of arguments, that the greatest evil resulting from submission to pleasure and pain is the compulsion to believe falsely that the source of the *pathos* is most real and true (83c). The pleasure of hope for immediate knowledge of the beings, Socrates implies, and the pain of frustration in obtaining it cause a man to believe in the clarity and truth of the pure wisdom he desires, hence the insufficiency of what is accessible through *logos*. This illusion, however, is in fact his own self-imposed obstacle: like the prisoner who incarcerates himself through his own submission to desire (82e), the misologist suffers the greatest evil, since he deprives himself of the only possible means to "the truth of the beings and knowledge." But the ambiguous status of this "and," which links truth with knowledge and does not clarify whether the "beings" are the object of one or both, points to the limitation of Socrates' present account of misology. It will be overcome only in his analysis of the *technē* of *logoi* that provides the escape from this danger; for, as Socrates will disclose in the course of that analysis, avoidance of misology depends precisely upon abandoning the desire for knowledge of the beings themselves, in order to preserve trust in the possibility of discovering "the truth of the beings" through *logoi* (cf. 99d–100a).

Socrates confirms, in this central interlude, his distance from the genuine philosophers in whose voice he delivered his initial defense. For his understanding of misology as the greatest evil could not be shared by those preoccupied with resentment of the body as *the* obstacle to the attainment of *phronēsis*, construed as direct contact of the pure soul with the pure beings. Given that goal, the genuine philosophers should direct no less resentment against *logos* than against the body, since it seems no more capable than sense perception of furnishing a receptive noetic vision of the beings themselves. The genuine philosophers thus appear to be the source of the disputatious; and just as the first half of the dialogue was determined, however implicitly, by the beliefs of the genuine philosophers, the second half will be no less determined as a reaction against the disputatious. The unwillingness of the disputatious, like that of the genuine philosophers, to admit their own deficiency results in the cynical belief that there is nothing firm or sound in *logoi* or *pragmata*. Yet Socrates concludes his account of misology by warning Phaedo of the need to guard only against the belief that there is nothing sound in *logoi*: he suggests that maintaining trust in *logos*, over against the cynicism of the disputatious, might require admitting, like the disputatious, the unsoundness of the *pragmata*—recognizing, that is, that the *pragmata* are not the beings themselves.

[90d9–91c5] Even when repeatedly disappointed by arguments, Socrates insists finally, we must assume that it is not the *logos*—from which we perhaps demand something impossible in principle—but we ourselves who are not yet sound, and who must therefore strive eagerly and manfully to become so. Socrates addresses this exhortation not only to the young men, but to himself as well, for, as he now admits, he fears he has not conducted the preceding arguments in a spirit of disinterested objectivity. He suspects that he has not spoken philosophically but rather, like "uneducated lovers of victory," who carry on disputation with eagerness not for the truth, but to make their opinions appear true to their listeners. Socrates differs merely in being eager to make his opinions appear true primarily to himself, only incidentally to others. But Socrates thus enacts the kind of self-accusation he just declared to be the necessary condition for maintaining trust in *logos*: he shows his distance from the motive of self-persuasion, which would stand in the way of concern for the truth, at the very moment when he stands back to accuse himself of that motive.[10]

Socrates elaborates—and in doing so complicates—his warning against the self-interest that has made the discussion thus far a reasonable wager. If what he says happens to be true, it would be beautiful to be persuaded of it.[11] Now, this might be the case for his companions, whose emotional state in the face of Socrates' death is motivating the desire for a proof of immortality. But for Socrates, self-persuasion that took the place of knowledge of ignorance could hardly be something beautiful. The most basic subject of their ongoing ignorance can be traced back to the agreement that "death is something" (64c)—at least if understood in contrast with the alternative Socrates now poses, that there is nothing for one who has died.[12] But even in that case, Socrates reasons, there would be a double benefit. For, on the one hand, turning their attention to the arguments for immortality has allowed him to avoid spending his time lamenting, being unpleasant to those gathered around him. And for himself, on the other hand, if death were indeed an absolute end, at least his ignorance or foolishness would not last forever, which would indeed be an evil.[13]

Socrates' worry about conducting the discussion like a lover of victory is supposed to be an accusation of himself; but he seems to be defending his conduct as a matter of both justice and prudence, providing a benefit at the same time to the young men at his side and to himself. That coincidence, however, is misleading and it puts each claim on its own into question. The failure to demonstrate immortality has created a despair of its own, though engaging in that attempt is said to be advantageous for Socrates' companions even if death is nothing. But it is death itself, so understood, in which Socrates claims to see a great good for himself, on rather shocking grounds: it would put an end to perpetual philosophizing without acquisition of wisdom. This final consequence must be Socrates' critique of the pragmatic wager, which depends on rejecting the worth of the life of examination. A discussion driven by that calculation, in abandoning the quest for truth, fails at the same time to serve Socrates' professed motive of self-interest: how could he be benefited by an inquiry that denies the good of Socratic philosophy?

After sharing his self-accusation with Phaedo, Socrates returns to Simmias and Cebes, urging them now to go back to the argument and fight against him, as he must fight against himself. Socrates first responded to their perplexities about the prohibition against suicide by advising them that they must be eager (*prothumeisthai*), and perhaps they might hear something (62a). He now advises them that they must raise any possible objections to the argument, lest Socrates in his own eagerness (*prothumia*) deceive himself and them alike. They must beware lest he, like a bee leaving his sting in them, prick them with arguments motivated by eagerness for self-persuasion and then depart without defending the assumptions or implications of those arguments.[14] The objections that they offered only reluctantly in the fear of disturbing Socrates must be continued not because of Socrates' philosophic indifference, as he first seemed to suggest (84e), but because of his urgent involvement. Just as Phaedo is to cut off his hair in mourning not for the death of Socrates, but only for the death of the *logos*, Simmias and Cebes are urged to resist any concerns that would stand in the way of a ruthless examination of the argument; only in that way could they participate with Socrates in the practice of dying.

Chapter Nine: Harmony

[91c6–92a6] Socrates encouraged his interlocutors to express their reservations about the argument by describing the conversation as his joyful swan song; he is now prepared to respond to them after issuing a warning about the distorting effects of his own self-interest. Socrates asks quite reasonably, therefore, to be reminded of anything he seems to have omitted from his summary of their objections. Simmias' distrust, as Socrates understands it, arises from his fear that the soul, although more divine and beautiful than the body, may nevertheless be destroyed first, being "in the *eidos* of a harmony." Cebes, on the other hand, appears to agree with Socrates that the soul is more enduring than the body but claims that no one can know whether, after wearing out many bodies, it might not finally be destroyed in departing from its last body, so that death would be nothing but this perishing of the soul. While Socrates drops altogether the image with which Cebes introduced his objection, he emphasizes the image that Simmias inadvertently turned into an account of the nature of the soul. Of course it was Cebes who spoke of the *eidos* into which the soul enters (87a), and he meant the human body, while Simmias never called the harmony an *eidos*. Nor did he declare it to be more beautiful than the body, but only to be the result of a beautiful mixing of the elements of the body, about which Socrates is now entirely silent. Nevertheless, Simmias and Cebes accept Socrates' formulation with no revision, for it sufficiently stresses their primary concern: the prior arguments have failed to supply a proof of the unceasing existence of the soul after death.

Socrates, however, does not announce any intention of attempting to satisfy that challenge. He seems interested, rather, only in discovering some inconsistency between their objections or between those objections and the presuppositions accepted in the preceding arguments. He finds the required basis in the one argument he himself did not initiate; for the *logos* that identifies learning as recollection, and thereby demonstrates that the soul must be "somewhere" before being imprisoned in the body, is the one argument that both Simmias and Cebes wholeheartedly endorse.[1] Since, however, their affirmation of the persuasive power of this argument may be for different reasons, Socrates must separate the objections he has put together. Turning first to Simmias, with the address "Theban Stranger," he foreshadows the conclusion of his refutation (cf. 95a).

[92a7–92e3] That Simmias has affirmed the recollection argument on the basis of an unexamined assumption concerning the existence and nature of "the beings" does not concern Socrates, at least not immediately. For, however inadequate his grounds may have been, Simmias has accepted a demonstration of the preexistence of the soul; he cannot maintain, consequently, that harmony is a composite *pragma*, and that the soul is some kind of harmony of elements of the body, which could never exist prior to that from which it is put together. Simmias does not take the opportunity to argue that perhaps harmony is not a composite *pragma*, or that the soul is a harmony, but not of corporeal elements,"[2] despite Socrates' explicit, if mysterious, remark that harmony is not that to which Simmias likens it. Socrates offers a clue to what he has in mind by reformulating Simmias' image: the lyre and strings and sounds come into being unharmonized, and harmony is the last to be put together and the first to be destroyed. Whereas, according to Simmias, the lyre and strings are the material elements from which harmony is produced, Socrates makes the crucial addition of "sounds." He thereby separates from the instrument itself the noise produced by it and, at the same time, separates from that noise the harmonic order imposed upon it. If the instrument, then, represents the body and the strings its elements, what is represented by the sounds produced by the strings and capable of being brought into harmony? It is precisely what Simmias left out of his image, Socrates implies by the conclusion of his response, that represents the soul and its *pathē*.[3] While the coming into being and perishing of the soul is thus dependent on the instrument of the body,[4] the harmonic order imposed on the soul is not itself necessarily dependent on the body.

But what then is this harmony itself separate from soul? Socrates offers a sign in his subsequent question to Simmias, as to how there can be harmony between the two *logoi*, that which identifies the soul as a harmony and that which identifies learning as recollection. Socrates seems to offer Simmias a free choice of which *logos* he prefers, as if neither could be shown to be more true than the other, as long as both are not held at once. But since he suggests only that certain presuppositions underlying Simmias' particular interpretations of each *logos* might have to be qualified or discarded in order for them to be reconciled, they may be no more a set of mutually exclusive alternatives than the alleged alternative Simmias was offered in the recollection argument—whether we are born with knowledge, or whether we recollect afterwards that of which we acquired knowledge before birth (76a–b). Simmias was indeed so perplexed by that choice that Socrates was compelled to replace it with the alternative that either all men can give a *logos* of the issues being discussed or they recollect what they once learned (76b–c). If Simmias is now being confronted with a parallel set of alternatives, the proper understanding of harmony would be connected with the capacity to give a *logos*, for both have been forced to compete, in an allegedly mutually exclusive opposition, with the identification of learning as recollection. This suggestion is confirmed by Simmias' response: he is willing to give up his image of the soul as a harmony because of his natural acceptance of the demand for harmony between *logoi*—his refusal, that is, to admit self-contradiction.

Simmias introduced his image of the soul as a harmony after a methodological reflection concerning the need to rely on the most irrefutable human *logos*, unless a more safe, divine *logos* is available (85c–d). He now justifies the abandonment of his image by admitting that it appealed to him, as to most men, not through demonstration, but through mere likelihood and plausibility, which can always be deceptive.[5] It is no wonder that Simmias still expresses such skepticism at the conclusion of the last argument (107a–b), or that he considers Socrates so indispensable for giving a *logos* (76b), if even the human *logos* that appears most irrefutable is convincing only because of likelihood and plausibility. And yet, Simmias is led to admit the deficiency of the harmony thesis by seeing its apparent conflict with the recollection thesis, and he is entirely convinced that the latter was based on a hypothesis worthy of acceptance. Now, Socrates is about to elaborate a procedure for positing a hypothesis, examining its consequences, and attempting eventually to defend the original hypothesis. But Simmias' remarks are, once more, a parody of Socratic procedure. For the premise in which he places so much trust is his unexamined assumption that nothing is so clear as the existence of the beautiful, the good, and the others of which Socrates always speaks (cf. 72a). Simmias' confident belief in the existence of "the beings," which are "seen" by the pure soul before birth, prevented him from investigating the meaning of giving a *logos*, just as it now prevents him from investigating a possible meaning of harmony other than his own image of the soul as a mixture of corporeal elements.

Socrates leads Simmias to give up that image without explicitly supplying an alternative answer to the question, "What is soul?". He nevertheless accomplishes two purposes at once. He attacks Simmias' unrecognized self-contradiction in conceiving of the soul, on the one hand, as naturally akin to the pure beings it contemplates apart from the body and, on the other, as a mere quality derived from a particular mixture of elements of the body. In what may seem to be a rather arbitrary refutation of Simmias' particular self-contradiction, Socrates points to the fundamental problem of the relation between soul as medium of cognition and soul as source of life. In using the recollection thesis, moreover, to reject the harmony thesis, Socrates exemplifies through the very form of the refutation his alternative interpretation of the meaning of harmony. Yet this interpretation of harmony as consistency of *logoi*—which Socrates will elaborate in the course of responding to Cebes' objection—proves to entail a denial of the assumption on which the recollection thesis depends; it denies, that is, the understanding of the beings as the object of a passive vision by the pure soul.

[92e4–93b7] This initial refutation seems to satisfy Simmias, in any case, more fully than Socrates.[6] Some implication of Simmias' image was, after all, apparently devastating enough to stop Socrates in his tracks when he first heard it, although only, perhaps, because it brought into the open what Socrates himself already recognized. Socrates' initial refutation of Simmias' image turns on the incompatibility between maintaining the autonomy and separability of the soul, on the one hand, its status as a derivative quality of the body, on the other. Socrates now adds a supplement to intensify that conflict. He begins by asking whether a harmony, like anything composite,[7] could ever be in any condition other than that of the elements of which it is composed, whether it could ever do or suffer anything other than what its elements do or suffer. Simmias offers no counterexample, although he might have proposed the relation between a word and its letters, a sentence and its words, an argument and its propositions; he is unaware of the nature of *logos* as a composite whole that has qualities other than those of its component parts.[8] Simmias agrees immediately that it would not be fitting for a harmony to lead, but only to follow, its elements, so that it would be unable to move or produce a sound in opposition to its own parts. He divines that a harmony is not some other thing alongside its parts but believes, unjustifiably, that this commits him to denying any special status to the ordered arrangement of those parts.

Rather than explore this question directly, however, Socrates adds a supplement to this supplement; before applying to the case of soul Simmias' agreement on the passive status of a composite harmony, he tries to support the latter with a new premise. If every harmony is by nature a harmony insofar as it is harmonized, Socrates reasons, it would be more and more fully a harmony insofar as it is more and more fully harmonized—if possible[9]—less and less fully a harmony insofar as it is less and less fully harmonized. Although Simmias had spoken of the soul as the harmony that results when the body is strung together neither too tightly nor too loosely, implying that soul is somehow itself a matter of degree, he is puzzled by Socrates' present suggestion. For what Socrates seems to propose is not the reasonable claim that the sounds produced by the strings of an instrument can be more or less harmonized, but that this is true of the harmony itself,[10] although every harmony as such, while it might be different from another, would seem to be necessarily no less a harmony than any other.[11] Socrates is proposing the reduction of all differences to those of degree. "Harmony," he implies, may be our unjustifiable construction of a substance that misrepresents the more or less harmonized quality of sound, just as "the child in us" who fears death was Cebes' construction of a being that misrepresents the mere quality of childish fear (cf. 77d–e).

If "soul" were of the same character, it would be only our name, which we mistakenly construe as an independent being, for the more or less "psychized" quality of living body. Now if Simmias had really understood his original image, he should have agreed to this consequence: the being of soul is as relative as a state of health. But Socrates appeals to Simmias' ordinary understanding of soul as a substance, which might be exemplified by different kinds, none of which, however, could be more and more fully a soul or less and less fully a soul than another.[12] Each would be equally a member of the same class, not simply relatively characterized by its participation in the principle of "the psychic." While Socrates gains Simmias' agreement without having to offer any further defense, he does not immediately draw the consequence that soul could not then be a harmony. He has argued, in any case, only that each harmony is more or less a harmony if it is possible for it to be more or less harmonized, and he does not attempt explicitly to affirm or deny that possibility.[13]

[93b8–94b3] Socrates proceeds instead to bring to light the consequences of the agreement about the nature of the soul by reinterpreting the meaning of its likeness to a harmony. One soul, Socrates reminds Simmias, swearing by Zeus,[14] is said to possess mind and virtue and to be good, another to possess mindlessness and wickedness and to be bad. Since these are, of course, characteristics of human beings, they seem to differentiate not one kind of soul from another, but a hierarchical range within one kind—at least this would be self-evident if Socrates had not just sworn by the highest god. But what is it, in any case, to which these characteristics are ascribed? They certainly don't appear to have anything to do with the excellence of the mixture of hot and cold and wet and dry. Socrates, in fact, simply replaces Simmias' doctrine with another traditional image, according to which virtue is a harmony and vice a discord; he does not acknowledge that it is an image, nor does he clarify exactly what it is that is thought to be harmonic in the virtuous soul or discordant in the wicked one. He assumes, rightly, that Simmias will accept this traditional image and will find himself, consequently, in a dilemma.

Will someone who claims that the soul is a harmony, Socrates asks, have to admit that the good one that is harmonized has within it a harmony while being a harmony, and that the other is disharmonic and has no other harmony within it? Although Socrates has just asked about the possibility of a harmony being more or less harmonized, Simmias cannot figure out how anyone could justify this allegedly absurd claim. He might have proposed that a certain mixture of bodily elements provides the necessary conditions for life—that is, the harmony constituting the soul that is just soul and never more or less so—while the human soul has an internal structure that may be characterized as more or less harmonious or discordant, which we call being virtuous or wicked. But Simmias proves unable to defend the proposal offered to him. He has given no thought to how his physiological account of the soul as the vital principle in any living organism is related to the ordinary understanding of the moral character differentiating one human soul from another, any more than he thought about how either is related to the cognitive function of the human soul.

Since Simmias does not take advantage of his implicit proposal, Socrates simply reminds him of their agreement that one soul is no more nor less a soul than another, which would be equivalent to the claim that one harmony is no more nor less a harmony than another, hence no more nor less harmonized.[15] With an apparently superfluous consideration, Socrates leads Simmias to agree, further, that whatever is no more nor less harmonized "participates" not to a greater or lesser degree in harmony but to an equal degree.[16] Yet, with this addition Socrates corrects his original reduction by acknowledging that "more or less" applies only to the degree of participation, the degree to which something is characterized by a particular quality, but not to that in which it participates in order to be so characterized at all. Socrates thus implicitly lays down the principles required to establish that every soul, which as a kind cannot be more nor less of a soul, can nevertheless participate more or less in harmony, and hence would be a more or less fully harmonized soul. Although he claims to conclude, on the analogy with a harmony, that every soul that is no more nor less a soul can he neither more nor less harmonized, he would be justified in concluding only that one soul could be no more nor less "psychic" than another.

If, Socrates infers, wickedness is disharmony and virtue harmony, one soul could participate no more in wickedness or virtue than another; or, more precisely, no soul could participate in wickedness at all, for if harmony is itself wholly harmony, it could not participate in discord, and likewise the soul, being wholly soul. That which is "wholly harmony" could participate in disharmony no more than in harmony, for it would *be* harmony "itself by itself." But Socrates has spoken nowhere of that which is more or less psychic because of the degree of its participation in soul itself. And whereas harmony has as its opposite disharmony, so that whatever is not wholly harmony would participate in that opposite, soul has no opposite in which whatever is not wholly soul could participate. Socrates states the conclusion that follows, as he emphasizes, "according to this *logos*": if all souls were by nature equally souls, so that none could participate in evil any more than harmony could participate in disharmony, then all souls of all the living—not even restricted to human beings—would be equally good. Compelled by the *logos*, Simmias reluctantly agrees. But since his desire to distinguish the good from the wicked prevents him from willingly affirming this conclusion, he feels obliged to abandon his claim that the soul is by nature a harmony.

[94b4–95a5] Socrates himself, however, seems to be no more satisfied by this refutation based on an appeal to Simmias' moral standards than he was by the original one. He has drawn attention to Simmias' conviction of the hierarchical range of human souls by reducing the substance harmony to the quality of being harmonized, but without ever connecting that to their previous agreement on the nonautonomy of a composite whole. That agreement, it seems, could not alone provide the means of refuting Simmias' image without some understanding of the soul implicitly introduced by the apparent digression on virtue and vice. Socrates now brings that connection to light by asking Simmias whether anything in man is fit to rule other than the soul (cf. 80a), especially if it is prudent (*phronimos*). Socrates brings to light with this reminder the limitations of any physiological account of the soul as such. The question of its autonomy, he indicates, is specifically concerned with the conduct of human beings, and the description of the harmonic or discordant soul must be relevant to that concern.

Simmias originally agreed that a composite harmony could never produce a sound in opposition to the tension and relaxation of the strings of an instrument. Reminded now of the standard of *phronēsis*, however, he readily agrees that the soul is not always and necessarily compelled to follow the *pathē* of the body: it may prohibit the body from drinking even when it is thirsty or from eating when it is hungry and may oppose the body in countless other ways. The soul, however, does not oppose the dryness of the throat, only the desire for drink, not the emptiness of the stomach, only the desire for food.[17] Socrates' simple examples, intended presumably to reveal the struggle of the soul against the body, in fact reveal the struggle of the soul against itself, and thus illuminate what it means to characterize the soul as internally harmonious or discordant. Even if the soul were understood as a composite harmony, Socrates implies, its components would not be the hot, dry, cold, and wet, as Simmias proposed, but its own *pathē*. Simmias is compelled to admit, in the light of Socrates' examples, that the soul actually leads those elements from which it is said to be composed; in fact it opposes them, he agrees, in almost everything throughout life, sometimes inflicting harsh and painful punishments, sometimes milder ones, sometimes threatening, and sometimes admonishing. Socrates identifies the harsher punishments with medicine or gymnastics, and thus reinforces the explicit claim that the soul is involved in an effort to rule over the body, which is alien to it. Yet the only thing that the soul could "threaten" or "admonish" would seem to be itself. The attempted tyranny of the soul, Socrates implicitly indicates, results from its misdirected resentment of the body, which should be directed against its own *pathē* in their recalcitrance to reason.

The soul attempts to gain control, Socrates elaborates, by "conversing with" (*dialegomenē*) its desires and angers and fears as if they were alien *pragmata*. This is how Homer describes Odysseus: "He smote his breast and rebuked his heart in speech: 'Endure, heart, you have endured a more outrageous thing than this!'"[18] Through a personification, Homer represents an internal struggle in which Odysseus addresses his own heart—that is, his passionate anger—as if it were another subject with a will of its own. Now Socrates uses Homer's image of opposition within the soul in order to illustrate the opposition of the soul to the body; he can do so, of course, only by ignoring its status as an image. In fact, it is just this passage, supplemented by another with the same structure, that Socrates employs in *Republic* Book 4 in order to establish a division—presumably tripartite—within the soul, based on the principle that the same thing cannot do or suffer opposites at the same time.[19]

Odysseus' self-reproach, which Socrates interprets as the struggle of reason against *thumos*, is juxtaposed with Leontius' angry reproach against his own eyes—"There, ye wretches, take your fill"—which Socrates interprets as the struggle of *thumos* against the desire to see. Moved by anger, a part of the soul identifies itself as the whole and regards any conflicting internal force as a personification of some part of the body. The soul, consequently, is understood as monoeidetic, and its own self-control as despotism over the alien. Socrates appeals to an image of this psychological struggle to "rule" oneself in order to refute Simmias' image of the soul as a composite harmony derived from elements of the body. But what Socrates tacitly shows, is *thumos* at work in constructing the ideal of the pure soul separate from the body and compelled to tyrannize it.[20] The construction of the pure soul, moreover, has been shown all along to be parallel to that of the pure beings: their origin, Socrates now seems to hint, is willfulness and moral indignation.

If Socrates had not suppressed recognition of Homer's image as an image, it would have indicated the difference between an internally harmonized, rather than discordant, state of the *pathē* within the human soul. This potential would suggest how it can be, in contrast to the derivative harmony to which Simmias likens it, "a far more divine kind of *pragma*"—to which Simmias agrees, by Zeus, with an unconscious irony. He accepts Socrates' conclusion that we cannot speak beautifully of the soul as some kind of harmony, since we would be in harmony, it seems, neither with the divine poet Homer nor with ourselves. Yet he does not seem to grasp Socrates' implication that the common ground of harmonization, understood as the well-ordered state of the parts of the soul in relation to the whole, and harmony, understood as consistency of *logoi*, must be the law of noncontradiction.[21] Having suffered, in any case, from

an unrecognized state of discord, based on the inconsistency of unexamined presuppositions, Simmias, the Theban Stranger, has finally been
harmonized, thanks to Socrates' "musical" skill, with Homer, as well as
himself. But Socrates has refuted Simmias' particular interpretation of
the soul as a harmony, without ever showing that the soul could not perish
before the body—the intention that, according to Socrates, motivated
the image Simmias proposed (cf. 91d). Socrates is understandably thank-
ful to Harmonia, the Theban goddess, for being, so it seems, measurably
gracious to them.[22]

[95a5–95e6] But what kind of *logos* is now needed, Socrates asks, to pro-
pitiate Cadmus? He joins the challenge of Cebes with that of Simmias
through the image of husband and wife,[23] and thus seems to confirm his
original plan of attacking the objection of each by discovering some contradiction between them. But while Cebes has experienced such encouragement from Socrates' sudden overturning of the distrust engendered
by the *logos* of Harmonia that he would not be at all surprised if the *logos*
of Cadmus suffered the same defeat, Socrates now expresses his lack of
confidence, admitting that he has conquered one threat only to confront
a more imposing one. After warning Cebes not to boast, lest the coming
argument be routed, he entrusts the *logos* to the care of the god and gathers
up his strength, in Homeric fashion, to mount the attack.

Socrates offers once more a summary of Cebes' objection and asks him
to make sure that nothing escapes their examination. What you really seek,
he explains to Cebes, is a truly worthy demonstration that our soul is imperishable and immortal. That it has been shown to be strong and divine
and to exist before birth implies, according to Cebes, only that it may endure for an immeasurably long time, capable of knowing and performing
other deeds; but this does not preclude the possibility that its entrance
into the human body is the beginning of its destruction, as if life were a
disease. That human life is a long illness from which the soul wishes to be
healed Socrates has not explicitly denied.[24] It is the basis of the resentment
he ascribed to the genuine philosophers and the assumption justifying
their longing for death as the separation of the soul from the body. But it
is precisely that understanding of death, Cebes argues, that avoids the
crucial question of destruction. "Death" is the name we apply to the termination of any particular life, but, according to Cebes, it should really
apply only to the termination of that life in which the soul finally perishes
with the body. And since no one knows what particular occasion of sepa-

ration from the body will bring destruction to the soul, one would be altogether foolish not to experience fear at the end of this present life.

Socrates clarifies, in this final repetition, the grounds of Cebes' demand for a proof of immortality as imperishability. Yet he puts into question, at the same time, the worth of Cebes' physiological account as an attack against the philosopher's confidence in dying. For the latter, Socrates has repeatedly implied, must be identical with confidence in the way one has lived one's life. Whether it is prudent or foolish depends, then, not on possessing a truly worthy demonstration of the imperishability of the soul, but on understanding the criteria that make any demonstration truly worthy; for, without that understanding, one would be threatened by the danger of losing all trust in *logos*. And to deprive oneself, in that way, of the only means for investigating "the truth of the beings" is to destroy the basis for confidence in the one life worth living. Before he confronts Cebes' challenge, Socrates points to the direction that confrontation must take if it is to be sufficiently fundamental.

Chapter Ten: Second Sailing

[95e7–96e7] While Cebes was eager to hear Socrates' response to his objection, Socrates himself fell silent for a long time, Phaedo reports, investigating something in relation to himself. Absorbed in his own thoughts, Socrates prepares himself not simply to refute Cebes' objection, but to explore the fundamental question it raises. What Cebes seeks, Socrates now informs him, is no trifling matter, for it requires a complete investigation of the cause of coming to be and passing away as a whole. For the sake of this inquiry, Socrates offers to relate the history of his own experiences; Cebes, of course, is free to use it for the persuasion of which he speaks. After identifying the concern with one's own *pathē* as the obstacle standing in the way of the concern with the *logos* (cf. 90d, 83c–d), Socrates offers a report of his own *pathē*. But this report reveals the problems that require a *technē* generating trust in *logos*, and Socrates' own intellectual development reflects a necessary progression of philosophic thought itself.[1]

Socrates offers this intellectual autobiography to Cebes, because he sees in him, perhaps, a mirror of himself when young, when he was wonderfully eager for that wisdom called "investigation of nature." He thought it magnificent to know the "causes" of each thing,[2] why each comes to be and perishes and—as if it belonged to the same inquiry—why it is. "I used to toss myself up and down,"[3] Socrates admits, investigating these questions. He wanted to know whether it is heat and cold, by some kind of fermentation, that result in the organization of living animals, then whether it is because of blood or air or fire that we think, or rather, because the brain furnishes sensations from which memory and opinion arise, from which, in turn, knowledge comes into being.[4] Despite Socrates' professed desire to discover the causes of everything, his examples reveal a particular focus: by investigating the causes of life and knowledge, what Socrates really wanted to know was the human soul.[5] But he could not have been aware of that goal since, he claims, he continued to study the conditions of heaven and earth. What he in fact discovered, however, was his own natural unfitness for this sort of investigation, for he felt "intensely blinded" by inquiries that put into question even those matters he formerly believed he had grasped. Not only did Socrates pursue the investigation of nature to learn about the human soul, but the result of his inquiry was the acquisition of what seems to be the familiar Socratic knowledge of ignorance.

That distinctive "human wisdom" is typically represented in the Platonic dialogues as the result of Socrates' examination of the moral and political opinions of others; but it does not appear to be those sorts of opinions that Socrates now claims to have held before, and to have questioned after, his investigation of nature. Rather, Socrates confesses, he believed he knew, like most others, that the cause of a man's growth is eating and drinking, since when flesh is added to flesh, as like to like, the small bulk becomes greater, and the small man great. Cebes innocently agrees to the reasonableness of this belief in a physiology of addition, without realizing the threatening perplexities lurking behind it, which Socrates attempts to indicate through an increasingly abstract series of examples. He believed he knew that a big man or horse standing next to a smaller one is greater "by a head," or turning to even clearer matters, that ten is greater than eight by the addition of two, and a two-cubit length greater than a one-cubit length because it exceeds it by half.

Cebes, who wants to know what Socrates thinks now, must still find these claims self-evident. But Socrates, swearing by Zeus for the third and final name in the conversation,[6] admits he is far from thinking he knows the cause—no longer the causes—of these matters. Socrates' former opinions were put into question, it seems, by the goal of discovering one comprehensive cause, at least of becoming and being greater, applicable to growth, magnitude, and number; yet he still has not achieved that goal on the last day of his life. Socrates may have been "awakened from his dogmatic slumbers" by his attempted investigation of nature; but it was that pursuit, he confessed, by which he was intensely blinded. If that is the same blindness that results from any attempt to look directly at things and grasp them through the senses (cf. 99e), it is not at all evident how it could have brought to light the perplexities concealed in Socrates' prephilosophic opinions, or in the logical structures they presuppose.

[96e7–97b7] What then are the puzzles that led Socrates to knowledge of his own ignorance? He cannot even understand, he explains, when one is added to one, whether the one to which the addition was made becomes two, or the one which is added or both together become two by the addition of each to the other. He finds it amazing that, when separated, each was one and not two, yet mere juxtaposition is the cause of their becoming two.[7] Socrates cannot take for granted what appears to be the most simple arithmetic operation. Is addition, he wonders, a performance executed in space? And, if not, how is it to be understood? To give a physiological account of how someone grows larger requires an understanding of what addition is; but to give an account of addition requires, in turn, an understanding of the relation between "each" and "both." And Socrates sees in the grammatical problem of what the subject is to which we ascribe the predicate "comes to be two" the ontological problem of how a common quality comes to characterize a whole whose elements are not characterized by it separately.[8]

These perplexities throw Socrates into a state of wonder—the beginning of philosophy.[9] No less amazing is the claim that one becomes two by being divided in half. Is division too, Socrates wonders, a spatial operation? But isn't the one on which the operation is performed thought to be an indivisible unit? And if, somehow or other, the operation is performed, does it transform halves of one into two ones? But in that case— if no further qualifications are stipulated—addition and division would be opposite causes of the same result. And as long as they are taken to be the cause of *what* something becomes or is, these opposites would appear to violate the law of noncontradiction and thus fail to satisfy the minimal condition for intelligibility.

The juxtaposition of two accounts of how two comes to be, through the division of an original unit or through the addition of originally separate units, was just the perplexity Socrates introduced in his opening description of pleasure and pain, which seemed to him wondrously related to each other (60b–c). And that description furnished in turn the model for a double account of the relation between body and soul. Does body become alive, then, by having soul brought near to it, or does soul become thereby embodied? And if both together become two by mere juxtaposition, how can they also become two by the separation of one from the other? In fact, as Socrates realizes in conclusion, he cannot yet persuade himself that he knows how one comes to be. For not only do there seem to be opposite causes that both produce two, but the same causes, and the same opposition, could also produce one: if body and soul are really united, they make a single living animal, but if they are really separated, each is a single entity—the corpse, at least, is a unit, whether or not the soul proceeds by itself on its journey to Hades.

Socrates has now reached the extreme stage of his knowledge of ignorance. Since he does not know how one comes to be, and since, furthermore, whatever is, is one,[10] he cannot claim to know how anything comes to be or ceases to be or is at all. His perplexity about two deepened to a perplexity about one; but since to be is to be something, and to be something is to be one, the perplexity about one pushed him beyond the problem of numbers to the problem of being. Socrates tried to think about being by thinking about becoming and perishing, and about that in turn by thinking about combination and separation; but in doing so, he discovered contradictions that he lacked any means to avoid, let alone resolve. Having set out with the desire for the knowledge of nature, Socrates was compelled by the perplexities of the *logos* to investigate the presuppositions of his own reasoning.[11] He draws a radical conclusion, therefore, from the wonder-inspiring puzzles he has described. He must consider the mathematical operations of addition and division a paradigm for all mechanistic explanation; for once he recognized the perplexities of how two and one come to be, he claims, he found himself no longer able to follow "the way of the method" of natural science.

Socrates turned instead to another way of his own that he "mixes up at random" (*eikē phurō*). He seems to allude to the mixed-up condition of human life before Prometheus' introduction of the arts: men had eyes but saw nothing, they had ears but did not understand, and, like shapes in dreams, throughout their lives, they mixed up everything at random.[12] Socrates' mixed-up way of his own is designed to deal with the threat of contradiction in *logos*, which he discovered by reflecting on the problem of the cause of two and one and being; but the allusion with which he refers to his own path identifies it as a regression behind all knowledge of cause, a reversal of the apparent progress Prometheus brought when he bestowed his fateful gift of numbers, letters, and the arts. The very order of Socrates' presentation, moreover, seems to reflect his own mixed-up way; for after simply referring to it, he returns to the recital of his philosophic development, without clarifying whether this subsequent stage followed from, or preceded and perhaps inspired, his discovery of the perplexities to which his own procedure should provide an answer.

[97b8–99c9] Once, Socrates continues, he heard someone reading from a book said to be by Anaxagoras, claiming that it is mind (*nous*) that arranges and is the cause of all. Socrates seems to go out of his way to identify the communication of this teaching in a written work: he arouses our suspicion about teleology as a questionable application to nature of the character of a human work of art. The Anaxagorean position pleased Socrates in any case; for to say that mind arranges all must mean, according to Socrates' interpretation, that it does so with a view to what is best.[13] To discover the cause of how anything comes into being and perishes, therefore, one need only discover how it is best for it to be or suffer or do, and by the same knowledge, one would necessarily know what is worse as well;[14] knowledge of what is best and what is worse, of course, would not entail knowledge of what is actual, unless the good could be shown to operate unlimited by any conditions of necessity. Socrates points to that problem when he admits his delight in finding in Anaxagoras a "teacher of the cause of the beings to my liking" (*kata noun*), literally "in accordance with mind." The pun Socrates constructs out of a colloquial expression discloses why the claim of teleology should be suspect: a universe constructed "in accordance with mind" is so pleasing to us, just because it projects onto the whole the operation of the human mind, without necessarily acknowledging that projection.

From Anaxagoras Socrates hoped to discover whether the earth is flat or round or in the center of the cosmos, with an explanation of the necessity of its being as it is, based on an account of what is best. Teleology identifies the good and the necessary without confronting the possibility of a tension between them.[15] Socrates expected that Anaxagoras would, in assigning the cause of each and of all in common, go on to explain the best for each and the good for all in common. Teleology cannot treat a part except as part of a whole; but the possible tension between them reflects the tension between the necessary and the good, since what is best for the particular, considered alone, may not be good for the whole of which that particular is only one part among many.[16]

Teleology could be saved, one might conclude, if reflection on the relation between part and whole led to recognition of the distinction between the good and the necessary, the former identified with purpose, the latter with the means through which it is carried out. In that case, however, an explanation would still be required of how the one functions as the condition for the realization of the other. But if means and end had to be added together or separated from an original unity, teleology would lead back to the same perplexities Socrates discovered in all mechanistic explanation. A comprehensive teleology would require a defense of the superiority of life, or of death, not merely for one individual but for that individual as a single part of a cosmic whole. And to defend the belief that life is good even for one individual, a teleological account would have to answer this question: Does union with the body serve as the means by which the good of soul can be realized, and, if so, how? But if, at least for some and on some occasions, death is preferable to a life not worth living, teleology would have to account for the goodness not only of the union, but also of the separation of soul and body. To be guided by the good teleology requires mind, and mind requires soul; but soul, with its apparently incompatible ends, seems to make teleology impossible.

Socrates reveals the attraction of teleology, despite these difficulties, with his admission that, if he could be shown what is best, he would no longer yearn for any other kind of cause.[17] But he silently points to the danger of such satisfaction. To possess knowledge of the good would put an end to all inquiry: the impossibility of teleology is, paradoxically, the hidden good that renders philosophy necessary and possible. The implicit irony with which Socrates first expressed his great hope in discovering the teaching of Anaxagoras is repeated, therefore, in his description of being let down by it. If mechanical explanation is open to the danger of self-contradiction, teleological explanation is open to the inevitable disappointment that results from a reliance on inappropriate standards: each alone and both together threaten to produce that experience of misology that Socrates considers the greatest evil. Their common ground is indicated by the failure of the Anaxagorean promise, which consists in its regression to mechanical cause. For Anaxagoras in fact made no use of mind, Socrates complains, to explain the ordering of things but assigned as causes air and ether and water and many other absurdities; despite his assurance of an intentional design of the whole, Anaxagoras could present only the means, without revealing their status as mere means.[18]

Socrates alluded, in the first argument, to the Anaxagorean cosmology, according to which the appearance of mind is preceded by an original condition of chaos. He introduced that argument with a reference to the Aristophanic portrayal that made him appear indistinguishable from Anaxagoras. But Socrates distinguished himself by admitting how much the present discussion would be motivated by self-interest: he implicitly criticized Anaxagoras for constructing a cosmological theory of mind without reflecting on his own human perspective in doing so. Socrates now confirms that attack when he turns, for the first and last time, to the silent context of the entire conversation. He likens Anaxagoras' teleological cosmology to an explanation of his own present situation, sitting in the Athenian prison and talking with his companions.

It is as if someone—not Socrates himself—were to claim that Socrates does all that he does "by mind." But what Socrates, in contrast to Anaxagoras, must have understood, is that mind requires soul; and since soul is no less the locus of desire, fear, anger, and all the other passions, it would seem impossible for any human being to do all that he does "by mind." Anaxagoras' teaching, in any case, would be equivalent to someone claiming that Socrates acts by mind but then proceeding to argue that the cause of his sitting in prison is the operation of his bones and sinews—of which Socrates gives a surprisingly detailed description[19]—or to argue that the cause of his conversing is the operation of voice and air and hearing. Having indicated the problematic assumptions of teleology, which treats natural phenomena on the model of human action, Socrates criticizes its reversion to mechanism, which treats human action on the model of natural phenomena. Such an account, Socrates charges, necessarily neglects what are truly the causes of his situation, namely, that the Athenians believed it better to condemn him, hence he believed it better to sit there, more just to remain and undergo whatever penalty they commanded.

Socrates assigns equal responsibility to the Athenians, who thought him guilty of injustice and impiety, and to himself, whom he called a divine gift to the city and its greatest benefactor;[20] he is willing, in this case, it seems, to accept opposite causes of the same effect. Nor does either of these causes express the operation of mind based on knowledge of the good, for each is simply an opinion of what is better; such opinions were apparently of no interest to Anaxagoras, but they are decisive for Socrates. At the same time, however, that Socrates juxtaposes his own opinion with that of the Athenian *dēmos*, he indicates the difference between them. His own opinion of what is better is based on a consideration of what is more just and would otherwise have been in conflict with the city: his bones and sinews might have been in Megara or Boeotia long ago, carried away by an opinion of what is best, had he not believed it to be more just and more beautiful to undergo the penalty ordered by the city instead of, or at least before fleeing and running away.[21]

Socrates brings to light the inseparability of mechanism and teleology, and with that of body and soul; for his opinion of the best, which should represent the intention of soul in contrast to the mechanical operation of the body, would have been carried out not only through the bones and sinews but in their service. What he believes to be good, Socrates makes clear enough, is life and its preservation; he was motivated to face his death sentence only because of reflection on the just and the beautiful, which are not only distinct from what is simply good but apparently incompatible with it. The just and the beautiful are examples of the *eidē*, which Socrates is about to introduce as *the* cause "in *logos*"; but since they do not in themselves lead to any action, only the particular intention based upon them can be designated truly a cause "in being" (*tō onti*), which must be distinguished—despite its inseparability—from that without which it would not be a cause. To fail to do so, Socrates charges, is to be groping in the dark,[22] to be as blind as those who mistake the *pragmata* for the beings themselves (cf. 99d–e).

To illustrate this danger, Socrates returns to his critique of cosmology. One theory after another offers a mechanical account of the position of the earth,[23] without searching for the power that causes things to be placed as is best. No such theory satisfies the principle of sufficient reason,[24] for none explains why the cosmos *must* be ordered as it is, since they all ignore the good and binding that truly binds and holds all together.[25] Anaxagoras identified mind as the cause of separation; but if it is to operate in the service of the good, Socrates now stresses, it must be just as much a cause of combination. It must unite, Socrates reminds us, the good with the necessary; but he thus confirms the problematic status of teleology, even while using it as a standard to criticize the insufficiency of mechanistic physics. Socrates could explain his own deed of remaining in prison by articulating the combination of mechanical cause and an opinion of what is better; to account for why the earth remains in place in the center of the heavens, however, requires an analysis of mechanical cause in conjunction with the intention of mind based on knowledge of the good. Socrates would gladly have become the pupil of anyone who possessed knowledge of such a cause, he tells Cebes, but he could neither find a teacher nor discover such knowledge himself.

[99c9–100a3] Having shown that teleological cause, even if it seems desirable, is not available, Socrates asks Cebes if he wishes to hear a demonstration of "the second sailing in search of the cause" with which he has busied himself.[26] Since this would seem to represent a third mode of inquiry, only the common ground of mechanism and teleology as "investigation of the beings" can explain why Socrates' replacement of that enterprise constitutes what is presumably a second-best alternative. But

Socrates' second sailing would be a compromising alternative only if the first way were both desirable and possible, and that is precisely what he proceeds to deny in his subsequent consideration of the danger inherent in all investigation of the beings.[27]

Socrates likens this danger to the misfortune that befalls those who attempt to look directly at the sun during an eclipse: they risk the destruction of their eyes, which they might have avoided by investigating the sun through an image in water or something of that sort. The image of blinding one's eyes instills fear in Socrates by leading him to conceive of the danger of blinding his soul. Visual blindness thus serves as an image for noetic blindness, but the image for "noetic vision" cannot be aesthetic vision, since the latter, or at least a certain attitude toward it, is in fact the cause of noetic blindness: the danger of blinding one's soul arises precisely from looking at things (*pragmata*) with one's eyes and trying to grasp them with one's senses. Those who will be visually blinded because of their unwillingness to look at a reflection in water, mistake the concealed sun for the sun itself; those who will be psychically blinded by their unwillingness to rely on reflections, in accordance with the analogy, mistake the *pragmata* grasped through the senses for the beings themselves.[28] If these *pragmata* were simply perceptible objects as such, the senses would be the source of the eclipse, and the body the only obstacle to direct contact of the soul with the beings. But that is precisely the belief against which Socrates' image is meant to be a warning. It is the belief that Socrates ascribed to the genuine philosophers (cf. 66e). But Socrates' indications of his own distance from them suggests a very different understanding of the cause of the eclipse: it is not the body, but the needs and desires, and hopes and fears of the soul—our attachment to "the visible" for example (cf. 83c–d)—that lead us to mistake the *pragmata* for the beings themselves.[29]

Striving for direct contact of the soul with the beings is not, then, the means of escape from, but rather the cause of, this deceptive condition, as Socrates confirms by explaining his own way of overcoming it: just as it is necessary to observe the sun through a reflection in order to avoid blinding one's eyes, it is necessary, in order to avoid blinding one's soul, to "take refuge in *logoi*" and to investigate through them "the truth of the beings." This second sailing on the vessel of *logoi* might appear to be a compromising alternative to direct observation of the beings themselves. But the necessity of observing the eclipsed sun through its image in water is itself a visual image for the necessity of turning from vision to *logos*; it is an image, therefore, whose very content demands that, in leading beyond itself, it deny itself.[30] Socrates attempts to correct its possibly misleading implication by insisting that investigation through *logoi* is no more a compromising reliance on mere images than investigation "in deeds" (*en tois ergois*) would be:[31] his own deed of remaining in prison, which Socrates chose in order to illustrate the problematic character of teleological cosmology, was no less an image than the *logoi* about the just and the beautiful that provided its motivating grounds.

Socrates does not, therefore, present his turn to investigation through *logoi* as a complete replacement for investigation in deeds but suggests, rather, their complementary relation. The model for the turn to *logos* that does not ignore the necessary connection of *logoi* and *erga* as equally images of the beings is the Platonic dialogue: Socrates' deed of remaining in prison provides in the *Phaedo* the proper context for the speeches on immortality. What it would have meant to investigate deeds alone is illustrated by Echecrates' opening remark—the Phliasians know only that Socrates drank the poison and died. To look directly at things, without turning to speeches, would be to look directly at the corpse of Socrates and expect to understand everything at stake in this last conversation. But if, on the other hand, investigation of *logoi* were sufficient in itself, the *Phaedo* would have consisted in a treatise outlining several possible arguments for the immortality of the soul, without illuminating their context, the effects they produce, and the interests from which they arise, nor, consequently, the clues for determining the intention behind any unsoundness in the arguments. Yet, what is dramatized in the *Phaedo*, of course, is only the representation of deeds in speech: the dialogue points to the limitations of *logoi*, without violating that turn to *logos* that Socrates presents as the only way to escape the danger of blinding one's soul.

To pursue the Socratic second sailing is to replace investigation of the beings themselves with investigation of their truth. Like the light, in Socrates' image, that serves as a bond between the eye and the visible object, the truth must be the bond between the mind and the noetic object. Just as the light makes possible the visibility of the phenomena, as well as the capacity of the eye to see, truth makes possible the knowability of the beings, as well as the capacity of the mind to know:[32] investigation of the truth of the beings is investigation of what makes knowledge possible. To neglect the latter because of having blinded one's soul is to suffer the same danger as that of misology, through which one deprives oneself of the possibility of discovering the truth of the beings (cf. 90d). But what it means exactly to investigate the truth of the beings through *logoi*, and thus gain protection against the psychic blindness of misology, Socrates has yet to clarify.

[100a3–100e4] He begins in each case, he explains, by laying down (*hupothemenos*) the *logos* he judges the strongest. Then whatever seems to him to harmonize (*sumphōnein*) with that, he posits as being true—concerning both cause as well as everything else that is—and whatever does not harmonize, he posits as not true.[33] Socrates first asked Cebes if he wished to hear about his "second sailing in search of the cause." But he seems to have demoted the importance of that particular object when he now claims to pursue this mode of investigation in regard to "all the beings." The procedure he describes indicates, nevertheless, what it means to give up the attempt to gain knowledge of the beings themselves; for it seems to define truth as nothing but consistency of *logoi*, without suggesting any possibility of overcoming the positivity of the premise in accordance with which such consistency is determined. Socrates' description of hypothesizing the *logos* judged to be the strongest, which presents no criteria for that judgment, echoes Simmias' reflection on the necessity of accepting the most irrefutable human *logos*, given both the impossibility of discovering the truth and the unavailability of a divine *logos* (85c–d). But in contrast with Simmias, Socrates does not deny the possibility of determining the truth, although he does stress the status of his hypothetical starting point when he claims to posit as true whatever is consistent with it.

Socrates quite reasonably expects Cebes not to understand fully; yet he insists that what he says is nothing new, but only what he is never ceasing to say, both elsewhere and throughout the preceding conversation. He attempts to thematize what has already been in practice apparently by showing Cebes the kind of cause with which he has been occupied: this *eidos* of the cause is the *eidos* as cause—not, however, of the coming into being and perishing of something, but of its being *what* it is. To treat the *eidos*, or "the what it is" (cf. 75d, 78d), as the cause of the determinacy of something else would seem to demand that we inquire what it itself is, and that in turn to presuppose that it is "itself by itself" something. Socrates first asked Simmias if he believed that death is something before offering a definition of it (64c); and he first asked Simmias if he thought "the equal itself" was something before asking if he knew what it is (74a–b). The being of the *eidos*, Socrates now clarifies, is not given in some "noetic vision" but must be laid down in a hypothesis as the necessary condition for inquiry. If the *eidē*, then, are "the truth of the beings" that must be sought through a second sailing, the hypothetical method of reasoning and the particular hypothesis of the causality of the *eidē* are not so arbitrarily connected as Socrates' presentation has led some readers of the dialogue to think.[34]

To illustrate the hypothesized causality of the *eidos*, Socrates informs Cebes, he must go back to those "much-babbled about things" (cf. 65b, 76d, 78c) and, in returning, set out from them: "the much-babbled about things" are what language renders always already familiar, and Socrates has appealed to them throughout the conversation, but without yet presenting his interpretation of their status. He begins to do so by laying down the hypothesis that the beautiful itself by itself is something, and the good and the great and all the others. Socrates speaks as if each itself by itself were entirely independent; yet his list of examples raises the question of their relation to each other.[35] Included in this list, moreover, is the good, although Socrates has just admitted that it was lack of knowledge of the good that compelled him to abandon the Anaxagorean project in favor of the procedure he is now describing.[36] Socrates introduced this *technē* of *logoi* in an attempt to turn attention away from all self-interest, particularly the urgent self-interest aroused by the present situation, which was determined, Socrates acknowledged, by his "opinion of what is better." The good, it would seem, cannot be divorced from self-interest; and if it cannot, for that reason, be treated hypothetically, it would be incapable of being assimilated to the Socratic *technē* of *logoi*.

But Socrates does not explore these questions. He is eager to gain Cebes' agreement to the hypothesis that each itself by itself is something; for he can then attempt, Socrates promises, to demonstrate the cause and to discover how the soul is immortal. While we would expect, instead, a demonstration of the immortality of the soul and a discovery of the cause, Socrates' interlacing of words suggests that the final argument for immortality will be in the service of his demonstration of the *eidos* as cause, rather than the other way around.[37] Cebes, in any case, quickly offers his assent— and Socrates just as quickly accepts it—to the hypothesis that the beautiful itself is something; it furnishes the required basis for the further claim that, if anything else is beautiful other than the beautiful itself, it is only because it participates (*metechei*) in that beautiful. Cebes again immediately agrees, without raising the question of the difference between the being of the itself by itself and its being the cause of something other having the quality that it is.[38] In fact, however, Socrates seems now to have identified the cause of such an attribution not with the *eidos*, but with the relation of "participation." Of course, he is unwilling to make any confident claim about how it works, whether by presence (*parousia*) or communion (*koinōnia*) or whatever else one wishes to call it—just as, in public prayers, one addresses the gods, because of ignorance of their correct names, by whatever name is pleasing to them.[39]

If someone tries to fill in this formula for an unknown "how"[40]—to suggest that something comes to be beautiful because of a lovely color or shape or anything of that sort—Socrates claims to be confused, compelled to bid farewell to all these other wise causes.[41] He insists only on the explanation that "all the beautiful come to be beautiful through the beautiful." This is the safest answer Socrates can give to himself and to others, but not absolutely safe, since, as a claim about *genesis*, it betrays its ignorance of cause in the ordinary sense. It implicitly raises the question as to whether anything can come to be beautiful simply or whether, rather, it only comes to be more beautiful than it was previously, or more beautiful than something else with which it is compared. Socrates confirms the limitation of his first claim with an apparently superfluous repetition: the claim that "through the beautiful the beautiful (are) beautiful"—because it is restricted to the question of something *being* what it is—provides an answer that is safe, Socrates promises, not only for him but for anyone else to give. The safe raft on which to sail through the dangers of life that Simmias sought in some divine *logos* (85d) Socrates has now replaced with a safe raft on which to sail through the dangers of *logos*. But the price he pays for this safety is restriction to a "simple and artless and perhaps foolish" answer that is indeed pre-Promethean, an *eidos* of cause that abandons any falsifiable claim to knowledge of how something comes to be or ceases to be what it is.

[100e5–101d1] Socrates seeks Cebes' acceptance of this safe answer before extending it, for, in doing so, he points to certain perplexities concealed by his original model. Through greatness, Socrates inquires, are the great great and the greater greater, and through smallness the smaller smaller? Socrates does not mention "the small" but only "the smaller"; he calls our attention to the fact that "greatness" is the name not only for one member but for the pair of opposites. That something said to be small is actually only smaller than something else, however, makes one wonder how anything could be said to be great without further qualification. The latter ascription seems, rather, to be a misleadingly abbreviated way of expressing the relation of one thing being greater than another. When, in fact, Socrates just described his perplexities about greatness, he spoke of one man or one horse being greater than another; his reference to members of two species suggests that, even if something were said to be great, it would be relative to the kind of thing it is. Socrates does not go back to ask, although perhaps he should have, whether any of the so-called beautiful things is only more beautiful by the relative absence of ugliness, either in comparison with other members of the same kind or as a superlative instance of one kind, which would have to be compared to other kinds.[42] To be beautiful, then, would always be a matter of being more or less so.

Socrates' example of greatness and smallness recalls, in any case, the difficulties he eventually came to recognize in his prephilosophic opinions about cause—how a man grows larger, "by what" one man or one horse is greater than another, or ten greater than eight, or a two-cubit length greater than a length of one cubit (96c–e). He is preparing to instill in Cebes the very perplexities he himself experienced when he found himself blinded by the investigation of nature and recognized that he could no longer claim to possess knowledge of how something becomes greater, or how anything comes to be at all. Socrates must replace the fear of death, which led Cebes to seek a demonstration of the imperishability of the soul, by the fear of self-contradiction, which must compel Cebes as it does Socrates to maintain the safety of *logos* at all costs.

Cebes would not accept the claim, Socrates advises, that one man was greater or smaller than another "by a head" but would insist that one thing can be greater than another only by greatness and because of the great, one thing smaller than another only by smallness and because of the small. Socrates emphasizes that Cebes would *speak* in this way—he may apparently *think* otherwise—for if he were to speak of one man as greater or smaller than another by a head, Socrates warns, he would fear the attack of an opposing *logos*, charging, first, that the greater would be greater and the smaller smaller by the same thing, and further, that the greater would be greater by a head, which is small, and that would be monstrous! Cebes quite understandably laughs at Socrates' warning: the laughter that has all along accompanied the fear of death is being transformed, along with that fear, into the laughter appropriate to the fear of self-contradiction. What Cebes is to fear is an attack against the claim that one cause could produce opposite results, or that one result could be produced by a cause opposite to it. This is precisely the structure Socrates outlined for Simmias in describing that exchange of greater and lesser through which courage and moderation come into being from their opposites (68d–69a).[43] From that irrational "shadow-painting," Socrates assured Simmias, the true character of virtue together with *phronēsis* is a "purification." He must now spell out for Cebes what is required for another "purification," this time from the threat of any apparent contradiction in causal analysis, which could be exploited by the disputatious to arouse distrust in *logos* (cf. 90c, 101e).

Socrates proceeds to warn Cebes of the danger in claiming that ten is greater than eight by two and because of this, or that a two-cubit length is greater than a one-cubit length by half; he must seek safety, rather, in the claim that ten is greater than eight by number and because of number, a two-cubit length greater than a one-cubit length by magnitude.[44] But the fear motivating these answers is only "somehow" the same as in the previous case, Socrates admits; for Cebes would now have to claim, in following Socrates' advice, that ten is greater than eight and eight smaller than ten by the same thing, number, or a two-cubit length greater and a one-cubit length smaller by the same thing, magnitude. Since, indeed, Socrates has just established that everything greater must be so only because of the great, everything smaller only because of the small, number should be the cause, presumably, only of something being countable, magnitude only of something being measurable.

Socrates does not stop to explore these difficulties concerning number or magnitude and the relations of being greater or smaller. He approaches, rather, the final perplexity that led him to recognize the deficiency of the whole series of his prephilosophic claims to knowledge of cause. If one is added to one, or if one is divided in half, he warns Cebes, you would not say that addition or division is the cause of two coming to be; but "in a great voice"—not apparently in thinking—you would say you know of no other way each comes to be than by "participating in the proper being (*ousia*) of each in which it participates." Cebes must accept no cause of the coming to be of two other than participation in the dyad, while whatever is to be one must participate in the monad. Cebes does not ask whether whatever is to be two participates at the same time in number, or whether, in being greater than one, it also participates in the great. Socrates supposedly wants Cebes to stick with the safe answer he has proposed when he commands him to bid farewell to additions and divisions and all such refinements, leaving these for wiser men to deal with; but whether the safe answer is truly free from these refined perplexities has been put into question by the very examples Socrates furnished to illustrate it.

131

Whatever perplexities Socrates may have concealed from Cebes, however, he has reasons for doing so. For Cebes must learn, Socrates warns, "to distrust his own shadow and inexperience." It is the inexperience that, without a *technē* of *logoi*, would lead to the danger of misology, for the disputatious who would attack his self-contradictory claims are voices that Socrates compels him to internalize. Cebes must undergo a risky development, becoming, on the one hand, similar enough to the disputatious to take seriously a purely verbal contradiction, while remaining, on the other hand, unlike the disputatious, whose discovery of contradiction leads them to abandon all confidence in *logos* as a means for pursuit of the truth. Socrates can use their attack against any claim to knowledge of cause in the ordinary sense in order to overcome their simultaneous attack against *logos* itself only because of his discovery of the safe raft that consists in a *technē* of *logoi*. Of course, the art of reasoning Socrates has described, and the final argument in which it will be applied, thus seem to be as dependent on the disputatious as the series of arguments in the first half of the dialogue was on the genuine philosophers. Socrates has satisfied Cebes, in any case, with his proposed solution to the problem of the cause of two and one; he has presumably completed a model invulnerable to any disputatious attack exploiting the perplexities that compelled him to abandon his original claims to knowledge of cause. He is prepared on that basis to return to his account of the procedure of hypothetical reasoning; that general account seems to have been merely interrupted, although it will in fact be significantly affected, by the consideration of its application to the Socratic *eidos* of cause.

[101d1–102a1] With the fear of the disputatious instilled in him, Cebes must hold fast, Socrates warns, to that "safety of the hypothesis" that precludes the possibility of self-contradiction. And if someone were to attack the hypothesis itself, Socrates continues, you would bid farewell to him and would not respond until you had investigated the consequences of the hypothesis, whether they harmonize (*sumphōnei*) with each other or are in discord (*diaphōnei*).[45] Socrates' account might appear to agree thus far with the initial statement that he feared was not yet clear enough for Cebes to understand (100a). But Socrates has now transformed a description of his own practice into a recommendation for Cebes' practice; and he no longer speaks of laying down as true whatever harmonizes with an accepted hypothesis, but rather, of determining the harmony or discord with one another of the consequences that follow from it. In his initial account, Socrates identified truth with consistency, since his primary concern was to confirm the impossibility of trying to grasp the *pragmata* through one's senses, and to replace it with the safety of investigating the truth of the beings in *logoi*. But the safety of consistency with a given starting point did not necessarily extend, in Socrates' first account, to the starting point itself, which was simply whatever *logos* he judged to be strongest. That starting point is now specified, in Socrates' present elaboration, to be a hypothesis safe in itself from all possible contradiction.[46] Yet Socrates only now seems to admit the possibility that consequences that contradict each other might be entailed by the one hypothesis with which they are severally in accord.[47] He has, after all, just offered the example of number as a safe answer to the question of the cause of ten being greater than eight as well as of eight being smaller than ten. He can no longer claim, therefore, to identify as true whatever follows from the hypothesis, and in fact ceases to speak of truth at all.

Socrates confirms this adjustment by the further step he now adds: when it becomes necessary to give a *logos* of the initial hypothesis itself—Cebes is not told when that would be—he must give it in the same way, laying down another hypothesis that would appear best among the higher ones. According to the original account Socrates presented, the hypothesis laid down as strongest could not itself be rejected, for whatever comes to light as inconsistent with it is simply identified as not true. But Socrates now acknowledges the necessity of defending that hypothesis "in the same way": once the consequences of the initial hypothesis have been shown to harmonize with it and with each other, the initial hypothesis must be defended by showing that it harmonizes with a hypothesis from which it can be derived, as well as with other consequences derivable from the same hypothesis. Since the call for justification of the initial hypothesis follows upon the examination of the harmony of its consequences, that very examination must be capable of bringing to light the presuppositions of that hypothesis not yet recognized or thematized in the initial agreement on it. The "higher hypotheses," then, to which appeal is made for justification, must be those implicit presuppositions of the initial hypothesis;[48] and the "best" among them would seem to refer to that which would entail the most comprehensive set of consistent consequences, including the initial hypothesis itself.[49] The ascending movement to a higher hypothesis is thus an archeological movement uncovering the deeper levels of assumption concealed in the initial hypothesis: every step forward would actually be a step backward in recognizing an apparently self-evident starting point to be in fact derivative.

133

This process must be carried on, Socrates concludes, until reaching "something sufficient," a starting point that is alone self-justifying, presumably, because it conceals no more implicit presuppositions from which it could be derived. Socrates' description of this procedure as a dialogic activity, however, suggests that "something sufficient" is nothing but that higher hypothesis that would defend the initial hypothesis against a particular questioner and thus silence any further attack. Simmias was persuaded of the preexistence of the soul because he was so certain of the existence of the beings themselves that no further examination seemed to him necessary (77a, 92d–e). Cebes is about to be persuaded by Socrates' final argument on immortality because of consequences drawn from the hypothesis, with which he is completely satisfied, that things are what they are by virtue of participating in the proper *ousia* of the various qualities ascribed to them. He demanded no further examination, therefore, when Socrates insisted that he could not yet consider whether this participation was to be construed as *parousia* or *koinōnia* or in some other way. It is an anonymous interlocutor who will bring just that problem to light by "attacking the hypothesis," questioning the relation between the *eidē* and the things said to participate in them (103b). And Socrates, in accordance with his own recommendation, will delay an adequate response—until it is too late!—before establishing the immortality of the soul as a consistent consequence of his hypothesis.

The point of sufficiency Socrates reaches in his conversation with Cebes and Simmias thus seems to be only a provisional stopping point: while Cebes' satisfaction with the final argument brings the discussion to an end, Socrates confirms the truth behind Simmias' dissatisfaction by insisting that they would have to examine more clearly their first hypotheses (107b). Socrates would have to show, in accordance with the procedure he has outlined, how the causality of the *eidē* could be derived from a higher hypothesis: he would have to confront the problem of participation to which the objection of the anonymous interlocutor points. Were Socrates directing the conversation toward this anonymous interlocutor, he would be challenged, then, by a different determination of "something sufficient"; and in that case, as the dramatic action of the dialogue suggests, he might not have succeeded in accomplishing a demonstration of the immortality of the soul. Not the *Phaedo* alone, but every Platonic dialogue, points to this tension between the meaning of "something sufficient," on the one hand as a provisional stopping point determined by the subjective satisfaction of particular conversants and the contingencies of the occasion, and, on the other, as that asymptotic standard of presuppositionlessness toward which all examination of hypotheses by way of higher hypotheses ought to proceed.[50] The formula for the impossible reconcilation of this tension is "the good": no further inquiry would be needed, Socrates admitted before introducing his second sailing, if only he possessed knowledge of the good.

Socrates concludes his address to Cebes with the advice that he must not mix up the starting point and its consequences as the disputatious do. Socrates might seem to allude to his own "mixed-up" way (97b), according to which examination of the consistency of consequences derived from a given hypothesis leads to the discovery of a presupposition from which that hypothesis is itself a consequence. But the disputatious—those, apparently, whom Cebes was warned to dismiss when they attack the hypothesis itself before considering its consequences—do not recognize the difference between the way from, and the way to, first principles.[51] Instead of aiming at a truly sufficient starting point, they believe their own wisdom so sufficient, Socrates charges, that they are content even when mixing everything together (*homou panta*): they are satisfied with the epistemological equivalent of Anaxagorean chaos, the state of the cosmos before the appearance of mind, in which the one *genesis* of combination is not balanced by the opposite *genesis* of separation (cf. 72c). Refusing to abandon confidence in their own wisdom, the disputatious cast blame on the weakness of *logos* itself; their assumption that *logoi* have no more stability than the *pragmata* is precisely the belief that, Socrates warned, is the source of misology, the greatest evil (cf. 90c).

Cebes must proceed in the way Socrates has described if he wishes "to discover something of the beings." Such a wish would hold no attraction for the disputatious, who are content with their undefended claim to its impossibility. Yet, once again, it is Socrates himself who seems to hide behind the mask of the disputatious.[52] For he admitted that, confronted with the verbal contradiction lurking behind all claims to knowledge of cause, he was forced to abandon the desire to discover the beings themselves; he did so, however, precisely because of recognizing the necessity and possibility of investigating "the truth of the beings" by means of the *technē* of *logoi* he has just elaborated. Cebes will do as he says, Socrates concludes, if he is "one of the philosophers." Socrates intends, perhaps, to test Cebes' awareness of the difference that should by now be evident: Does he belong to the class of the "genuine philosophers" who desire knowledge of the beings, or is he one who recognizes the need to abandon that impossible pursuit in favor of a second sailing?

[102a2–102b2] Cebes provides no explicit evidence of whether he has passed this test. Moved, apparently, simply by the appeal to their status as philosophers, Cebes, in union with Simmias, assures Socrates, "You speak most truly." Yet their enthusiasm is suspicious: they have never even asked if the hypothesis of the causality of the *eidē* is only one illustration among others of the general procedure of hypothetical reasoning, and, if not, what the necessary connection between them is. Their sudden affirmation of clarity calls to mind the sudden disillusionment they expressed in common at the conclusion of the first series of arguments. Indeed, just as Echecrates interrupted then to announce his sympathy with Phaedo's description of the confusion and mistrust generated by the objections of Simmias and Cebes (88c–e), he now interrupts to confirm the satisfaction of "we who were absent" and are simply listening to Phaedo's report. The boundaries marked by this intrusion thus constitute a frame around the core of the dialogue, which moves from the threat of misology to the security of Socrates' *technē* of *logoi*.

Imitating the enthusiasm of Simmias and Cebes, Echecrates praises Socrates for having made these matters wonderfully clear, even to a man with little sense (*smikron noun*)! Echecrates' mere figure of speech confirms the independence of the Socratic *technē* of *logoi* from any account— teleological or otherwise—of soul as mind. But since Echecrates shows no awareness of the significance of his figure of speech, he makes us wonder whether Plato intends his reader to share in this feeling of clarity. Socrates does seem to have succeeded in turning attention to the *logos* itself: whereas Echecrates first requested to hear both what Socrates said and what *pathē* he suffered (88e), he now requests simply to hear what was said next. But whether Socrates has been equally successful in explaining the *technē* of *logoi* illustrated by the hypothesis of the causality of the *eidē* is put into question by Phaedo's response to Echecrates. After imitating in detail the speeches of a daylong conversation and narrating the matter between them,[53] he suddenly turns to indirect discourse and merely summarizes the discussion providing the grounds for the application of Socrates' methodological reflections to the final argument on immortality.

Socrates went on, Phaedo thinks, after these matters had been granted "and it was agreed that each of the *eidē* is something, and the others, participating in them, take their names from these very things." What should presumably constitute the philosophic peak of the dialogue, Phaedo presents as a mere conclusion with no argument in defense, introduced by the qualification, "I believe." His only prior moment of hesitancy was in expressing his belief that Plato was sick on the day of Socrates' death, and the only subsequent one his admission that he cannot remember the name of the interlocutor who raises the question of the relation between the *eidē* and the *pragmata*—the very problem he now passes over so quickly in a single summary statement. Phaedo's insufficient report of the discussion on participation, which might have pointed to the higher hypotheses justifying the first hypotheses of the conversation, seems to cast doubt on his trustworthiness as narrator; yet precisely that deficiency allows him to proceed with his report of the final argument on immortality. Exemplifying, however unwittingly, the inevitable "impurity" of the procedure of hypothetical reasoning,[54] Phaedo shows himself to be a most appropriate Iolaus to Socrates' Heracles in the battle for the salvation of the *logos*.

137

Chapter Eleven: Immortality

[102b3–103a3] Having summarized the agreement on the being of the *eidē* and their relation to the *pragmata*, Phaedo resumes direct discourse to report the argument based on that agreement, through which Socrates has promised to discover the immortality of the soul. Particular things, Socrates begins, receive their names from the *eidē* in which they participate. He is talking about attributes of a subject—Simmias greater and smaller—but his reference to "names" might call to mind the identity of an individual: a proper name operates like the Athenian *logos* that each year declares the sacred ship, worn away bit by bit, to be the very "ship of Theseus" that once made its legendary journey to Crete (58a). Socrates points to the rhetorical power of the proper name when, just before drinking the poison, he tries to comfort Crito by commanding him not to say, as he buries the corpse, that he is burying "Socrates," for to speak in that way produces terrible effects (115e). By means of this restriction, Socrates hopes to convince Crito of the identification of the self with a soul that is unaffected by death and burial; the proper name betrays the *pathē* that motivate our particular interest in positing the identity of the self that remains the same through all change. But while Socrates now chooses Simmias as an example of a *pragma*, he does not ask in which *eidos* he must participate in order to receive the name Simmias. Socrates suggests, by this silence, that what the proper name in fact illustrates is the mistake in construing any *pragma* as a neutral substratum that remains the same despite the plurality of *eidē* in which it participates. Rather, each *pragma* is an inseparable unity of a subject and a quality ascribed to it, and when the opposite quality is ascribed to that subject, that inseparable unity constitutes the opposite *pragma*.[1]

Socrates therefore chooses an example in which Simmias is nothing but the accidental center of two opposite relations. In calling Simmias greater than Socrates but smaller than Phaedo, Socrates asks Cebes, would he be saying that there is in Simmias greatness and smallness? Socrates emphasizes the speech through which this predication is made. For the greatness or smallness in Simmias is the product of our act of comparing him with another. While, therefore, the two relations in which he stands might seem to exist at the same time, that may be an illusion that results from forgetting the two acts of comparison, which cannot, perhaps, be performed simultaneously. Only an observer who suppresses his own acts, when he looks at Simmias standing in the middle of Socrates and Phaedo, can grant Simmias "the eponym, to be great and small."[2] The independent status of the two opposites in which Simmias participates disappears in the name referring to one continuum of more and less, along which Simmias occupies a particular position.[3]

Even to speak with the proper qualification, however, and to say that Simmias is greater than Socrates and smaller than Phaedo, is not true "in these words," Socrates explains. For it implies that Simmias is greater or smaller because of being Simmias, or because of Socrates who is smaller being Socrates, or Phaedo who is greater being Phaedo. But none of them is great or small apart from the relations between them, or rather, as Socrates now insists, between the opposite qualities themselves. Expressed correctly, therefore, it is only the greatness in Simmias that exceeds the smallness in another, while the smallness in him is exceeded by the greatness in another. Of course, the greatness in Simmias that exceeds the smallness in another is simply his height, the very same height that constitutes the smallness in Simmias exceeded by the greatness in another. Just as Cebes laughed at Socrates' warning of a potential disputatious attack (101b), Socrates now laughs at the precision of a speech that sounds like a written legal contract, which is designed, presumably, to provide protection against the same threat of verbal contradiction.

Socrates hopes, consequently, to make it appear to Cebes as it does to him, that not only would the great itself never wish to be great and at the same time small, but also greatness in us would never admit the small nor wish to be exceeded. While Simmias can become smaller, having been greater, greatness in him, since it is unwilling to admit its opposite, must, when the small approaches, either flee and withdraw or have already been destroyed.[4] Now, the alternative of flight or destruction is not applicable to the great itself, since it is presumably not present in the first place in the *pragma* characterized as greater; and it is not clear how, when *we* become smaller, greatness *in us* could withdraw rather than be destroyed. But this alternative, which will turn out to be crucial for the argument,

Socrates is not yet prepared to explore. He must establish only that great-ness in us does not wish to abide and admit smallness, thus becoming other than what it was, nor does the small that is in us wish to become or be great, but rather, like any opposite, it must either depart or be destroyed in the change. Greatness or smallness in us, according to Socrates' for-mulation, only "wishes" to remain what it was: it might be compelled, against its inclination, to admit its opposite, which would constitute its own destruction. The "wishing" of greatness or smallness not to coexist with its opposite—not to violate, that is, the law of noncontradiction—looks like the "wishing" of pleasure or pain not to become present in a man at the same time as the other (60b). But such a personification, Socrates suggested in his opening remarks, is the unrecognized projection onto apparent opposites of the human will to separate them.

Socrates might appear, in any case, to contrast the mutually exclusive opposite qualities with the subject that can persist through the change from one opposite to the other while remaining what it is: "I (*egō*), having admitted and abided smallness, and still being what I am, am this same one, small." But his formulation does not in fact affirm the identity through this change of a neutral subject; it suggests, rather, that "Socrates great" is one *pragma* and "Socrates small" its opposite.[5] How, then, can the immanent qualities, greatness and smallness in something, that de-termine the opposite *pragmata* generated from each other, at the same time preserve the safety of *logos*, which requires that no opposite "dare" to be or become its opposite? Socrates describes this battle of opposites in us metaphorically, by borrowing the military language of advance and attack, flight and withdrawal, destruction or abiding.[6] But his obscurity about the status of that mediating level on which *genesis* is actualized only confirms his own silence in specifying the nature of "participation" (100d); it suffers from the same incompleteness as Phaedo's report on the discussion concerning the relation between the *eidē* and the *pragmata* said to participate in them.

[103a4–103c9] The claim that no opposite that is still what it was can ever become or be its opposite brings the discussion full circle round to the first argument, although Cebes, to whom the two arguments have been addressed, seems unaware of it. But someone whose name Phaedo does not remember expresses surprise—he swears by the gods—at Socrates' apparent denial of their original premise, according to which the greater comes to be from the smaller and the smaller from the greater, exemplifying the necessary *genesis* of all opposites from each other (70e). The anonymous interlocutor, who seems to be the only one following the conversation with sufficient attention,[7] enacts a Socratic second sailing: he brings to light the fact that the two arguments concerned with the relation between opposites are themselves the manifestation in *logos* of the relation between opposites.

Listening most attentively to this objection, Socrates, Phaedo reports, threw his head to one side, looking away perhaps from the speaker. Socrates commends the speaker's manliness while reproaching him for neglecting the difference between the two arguments; that difference is rendered explicit, nevertheless, only as a result of this objection. The first argument, Socrates now contends, was concerned with the coming to be of one *pragma* from its opposite, whereas the present one is concerned with the opposite itself, either in nature or in us, which cannot come to be from its opposite. Whereas the first argument dealt with those things possessing the opposites and named by their names, the last deals with the things themselves according to which the *pragmata* are named. In presenting this response, Socrates addresses his anonymous interlocutor "dear one"; he addressed Cebes in the same way when he completed his argument for the necessity of a cyclical *genesis* between opposites (72c). Socrates claims now to clarify the distinction between opposite *pragmata* and opposites themselves, though without specifying any further consequences of the division within the latter, between those "in us" and those "in nature." Yet the qualities in us through which *genesis* is actualized would seem to belong on an intermediate level between that of opposite *pragmata*, on the one hand, and opposite *eidē*, on the other. Despite Socrates' affectionate address to his anonymous interlocutor, his response seems to repeat once more the insufficiency of Phaedo's summary of the fundamental hypothesis on the participation of the *pragmata* in the *eidē*.

The anonymous interlocutor has put into question the compatibility of the premises of the first and last arguments; an adequate response to his objection would seem to require, therefore, a more thorough examination than Socrates conducts of the relation between the two halves of the dialogue. But such an examination is in tension with the immediate challenge of providing a demonstration of the immortality of the soul. It is a task assigned by Plato to his reader, therefore, not by Socrates to his companions. Socrates is able to avoid it, because he answers the anonymous interlocutor while at the same time looking up at Cebes, who admits he is not disturbed by the objection. Socrates is eager to agree with Cebes on "this simply"—that no opposite will ever *be* its opposite. He transforms the claim, uttered just before he was interrupted, that no opposite will ever be or *become* its opposite; and since the question of becoming is relevant not to opposites in nature, but only in us, Socrates thus avoids having to clarify the status of the latter.

[103c10–104c6] Having established, however dogmatically, their fundamental premise, Socrates asks Cebes to investigate whether he will agree that he calls something hot and cold, qualities which are other than fire and snow. Yet in accordance with what was said previously, it must seem that snow, though other than the cold, will never admit the hot while still being what it was but will, when the hot approaches, either withdraw or be destroyed; and again fire, though other than the hot, will, when the cold approaches, either go away or be destroyed but will never dare admit coldness while still being what it was. Socrates seems to have complicated the argument unnecessarily with these examples. In fact, however, they raise a crucial question for the application of this model to the conclusion of the argument. If fire bringing forward heat is equivalent to soul bringing forward life, what is the equivalent to snow bringing forward cold? The drama of the dialogue indicates the answer: the poison (cf. 63d, 118a). But while death itself might be the opposite of the *eidos* life, Socrates will be silent about the carrier of death, parallel to soul as carrier of life. We will soon have a vivid portrayal in deed of hemlock bringing death through chilling the body; but that makes all the more vivid the mystery of how soul is affected by this corporeal change. Our knowledge of the causality involved in the role of soul as carrier of life must be as limited as our knowledge of how it is affected by the causal operation of the poison.

Socrates' description of snow and fire, characterized essentially by the cold and the hot, seems to be parallel to his previous description of the immanent qualities of greatness and smallness in us. While these latter, however, are themselves opposites that derive their names from the great or the small while coming to be present in some other thing, fire and snow are not themselves opposites, but each seems to be a *pragma* characterized by one opposite quality. On the basis of this extended model, Socrates can conclude that there are some cases in which it is not only the *eidos* of an opposite that is worthy of having the same name for all time, but also something other that always possesses the shape (*morphē*) of that *eidos*, whenever it is. Whereas Simmias would never deserve for all time the name "great" or "small" because he is always greater or smaller in relation to some other, fire or snow always deserves the name "hot" or "cold," since each always—as long as it exists at all—possesses the shape of the *eidos*, hot or cold. Of course, since being hot or cold is a matter of degree, fire would be only hotter than something else, and snow colder, even if it does appear to be contradictory to speak of cold fire or hot snow.

Socrates hopes to make the argument clearer, as he did previously (cf. 96d–97b, 101b–c), by considering the example of numbers: since every number is determined by participation in one of two opposites, the even and the odd, it could never admit the other and still be what it is.[8] When Socrates formulates the principle in terms of names, however, asking whether the odd must somehow always have this name we now utter, Cebes agrees immediately, without considering the fact that, if Socrates referred to whatever is characterized as odd, it might just as well be called "uneven" (cf. 104e). But Socrates clarifies the status of "the odd" as a principle when he asks whether "this among the beings," or also some other that is not itself the odd, must nevertheless always be called "odd" together with its own name, since it is of such a nature that it is never separated from the odd. The triad (*hē trias*), for instance, can always be addressed by its own name as well as that of the odd. The pentad also, and indeed half of all numbers, are by nature such that each, while not the same as the odd, is nevertheless always odd; and again, two and four and the whole other row of numbers, while not the same as the even, is each nevertheless always even.[9] Socrates articulates for Cebes the point he wanted to clarify through the example of numbers: not only do opposites themselves *appear* incapable of admitting each other, but also those things that, while not being opposites always possess opposites, *seem* incapable of admitting the *idea* that is the opposite of that which is in them,[10] so that when this comes, they must either be destroyed or withdraw.

Three (*ta tria*), Socrates offers as an example, will be destroyed or suffer anything else before submitting to becoming even while still being three and odd. Socrates necessarily shifts, although almost imperceptibly, from the triad to three; for, like the monad or dyad in which anything that is to be one or two must participate (101c), the triad, in which anything that is to be three must participate, could not be destroyed, since it would not enter into arithmetical operations at all. Three, by contrast, must be a countable collection that would be destroyed as three if, for example, one were taken away. Yet the subject is presumably not a collection of sensible objects, which could be spoken of as three, but would not themselves be called "odd."[11] The passage must point, then, to the distinction, which

Aristotle reports, between two kinds of number:[12] while the mathematical number, like the eidetic number, could be characterized as essentially even or odd, it could also be said, unlike the eidetic number, to be destroyed when involved in an arithmetical operation that produces the opposite of the *idea* it always possesses. As an intermediate between a collection of objects and the eidetic number, it would allow for the "generation and destruction" of numbers in arithmetical operations, while remaining subordinate to the safe answer, that the cause of any countable collection being what it is, is participation in its proper *ousia* (cf. 101c).

[104c7–105b4] The ambiguity of the conclusion Socrates draws from his consideration of numbers—that not only opposite *eidē* but also "certain others" do not abide the approach of an opposite—justifies his subsequent invitation to define what sort these are. Yet Cebes is quite understandably confused by Socrates' new formulation: the nonopposites that refuse to admit opposites must be those things that always compel whatever they occupy to have not only their own *idea* but also that of some opposite. For the exclusion of an opposite is here assigned to something that is intermediary between an eidetic opposite with which it is inseparably connected and some other thing that it occupies; it has, moreover, its own *idea* that it imposes, together with that of the eidetic opposite, on that which it occupies. To clarify this new formulation, Socrates renders explicit the implied distinction between the triad and three: the triad, it seems, is the *idea* of three, which compels the collection of units it occupies to be three as well as odd.[13]

Just when Socrates seems to have arrived at an adequate clarification, however, he exploits the ambiguity of his original formulation by expanding, while apparently merely repeating, it: such a thing—now, presumably, whatever is occupied—would never admit the *idea* that is the opposite of the shape (*morphē*) responsible for producing its own characterization.[14] A collection of three units occupied by the *idea* of three would never admit the *idea* of the even, for the latter is the opposite of the odd, which is, as Socrates goes on to confirm, the *morphē* that produced its characterization as three and odd.[15] And since three has no part in the *idea* of the even, Socrates concludes, the triad is uneven. Socrates seems to have pursued a rather circuitous route merely to establish that the *idea* of any odd number must be uneven. In doing so, in any case, he casts doubt on his original claim that not only the odd itself, but also some other—the triad, for example—must always have the *name* "odd" whenever it is (104a). He has furthermore implicitly put into question the appropriateness of applying the model of numbers, with its division into two kinds, to the case of soul: Socrates will never speak of an *idea* of soul, in which each particular soul must participate, corresponding to the eidetic number that is itself an *idea*, imposed together with the *idea* of the even or the odd on any mathematical number participating in it.[16]

Rather than explicitly raise this question, however, Socrates proposes to define once more, with further unacknowledged variations, what sort of nonopposites do not admit opposites themselves. The triad, though not the opposite of the even, not only refuses to admit it, but also brings forward against the even the opposite with which it is always connected; and in the same way, the dyad always brings forward the opposite of the odd, and fire the opposite of the cold, and all the numerous others.[17] Socrates has expanded his military metaphor, for the intermediary is now not only an occupying force, but it actively brings forward the opposite with which it is allied in self-defense against the approach of the hostile opposite. Socrates asks Cebes to examine the revised formulation that results from this addition: not only do opposites themselves exclude each other, but also that which always brings forward some opposite to that which it approaches will never admit "the opposition" of that which is brought forward. Socrates no longer speaks of the opposite itself approaching—either its own opposite, or something that always possesses its opposite, or something that compels whatever it occupies to have its own *idea* as well as that of an opposite, or whatever is occupied by that which always possesses an opposite. He points ahead to the problematic application of this principle. For when his silence about the poison as the carrier of death compels him to speak of death itself as approaching a man, we do not know the causal operation of this active agent. At the moment, in any case, the opposite itself is treated as passive, and its own opposite is said to be excluded, not necessarily by what is approached, but by the active intermediary that brings forward an opposite to whatever it approaches.

After transforming the general principle of the exclusion of opposites through so many twists and turns, Socrates offers to refresh Cebes' memory, since it cannot hurt to listen to it over and over again! Just after this warning, however, in response to an alleged repetition that in fact puts into question the application of the general principle,[18] Cebes claims to be following Socrates and to agree "most intensely." Socrates is therefore saved from having to specify whether the exclusion of an opposite has been attributed to the nonopposite that always brings forward an opposite to something it occupies or to that which is thus occupied, or to both at once. The argument has progressed from the example of Simmias great and small, through the example of hot fire and cold snow, to the example of odd three and even two. There is, in the first case, nothing in the nature of the subject that connects it inseparably with one opposite or the other, since Simmias can become greater having been smaller, or he can be greater in one relation, smaller in another. The principle of exclusion of opposites applied, consequently, not to the subject that admits both contraries, but to the greatness in him, which is in fact an abbreviated expression for one relation, and the smallness in him, which is an abbreviated expression for another. In the case of fire and snow, by contrast, each subject is essentially characterized by one of two opposite qualities, although its being so characterized is a matter of degree; heat can be transferred by fire, moreover, to some other thing, which is not itself essentially hot or cold but can change from one to the other. Only in the third case is each subject not only essentially even or odd, but never merely more or less so; and in this case there is no neutral subject that can change from one opposite to the other. Socrates does not clarify which is the proper paradigm to be applied to the case of soul and its characterization, which is presumably the point of the argument.[19]

[105b5–105d5] Socrates is prepared, without that clarification, to offer Cebes a model for a "more refined" answer that goes beyond the first "unlearned" one, whose own safety is nevertheless guaranteed by the preceding argument. If Cebes were to ask, "By what coming to be present in something will it be hot?", Socrates would no longer be restricted to the simple answer, "By heat," but could now give the more refined answer, "By fire." And if he were to ask, "By what coming to be in a body will it be ill?", Socrates would no longer cling to the simple answer, "By illness," but would boldly respond, "By fever." If Cebes were to ask, finally, "By what coming to be in a number will it be odd?", Socrates would no longer be compelled to answer, "By oddness," but can now reply, "By the monad." Socrates' refined answer represents an advance in knowledge of cause in the ordinary sense, but only at the price of giving up irrefutability. It assigns a cause that is neither sufficient—since its safety depends upon its essential connection with some independent opposite—nor necessary—since the result it produces might just as well have been produced by some other cause.

The argument that prepares for this refined answer has established that fire can be the cause of heat only and not of cold, but it did not and could not have established that fire is the only cause of heat; conversing might just as well be the cause of heat (cf. 63d), or even fever, as Socrates suggests by adding it between his original examples of fire and number. And cooling might just as well as fever be the cause of illness, or at least of death (cf. 118a). That it is the monad that renders some number odd may seem to be an advance over the simple answer, "By oddness"; yet it is no longer a necessary answer, for Socrates has just admitted that the *idea* of the odd can be brought forward by the *idea* of any odd number. The monad, moreover, which is now identified as the refined cause of any number being odd, was first presented as the safe answer to the question of the cause of anything—apparently even or odd, or perhaps not to be construed in a mathematical sense at all—being one (101c).[20] While the monad, in its mathematical function as an intermediary, is subordinate to oddness, that might not be the case for the monad as the eidetic cause of unity. Socrates thus points with this last example to the problematic subordination of soul, which will soon be assigned a merely intermediary function as the cause of life in the body.[21]

The model for the refined answer furthermore preserves, rather than resolves, the equivocation of the preparatory argument on the exclusion of opposites; for it does not indicate whether the quality in question characterizes only that which is approached or that which brings it forward, or both. Fire, which is essentially hot and therefore never admits the cold, can also bring forward heat to whatever it approaches, making it too hot. But fever, though it brings forward illness to the body it approaches, could not itself be said to be ill any more than healthy. And even if the monad were to make the number in which it comes to be present odd, it is questionable whether it is itself necessarily odd and not also even,[22] or neither odd nor even. Socrates thus distinguishes between a cause that transfers to something else the quality of an opposite by which it is itself characterized and one able to transfer a quality that is not its own characteristic: he does not specify which is the proper model to be applied to the case of soul, which he is finally about to introduce.

Since Cebes believes he has followed the model "very sufficiently," Socrates instructs him to imitate by answering in turn the question: "By what coming to be in some body will it be alive?" Socrates connects his question about the cause of life "in the body" most closely with his example of fever as the cause of illness in the body: he recalls Cebes' image, with its implication that the entrance of the soul into the body is the beginning of its destruction, as if life were a long disease (95d).[23] Socrates' formulation implies, furthermore, that soul could not itself be characterized as living any more than fever could be characterized as ill. By asking about the cause of life "in the body," finally, Socrates compels Cebes to answer, "By soul." He precludes the answer, "By the union of body and soul," which would have recalled the original definition of death as their separation, while clarifying that the attribute "living" belongs properly only to the compound being.

Socrates asks Cebes the one question he never raised in the preceding model when he inquires whether soul is always the cause of life in the body. Cebes is convinced that it is, without considering the possibilities, suggested by the first series of arguments, that soul could be understood as the cause of death no less than of life, or that body no less than soul could be understood as the cause of life. In giving up the nonfalsifiable answer—that the body comes to be alive by participation in the *eidos* of life—for the sake of answering "by what" that participation takes place, the refined answer might thus seem to lose the safety Socrates sought, motivated by a proposed disputatious attack. But to overcome that attack requires, as Socrates has shown, not a nonfalsifiable answer but only a noncontradictory one; and to account for something being what it is by referring to one possible refined cause, which is not itself the opposite of another such cause, might be empirically wrong but could not be logically contradictory.[24] A threat to the *logos* would be constituted, therefore, not by a claim that something besides soul is the cause of life, but by the claim that, in causing life, soul produces a result opposed to its own essential nature, or that soul is both the cause of life, through its attachment to the body (cf. 81d–e, 83d), as well as of its opposite, death, through its longing for *phronēsis* (cf. 67c–e). Socrates defends himself against this possible attack, once more, by the way he formulates his question, whether the soul always comes to whatever it occupies bearing life. With this repetition he manages to avoid, at the same time, the unsettled question of whether the quality "living" characterizes the soul or the body it occupies, or only both together.

[105d6–105e9] To apply the general principle of the exclusion of opposites to the case of soul as the cause of life, Socrates must establish, first, that there is something that is the opposite of life and not, as he goes out of his way to suggest as an alternative, nothing. That this alternative is not explored depends upon the unquestioned premise of the entire discussion—that we believe death is something (64c)—which was agreed upon before the subsequent consideration of what it is. Death was then defined as a double separation—the body becoming separate from the soul and the soul being separate from the body; and it was with that definition in mind that Cebes originally posited the opposition of "being alive" and "being dead" (71c). When Cebes now affirms death, without further specification, to be the opposite of life, Socrates does not raise the question of whether this opposition is equally intelligible on the basis of the ordinary understanding of death as annihilation. The opposition between being alive and being dead looks like the opposition between even and odd, not like that between hotter and colder, which is a matter of degree, or greater and smaller, which is a relation dependent on an act of comparison. Perhaps this range of examples has been introduced, though, just because of the questions it raises. Physiologically, of course, one is either alive or dead. But doesn't Plato's portrait of Socrates suggest what it might mean to be, in some important sense, "more alive"?

Given the current conception of soul, in any case, Cebes' assertion about the opposition of being alive or dead leads to the desired conclusion from the final formulation of the principle of exclusion of opposites (cf. 105a): soul, which always brings forward life to the body it occupies, could never admit the opposite, which has been identified as death. If the original definition of death were read into this conclusion, the impossibility of "dead soul" would be tantamount to a denial of its possible existence apart from the body. The present argument was introduced, however, in response to Cebes' objection, which amounted to a redefinition of death as the perishing or destruction of the soul (91d, 95d). It must demonstrate, accordingly, that soul cannot admit death, understood as its own destruction.[25] This indestructible quality would have to belong, however, not to a separate soul existing after death, but as the present argument requires, to soul as carrier of life to the body. The impossibility of soul remaining what it is and becoming dead may look like the impossibility of three remaining what it is and becoming even. Yet, while three cannot become even because it is itself odd, soul cannot become dead, not because it is itself alive, but only because it is, and as long as it continues to be, the cause of life in the body.

Before stating the expected consequence of the claim that soul will never admit the opposite of life, which should bring the argument to its conclusion, Socrates introduces a digression on names. When he asks what we *now* call "the nonadmitting of the *idea* of the even," he encourages Cebes to remember the characteristic of nonopposites that do not admit the *idea* opposite to that which is in them (cf. 104d–e). Cebes would be thinking, then, of an odd number and its essential characteristic with his answer, "uneven," preparing for the characterization of soul as "deathless." But Socrates holds off and proceeds to ask what names we give to "the nonadmitting of the just" or to "that which does not admit the musical," and Cebes confirms the linkage of the two when he answers in reverse, "Unmusical, and the unjust." Why should Socrates interrupt his argument about the essential character of soul with this apparently superfluous pair of examples? At the outset of the conversation, Socrates expressed his possible guilt for a lifelong misinterpretation of the recurrent dream ordering him "to make music," which he identified with philosophy as "the greatest music," while neglecting "demotic music" (60d–61b). The purification he claimed to be seeking now takes the form of the purely logical argument he is about to complete—soul as bringer of life to the body is by definition "deathless"—which manages at the same time to address his interlocutors' hope for immortality as eternal life.[26]

Socrates asks finally what we call that which does not admit death, and Cebes, imitating the established model, replies "*athanaton*." On the basis of certain steps in the preceding argument, this characterization could belong to the body as long as it is occupied by soul no less than to the soul as long as it occupies a living body.[27] Body as such, of course, has no essential connection with one opposite *eidos*; it is therefore capable, in contrast with soul, of still remaining what it is while undergoing the *genesis* from being alive to being dead. It is only the ensouled body, then, that participates in the *eidos* of life, since it is not by virtue of being body that it does so. But it is equally true that only embodied soul can be called "deathless."[28] For soul earns this ascription by virtue of being the cause of life in the body it occupies, and to say that it cannot be dead is to deny the possibility of its existence apart from that defining function.[29] Nevertheless, when Socrates reaches the conclusion, "Then the soul is something *athanaton*," what Cebes hears is the ordinary understanding of the term *athanaton*, which would be ascribed only to the gods, who are deathless because they never cease to exist. Cebes enthusiastically assures Socrates that the demonstration has been "very sufficient."

[105e10–106b3] Cebes seems to be entirely satisfied that Socrates has at last fulfilled the demand for a demonstration of the immortality of the soul as imperishability (cf. 88b, 95b–c). But it is precisely the nonidentity of these qualities that compels Socrates to pursue the argument beyond its present conclusion. He has established the immortality of the soul only as an inability to abide the approach of death, the opposite of life, which the soul always brings forward to the body it occupies. But Socrates originally specified a subsequent alternative for something that cannot remain behind and admit an opposite; the supplement he now adds to his argument must attempt to demonstrate that the soul that cannot admit death necessarily withdraws rather than allow itself to be destroyed at its approach.

To accomplish this purpose—or to show that it cannot be accomplished—Socrates returns to the original examples in the preceding argument. If the uneven were necessarily imperishable, he asks, with no support for this premise, wouldn't three be imperishable?[30] When Cebes responds, "How could it not be?", he points, however unintentionally, to the unresolved ambiguity of the argument. For the imperishability of three would follow necessarily, only if the uneven referred to a class, each of whose members would be imperishable; if the uneven were construed, on the other hand, as a class characteristic, nothing would prevent the number three from "perishing" in a mathematical operation that produced an even number, while the quality of unevenness would "withdraw."

However metaphoric this language about number, Socrates' expansion of the model to natural phenomena looks all the more like a reductio ad absurdum. If the unhot were imperishable, he asks, whenever heat came against snow, wouldn't the snow withdraw, unmelted? For it would not be destroyed, nor could it remain and admit heat. Before giving Cebes a chance to answer, Socrates affirms the parallel case:[31] if the uncoolable were imperishable, whenever cold came against fire, it could never be quenched or destroyed but would withdraw unaffected. The comic picture of snow or fire taking off in safety might lead to rejecting the imperishability of the unhot or uncoolable in any subject with that characteristic. What can we conclude about the imperishability of the immortal and its consequence for soul? Socrates began by asking about three being imperishable (*anōlethros*), if the uneven were so; but he speaks of snow or fire not being destroyed (*ouk appolusthai*), by ceasing to be cold or hot. For a subject to be destroyed at the approach of an opposite means to lose its essential attribute and no longer be what it is, whereas to perish is simply to cease to exist.[32] If snow or fire is the closest model, Socrates would be asking whether, at the approach of death, soul could lose its essential attribute and be destroyed, analogous to snow melting or fire being quenched.

Having established the consequence entailed for a member of any class hypothetically taken to be imperishable, Socrates asks finally if it is necessary to say the same about the *athanaton*.[33] If it is also imperishable, he reasons—dropping the "unreal" form through which the premise of the previous examples was expressed—then it is impossible for the soul, when death comes toward it, to be destroyed. For it will not admit death, nor will it be dead, Socrates concludes, thus confirming the meaning of destruction as the fate of something essentially characterized by one opposite that becomes other than what it was by admission of the other opposite. Yet, if the immortal soul cannot become other than what it is, it may, at the approach of death, have to cease to exist altogether. If the soul cannot be dead, what indeed would it mean to say that it "withdraws," presumably to Hades, when it ceases to occupy a living body?

[106b3–106d1] Just as the soul will not be dead, Socrates continues, three will not be even, nor again will the odd be even, nor will fire be cold, nor the heat in fire. But the distinction Socrates now suppresses—between the odd or the hot, which never become even or cold, and three or fire, which cannot be even or cold as long as they are at all—leads him to imagine the objection of an unnamed critic. It was the objection of an anonymous interlocutor at the outset of the argument that compelled Socrates to articulate the distinction between opposite *pragmata* that come to be from each other and opposite *eidē* that exclude each other. But Socrates has now extended the principle of exclusion of opposites beyond the safe answer to a more refined one, a subject essentially characterized by an opposite, like fire or snow. Unlike the opposite *eidos* itself, however, it looks as if the refined cause could be destroyed or cease to exist altogether at the approach of an opposite it cannot admit while remaining what it is.

Motivated, apparently, by that thought, Socrates' imaginary critic is willing to admit, in accordance with their prior agreements, that the odd does not become even at the approach of the even, but he sees nothing to prevent it from being destroyed, while the even comes to be in its place. Socrates does not clarify the ambiguity of "the odd" by distinguishing the characteristic of being odd, which does not become even, from the number that is odd, which can be replaced by one that is even. Nor does he confront the question of what it would mean for three to be "destroyed," in the sense of turning into an even number. He has argued only that three would be imperishable if the uneven were imperishable; and though he now rejects the truth of that premise, he insists that, if it were true, three and the odd would withdraw together at the approach of the even. In the same way, fire would withdraw from the cold if the hot were imperishable, and so for all the rest. Since the same reasoning should be applicable, Socrates implies, to soul, if the immortal were imperishable, he need only distinguish that case from the former ones by establishing the truth of its premise.

If the immortal is agreed to be imperishable, Socrates had argued before he interrupted himself with an imagined objection, then the soul could not be destroyed when death approaches it. But he now transforms that consequence, in accordance with the model of three and the uneven, when he claims that soul would be, with regard to the immortal, also imperishable. "With regard to the immortal" must mean insofar as soul is a member of the class of the immortal. For if the latter were simply a class characteristic, it could be objected that, when the man dies, his soul, although it could not remain soul and become dead, could indeed cease to exist, while its deathlessness would "withdraw" and come to be or remain present in some other soul occupying a living body.

Socrates must demonstrate, then, that it would be a self-contradiction to claim that what cannot be dead could nevertheless cease to exist. He must establish the identity of life and existence, which was not presupposed by the first part of the argument and was denied by the series of arguments in the first half of the dialogue. Unless this necessary connection between immortality and imperishability can be affirmed, Socrates concedes, some other *logos* would be needed (cf. 70d, 76e). Of course, the agreements that represent "something sufficient" for the interlocutors who accept them, on the basis of which further consistent inferences may be drawn (cf. 101d), should be for the reader of the dialogue precisely those points at which an affirmation of self-evident truth must be transformed into a question for further examination.

[106d2–106e4] But Cebes does not hesitate to grant Socrates his agreement: if there is anything at all that would not admit corruption, he believes, it must be the immortal, which is everlasting. Cebes replaces the question about imperishability with a claim about what is subject to corruption (*phthora*), which would seem to be especially applicable to natural things: perhaps he still has not forgotten the common human fear that the soul is something like breath or smoke (70a). Nor does Cebes specify how he understands "the immortal" whose invulnerability to corruption he affirms simply by asserting that it is everlasting (*aïdion*),[34] thus presupposing exactly what is in question. He must consider this justified by the necessity of rejecting the consequence he thinks would otherwise follow, namely, that everything would sooner or later cease to exist. Cebes seems to remember the conclusion of the first argument, in which the assumption that there must always be something living, unless everything were to end up dead, led, as its necessary condition, to the agreement that there must be something always capable of coming to be alive again, namely the souls of the dead (72c–d). The assumption that there must always be something that escapes destruction now leads Cebes to conclude that there must be something that always escapes destruction, namely the immortal, which is everlasting.[35]

Socrates offers Cebes his qualified support: it would be agreed by all that the god at least and the *eidos* of life itself and anything else immortal, if there were such, could never be destroyed. That it is something immortal only in the ordinary sense, rather than in the reconstructed sense at stake in the first part of this argument, that could be characterized as everlasting, Socrates confirms by his reference—for the first time in the argument—to the god, who is by definition always living. Yet this would hardly constitute the grounds for the indestructibility of the *eidos* of life itself. Socrates is silent, in any case, about the human soul. But he does put the ordinary understanding of its immortality into question when he emphasizes the hypothesis that *if* there were anything else immortal, it too would be indestructible. With an irony he himself is not likely to recognize, Cebes affirms the universal acceptance of Socrates' claim, "By all, by Zeus, men. and even more, I believe, by the gods."

Eager, apparently, to reach the conclusion of the argument, Socrates immediately accepts Cebes' agreement and poses on that basis his final question: Since the immortal is incorruptible, would the soul, if it happened to be immortal, be anything but imperishable? The model for this question was the imperishability of three, if the uneven were imperishable. But that model is a reminder now of the questionable grounds for their agreement on the imperishability of the immortal. It is a reminder, moreover, that while three was said to be determined not only by the *idea* of the odd, but also by its own *idea*, Socrates has nowhere established a parallel *idea* of soul. When Cebes responds to Socrates' question, "Most necessary," he must ignore its optative mood and the hypothetical condition contained within it. But Socrates' stress on that hypothetical condition suggests that what is required for a demonstration of imperishability is not the immortality established in the first part of the argument, but rather immortality in the ordinary sense. Socrates would have had to demonstrate—but he did not—that soul could not cease to be alive, because it could not cease to exist.[36] The imperishability of the soul has not been, and could not be, established, that is, without assuming what is supposed to be deduced from it.

[106e5–107a1] Socrates manages, nevertheless, to reach a justifiable conclusion that avoids just this problem: "When death approaches the man, the mortal, as it seems, of him dies, while the immortal departs, going away safe and incorruptible, withdrawing from death." Socrates is silent about the immortal as a characterization of the soul and conspicuously refrains from referring to "the immortal (part) of man" parallel to "the mortal of him." If the mortal that dies when death approaches is the living being as such, the union of body and soul, then the immortal that withdraws "safe and incorruptible" must be nothing other than the quality of deathlessness that characterizes every ensouled body or embodied soul, whenever it exists. Cebes transforms his previous exuberant response into the rather subdued, "It appears so"; for Socrates has finally compelled him, and perhaps the others as well, to realize that it is the man whom death approaches, the man Socrates, whose imminent death they pity and fear.

As if to combat the moderation of the conclusion they have justifiably reached, Socrates enthusiastically proclaims one last consequence: "Then above all, Cebes, soul is immortal and imperishable, and our souls will really be in Hades." Socrates' surprising certainty about this conclusion "above all" (*pantos mallon*) echoes the certainty he expressed at the conclusion of the first argument he conducted with Cebes (cf. 72d). That echo is confirmed by Socrates' sudden reference to plural "souls" for the first time in this argument and his sudden mention of Hades for the first time in the second half of the dialogue. In fact, however, whereas the first argument was supposed to investigate whether the souls of the dead are in Hades, it concluded only that they exist. And while the present argument concludes that "our souls" will be in Hades really, the first argument affirmed that there really is coming back to life. Socrates does not explain how he can be certain that our souls will be in Hades if, as he has just demonstrated, the soul cannot be dead. He expresses his certainty, moreover, at the very moment he recalls, but does not renounce, his previous certainty that the living come to be from the dead. The echo of the first argument's conclusion in that of the last thus serves only as a reminder of the anonymous interlocutor's observation of their apparent contradiction.

In the transition from the first to the last argument, the consideration of one *pragma* coming to be from its opposite is transformed into the consideration of one *pragma* coming to be *what* it is, characterized by a quality that necessarily excludes its opposite.[37] The final argument asks no longer about the coming to be or passing away of a living being, but rather, about the cause of the body being, coming to be, or ceasing to be alive; for this question the safe but simple answer, "Participation in the *eidos* of life," can be supplemented by the refined answer, "*Psychē*, which always brings forward life to the body it occupies." Yet Socrates' reminder of his first argument at the conclusion of his last does not appear where it does by accident: the move beyond the demonstration of immortality to the issue of imperishability is a return to the question of the necessary existence of the soul, rather than of its necessary characterization as what it is. Socrates indicates the problematic status of this return when he concludes his last argument, like the first, with the announcement that our souls will be in Hades "really" (*tō onti*), literally "in being," rather than "in *logos*."[38]

[107a2–107b10] Cebes first admitted the "great encouragement and trust" required to show that the soul of the dead man has some power and *phronēsis* (70b); he now admits only that he has nothing more to say against the argument, nor can he distrust these *logoi*. He encourages Simmias and the others, nevertheless, not to be silent, since there may be no other opportunity to speak or hear about these matters: all Socrates' efforts have not removed Cebes' fear that the *logos* will die with the death of Socrates. Simmias, on the other hand, although he too can think of no further objections, cannot help but distrust these *logoi*, given, he explains, the magnitude of the subject in contrast with our human weakness.[39] Like the reflections with which Simmias introduced his earlier objection (85c–d), his present ones turn out to be a parody of the principles of Socratic inquiry. For Socrates, too, acknowledges that a clearer investigation is required of their first hypotheses, however trustworthy they may seem. But despite their apparently common recognition of our human weakness, Socrates, unlike Simmias, does not abandon the goal that would motivate continuation of the investigation. Only if one could go through it sufficiently, Socrates adds, would he follow the *logos* as far as humanly possible. The process of defending a hypothesis on the basis of a higher one, Socrates explained to Cebes, must be carried on until "something sufficient" is reached; at that point, he now promises Simmias, you will seek nothing further.

The hypothesis that underlies the argument as a whole—indirectly, the entire series of arguments—is the agreement, which Phaedo only summarized, on the being of the *eidē* as the cause of the *pragmata* being what they are. The investigation that Socrates now recommends would have to justify, then, the separation of *eidē* from *pragmata*, while clarifying the mediating level that allows for the relation of "participation." This would entail in turn a reconstruction of the unity of the dialogue divided in two halves, the first beginning with the principle of the mutual generation of opposite *pragmata*, the second with the principle of the mutual exclusion of opposites themselves. But the complementary relation between these principles does not resolve the apparently contradictory content in the two halves of the dialogue based upon them. While the series of arguments in the first half assumes the separability of the soul from the body after death, when it is in contact with the beings themselves, to which it is akin, it is precisely that assumption that is denied by the final argument. It alone demonstrates the immortality of the soul; yet that immortality is not eternal existence after death, but rather, the essential relation of soul—and not a cognitive one[40]—with one *eidos* only, that of life, which it brings forward to the body it occupies as long as it exists.

Reconstruction of the unity of the dialogue would thus appear to require a resolution of the tension between soul as a principle of life and soul as mind; but what the *Phaedo* suggests, rather, is an alternative to the latter. A psychological analysis of thinking and knowing is replaced, that is, by a logical one, and precisely because of the passions shown to lie behind the positing of the pure soul as nothing but a medium of cognition. In the second half of the dialogue, "mind" appears only when Socrates imagines a claim that all his actions are directed by it,[41] motivated, presumably, in no way whatsoever by desire, fear, hope, anger, or any other passion; such a claim thus implies the absence of soul, even though mind would seem to be impossible without soul. Socrates indicates in this way the problematic character of the premise of Anaxagorean teleology—that mind is the cause of all, arranging the best for each and the good for all in common. It was the unavailability of such knowledge of the good, Socrates confessed, that compelled him to replace teleology with his own second sailing. Yet when Socrates labels the procedure he adopts in that second sailing a "*technē*," he arouses our suspicions about its status. For Socrates certainly has not solved all the unanswered questions that remain in his elaboration of this art of reasoning, and in fact, just to the extent that it is an art, it could not determine the ends for which it serves as a means. It is, rather, the motivation of the practitioner of the *technē* of *logoi* that guides the direction in which it is applied. What the *technē* of *logoi* replaces is not the human soul as such, but precisely and only the notion of soul as mind, abstracted from all human *pathē*.

The final argument of the *Phaedo*, which results from that replacement, ought to be, apparently, a "purification" of the *logos* from all rhetoric motivated by self-interest; this of course implies some relation between them, at least an understanding of the self-interest from which the *logos* is supposedly liberated. The purification of the *logos* is, one might say, an idealization. For not only does the presumably discarded rhetorical element come back with a vengeance to haunt the ensuing *mythos*, but it is already present in the abrupt conclusion of the final argument. In fact, even before that point, the argument has a persuasive appeal, to Cebes among others, based on the assumption of the ordinary understanding of "immortality." It is, nevertheless, the definitions and principles stipulated in the argument that provide the means to correct its merely persuasive appeal. The interpretation resulting from that correction separates in *logos*, and for the sake of *logos*, only the mutually exclusive opposite *eidē*, while identifying soul as nothing but the inseparable cause of life in the body. The separability of pure *logos* exemplified by the final argument may be an idealization, but it is one—unlike the idealized separate soul—that precludes its illusory identification with the self. It precludes, consequently, the paradoxical combination of resentment of life and the longing for eternal existence.

Chapter Twelve: *Mythos*

[107c1–107d4] When asked whether everyone could give a *logos* of these matters, Simmias betrayed his fear that on the morrow there would no longer be any man able to do so (76b); when warned of the need to sing charms daily to comfort the child in us moved by the fear of death, Cebes betrayed his fear that someone able to do so could nowhere be found, since Socrates was about to leave them (77e–78a). The speeches have grown longer, the day shorter, and however successfully the *logos* may have been preserved, "this Socrates who is now speaking and arranging what is being said" (115c) will not be present much longer to protect it. That fact is nowhere more striking than in Socrates' acknowledgment of the need for further examination of the first hypotheses of their arguments, which would have to be continued, he insisted, until arriving at "something sufficient." But Socrates now replaces that task, in the short time left before he must drink the poison, with a *mythos* about the fate of the soul after death. He knows a "likely story,"[1] it seems, that can take the place of that sufficiency he claimed to have sought in knowledge of the good, showing the work of mind arranging things as is best for each and good for all in common (cf. 98a–b). Relative to that standard of sufficiency, life is always too short; *mythos* would seem to be necessary in some form, consequently, for any inquiry.

Socrates opened the conversation by remarking on the strange character of what we call "pleasure"; he addressed those remarks, just after sending Xanthippe away in tears, to his interlocutors as "he men" (*andres*, 60b).[2] He now addresses them in the same way once again, when he introduces his concluding *mythos* with a remark on what we call "life." Yet despite that qualification, he transforms the conclusion of the last argument into a hypothesis: It is just to consider that, *if* the soul is immortal, it is necessary to care for it not only for this time we call "life," but for all time.[3] In making his exhortation conditional, Socrates implies that the immortality legitimately demonstrated in the previous argument does not mean the continued existence of the soul apart from the body after death. But he indicates, at the same time, that the necessity of care for the soul in what we call "life" is entirely independent of the question of our future existence. That familiar Socratic care for the soul that has emerged only implicitly at fleeting moments throughout the conversation cannot come to the foreground until the completion of the last argument, which was intended to illustrate the turn from concern with the self to concern with the *logos* itself. In order to carry out that turn, Socrates transformed the danger of sailing through life, for which Simmias sought a safe vessel, into the danger of contradictory speech, for which the *technē* of *logoi* was to provide a safe defense. He transforms it once more when he adds that to neglect care for the soul would now appear to be a terrible danger; and it is safety in the face of this danger that is to be provided, presumably, by the *mythos* Socrates is about to deliver.

Before offering his defense of philosophy as the practice of dying, Socrates expressed the hope that "there is something for the dead and, as it is said of old, something better for the good than for the bad" (63c). It is to such a hope—which has hardly been confirmed by the preceding series of arguments—that Socrates now returns. Death would be a blessing for the bad, he argues, if it were a release from everything;[4] for in being freed from the body, they would be freed at the same time from their own evils and—he admits explicitly for the first time—from the soul to which such evils must belong. Death would be a benefit to himself, Socrates claimed earlier, simply in being released from his ignorance (91b)—if, at least, the continuation of that condition would really be an evil. Socrates now asserts the desirability of escaping any real evils that belong to the soul itself while denying that the termination of life is the condition for that escape; for given its manifest immortality, there would be no salvation for it except by becoming best and most prudent (*phronimos*). Socrates refers, one can assume, to the soul; but its manifest immortality is only its inability to be dead whenever it exists, and the evil from which it must escape is not life itself as the genuine philosophers believe—but the opposite of being good and prudent.[5] The *phronēsis*, therefore, that Socrates identifies as the only salvation cannot be that which the genuine philosophers seek as the automatic result of dying, when the soul is separated from the contamination of the body.

Death alone is no escape, Socrates argues, because the soul takes with it into Hades its education and nurture.[6] Just this consideration has been absent from Socrates' attempts to demonstrate, in the first argument, that "the souls of the dead are in Hades" (72d), in the second, that "our souls are before we were born" (76e), and in the last, that "our souls will be in Hades" (107a). In the third argument, on the other hand, Socrates admitted that not every human life is conducted in accordance with the true nature of the soul, and it is the manner of life a man has led that determines what the destiny of his soul is "like." That the invisible soul, in any case, departs into Hades as the place most like itself (80d), is the sort of charm we ought to chant to ourselves, Socrates insisted, in order to assuage our childish fear of death. Now the story he is about to tell about the "journey abroad" after death is, Socrates admits at its conclusion, a magic charm designed to work on the experiences of the soul. As such, it must represent a continuation of the third argument, which brought the first half of the conversation to an end. Only the comic imagery of that speech, which concluded with a description of the hierarchy of classes of human souls ranging from the bestial to the divine, foreshadows Socrates' present attempt to lend support to the hope that death brings something better for the good than for the bad.

[107d4–108c5] Shifting to indirect discourse in the middle of his sentence about the education and nurture of the soul—"which are said to benefit or harm the dying man greatly from the outset of his journey"— Socrates continues his report, although he begins referring not to the soul, but to the man who has died. The *daimōn* allotted to each man leads him after death to a certain place, where all are gathered together to be judged;[7] then, after journeying into Hades led by one guide and experiencing there what is necessary for the requisite time, another guide brings him back. Socrates recalls the ancient *logos* about the cycle of living and dying, which provided the hypothesis of his first argument. He intended then, apparently, to guarantee the necessary eternity of the cycle (cf. 77d) by demonstrating the impossibility of a *genesis* in the direction of one of two opposite states without a return *genesis* in the direction of the other. But it is precisely such an irreversible linear motion that Socrates is about to describe as the fate of any human beings who are perfectly impure or perfectly pure—if there are any.[8] In the present tale, moreover, Hades represents the place of imprisonment after the judgment of the dead man; but it represented in the first series of arguments an at least temporary escape from the perceived punishment of life that consists in the imprisonment of the soul in the body.

163

Although he claimed to be no mythmaker (61b), Socrates now competes with Aeschylus, whose Telephus asserts that a simple road leads into Hades: if there were one simple path, Socrates reasons, there would be no need of guides, yet there seem to be many divisions in the path, as the holy rites and laws here give witness.[9] Socrates does not explicitly offer his own interpretation of the complexity that characterizes the road into Hades. But his account of the *daimōn* who leads the dying man recalls the role previously assigned to a personified philosophy, who takes hold of the soul when it is welded to the body and encourages it gently, trying, although not necessarily succeeding, to set it free (82e–83a). Socrates proceeds to distinguish the orderly and prudent soul, which follows its guide and is not ignorant of its circumstances, from the soul that is desirous of the body and therefore flits about the visible place for a long time until after much struggling it is led away by force. Socrates will try to persuade Crito, at the conclusion of this tale, that he himself, being aware of his circumstances, has no interest in flitting about the Athenian prison any longer, but is prepared to follow, without any struggle, the guidance of the man in charge of administering the poison.

In contrasting the fate that awaits the pure souls with that of the impure, Socrates recalls the language of the mysteries (cf. 69c): while the soul that has lived purely and measurably enjoys gods as companions and guides and dwells in its fitting place, the soul that is impure and responsible for impure acts, like unjust homicides, is shunned by all and left to wander about in perplexity.[10] Now, Socrates had originally contrasted the orderly and prudent soul with one that cannot give up its attachment to the body. But whereas the prudent soul might reasonably be identified as one having lived purely and measurably, it is far from evident why its opposite, the body-loving soul, should be represented by the murderer. Perhaps Socrates is thinking of those who committed murders in the belief, based on their love of the body, that the greatest punishment is death—that is, separation from the body. If Socrates exemplifies the orderly and prudent soul, his contrary might be exemplified by the Athenian *dēmos*, which condemned him, presumably unjustly, to the punishment of death, believing it to be the greatest evil.[11]

[108c5–108e3] Socrates' speech, introduced to show why we must care for our soul through all time, seems to be completed; his mere mention of the fitting dwelling places of the various kinds of souls explains the multiplicity of paths and places in the other world as an image for the multiplicity of ways of life, based on the education and nurture by which every soul is said to be harmed or benefited greatly on its journey. But Socrates suddenly makes the surprising announcement that there are many wonderful places on the earth, and that the earth itself, he is persuaded,[12] is not what it is thought to be, in size or shape or any other way, by those who usually speak about it. When Simmias interrupts to express his interest in this cryptic allusion, Socrates agrees to speak about the earth from hearsay. He was willing to speak from hearsay about the prohibition against suicide, Socrates told his interlocutors at the outset of the conversation, since he found it most fitting to investigate and mythologize, in the time between dawn and sunset, about his imminent journey abroad (61d–e); he could not, therefore, be accused of idle chatter even by the comic poet who portrayed him as an investigator of things above the heavens and beneath the earth (70b–c).[13] Plato portrays Socrates, at the end of the *Phaedo*, carrying out precisely that investigation: he has Socrates take revenge, just before the execution of the penalty assigned by the Athenian *dēmos*, against the comic poet who is accused of being the original source of his conviction.

Socrates offers to tell Simmias about the *idea* of the earth and its places, but his reference to this *idea*—which seems rather surprising after the use of the term in the preceding argument—calls for a careful qualification: he needs no art of Glaucus simply to relate what he is persuaded of, but to demonstrate its truth would be too difficult for the art of Glaucus.[14] Even if there were a sufficient art, he himself might not be adequate to practice it, Socrates humbly admits, recalling his ironic judgment not on the impossibility of investigation of nature, but on his own natural unfitness for it (96c). And in any case, he adds, his own life would not last long enough for completion of the *logos*; with this last painful reminder Socrates brings to mind the incomplete investigation of the first hypotheses of their arguments, for which the present speech must serve as a replacement.

[108e4–109a8] Socrates identifies the premise of his account, before and after stating it, as "the first of which I am persuaded": *if* the earth is in the center of the heavens and is round, then it needs neither air nor anything else to prevent it from falling, but the homogeneity of the surrounding heavens and its own equipoise suffice to hold it. The shape and position of the earth, and why it is necessarily best for it to be as it is, is precisely the knowledge Socrates claimed to have sought so eagerly in the teaching of Anaxagoras (97d–e), which turned out to be no less disappointing than all the other theories that neglected the causality of the good. Yet the explanation Socrates now offers for the hypothetical position of the earth in the center of the cosmos seems to satisfy the principle of sufficient reason without being a teleological explanation based on knowledge of the good: it simply assumes that there is no reason why something completely balanced would ever incline in one direction rather than another.[15]

Socrates implicitly criticized Anaxagoras for trying to construct a theory of the cosmos governed by mind in accordance with the good while neglecting all consideration of the human good. He chose, therefore, to illustrate the failure of the Anaxagorean project—its inability to distinguish between a cause and that without which it could not operate as a cause—by considering the cause of his present situation: it would be as if someone were to claim that Socrates does all that he does through mind, then go on to assign as the cause of his sitting in the Athenian prison the mechanical operation of his bones and sinews, rather than his opinion of what is best. But while Socrates could thus explain his disappointment in Anaxagoras, he was not himself able to carry out the intention of demonstrating how the arrangement of the cosmos reflects the power of the good. He seems prepared finally to confront that challenge. Yet the knowledge Socrates now claims to possess is not of the good as a cosmological principle, but only that the soul must become as good and as prudent as possible: his present speech is only a magic charm designed to make a man courageous in living or dying (114d). The account Socrates has just offered of the earth at rest in the center of the heavens may be his answer to Anaxagoras; but rather than provide a cosmological theory demonstrating the best arrangement for each and the good for all in common, it seems in fact to be only an image of his own action, or nonaction, of remaining at rest in the Athenian prison.

Socrates has found an appropriate subject of investigation for the short time left before he will be transformed by the poison into a corpse devoid of all self-motion. For the earth that is characterized by the absence of motion would seem to represent pure body separate from soul; Socrates' account, as will soon become evident, is in fact an autopsy that renders visible the hidden insides of this gigantic corpse. Socrates' cosmological geography is an image of the body "writ large"[16]—a paradoxical choice, it would seem, to illuminate the fate of the soul after death in light of the purity or impurity of its way of life. But purification was first identified as the effort of the soul to separate itself from the body, accustoming itself to collect and gather itself together from "everywhere" (67c–d). And if the soul is imprisoned in the body, as Socrates affirmed in concluding his argument on its likeness to the invisible, by means of its own desires, nailed in by every pleasure or pain it experiences, then its character should be revealed in and through the nature of its attachment to the body. That is precisely what Socrates is about to illustrate by describing the places of the earth in which various kinds of souls belong.

[109a9–110a8] The earth is so gigantic, Socrates is persuaded, that those who dwell between the pillars of Heracles and the river Phasis—the inhabitants of the Mediterranean region—could be likened to ants or frogs around a pond, unaware of the other inhabitants of other regions. But the earth is in fact covered by many hollows of all different forms (*ideai*) and sizes, filled with water, mist, and air that are the sediment of what is called by the physicists "ether," the pure heaven in which the earth itself (*autē hē gē*) lies in its purity. The pure soul, itself by itself, released at death from the contamination of the body, has as its counterpart in Socrates' tale the pure earth itself, beyond its briny hollows.[17] Like the genuine philosophers who claim to have knowledge of the pure soul while alive and imprisoned in the body, Socrates claims to have knowledge of the earth itself while remaining sunk in one of its hollows. To account, consequently, for our systematic deception, Socrates must rely on analogy: like creatures dwelling on the bottom of the sea, believing it to be the heaven and never rising above the surface to see how much more pure and beautiful the region beyond is, we dwell in one hollow of the earth but believe we live on its upper surface, and we call the air *ouranos*, as if it were the heaven in which the stars move. But just as the things in the sea are covered with mud and brine, so those here on earth are corrupted and corroded, while the things beyond are as superior to those of our region as ours are to those in the sea. Only if one of us could fly up on wings and lift up his head, just as a fish could lift up his head from the water, would he see what is beyond;[18] and if his nature were sufficient to bear the sight, he would know that it is the true *ouranos* and the true light and the true earth.

Looking down on the inhabited world from the viewpoint of the true heavens, Socrates offers an image of the cave; but now the walls of the *polis* within which we are chained prisoners are replaced by the boundaries of the known world, the shadows cast on the wall by artificial objects reflected in the light of man-made fire replaced by the natural phenomena of our environment systematically misperceived through our murky depths.[19]

167

Socrates thus prepares to elaborate his earlier description of the imprisonment of the soul in the human body, chained by its attachment to pleasure and pain and compelled to view the beings through the prison bars of the senses (82e). The winged flight of that rare inhabitant able to lift his head out of this region should represent the philosopher's longed-for flight from the body, as the condition for direct contact of the pure soul with the pure beings; yet, like the pursuit of pleasure that always brings in its wake its opposite, the pursuit of the purified region beyond our own leads to the vision of the earth itself—an image of pure body separate from soul.

[110b1–111c3] Socrates uses the word "*mythos*" for the first time when he offers to tell Simmias something worth hearing about the things on the earth beneath the heavens. Socrates begins this *mythos* as he did his account of the *idea* of the earth, with "what is said first": if the earth itself could be observed from above, it would appear like those twelve-sided leather balls, divided into a patchwork of colors.[20] These are brighter and purer, more and more beautiful, than any we have seen here, and from that perspective even these hollows filled with water and air furnish some kind of *eidos* of color, so that the whole produces the glistening illusion of one continuous multicolored *eidos*. Correspondingly beautiful are the trees and flowers and fruits that grow on the true earth. And while our precious stones are corroded by the vapors and liquids that run together here, the earth itself is adorned by jewels that are pure and smooth and transparent; gold and silver, moreover, are not hidden as here but lie in open view, a blessed sight for the observer.[21] The pure earth offers, not the noetic vision by the soul of invisible ideas, but a purified aesthetic vision by purified body. *Eidos*, which in the last argument meant a determination in *logos*, is now only an embroidered *phantasm* of color, and the earth "patched up" by those hues replaces the soul "patched up" by its contamination with the somatoeidetic (81c).

On this true earth, Socrates continues, live many animals and men, some dwelling inland, others on coasts about the air, just as we dwell about the sea, and others on islands surrounded by air. The seasons there are so tempered that its inhabitants have no diseases and live much longer than we do here—although they will soon be identified as one class of the dead![22] In sight and hearing and *phronēsis* and all such, they are as superior to us as air is superior in purity to water, and ether to air. This ratio of elements, with the highest unknown to us, presumably accounts for our state of systematic delusion,[23] but to rise above the indented surface of the earth on which we dwell is only to reach the same element in its purest form.

Phronēsis, moreover, which the genuine philosophers claim to seek through the separation of soul from body, seems to have become nothing but one more faculty of perception and to belong apparently to men and animals alike. The inhabitants of this paradise of the body, with their intensified sensation to which all cognition has been reduced, need not imagine or fabricate images of absent gods: they enjoy communion face to face in sacred groves or temples where the gods dwell really (*tō onti*).[24] And since, furthermore, the sun and moon and stars can be seen just as they really are, there is no need to rely on observation through images:[25] given this direct contact with the *pragmata* themselves, no second sailing is required (cf. 99d–e). In all other ways, Socrates concludes, their blessedness is in accordance with this.[26]

[111c4–113c8] From his account of the true earth, Socrates turns to the hollows (*koila*)—the bellies or bowels of the earth[27]—sunk under its outer surface. Of these, some are deeper and wider in comparison with our own, some deeper but narrower, and some less deep but broader: the one in which we live is at least not the most inaccessible to the region beyond. The hollows are connected, Socrates continues, by subterranean channels through which water flows from one into another, as in mixing bowls.[28] And in the depths of the earth are "everlasting rivers of incalculable magnitude," which fill the various regions through which they run, moving up and down as if by some kind of oscillation. Preparing to explain the nature of this oscillation itself (*hautē hē aiōra*),[29] Socrates refers for the first time to *phusis* and drops the preceding indirect discourse that was prefaced by "It is said." While he appeals to Homer and the many other poets who gave the name "Tartarus" to the greatest of the chasms bored right through the whole earth,[30] Socrates does not need the poets to explain the cause of all the rivers flowing into and back out of this chasm: since the liquid there has no foundation, it oscillates up and down, running toward one side of the earth and then the other. The earth itself, according to Socrates' explanation, requires no foundation as the cause of its motionlessness, since there is simply no reason for it to move in one direction rather than another. Socrates now offers a correlative explanation for the motion of the rivers within the earth, whose oscillation from one direction to its opposite is caused simply by the absence of any foundation. This mechanical oscillation, which provides the source of motion for the circulatory system of the earth body, has taken over the function of soul as the source of motion for any living body.

169

When the liquid is set in motion, Socrates continues, the wind and air follow, and their oscillation produces terrible and irresistible blasts rushing in and out: just as the water flowing through the channels within the earth operates like blood flowing through the veins of the body, the wind rushing through the inner earth operates like the inspiration and expiration—or any other release of air!—in a living animal.[31] When the water flows out of Tartarus and withdraws to the so-called lower regions,[32] it runs through the earth, filling the streams there as if pumped into them, and when it is set in motion toward this side, it fills the streams here, just as the blood circulating through the veins fills the places in the body that have been emptied.[33] These streams produce seas and rivers and springs at various places and then pass back under the earth again. And each river gains its particular quality and color from its mixture with the parts of the earth through which it flows, just as the colors of the streams of nutriment are produced as they flow through various parts of the body.[34] Finally, all flow back into Tartarus, on either the opposite side from which they flowed out or the same side. And some empty at the lowest possible point into Tartarus, after circling like serpents around or within the earth once or many times, just as the intestines coil through the lower belly.[35] Yet all must descend below the point at which they flowed out, closer to the center of the earth, but not beyond it.[36]

As the locus of origin and return for all the great subterranean rivers, Tartarus takes the place of the heart, the source of circulation for the blood that flows to the limbs and back again in the body of a living animal. The heart is set in the body, according to one "likely story," like a guard chamber in the acropolis of the city, which allows for the rule of the best:[37] for while the wrath of *thumos* boils up whenever *logos* announces some unjust action, either from without or from the desires within, the circulation impelled by the heart delivers to the organs of sensation the commands and threats that are to be obeyed by all in all ways. A political metaphor thus allows for a teleological account in which the structure of the body is determined in accordance with the passions of the soul. Socrates is about to accomplish the same purpose now that he has described the circulatory, respiratory, and alimentary systems of the great earth body as a metaphor for those of a living animal. In place, however, of the food particles digested by the inner fire and transported through the bloodstream, nourishment for the earth body is provided, as Socrates will shortly indicate, by the ingestion, digestion, and excretion of human souls!

Appealing once more to the authority of the poets, Socrates attributes a particular significance to four—two pairs of opposites—of the many great streams circulating through the body of the earth.[38] The greatest and outermost, which winds in a circle, is called Okeanus,[39] and opposite to it, pouring through many desolate places in the opposite direction, is the Acheron. The Acherusian lake, at which this river finally arrives, is the gathering place of most of the souls of the dead, who must remain there for some appointed time before coming back to life again. The third river, which is called Pyriphlegethon, pours out between the first two, comes to a place burning with fire, produces a lake boiling with water and mud, and then winds many times around the earth before flowing back into Tartarus. And the fourth river, which issues opposite to it, comes first to a terrible place the color of lapis lazuli, takes "terrible powers" into its waters as it passes under the earth,[40] then circles in the opposite direction of the third river, before emptying on the opposite side into Tartarus. The lake produced by this river is the Styx, the river itself the Stygian, but called by the poets Cocytus.[41] As the name-givers of the great and terrible rivers of the underworld, the poets appeal to our fear and guilt by fabricating images of human *pathē*[42]—Pyriphlegethon, burning fire of passion; Styx, icy frost of hatred; Cocytus, sorrow of shrieking and wailing:[43] they justify Socrates' transformation of the mechanistic circulatory system of the earth body into the fitting context for a story about the destiny of the human soul.

[113d1–114c6] After completing his account, then, of the outer surface of the true earth and its inner circulatory system—both invisible, to human eyes at least (cf. 79b)—Socrates returns to his description of the journey of the dead into Hades. Arriving at the region to which each is led by his *daimōn*, each is judged as to whether he has lived beautifully and piously or not: Socrates does not yet raise the question of whether a noble or beautiful life is identical with a pious one. He implicitly admits the possibility of deception in this judgment, furthermore, by repeatedly affirming, in the following account, that the dead—who are not simply souls—only *appear* to belong to one class or another.[44] To link this division of classes with the system of four great rivers, Socrates begins, not accidentally, with the only one for which he acknowledged such a purpose: the Acherusian lake is the destination of all who are found to have lived in the middle state, neither a beautiful or pious life nor the opposite. But while Socrates first assigned to this place most of the souls of the dead, it must in fact be the source of all living men, since it is the only region from which souls were said to be sent back to be born again into living beings. Yet when he now announces that those who dwell for the appointed time in the Acherusian lake are there purified, Socrates no longer speaks of a return to life, and he is as silent about the nature of this purification as he is about the deeds that render it necessary.

Why Socrates begins his account with the middle condition of those sent to the Acherusian lake, while remaining silent about their eventual departure, is revealed by the role they play in the fate of the others. At one extreme from this mean are those who seem to be incurable, having committed many great acts of sacrilege or many unjust and lawless homicides or other such deeds.[45] It is a fitting fate that these should be thrown into Tartarus and should never emerge, for their interminable punishment is nothing but an image of their incurable evils. Those, on the other hand, who committed an act of violence out of anger against father or mother, then lived the rest of their lives in repentance, or those who committed any homicide in the same way, appear to belong in Tartarus as well; but since to repent is, by definition, to be released from that region, they are cast out after one year by the wave pulsing through Tartarus, the homicides through Cocytus, those who attacked father or mother through the Pyriphlegethon. Carried by the current to the Acherusian lake, the repentant call out to those they have slain or attacked, begging to be allowed to come into the lake; if they persuade their victims, they come out and leave behind their sufferings, but if not, they are carried back into Tartarus and then into the rivers, and this is repeated until they are able to persuade those they have wronged.

This is the penalty, Socrates adds, imposed by their judges. But it is the purely mechanical operation of the circulatory system of the earth body that accomplishes the purpose of the homicide law that requires an involuntary slayer to absent himself for a year from the region inhabited by his victim, in order to allow the dead man's wrath to abate.[46] The goal of the recycling of sullied souls in the invisible rivers of the underworld is purification, and the deeds thought to induce pollution—sacrilege, murder, violence against parents—are those that form the material of tragic drama.[47] Like the legal code for the treatment of pollution laid down by the Athenian Stranger in Plato's *Laws*, the system of purification in Socrates' Hades is based not on punishment, assuming responsibility, but on the psychological phenomena of guilt and absolution, anger and forgiveness; in Socrates' Hades, however, where the dead can speak for themselves, the victims have complete power to decide whether or not to pardon those who have wronged them.[48] The fate of the impure who repent is determined, therefore, not by evidence of moral improvement, but rather by skill in the art of rhetoric: the necessary condition for release is successful persuasion, by which the guilty man transforms his victim's anger into forgiveness. But Socrates has concealed a crucial problem: there is no guarantee that the victim was or still is an inhabitant of the Acherusian lake. A crime committed against either one who has been purified and released or one doomed to Tartarus forever could never be forgiven: justice can be carried out only if there are no extremes, with all men remaining in purgatory. Otherwise, the repentant murderer is automatically doomed to exile in the rivers of the underworld:[49] Socrates, who may never have to pay a penalty for injustice in the Acherusian lake, would thus condemn to eternal punishment in Hades the Athenian *dēmos*, who condemned him to death in one day and then lived to repent it.[50]

Socrates supports this possibility in the account he now offers of the fate of the pure, to balance that of the incurably impure—for otherwise nature would be lame (71e): those who are found to have excelled in pious living, liberated by their own weightlessness from the regions of the earth as from prisons, rise upward into their pure abode on the outer surface of the earth (cf. 82e–83a).[51] The pious, who sought throughout their lives separation from the body construed as a prison of the soul, are rewarded at death by release from imprisonment within the body of the earth; but their pure dwelling place is only the surface of the earth itself, which has been described as an intensified realm of the body and the senses. Those who, like the genuine philosophers, desire nothing but "noetic vision," contact of the pure soul with the pure beings, Socrates now condemns to the abode of aesthetic vision—forever! The inhabitants of the Acherusian lake who lived a life in the middle, as well as those who paid the penalty in Tartarus for their great sins but then obtained forgiveness from their victims, all receive another chance, another life on earth; only those who have lived a pious life, together with the incurably evil, are precluded forever from release from the body, banned eternally from contemplation of the "ideas."

Socrates confirms this terrible condemnation in the conclusion through which he finally brings to light a division within the class of the purified: whereas those who are found to have devoted themselves to the holy mount upward to dwell on the surface of the earth, only those "sufficiently purified by philosophy"—for the first time, Socrates does not say they merely appear so—live altogether without bodies, passing to even more beautiful abodes. Socrates removes, through this explicit distinction, the mask behind which he has, for certain purposes, provisionally hidden himself: release from the body is a reward not for those who pursued it as a goal—the initiates who will dwell with the gods (69c, 111b–c)—but only for those whose separation from the body is simultaneously separation from the self, from the inseparable union of soul with body. That this "sufficient purification by philosophy" consists in the turn to investigation through *logoi* Socrates suggests by admitting his inability to describe, in the context of this *mythos*, the abodes beyond the surface of the earth in which the bodiless philosopher belongs. In any case, Socrates concedes, his remaining time on earth would not suffice for the task—the very reason he gave for his inability to demonstrate the truth of the *mythos*, to which this account must be equivalent, and which was itself in turn equivalent to a continued examination of the first hypotheses of their arguments.

[114c6–115a2] But Socrates does not need to reach this point of sufficiency in order to affirm, in closing his address to Simmias, that it is necessary to participate in virtue and *phronēsis* "for the sake of these things"—namely, the "beautiful prize and great hope" of Tartarus for the evil and paradise for the pure. Of course it would not be fitting for a man with sense, Socrates acknowledges, to insist that everything is just as he has narrated. But it would be fitting to admit that something like it is true—since the soul is manifestly immortal—of our souls and their dwelling places: the paradoxical truth revealed by the *mythos* is that attachment to the soul entails attachment to the body.[52] It is worthwhile to risk accepting this, Socrates adds, for the danger is beautiful. Against the terrible danger of neglecting care for the soul (107c), one must risk the beautiful danger of chanting such a story to oneself, as if it were a magic charm—which is the reason, Socrates claims, that he has expanded the *mythos* for so long, given the brevity of the time left to him.

After reflecting in this way on the status of the *mythos*, and no longer addressing Simmias alone, Socrates announces once again what is required "for the sake of these things";[53] only now the motivation of hope for the beautiful prize has been replaced by acceptance of a beautiful danger, and what is necessary is only confidence about one's own soul, based on the way one has lived one's life. One would exhibit a very foolish confidence in dying, Cebes insisted, unless one possessed a complete demonstration of the immortality and imperishability of the soul (88b; cf. 95d). Socrates now concludes his *mythos*—as he did his initial defense (69c), as well as the first series of arguments (84a–b)—with his third and final affirmation of the alternative grounds for such confidence.[54] Socrates announced his wish, at the beginning of his initial defense, to explain why it appeared likely to him that a man who really spent his life in philosophy would be confident when about to die and of good hope for attaining great blessings there when he has died (63e–64a); like the mixture of *mythos* and *logos* introduced by that defense, which has been separated in the second half of the dialogue, the hope for reward after death and the confidence in dying that Socrates first combined have now been properly separated from each other.

He is confident about his own soul, Socrates concludes, who in his life "bid farewell" to the pleasures and adornments of the body as being alien, but was serious about those of learning. Socrates recalls the speech concluding the first half of the conversation, in which he described the "lovers of learning" who do not care for the body but for their own soul, who bid farewell to the lovers of the body while turning to follow philosophy wherever it leads (82c–d). But whereas the soul was then said to be enslaved to the body by submission to pleasure in general—since its source, Cebes agreed, is "mostly the visible things"—Socrates now, for the first time, admits the possibility of pleasures that belong properly to learning. To pursue these, Socrates adds, is to adorn the soul with no alien adornments, but with those that belong to it—moderation and justice and courage and freedom and truth. In his account of true virtue at the conclusion of his initial defense, Socrates added to moderation and justice and courage "*phronēsis* itself" (69b); he now replaces the latter, in his final description of the proper "cosmos" of the soul, with freedom and truth. He indicates the perhaps surprising distinction between, on the one hand, participation in *phronēsis* based on hope for the beautiful reward of a particular fate after death and, on the other, pursuit of the pleasures of learning and adornment of the soul with freedom and truth, based on the need to be confident about one's own soul in living and dying. But the distinction Socrates presents in reflecting on the status of his *mythos*, addressed to a man with sense, should be no more surprising than his separation of the pious, whose reward has been described most beautifully, from the philosopher, whose fate after death has been shrouded in silence.

Chapter Thirteen: *Pharmakon*

[115a3–116a3] Socrates concludes his *mythos* with a description of the man who is confident about his own soul and is therefore prepared for his journey into Hades when fate calls him. Indeed, his own time has now arrived, Socrates announces to his companions, "as a tragic man would say." Having described the journey of the souls of the dead into Hades and their cleansing in the rivers of the earth body, Socrates declares his intention, before departing on that journey, of cleansing his own body.[1] He betrays the corporeal root of the notion of purification and the metaphorical status of its interpretation as a separation of soul from body.[2] Despite his allusion to the call of fate, Socrates—who appears to have taken responsibility for attending the trial, for provoking the conviction, or at least the death sentence, and for having it carried out[3]—is determined now to bathe himself. For to do so is better, he believes—though perhaps a violation of established ritual—than to give the women the trouble (*pragmata parechein*) of bathing the corpse. Socrates' concern for the women seems to be his way of expressing the shame he feels at the thought of becoming, after death, a mere *pragma*. Yet Socrates attempts, precisely by speaking of the corpse, to separate "himself" from his body and to identify the latter as the alien *pragma* that is about to "admit death." The problematic character of this attempt is immediately indicated, however, by Phaedo's continuation of the narrative; for his reference to Socrates "himself" (*autos*) recalls the first word of the dialogue, which designated the living being as an inseparable whole consisting of body and soul. Just this question of the identity of the self becomes the explicit theme of the exchange Socrates shares with Crito in a brief interlude between announcing his intention of bathing himself and actually getting up to do so.

Crito, who has been silent ever since his initial interruption to report the warning concerning the effects of the poison, now returns to offer his aid to Socrates in carrying out any last wishes. Appearing only in the outer frame of the *logos*, Crito is the necessary support for Socrates' deeds. Asking Socrates for instructions regarding his children or anything else, Crito displays the same concern he showed in their private conversation.[4] And Socrates answers Crito, as he did throughout that conversation, that he has nothing new to request but only the same old demands:[5] if they take care of themselves—not only their souls!—they will serve Socrates and what is his, as well as themselves; but if they neglect themselves and the traces of the speeches uttered just now and long ago, no matter how intensely they might make promises at the moment, they would accomplish nothing. Just when Crito promises to strive eagerly to do as Socrates asks, however, he betrays the limitations of his eagerness;[6] for his very question—in what way Socrates wishes to be buried—violates just what Socrates claims to have been trying to establish throughout the conversation.

Bury me however you wish, Socrates responds, "if you can catch me and I don't escape." With that remark he laughed gently, Phaedo reports, while looking up at the others. Socrates displays the same painful pleasure as he did when he laughed gently at Simmias' hesitation to disturb him with an objection, wondering how he could persuade others that he was facing no misfortune, when he could not make even those present believe it (84e). Socrates cannot now persuade Crito, let alone others, that "I am just this Socrates who is now conversing and arranging each of the things spoken," for Crito could hardly be convinced that Socrates, his lifelong friend, is nothing but the *logos*. He seems to think, Socrates reproaches him, that all these speeches about his departure to the joys of the blessed have been uttered only to encourage his companions as well as himself.[7] But this is precisely the warning Socrates himself issued to his companions (91a): Socrates' attempted persuasion of Crito, who represents the human perspective as such, is, as always, an attempted persuasion of himself.

Continuing his bittersweet playfulness, Socrates requests that the young men give security to Crito, only the opposite of that which Crito offered the judges at the trial: Crito gave security that Socrates would remain in the Athenian prison,[8] whereas the young men are to give security that Socrates will not stay behind when he dies but will go away and withdraw. While Crito pledged that Socrates would not leave his cell, he devoted all his efforts to persuading him to run away; Socrates asks the young men to give assurance of his withdrawal at death, with full recognition of their desire that he remain at their side.[9] If Socrates were to withdraw, rather than remain behind and be destroyed at the approach of death, he would confirm in his own deed the *logos* concerning opposites themselves, or that which is essentially characterized by an opposite. Socrates thus recalls his description of the immortal that withdraws, in contrast with "the mortal of us" that dies when death approaches the man (106e). But to ascribe withdrawal at death to himself, Socrates must identify the soul with the self as a whole, while at the same time assuming its separation from the body.

Socrates indicates his awareness of this difficulty by emphasizing the way it is necessary to speak: in order that Crito may bear it more easily when he sees the body of Socrates being burned or buried and may not be troubled by the belief that Socrates himself will be suffering something terrible, he must not say that he is laying out "Socrates" or carrying away "Socrates." Such speeches, which are not beautifully spoken, implant some kind of evil in souls: the very name "Socrates," which presupposes the identity of him who is now conversing with that which will soon be laid out, borne to the tomb, and buried, produces that monster, the fear of death, which they have striven manfully to overcome. The separation that may be unintelligible in deed must be preserved in speech, for Crito must be confident—like the man who must be confident about his own soul (114d)—and say that it is only the body of Socrates that will be buried. It can be buried, therefore, in whatever way he finds most dear and lawful. While the characteristics of being dear and being lawful may not be identical for Crito—as his private conversation with Socrates indicates—Socrates tries, just as he did in that conversation, to satisfy simultaneously his own principle, the wishes of his friend Crito, and the demands of the law.[10]

Phaedo introduced this exchange by reporting that Socrates *autos* announced his intention of going to bathe; he concludes it by reporting "that one spoke these things, and then went inside to bathe and Crito followed him (*autos*)." Phaedo's narrative frame belies the theme of the exchange it surrounds: it reveals the limitations of mere speech in establishing the separation Socrates demands between himself and the silent, motionless corpse he will soon become. But "this Socrates now conversing and arranging each of the speeches" is in fact only a representation in Phaedo's narrative report: the reality behind the separation of Socrates from Socrates, of which he cannot persuade his companions or perhaps himself, is the separation of the living Socrates, whose life is about to come to an end, from the written image, created by the Platonic art of writing.

[116a4–116b8] Phaedo began his report with a description of the young men commanded by the jailer to wait outside the prison while the Eleven were releasing Socrates from his chains (59e); he now describes how they were ordered by Crito to wait outside the inner chamber of the prison cell while Socrates bathed himself. In this interval, Socrates performs an experiment, as it were, testing the young men's response to his absence. They began by conversing with each other about what had been spoken, Phaedo reports, but then turned to discuss in detail the misfortune that had befallen them. The speeches that may have convinced them that Socrates suffers nothing terrible in dying have only confirmed their own sense of being abandoned. The *pathos* they suffer is not pity but self-pity: Socrates' test run of his own absence testifies to his greater success in defending the prudence of his willingness to die than his justice in running away from friends and masters (cf. 63b).

"We felt simply as if we were being deprived of a father and would spend the rest of our lives as orphans,"[11] Phaedo admits, and then immediately reports that Socrates completed his bath and prepared for the visit of his own children, who were about to become real orphans.[12] The outer frame preceding the *logos*, when Crito helped carry out Socrates' wish of having Xanthippe taken home, is now complemented by the outer frame following the *logos*, when Crito remains with Socrates in the inner chamber to help carry out his directions to the women of the family. Socrates returned to them, Phaedo continues, only after spending a long time within—perhaps part of it alone[13]—for it was nearly sunset. Despite his promise to try to narrate everything, Phaedo's bodily absence from the inner chamber has the same effect, paradoxically, as his nonbodily absence from the philosophic peak of the discussion, which he could only report in the same summary outline. Phaedo's narration has progressed, in any case, almost completely from speech to deed, for when Socrates returned and sat down, "not much more was said."

[116b8–116d7] This closing of the frame around the *logos* is indicated by the entrance of the servant of the Eleven, the same man, presumably, who released Socrates from his chains at the outset of the day and gave directions about how he would die.[14] Despite, or perhaps because, he has taken no part in the discussion, only the servant of the Eleven acknowledges its suppressed political context. Just because he has not heard Socrates defend his belief that death is not an evil, he alone grasps Socrates' invisible anger and the knowledge on which it is based:[15]

Oh Socrates, I will not blame you as I do the others for being angry and cursing me when I, compelled by the rulers, pass on the order to drink the poison; but you I have known in all this time to be the noblest and gentlest and best man of all who ever arrived here, and now especially, I know that you are not angry with me but with those others, for you know who are to blame (*tous aitious*). (116c)

It is no accident that the man most concerned with the question of responsibility should bring to light the practical reflection of Socrates' theoretical analysis of cause (*to aition*): he hits upon the truth of Socrates' charge against those who are groping in the dark when they name as cause those subordinate conditions necessary for carrying out the intention that constitutes the true cause. As if he had heard Socrates acknowledge that the true causes of his situation were the Athenians' belief that it was best to condemn him and his own subsequent belief that it was best and most just to undergo the penalty they commanded (98c–99b), the servant of the Eleven expresses gratitude for Socrates' recognition of his subordinate status. He suggests, however inadvertently, that Socrates' anger might be directed justifiably even beyond the Athenian *dēmos*, insofar as it, too, is only a subordinate instrument for carrying out the intention of superiors: "It is perhaps not irrational," Socrates admitted, "that a man must not put himself to death before a god sends some necessity," as he judges to have now come to himself (62c).

The servant of the Eleven bids farewell to Socrates with words that Socrates might well address to himself: "Now, for you know what I have come to announce, farewell, and try to bear as easily as you can the necessities." As the man burst into tears with these words, Socrates looked straight up at him (*anablepsas*): Phaedo reports one more gesture, in a series of increasing intensity, that betrays the *pathē* concealed by speeches alone.[16] "Goodbye [*chaire*] to you too," Socrates responds, while promising to do what he advised. Socrates addresses to the servant of the Eleven the ambiguous farewell that he offered to none of his interlocutors but only asked Crito to deliver to the man in charge of administering the poison, when he issued the warning that Socrates should try to converse as little as possible (63d–e). But while dismissing the servant of the Eleven with the expression that has indicated delight in being rid of something troublesome, Socrates remarks to the others how "urbane" the man is; he has, after all, just praised Socrates as the best among the criminals he has known in the Athenian prison! Throughout the imprisonment, in fact, the man has been coming to visit and converse, Socrates mentions, and then praises him as the best of men. For while the others, moved by resentment concealed as pity, construe Socrates' death as evidently self-willed and have therefore put him on trial for injustice and imprudence, only the servant of the Eleven recognizes Socrates' noble and gentle anger, which is based on a true understanding of responsibility. As if foreseeing that the others are about to weep at their own misfortune, Socrates marvels at how nobly the servant of the Eleven weeps not for himself, but for Socrates.

[116d7–117e3] Having promised to try to bear as easily as possible "the necessities," Socrates asks Crito to have the poison brought out, or at least prepared. But Crito is as eager as ever to postpone these necessities: the sun has not yet set, he argues, and others have drunk the poison very late after the order was issued, meanwhile feasting and drinking and having intercourse with those they desired. Socrates does not repeat his account of the philosopher's disdain for the pleasures of the body; he acknowledges only that they would act suitably if they believed that they would profit from such actions, but he believes there is no profit in drinking the poison a little later. Just this realization that life no longer had any profit must have moved Socrates to embrace, rather than struggle against, the "call of fate," not simply at this final moment with the sun still upon the mountains, but from his first recognition of the intention of the Athenian *dēmos* to force him to give up the practice of philosophy.

Socrates is as successful in persuading Crito as he was, apparently, in persuading the Athenians that there was no point in continuing a life no longer worth living.[17] But, against his wishes, Socrates had to wait a long time, Phaedo remarks, after Crito signaled to the boy standing near that it was time to bring the man who was to administer the poison, to whose authority Socrates at last submits, after a daylong delay. When he asks, however, what he must do (*poiein*), he is told he must do nothing, only walk until his legs become heavy, then lie down, and the *pharmakon* will act of itself (*auto poiēsei*). Despite Socrates' will to maintain control over the act of dying, his transformation from an agent carrying out his own intentions to a motionless corpse will be fittingly accomplished as a mechanical result of the self-acting poison.

Socrates' painful recognition of this fact is both concealed and revealed by Phaedo's account of his response when handed the cup of poison. Interrupting his narrative to address himself to Echecrates—as if to relive as closely as possible the intense *pathē* of that moment—Phaedo describes how Socrates took the cup gently, without trembling or changing color or expression. But Phaedo's careful observation, which is in conflict with his own interpretation of it, betrays the truth of Socrates' experience: at the moment he took the cup so steadily, Phaedo adds, Socrates looked up at the man from under his brows, bull-like (*taurēdon hupoblepsas*). Socrates suddenly turns into an image of the Minotaur, the mythical monster symbolizing the fear of death. Socrates/Theseus has been victorious over that monster, thanks to his discovery of the safety of taking refuge in *logoi*. But the salvation of the *logos* is not, or is only in a sense, the salvation of Socrates himself:[18] with the cup of poison in his hands, Socrates betrays his realization that "this Socrates now conversing" is not identical with the *logos* itself. For this brief moment, perhaps, Socrates succumbs to the fear of death, or at least he presents that appearance to his audience.

Socrates asks, at the same moment, whether he might pour a libation from the drink to someone.[19] His request seems to be an accusation against the gods for imposing on him the present necessity;[20] that claim, after all, furnished Socrates' only defense against the charge of injustice in running away from life, and the implicit charge of impiety underlying it. But Socrates is prevented from expressing his ironic gratitude to the gods, for he is told that the authorities have prepared only as much poison as they believe measurable—enough, presumably, to end a man's life. When Socrates was warned originally, however, not to get heated up by conversing all day, or a greater quantity of poison would be required to produce its effect, he had boldly responded, "Let him prepare to give it twice, or if necessary thrice" (63e); that response calls to mind, in the present context, the formula of the libation, "Thrice to Zeus the savior."[21] Had Socrates remained silent all day, perhaps the cup of poison would have held enough to accomplish its primary purpose, with some to spare. The daylong conversation has replaced, it seems, a ritual libation to the gods: Socrates could not devote himself to the *logos* and at the same time display his piety, even in its most ironic form.

He must, nevertheless, offer to the gods at least a prayer, Socrates insists, that his change of abode from here to there be a fortunate one. With the simple wish, "May it come to be so,"[22] Socrates raised the cup to his lips and drank the draught, according to Phaedo, very readily and calmly. But the others, at the sight of this act, could no longer contain themselves; while Crito had been compelled to leave even earlier in tears, and Apollodorus had burst into wailing, making everyone but Socrates lose control, Phaedo wrapped his face up in his cloak,[23] he confesses, and wept for himself. Socrates reproaches the men—"Oh, wondrous ones"—for behavior he expected from the women he sent away, having heard that "it is neces-sary to die in silence" (*en euphēmia*).[24] Yet, since Socrates might have cho-sen, presumably, to remain in the inner chamber and die alone, he seems to have gone out of his way to compel his companions to watch him die.[25] He makes the occasion of his own death an experiment, intended to test the power of *logos* over the *pathē*;[26] but it is a test that none of his com-panions passes, for they check their tears finally only out of shame at Socrates' command—"Keep quiet and overcome."

[117e4–118a8] After walking about until his legs were heavy, Socrates lay down, Phaedo recounts, and the man administering the poison touched him, examining his feet and legs, until when he pinched his foot hard, Socrates felt nothing. After being released from his chains at dawn, Socrates sat up and rubbed his own leg, remarking on the paradoxical experience caused by release from the pain of being fettered, which was itself recog-nized only in retrospect as the condition for the subsequent feeling of pleas-ure. Now at dusk, Socrates can no longer actively rub his own leg, which has been rendered motionless and numb by the poison: Socrates is being released from the self-imposed chains of attachment to pleasure and pain.[27]

As the poison extended its effect, the attendant continued his exami-nation upward, demonstrating to the others—apparently having them, too, feel Socrates' body—that he was growing cold and rigid. A war of op-posites—heat and cold, life and death—is being played out on the battle-field of the body of Socrates. As soon as the cold reached the heart, the attendant explained, he would depart:[28] just as the servant of the Eleven unwittingly confirmed Socrates' theoretical analysis of cause, the man who administers the poison unwittingly confirms his account of that which must withdraw, if it is not to be destroyed, at the approach of an opposite. When the numbness reached the area of the groin, Phaedo con-tinues, Socrates uncovered his head, for it had been covered some time, apparently, after he lay down on his back and the attendant began to ex-amine his body growing cold. Was Socrates, then, like Phaedo, compelled by shame at his fear or self-pity to cover his head? Or did Socrates, who just identified himself in relation to others, as "the Socrates who is now conversing," cover himself solely for the sake of his companions? Actually, we are not told that it was Socrates himself who performed the deed. The very fact that his head was covered is revealed, in any case, only in retro-spect, when Socrates uncovers himself—like the pain that is revealed as pain only when release from it is experienced as pleasure.

Socrates manifests this recovery when the numbness reaches the organ of generation. He addresses to Crito at this moment his last words: "To Asclepius we owe a cock;[29] but pay it and do not neglect it." Socrates marks his success in the practice of dying by remembering the god of healing; he believes it necessary, apparently, to supplement the hymn to Apollo he claims to have produced as a rite of purification.[30] Asclepius should be a model for the best physician, Socrates argues on one occasion,[31] since he was willing to heal those who could recover and lead a normal life, but not those who would go on living only with suffering or with constant pampering. Socrates contrasts his own view, however, with that of Pindar and the tragedians, who affirm that Asclepius, though a son of Apollo, was bribed by gold to heal a man already at the point of death. Asclepius, whom Socrates now thinks of in his last words, seems, then, to have a double significance. Does Socrates express his gratitude to the healing god, who knows when it is no longer worth living, for his own recovery from the disease of life?[32] Or does Socrates, who announced his call of fate "as a tragic man would say," offer at the last moment a bribe to the healing god to fight off the approach of death—one last affirmation of the goodness of life?[33]

Whatever union of opposites Socrates is portrayed as experiencing at his release from life, Plato has him express appreciation for another recovery that is concurrent with the portrayal of that release. From Phaedo's narrative we know of one case of illness—the cause of Plato's absence from the scene of Socrates' death (59b); and the sign of recovery from that illness is nothing but the Platonic dialogue itself, which has provided this image of the dying Socrates. The *pharmakon* that Socrates drinks is simultaneously a poison that brings his life to an end and a remedy that cures a disease. But it is a different *pharmakon*—that of the written word[34]—that truly fulfills the practice of dying, as a separation of *logos* from the living self. The Platonic Socrates thus invests his dying words with an appropriate implication of gratitude—Thank god for Plato!

[118a9–118a17] Crito agreed to carry out Socrates' wish and was ready for any further requests; but Socrates made no reply, and after a little while, Phaedo remarks, he moved. Socrates' original formulation of what death is revealed it to be two things—the body becoming separate from the soul and the soul being separate from the body (64c). Socrates now enacts in deed this double determination in speech. If his last words mark the withdrawal of the soul, his last movement must be an involuntary reflex of the body; or rather, as the course of the dialogue has taught, what seem to be separate signs of soul and body are in fact the signs of soul as agent of thought or speech and soul as source of motion or life, with the former dependent on the latter. That Socrates' final intentional action must have been to re-cover his face after uttering his request to Crito is revealed, once again, only retrospectively: after that last unwilled movement, Phaedo reports, Socrates was uncovered by the attendant. But the final deeds are performed, of course, by Crito: without disclosing whether he remembered the speeches Socrates recommended to inspire confidence, Crito covered the eyes and mouth of the corpse.[35]

Having completed his account of everything said and done, Phaedo closes the frame around his narration: "Such was the end of our friend, of all those of his time the best and most prudent [*phronimos*] and most just." He pays tribute to Socrates only as the best of his contemporaries: Socrates *is* no longer. The true "cause" of his death, Socrates insisted, was his belief that it was more just and noble to endure the penalty imposed by the Athenians, who found him guilty of injustice and impiety. But it is with regard to the charges of injustice and imprudence, for which Socrates was put on trial on the last day of his life, that Phaedo pronounces the final judgment of exoneration. He is silent about Socrates' piety;[36] or, one could say, he replaces that question with the judgment about his superlative goodness.

Notes

Introduction

1. The variety of approaches to the dialogues might be divided into three kinds—subject to all the usual qualifications of any typification: (a) The tradition predominant in English language scholarship is interested primarily in analyzing the arguments, abstracted from their literary presentation; as a result, fallacies in the arguments are generally assumed to be due to Plato's failure to carry out his intention, while credit for our recognition of these fallacies is often given to contemporary tools of analysis. (b) The tradition represented primarily by the Tübingen school (see the works of Hans Joachim Krämer and Konrad Gaiser referred to in the bibliography) takes its bearings from the reports of Plato's "unwritten teachings" in Aristotle and later doxographic sources; it seeks, on that basis, to reconstruct the systematic character of Platonic philosophy, in contrast to which the dialogues are thought to have merely a protreptic function. (c) According to the tradition that can be traced back at least to Friedrich Schleiermacher (see also n. 11 below), the Platonic dialogue is a unified whole, whose philosophic content cannot be separated from its dramatic form, since the latter is no mere compromise but in fact the only proper mode for philosophic communication through the written word.

2. See Francis M. Cornford, *The Republic of Plato*, xxv.

3. See Hans Wagner, "Platos Phaedo und der Beginn der Metaphysik als Wissenschaft," 363–82.

4. See R. Hackforth, *Plato's Phaedo*, 3; see also A. E. Taylor, *Plato: The Man and His Work*, 176.

5. See Hackforth, 3.

6. For a review of the controversy, see Hackforth, 127–31. See also n. 24 below, and ch. 10, n. 1.

7. See G. M. A. Grube, *Plato's Thought*, 129.

8. See Leo Strauss, "Plato," in *History of Political Philosophy*, 7.

9. See *Phaedrus* 274d–278b; and Ronna Burger, *Plato's Phaedrus: A Defense of a Philosophic Art of Writing*—particularly the introduction and ch. 6, "The Art of Writing."

10. *Phaedrus* 264b–c.

11. On the approach to the reading of the dialogues advocated here, see especially Leo Strauss, *The City and Man*, 50–63; Jacob Klein, "Introductory Remarks" to *A Commentary on Plato's Meno*, 3–31; and Stanley Rosen, introduction to *Plato's Symposium*, xi–xxxviii.

12 This qualification was inspired by the recent appearance of two books on the *Phaedo*
that claim to be guided by the same hermeneutic principle: Jerome Eckstein, *The
Deathday of Socrates: Living, Dying, and Immortality—The Theater of Ideas in Plato's
Phaedo*; and Kenneth Dorter, *Plato's Phaedo: An Interpretation*. That this common
claim leads to very different results, which distinguish the two works from each other
and from the present study, is instructive. In *Deathday of Socrates*, Jerome Eckstein's
concern with how "psycho-dramatic reality pervades and tempers the dialogue's logic"
(51) leads him to see the arguments as "one prolonged blast of Platonic irony" (11),
motivated by Plato's primary intent to discredit the rationality of Socrates' "heroic
suicide." Of course it is not clear that this thesis could account for the specific ways
in which each argument is ironic, nor for the structure that relates them to one another.
That Socrates presents fallacious arguments for immortality, in any case, does not necessarily mean that he is portrayed as believing them, or even wanting to believe them;
in fact he repeatedly indicates his awareness of their deficiency, and when he acknowledges the true motivation for his acceptance of his death, it is not a belief in immortality to which he refers.

   In *Plato's Phaedo: An Interpretation*, Dorter seeks to synthesize the analytic with
the dramatic approach, which he takes to be influenced in part by Schopenhauer's and
Husserl's views of the superiority of direct to indirect evidence. But since Platonic
dramaturgy surely requires for its interpretation "inferring," not merely "intuiting,"
it hardly seems to be a direct means of conveying insights, in contrast to the "indirect
and often tendentious technique of argument" (ix). By attending to Socrates' rhetorical
purpose, Dorter recognizes that his attempt to demonstrate the personal immortality
of the soul is only an appeal to "popular religious imagination"; yet Socrates does
demonstrate, Dorter thinks, a meaningful sense of immortality, whose subject is the
"world-soul" of which all individual souls are portions (44, 157). It is not at all evident,
however, that a demonstration of such "impersonal immortality," any more than one
of "personal immortality," could avoid the fundamental misconceptions that Socrates
warns against when he insists on the necessity of replacing "investigation of the beings
themselves" by his own "second sailing" and illustrates that replacement in the final
argument of the dialogue.

13 The traditional Greek understanding of *psychē* (regularly translated here and elsewhere
as "soul") is brought to light in Aristotle's account of the views handed down by his
predecessors: the distinguishing characteristics of soul are thought to be its functions
as source of movement or life and of sensation or cognition (see especially *De Anima* 1.2).

14 This is emphasized by Schleiermacher in the introduction to his translation of the
Phaedo. See his *Platons Werke*, 2(3), 9. "Wir...treffen hier," Hegel remarks on the
Phaedo, "am wenigsten geschieden die Weise des Vorstellens und des Begriffes" (*Vor-
lesungen über die Geschichte der Philosophie*, 52).

15 Using the Greek word rather than a translation makes it possible to preserve the multiplicity of associations with *logos*, including the broad sense of speech as opposed to
deed and the precise sense of argument as opposed to myth.

16 See Aristotle *Metaphysics* 987b10–14, 29–32.

17 See Aristotle's critique of this doctrine, *De Anima* 407b20–24.

18 "Music" might seem, consequently, to be too restrictive a translation of *mousikē*; but
it is intended to capture Socrates' reconstruction—as well as its possible Pythagorean
source (see John Burnet, *Plato's Phaedo*, note on 61a3)—in labeling philosophy "the
greatest music," and thus indicating its continuity with, as well as difference from,

poetry as "demotic music." On the translation of *mousikē*, see Allan Bloom, *The Republic of Plato*, xiii. The command of Socrates' dream—*poiei kai ergazou*—might be translated "do" or "practice" music, but it seems here to have the connotation "produce" and "fabricate works."

19 See *Apology* 28d–29a.

20 See *Crito* 48b–e and the entire speech Socrates delivers in the name of the laws of Athens.

21 In the ordinary sense, which appears frequently in the Platonic dialogues (see, for example, *Symposium* 209a), *phronēsis* means practical wisdom, a capacity for sound judgment, especially in political affairs. When Cebes first raises the question of whether the *phronimos* man would not be most fearful of death (62d), he seems to understand *phronēsis* as the prudential pursuit of one's true self-interest. Yet this would seem to be a very odd capacity to ascribe to the disembodied soul, as the "genuine philosophers" do, and as Cebes asks Socrates to prove. The tension between the two demonstrations Cebes demands—of Socrates' prudence in accepting his death and of the possession of *phronēsis* by the soul after death—makes the meaning of *phronēsis* a thematic question of the dialogue.

22 *Pragma*, which is most often translated simply as "thing," is related to the word *praxis* and often has the connotation of being a matter of importance or concern. Socrates clarifies its particular usage in the *Phaedo* when he distinguishes "opposites themselves," which are always mutually exclusive, from "opposite *pragmata*," the things characterized by those opposites that come to be from each other (103b). A *pragma* in this particular sense is a subject characterized by a quality, like "Socrates greater" or "Socrates smaller"; while it is contrasted with the qualities "greatness" or "smallness," which remain what they are through all changes, it denies the possibility of an identical subject, "Socrates," which remains the same through all changes.

23 *Technē* is here translated "art" in the sense of a set of rules or method of making or doing. Socrates distinguishes it, in the *Gorgias* (465a), from mere practice based on experience (*empeiria*), which cannot give a *logos* of its subject and lacks knowledge of cause.

24 Socrates' pre-Socratic starting point therefore illustrates the necessity of beginning in error. If his intellectual autobiography were simply an account of an accidental development, rather than a necessary one, it would be hard to explain, as Michael Davis argues, why the *Phaedo* should reproduce that development in its own structure ("Socrates' Pre-Socratism: Some Remarks on the Structure of Plato's *Phaedo*," 574).

25 See *Phaedrus* 274e–275a; cf. Jacques Derrida, "La Pharmacie de Platon."

Chapter One

1 Within the Platonic corpus, four dialogues present a Socratic conversation through the perspective of a narrator other than Socrates himself: the *Phaedo* and *Theaetetus*, in which Socrates seems to choose the reporter who will reconstruct the conversation after his death, are complemented by the *Parmenides* and the *Symposium*, in which a young Socrates and Socrates' own report of himself when young, respectively, are represented through the recollection of multiple reporters. The *Theaetetus*, whose narrator and auditor appear among those present at Socrates' death, is the first, according to dramatic chronology, and apparently most aporetic, of the dialogues centering on Socrates' trial and death, the *Phaedo* the last and apparently most dogmatic. Socrates' account, in this last conversation, of his way of investigation through *logoi* recalls the lesson he learns in the *Parmenides* when criticized for his inadequate defense of the ideas and asked to

follow Parmenides' model of a "hypothetical method." The most emotional of those present at the conversation on the day of Socrates' death, which begins at dawn and ends at dusk, is the narrator of the *Symposium*, which begins at dusk and ends at dawn, when Socrates compels two poets to admit the possibility of the same man writing by art both tragedy and comedy. The dialogue on *erōs* and the dialogue on the "practice of dying" seem to form together one whole (see ch. 13, n. 29); they represent, Friedrich Schleiermacher suggests, "two aspects of the philosopher as such." See the Introduction to his translation of the *Phaedo* in *Platons Werke*, 2(3), 5–8.

2 Compare "*Platōn de oimai ēsthenai* " (59b) with Phaedo's introduction, "*hōs men egō oimai* " (102a) to his summary of what seems to be the philosophic peak of the dialogue.

3 The first word points ahead, at the same time, to the formula for the separate *eidos*, "*auto kath' auto*" (100b; cf. 65d, 66a, 74a, 75c–d, 78d, 103b, e, 106d).

4 The only other occasion is in the *Apology*, where Socrates mentions that Plato is present (34a), and that he, along with Crito, Crito's son, and Apollodorus, commanded Socrates to propose a fine, for which they would give security, large enough to satisfy the jury (38b). Eckstein interprets Plato's absence from the *Phaedo* as a sign of his disapproval of Socrates' decision to accept the death sentence (*The Deathday of Socrates*, 28, 30).

5 In no other dialogue, Schleiermacher remarks in his Introduction to the *Phaedo*, is the mimetic element so completely determined by, and unified with, its subject matter, and nowhere does it have a greater right to be so. See *Platons Werke* 2(3), 9.

6 Cf. *Phaedo* 117d, *Symposium* 173d–e, *Apology* 34a.

7 Phlius, home of Echecrates and the last of the Pythagoreans, is, according to legend, where Pythagoras first used the word "*philosophos*" (see Diogenes Laertius *Lives of Eminent Philosophers* 8.46; Cicero *Tusculan Disputations* 5.3). It provides the fitting context for Phaedo's reconstruction of the conversation Socrates is about to begin with an appeal to the "genuine philosophers."

8. Phaedo does not specify the length of time that passed between Socrates' trial and death, but Xenophon tells us that it was thirty days (*Memorabilia* 4.8.2).

9 See Plutarch's *Lives*, "Theseus," ch. 23.

10 While pity is distress at our neighbor's misfortune and envy at his prosperity, a man who comes to feel one, Cicero maintains, is always susceptible to the other (*Tusculan Disputations* 3.20–21).

11 On these individuals, and the other Platonic dialogues in which some appear, see John Burnet, *Plato's Phaedo*, 7–11; see also W. D. Geddes, *The Phaedo of Plato*, 195–202.

12 Consider the characterization of Menexenus in the *Lysis* (especially 211b–c) and of Ctesippus in the *Euthydemus* (especially 283e, 288b, 300d).

13 On the correspondence that makes the *Phaedo* a mythological account of Socrates' death, in which the "new and true Theseus" is Socrates, and the "old and true Minotaur is the monster called Fear of Death," see Jacob Klein, "Plato's *Phaedo*," 1–2.

14 Referring to the absent Aristippus, Cleombrotus, and Plato, Phaedo brings his list to seventeen. Five of those he names appear in the list of seventeen young men, together with their fathers or brothers, whom Socrates mentions at his public trial as those with whom he conversed (*Apology* 33d–34a). This list happens to be parallel, Leo Strauss observes, to the list of seventeen named or unnamed individuals—including the poets and their fictional characters!—with whom Socrates claims he would like to converse in Hades (*Apology* 41a–c). See Leo Strauss, "On Plato's *Apology of Socrates* and *Crito*," 160–63.

15 See *Phaedrus* 264b–c, and the discussion of logographic necessity in the Introduction above.

16 See *Apology* 30e–31a.

17 The phrase that literally means "for the sake of the holy" (*hosias heneka*) comes to mean "for form's sake." See Seth Benardete, *Sacred Transgressions: A Reading of Sophocles' Antigone*, 106, 110.

18 The first of the cases mentioned in Plato's *Laws* in which suicide is not to be punished—followed by the stress of cruel and inevitable calamity or desperate and intolerable disgrace—is the sentence of the city requiring self-slaughter (873c).

19 Cf. *Crito* 45e–46a.

20 See *Republic* 514a–520d.

21 See *Apology* 37e–38a.

22 See *Crito* 52e, 53d–e.

23 See *Crito* 53b–c.

24 Socrates does not tell Crito why he could not travel to far away well-governed cities like Sparta or Crete, which the laws mention (52e)—precisely the journey undertaken by the Athenian Stranger of Plato's *Laws*, whom Aristotle calls "Socrates" (*Politics* 2.6). See Strauss' remarks on the Athenian Stranger in *The Argument and the Action of Plato's Laws*, 2.

25 See *Theaetetus* 143a–c.

26 See W. K. C. Guthrie, *A History of Greek Philosophy*, 1:179.

Chapter Two

1 The dream speaks in the words of Achilles, who stubbornly rejects Odysseus' entreaty to return to the war by threatening to set sail for his homeland Phthia (*Iliad* 9.363). Achilles' homeland is in lawless Thessaly, where Crito proposes Socrates should escape (*Crito* 53d). But the beautiful woman in Socrates' dream must be the goddess Thetis, who warns her son Achilles that, if he avenges the death of Patroclus, "immediately after Hector, death is appointed unto thee" (*Iliad* 18.96). Achilles' rejection of a long but disgraceful life is the response Socrates cites in his public trial when he insists that he must remain at his appointed station of practicing philosophy (*Apology* 28d). By combining the two Homeric passages in the dream he relates to Crito, Socrates can affirm the journey to death as his true homeland, without abandoning responsibility to Athens. See the analysis of this passage by Leo Strauss, "On Plato's *Apology of Socrates* and *Crito*," 164–65.

2 See *Crito* 43a.

3 On the function of the Eleven and their connection with public execution, see Aristotle *Athenian Constitution*, 52. The jailer's reference to "the Eleven" in general anticipates the question of responsibility, which is appropriately brought up at the conclusion of the dialogue by the "servant of the Eleven" (cf. 116c).

4 Plato seems to go out of his way to let us know that Socrates, who is about to speak of the philosopher's desire to escape from the body, is the father of a child young enough to be held in his wife's arms (cf. *Apology* 34d).

5 In the *Crito*, for example, we are never told that Socrates rose from his reclining position for a conversation in which he conspicuously avoids the words "*psychē*" or "*philosophia*" (see 47d–48a).

6 What Xanthippe is reproached for, it seems, is the fact that she cried out (*aneuphēmēse*); when the men can no longer hold back their tears at the sight of Socrates drinking the poison, he reproaches them for acting like women, reminding them that "it is necessary to die in *euphēmia*" (117e, cf. ch. 13, n. 24).

7   Lamentation (*threnon*) stands at the center of Socrates' list of seven *pathē* in which the soul itself suffers from a mixture of pleasure and pain (*Philebus* 47d–e).

8   Socrates expresses the same wonder each time he confronts a problem of the relation of opposites (cf. 60b, 62a, 97a).

9   The "wishing" of pleasure and pain not to come to be present together is like the "wishing" of greatness or smallness in us not to admit the other, which may require the destruction of one at the approach of its opposite (see 102d–e).

10   Perhaps no one would ever claim that pain is simply the cessation of pleasure; but the more persuasive claim that pleasure is simply the cessation of pain can be denied only by establishing the possibility of an autonomous intermediate state that is neither pleasure nor pain (see *Philebus* 43d–44d; *Republic* 583c–585a).

11   On the command of Socrates' dream—to "make music"—see Introduction, n.18. The identity of Socrates' dream, despite its multiple variants (cf. *Apology* 33c) poses another version of the problem implicitly raised by the identity of the Athenian ship (see ch. 1, n. 9) and finally by the identity of an individual whose body is constantly being worn away and replaced within one lifetime (87d–e).

12   See *Apology* 23a–b.

13   On the possible Pythagorean source of the identification of philosophy as "the greatest music," see W. D. Geddes, *Phaedo of Plato*, 209.

14   Cf. *Apology* 20b–c; *Phaedrus* 267a.

15   The misunderstanding against which Socrates issues this warning is illustrated by the anecdote reported by Cicero (*Tusculan Disputations* 1.84): according to Callimachus, Cleombrotus of Ambracia was so convinced that death is no misfortune that he flung himself from the city wall into the sea after reading Plato's book.

16   Philolaus, said to be the first to put Pythagorean teaching into writing, taught at Thebes, to which he escaped after the expulsion of the sect from southern Italy (see W. K. C. Guthrie, *History of Greek Philosophy*, 1:179). Clement of Alexandria claims to quote Philolaus on the source of his Pythagorean teaching: "The ancient theological writers and prophets also bear witness that the soul is yoked to the body as a punishment and buried in it as in a tomb" (*Stromata* 3.17). Among other echoes in the *Phaedo* of doctrines ascribed to Philolaus is Simmias' image, supported by Echecrates (88d), of the soul as a harmony (see Guthrie, 1:312). For a critique of the authenticity of the fragments assigned to Philolaus and a defense of their post-Platonic source, see Erich Frank, *Platon und die sogennanten Pythagoreer*, especially 291–302.

17   Compare Diotima's warning that Socrates must be eager to follow her initiation into the mysteries of *erōs* (*Symposium* 210a), Socrates' acknowledgment of his eagerness to initiate Meno into the mysteries of the proper way to give a unified definition of virtue (*Meno* 77a), and Socrates' admission to Glaucon that his eagerness to reveal the idea of the good could make him look ridiculous (*Republic* 506d). Cf. the analysis of the latter passages by Konrad Gaiser, "Platons *Menon* und die Akademie," 348, and Hans Joachim Krämer, "Über den Zusammenhang von Prinzipienlehre und Dialektik bei Platon," 431–32.

18   For an analysis of proposed translations and interpretations of this passage, see David Gallop, *Plato's Phaedo*, 79–83, Kenneth Dorter, *Plato's Phaedo*, 12–16; and Geddes, 213–17.

19   This would seem to be the Platonic reversal of the "tragic" understanding of divine jealousy, according to which the gods would claim that death is better for man than life. Cf. Cicero *Tusculan Disputations* 1.113–15. Consider Herodotus' report of the

story Solon tells Croesus, which presents two contrasting responses to the question of human happiness: the point of view of the sacred is represented by the fate of Cleobus and Biton, through whom "the god showed it was better for a man to die than to live" (*Histories* 1.31.3). See the analysis by Seth Benardete, *Herodotean Inquiries*, 185, 212.

20 As Nietzsche puts it: "Man muß durchaus seine Finger danach ausstrecken und den Versuch machen, diese erstaunliche finesse zu fassen, daß der Wert des Lebens nicht abgeschätzt werden kann. Von einem Lebenden nicht, weil ein solcher Partei, ja sogar Streitobjekt ist und nicht Richter; von einem Toten nicht, aus einem anderen Grunde" ("*Das Problem des Sokrates*," §2, in *Götzen-Dämmerung*). Cf. Michael Davis, "Plato and Nietzsche on Death: An Introduction to Plato's *Phaedo*," 78.

21 The "simplicity" of the divine prohibition against suicide will inspire wonder, Geddes proposes (215–17), precisely because it is valid even for those and on those occasions when death is indeed superior. Or, as Hans Reynen argues, the dubiousness of the claim that life is always superior is meant to put into question the unconditional status of the divine prohibition against suicide ("Phaidon Interpretationen: zu Plat. *Phaed*. 62a und 69a–b," 42–46).

22 Olympiodorus interprets Socrates' cryptic formulation to mean that suicide is forbidden with regard to the body that it harms but justified because of a greater good to the soul (*Commentary on the Phaedo* 1.9).

23 Once this ambiguity is taken into account, it is no longer as easy to find in this passage, as Jerome Eckstein does, Plato's accusation of Socrates for the decision to take his own life (*Deathday of Socrates*, 13, 45).

24 Cf. the etymology of "Zeus," which Socrates derives from his two names (*Zēna* and *Dia*): together they signify the nature of "the god through whom all the living always have life" (*Cratylus* 396a–b).

25 See *Crito* 51b–e.

26 See *Apology* 28d–e.

27 The word *phroura*, which appears in a fragment assigned to Philolaus (DK 32B15), could mean either prison (see *Gorgias* 525a) or guard house (see *Critias* 117d; *Laws* 760a, c, 762c). Cf. Socrates' etymology of "body" (*sōma*) in connection with "to keep safe" (*sōzetai*, *Cratylus* 400c), which is juxtaposed with an etymology connecting "body" and "grave" (*sēma*), in which the soul is said to be buried (cf. *Gorgias* 493a).

28 Cf. *Laws* 902b, 906a; *Critias* 109b.

29 Cf. Phaedo's final judgment on Socrates as "the most *phronimos*" man of his time (118a). Cebes unwittingly puts into question the relation between the understanding of *phronēsis* as a state of the pure soul after death, which Socrates ascribes to the genuine philosophers, and Socrates' own understanding and exemplification of *phronēsis* (cf. 69a, b, c, 94b, 107d, 108a, 114c).

30 See *Apology* 26b–28a.

31 Cf. *Cratylus* 403a–404b.

32 See *Phaedo* 100d; cf. 114d; *Meno* 86b.

33 Appropriately, Simmias brings to mind the Pythagorean maxim—"Friends have all in common." (See Iamblichus, *Vita Pythagorae* 81, 87; cf. *Phaedrus* 279c; *Lysis* 207c; *Republic* 449c; *Laws* 739c). But just to the extent that Simmias does not share with Socrates the need he expresses, he puts into question the possibility of their "friendship."

34 See 60b–c and 103a–c.

35 Cf. 63e, 64c, 65c, 82d, 83d, 100d, 101e, d, 114e, 116d.

36 See *Apology* 29c–d.
37 Cf. *Gorgias* 498e; *Philebus* 59e–60a, *Laws* 957a; and the remarks of Paul Friedländer, *Platon,* 3:61.

Chapter Three

1   Contrast *Apology* 40a and 38c.
2   Paul Friedländer (*Platon,* 3:473) appropriately refers to Heidegger's description of *sein zum Tode* as a condition of which *Dasein* would be deprived by death itself.
3   The word "*philosophountes*"—which Simmias introduces and Socrates uses throughout his defense, along with "true philosophizers" and "correct philosophizers"—often seems to have a derogatory sense, indicating particularly the disdainful conception of the philosopher on the part of the many (cf. *Apology* 23d; or Callicles' speech in the *Gorgias* 485b, c, d.)
4   Socrates, who won't profess knowledge when conscious of his own ignorance, can hardly have the attitude toward life that he ascribes to the "true philosophers," as R. Hackforth argues (*Plato's Phaedo,* 16).
5   Cf. 65d, 74a, 100b, 102a–b. On the status of the agreement that something is, which seems to be the necessary premise for determining *what* it is, see Hans Wagner, "Die Eigenart der Ideenlehre in Platons Phaedo," 6.
6   At the conclusion of his public trial, Socrates defends the possibility that the death sentence he has received may be something good, on the basis of the presumably exhaustive alternative that death is either a continuation of his own life on earth, or that it is a "wondrous gain" simply in being virtually nothing, like the most unconscious dreamless sleep (see *Apology* 40c–e).
7   Cf. *Philebus* 47b.
8   Olympiodorus finds it puzzling that the attainment of *phronēsis,* ordinarily understood as the statesman's practical judgment (cf. *Symposium* 209a), should be designated as the goal of the philosopher's purification after death (*Commentary on the Phaedo* 3.6).
9   See ch. 2, n. 35.
10 Continuing, however ironically, his attempted unification of demotic music with the greatest music, Socrates appeals to the poets who are constantly "drumming into our ears" that the sight and hearing of men have no contact with the truth (65b); Socrates will characterize in the same way the *ousia* he is always "drumming into our ears" (cf. 76d–e, 100b1). Olympiodorus (4.13), surprised perhaps by Socrates' reference to the poets, suggests that they are Parmenides, Empedocles, and Epicharmus, as well as Homer, from whom he quotes *Iliad* 5.127–28.
11 Consider Socrates' etymology of "Phersephone" (*Cratylus* 404c–d), or of *sophia* (412b). Cf. Aristotle, *De Anima* 424a17–24, 429a13–18, 432a1–3; and the analysis by Stanley Rosen, in "Thought and Touch: A Note on Aristotle's *De Anima,*" 127–37, especially 132.
12 Cf. *Meno* 72d–e, *Philebus* 26b.
13 Cf. 78d, 92d, 101c; and David Gallop's note on this phrase (*Plato Phaedo,* 227, 230). See also Hans Wagner's account of *ousia* as the general title for the determination of the object, "that which each happens to be" ("Die Eigenart der Ideenlehre," 8). The connection between the philosophic sense of *ousia* and its ordinary meaning as "property" is preserved in our use of the word "substance."
14 Cf. 67c, 79a; cf. also *Sophist* 227c.

15 When Theaetetus is puzzled by the Eleatic Stranger's division of hunting into that of living and lifeless prey, the Stranger affirms that both exist, although no special name belongs to the latter (*Sophist* 220a); he brings to light Theaetetus' ignorance of their own effort. See also *Euthydemus* 290b–d, or the legislation about hunting with which the Athenian Stranger completes his regulation of education (*Laws* 823b–824c).

16 Either they are led themselves "together with the *logos*" to this conclusion (see Gallop, 11, 227), or, assuming Schleiermacher's transposition, they are led to recognize the hindrance of having "the body together with the *logos* in the investigation," echoing Socrates' prior description (66a) of investigating without dragging the senses along with *logismos* (see John Burnet, *Plato's Phaedo*, 36). In either case, the genuine philosophers are far more preoccupied with their resentment of the contamination of the soul by the body than they are with considering what the role of *logos* is.

17 It is on the basis of the principle, "Like knows like," Aristotle asserts, that his predecessors established their various accounts of soul (*De Anima* 405b14–16). In his concluding myth, describing those purified by philosophy, Socrates speaks, not of their knowing the pure beings, but living—without bodies—in pure and beautiful dwelling places (114c).

18 Cf. 82c, 83e. Socrates attempts to establish the combination of philosophic and "thumoeidetic" traits in the nature of the guardians of his best city by obtaining Glaucon's agreement, without examination, on the identity of love of wisdom and love of learning; the latter is supposed to be exemplified by the dog, who is friendly to the familiar and hostile to the unknown, regardless of benefit or harm (*Republic* 376a–c).

19 Socrates will recall this passage in his mythological description of the purified soul being released from the regions within the earth as from a prison (114b–c). Cf. *Timaeus* 69c–70a.

20 Cf. *Phaedrus* 265d–e, 266b; *Sophist* 253d; *Statesman* 282b, 287c.

21 See *Sophist* 226d.

22 But laughter, or even a gentle smile, may be a sign of fear, as the deeds reported by Phaedo suggest: see 59a, 62a, 64a, 77e, 84d, 86d, 115c. On laughter as a mixture of pleasure and pain, see *Philebus* 50a.

23 Cf. *Phaedo* 80d, 81a; *Gorgias* 493b; *Cratylus* 403a.

24 Cf. *Phaedrus* 227c, 257a–b, *Symposium* 177d–e; *Theages* 128b; *Lysis* 204b–e. In the conversation he conducts with Theaetetus after hearing of his indictment and before his trial, Socrates ascribes to himself an art not of erotics, but of midwifery, modeled on that of women who are too old to conceive and bear children of their own (*Theaetetus* 149b–150d).

25 The sign Socrates interprets as a "divine necessity" sanctioning this release may be the disappearance of his *daimonion*; for he attributes to its noninterference his decision to face the trial while aware of its likely outcome (*Apology* 40c). The *daimonion* does seem to provide or protect Socrates' life impulse: it kept him not only from unpromising associations (*Theages* 128d–130e), but also from participation in politics, which might have meant an early death (*Republic* 496c–d; *Apology* 31d).

26 That the love of pleasure is omitted here as a sign of love of the body (see Olympiodorus 7.5, Damascius 1.137) suggests that, while the genuine philosophers identify all love of the body with love of pleasure, Socrates silently rejects the identification of all pleasure as corporeal (cf. 114e).

27 Cf. *Republic* 580d–581c.

28 Cf. *Apology* 37c; *Gorgias* 512e; *Laws* 944e.

29 Socrates seems to adopt—as he did in his nonsymmetrical analysis of the so-called pleas-
    ant and the painful (60b)—the assumption of the severe men he describes to Protarchus,
    who claim that all pleasure is nothing but release from pain (see *Philebus* 43c–44d).

30 Cf. *Protagoras* 355b–356c. Aristotle begins his account of the specific moral virtues
    with courage followed by moderation, "for these seem to be the virtues of the irrational
    parts" (*Nicomachean Ethics* 1117b23–24).

31 If courageous action can be produced not only by courage itself, but also by cowardice,
    moderate action not only by moderation itself, but also by incontinence, not only would
    opposite causes produce the same result (97a–b), but also one cause would produce a
    result opposite to its own nature (101b); and if fear of pain could produce courage as
    well as cowardice, while fear of deprivation of pleasure could produce moderation as
    well as incontinence, one cause would in each case produce opposite results (101a).

32 If Socrates does face death courageously, is it not because he fears as a worse evil the
    way he would otherwise have to go on living (cf. 99a; *Apology* 29a–c, 37b–e; *Crito*
    47d–48d)? Of course, Socrates' claims may be, as he himself admits. the sign of his
    love of victory on this occasion (cf. 91a–b, 115d), so that his courage and/or moder-
    ation would be displayed only in spite of those claims. Cf. Aristotle *Nicomachean
    Ethics* 1117b10–13.

33 Cf. *Meno* 88a–d; *Protagoras* 332a–333b, 349e–350c, 360b–e; *Laches* 194d–195a, 199c;
    Charmides 165c–167b; *Laws* 688a–b, 963a–965e; Aristotle *Nicomachean Ethics* 1103a4–
    10, 1144b1–1145a.

34 Pains and fears should correspond, it seems, to pleasures and desires, but Socrates is
    silent about the last; he has, after all, just described demotic moderation coming into
    being not from desire for pleasures, but from fear of their deprivation.

35 The Eleatic Stranger contrasts the mathematical measure, concerned always with
    greater and lesser in relation to each other, and the measure of the mean (*Statesman*
    283d–285e). See Seth Benardete's discussion of the two measures in the chapter "Met-
    rics," *Plato's Statesman*, 3:113–19.

36 See the analysis of various translations and interpretations of this passage by Hans Rey-
    nen, "*Phaidon* Interpretationen: zu Plat. *Phaed.* 62a und 69a–b," 46–60.

37 Cf. *Republic* 583b, 586b–c; cf. also *Philebus* 42a–c; *Protagoras* 356a–357b.

38 It is unclear at 69c1–3—perhaps intentionally so—whether moderation and justice
    and courage are linked to "the true," which is some kind of purification, or to *phronēsis*,
    which is some kind of purgation. Cf. Aristotle's distinction between virtue, which
    makes us aim at the right mark, and *phronēsis*, which makes us take the right means
    (*Nicomachean Ethics* 1144a6–8).

39 Condemning the way the poets praise justice and condemn injustice, Adeimantus
    refers to their description of the impious and unjust buried in the mud in Hades (*Re-
    public* 363d); but Socrates takes up the same description as an image of "the eye of the
    soul sunk in barbaric mud," from which dialectics leads it upward (533c–d).

Chapter Four

1 Cf. Homer *Iliad* 23.100, and Socrates' criticism of such fear-inspiring poetry (*Republic*
    387b).

2 The claim that what is must necessarily be in some place and occupy space, but what
    is neither in heaven nor on earth has no being, is, according to Timaeus, what "we say
    as if seeing in a dream" (*Timaeus* 52b–c). The physicist must have knowledge of place,

Aristotle argues, for it is generally assumed that things that are, are in some place, while that which is not is nowhere (*Physics* 208a27–33).

3   Cf. the double determination of soul suggested by *Phaedrus* 245e and 249b–c, or by *Sophist* 248d–249b; cf. also Aristotle *De Anima* 403b25–27.

4   Socrates rebukes Polus for praising rhetoric as the most beautiful art before answering what it is (*Gorgias* 448d–e); he disapproves of his conversation with Thrasymachus, trying to consider whether justice is virtue or vice, ignorance or wisdom, and whether or not it brings happiness, before knowing what it is (*Republic* 354b–c); he criticizes his procedure with Protagoras, trying to determine whether virtue is teachable before asking whether it is knowledge (*Protagoras* 360e–361c); but although he first tells Meno that they cannot know whether virtue is teachable before knowing what it is (*Meno* 71a–b), Socrates then suggests that, like geometers who assume the nature of something as known and then argue from that as a hypothesis, they ought to assume that virtue is knowledge in order to deduce its teachability (86d–87c).

5   It is only to those who voted for acquittal at his public trial that Socrates suggests telling stories to each other (*diamuthologēsai*) as well as conversing (*dialegesthai*) about whether death is something good or not (*Apology* 39e).

6   See *Apology* 19b–c and Socrates' protest that Meletus must think he is prosecuting Anaxagoras when he charges Socrates with inventing theories about the sun being a stone or the moon earth (26d).

7   See *Apology* 19d.

8   See Aristophanes *Clouds* 1480; cf. *Republic* 488e and Socrates' apparent praise of Anaxagoras in the *Phaedrus* (270a).

9   On Aristophanes' critique of Socrates, which could be understood as an attack against his indifference to "demotic music," see Leo Strauss, *Socrates and Aristophanes*, 1–3. Cf. Stanley Rosen, *Plato's Symposium*, 121–23.

10   Although the subject *psychai* is not mentioned, it is implied by the participles in the feminine plural. On the ambiguity of *gignesthai*, which could mean "to be born," "to come into being" or, with a complement, "to become something," see David Gallop, *Plato Phaedo*, 105–6. If the subject is *psychē*, the verb should be translated "to be born," since the argument denies that it comes to be in the strict sense; if the subject is "the living," being born and coming to be would be identical.

11   Socrates uses only the last part of the ancient *logos* when he repeats as the antecedent of the argument that the living are born again from those who have died; otherwise the claim that the souls "are there arriving from here" would include in the premise that which is to be derived from it (see R. Hackforth, *Plato's Phaedo*, 59n2).

12   Cf. Aristotle's reference to soul as "the place of the *eidē*" (*De Amina* 429a27).

13   See Aristotle *Metaphysics* 987b1–4.

14   The beautiful and the ugly, furthermore, seem to exemplify the opposites themselves that are "unwilling" to coexist in something at the same time, whereas that which comes to be more beautiful in relation to one thing would still be less beautiful, that is, more ugly, in relation to something else. Cf. *Hippias Major* 289a–d.

15   Cf. the characterization by Timaeus of the aesthetic, in contrast to the noetic, as that which comes to be in some place and passes away out of it (*Timaeus* 52a).

16   Cf. also *Theaetetus* 159b–c.

17   By means of these opposite *geneseis*, the pre-Socratics could account for a plurality of phenomena, without having to admit coming into being out of nothing and passing away into nothing (see Aristotle *Physics* 187a12–b1, 188a19–32, b21–30, 191a23–34). On the

processes of cooling and heating, see Anaximander DK12A10; Anaximenes DK13B1; Philolaus DKA27; Anaxagoras DK59B8; and Heraclitus DK22B126. On separation and combination, see Anaximander DK12A9; Empedocles DK31B17; Anaxagoras DK 59B17. Cf. Aristotle, *On Generation and Corruption* 322b6–8, 329b25–30.

18 When Theaetetus admits that he is made dizzy by these puzzling cases in which something comes to be greater without increasing, smaller without decreasing, Socrates assures him that this sense of wonder is the beginning of philosophy (*Theaetetus* 154c–155d). See Seth Benardete's analysis in Plato's *Theaetetus*, 1:106–7.

19 Those who postulate one underlying substratum must identify coming to be and passing away as alteration, Aristotle reasons, while those who postulate more than one underlying substratum must identify coming to be and passing away with combination and separation (*On Generation and Corruption* 314b1–6, 315b16–24; cf. Damascius *Commentary on the Phaedo* 1.190).

20 The comparatives illustrate opposites that are contradictories, with no intermediary, so that a logical inference is possible from one to the other. Living and dead, on the other hand—like just and unjust or beautiful and ugly (see *Symposium* 202a–b)—are not contradictory but contrary opposites; since something may be neither dead nor alive, no logical inference is possible from the denial of one to the affirmation of the other. On this distinction, see Aristotle, *Metaphysics* 1055a38–63. On its role in the present argument, see P. W. Gooch, "Plato's *Antapodosis* Argument for the Soul's Immortality: *Phaedo* 70–72," 2:243.

21 Insofar as all things that come into being do not proceed from their opposite form but from their own privation (see Damascius 1.246; Aristotle *Physics* 191b13–17), Socrates could infer only that, if something comes to be alive, it must have been previously not alive.

22 Cf. Heraclitus DK22B88. In accordance with the model on which the argument has been based, "being asleep" should only mean being less awake, and by implication "being dead" should mean being less alive. If, Socrates claims at his public trial, being most awake, and by implication most alive, is to engage most constantly in the activity of examination, then most men are indeed more or less asleep—that is, throughout their lives, more or less dead. If death is not simply a continuation of his own way of life, Socrates surmises at the end of the trial, then it is like the deepest sleep with no awareness (*Apology* 40c–e); the Athenian *dēmos*, whom Socrates describes as a slumbering horse unwilling to be awakened by his gadfly activity (30e–31a), illustrates the truth of his claim that the unexamined life is not worth living.

23 But even if something that now awakens must have been previously asleep, or something that falls asleep must have been previously awake, it does not follow that something now awakening must have previously fallen asleep after first being awake. Socrates can argue, as Julian Wolfe puts it, that if the soul comes to be alive, it must previously have been not alive, but that doesn't mean it must have come to that state by dying ("Plato's Cyclical Argument for Immortality," 2:253). Being alive, he assumes, is to animate a body, dying to cease animating a body, and being "not alive" to exist apart from a body.

24 Cf. *Symposium* 207c–e; *Laws* 721c, 773e, 776b. In the context of criticizing the ideas as useless in accounting for *genesis*, Aristotle describes the coming to be of natural things, where the generator is of the same kind as that which is generated: man generates man (*Metaphysics* 1033b30–33).

25 Cf. Socrates' appeal to the general principle of *antapodosis* in *Republic* 563e, or Timaeus' account of the *antapodosis* of inspiration and expiration (*Timaeus* 79e).

26 Cf. *Phaedo* 81b–e, 83d–e, 113a; cf. also Anaximander DK 12A9, or Heraclitus DK 22B94. But Socrates' present argument, as the ancient commentators recognize (see Olympiodorus 10.14), would preclude the possibility of that eternal condemnation of the incurably wicked or eternal reward of the purified that Socrates describes in his concluding myth (113e, 114c).

27 See Kenneth Dorter, *Plato's Phaedo*, 45.

28 Socrates here introduces "always" for the first time, Hackforth argues (64), since it is only at this point that he attempts to demonstrate an everlasting cycle from one opposite to the other.

29 Cf. Aristotle's interpretation of the position of Heraclitus in *Eudemian Ethics* 1235a25–27.

30 The consequence that would result from the denial of opposite *geneseis*, as Socrates' ambiguous use of *gignesthai* may suggest, is that everything would cease coming to be anything at all (Gallop, 112). Is the cycle of *genesis* ceaseless, Aristotle asks, because the passing away of a this is the coming to be of something else (*On Generation and Corruption* 318a24–26)?

31 Socrates presents the equivalent in *logos* to Anaxagoras' cosmological chaos when he uses the same allusion to describe the confusion of the disputatious, who do not separate the positing of hypotheses from the derivation of their consequences but mix everything together (101e).

32 Given the indeterminacy of the Anaxagorean mixture as Aristotle interprets it, nothing could be truly predicated of the underlying substance (*Metaphysics* 989b6–20).

33 Cf. Aristotle *Metaphysics* 989a33–b4.

34 Cf. Damascius 1.228 and Strato's criticism of the argument (cited in Hackforth, 195). After asking whether the cyclical structure of becoming is accomplished in the same way by all things, Aristotle answers that only for those things whose substance is imperishable is the recurrence numerically the same, while in all others it is the same only in species (*On Generation and Corruption* 338b12–19).

35 The premise that nothing comes from nothing, Aristotle claims, is a principle held in common by all the pre-Socratics (*Physics* 187a27–30).

36 Cf. Aristotle *On Generation and Corruption* 318a13–24.

37 See Melissus DK 30B8; cf. Walter Bröcker, *Platos Gespräche*, 128.

38 The consequence of such a reduction, Aristotle argues, is the impossibility of explaining change—which requires that there *be* an "out of which" and a "to which"—as well as the denial of the law of non-contradiction (*Metaphysics* 1009a22–38, 1010a1–38).

39 Compare Socrates' silence about any nonmoving beings in his attempt to demonstrate that the indestructibility of "the whole heaven and all *genesis*" depends upon the ungenerated and indestructible *archē* constituted by self-moving motion, which could be "not shamefully" identified as the *ousia* and *logos* of soul (*Phaedrus* 245d–e); cf. *Laws* 895a–896a.

40 The disturbance of modern editors who bracket the manuscript reading of the final phrase of this conclusion—"And it is better for the good but worse for the evil"—is hardly surprising; if authentic, it would be Plato's acknowledgment of the inappropriateness of the argument to respond to Cebes' demand for a demonstration to justify the "great and beautiful" hope promised by Socrates' defense (70a–b). See Hans-Georg Gadamer, "The Proofs of Immortality in Plato's *Phaedo*," 25–26.

41 The expression "*tō onti*" appears seventeen times in the *Phaedo*—fourteen times in the first half of the dialogue, prior to Socrates' account of his turn from investigation of the beings to investigation through *logoi*. In the second half of the dialogue, which il-

lustrates that turn, the first occurrence distinguishes what is truly a cause "in being" from a mere co-cause, that is, teleology from mechanism (99b), both of which are contrasted, however, with the *eidē*; the last occurrence, in Socrates' myth, refers to the real presence of the gods with the purified (111b); the central occurrence is in the conclusion of the final argument, affirming that our souls will "really" be in Hades (107a). Compare the seventeen cases of false opinion that Socrates outlines for Theaetetus, the first fourteen of which are impossible, and only the last three possible (*Theaetetus* 192a–c).

Chapter Five

1   Cebes introduces the word "*athanaton*," while Socrates first promises to demonstrate the deathless character of soul in the final argument (100b, 105e ff.). He uses it in the third argument only as the principle to which the soul is akin (79d, 80b, 81a), and once as the characteristic, "so to speak," of the bones and sinews (80d).

2   Cebes also introduces the term "*eidos*," in its prephilosophic sense of body or figure, especially the living human body. On the relation between this colloquial sense and the technical use of the term in the arts of rhetoric, medicine, and mathematics, see A. E. Taylor, "The Words *Eidos, Idea* in Pre-Platonic Literature," especially 182, 251. See also Jacob Klein's discussion of how, from the ordinary meaning of *eidos* as looks or appearance, "Plato derives—by way of contrast, paradox, and pun—his understanding of the *eidos* as *aeides*," the invisible object of thought (*Commentary on Plato's Meno*, 50).

3   Cf. *Meno* 82b–86b. In the account Socrates first offers to Meno (81c–d), the identification of learning as recollection follows from the premise of immortality, whereas in Socrates' own reflections after his exhibition on the slave boy (86a–b), the immortality of the soul follows from agreement on the possibility of learning (Klein, 180). In the argument Socrates now conducts, the preexistence of the soul should follow from the account of recollection, but Simmias will affirm his acceptance of recollection on the basis of the preexistence of the soul (92d; cf. Klein, 132).

4   Cf. *Phaedrus* 249d–251a.

5   And yet, the example of the image provides the model for the rest of the argument, as J. L. Ackrill observes ("*Anamnesis* in the *Phaedo*: Remarks on 73c–75c," 185). The example of Simmias and his picture seems, moreover, to make *anamnēsis* indistinguishable from *eikasia*, that capacity to perceive an image as an image that Socrates assigns to the lowest section in his image of the divided line (*Republic* 509e–510a).

6   Cf. *Cratylus* 432b–d.

7   Cf. *Republic* 472d–e.

8   It is, perhaps, for this reason that Socrates illustrates the possibility of pure pleasure by referring to the sight of images, not of living beings, but only of geometric figures (see *Philebus* 51c).

9   Do we know it, what it is (*auto ho estin*)?, Socrates asks, where *auto*, referring to the equal itself, is simultaneously the direct object of "know" and the subject of "what is" (cf. 75b6, d1; see Gallop, *Plato Phaedo*, 119–20, 229). Cf. ch. 3, n. 5.

10 On the controversy over whether this refers to different observers or to different relations in which the phenomena stand, and for this translation, which is intended to preserve that ambiguity, see Gallop, 122–23, 220. See also the analysis of different interpretations by K. W. Mills, "Plato's *Phaedo* 74b7–c6," 128–33.

11 Sticks and stones may be equal in length, for example, but not weight (see Richard Haynes, "The form equality, as a set of equals: *Phaedo* 74b–c," 20). The problem,

then, with which Socrates is concerned is not one constituted by and correctable by perception itself, as in a dispute among different observers. He is concerned, rather, as his later discussion of opposites suggests, with the apparently contradictory claim that phenomena, while remaining the same, are both equal and unequal—a claim that would be corrected by specifying the different relations in which these opposite qualities are ascribed (cf. *Parmenides* 129c–e).

12 "The equals themselves" seems, then, to refer to the properties themselves that are equal and never seem unequal to anyone (see Michael Wedin, "*Auta ta Isa* and the Argument at *Phaedo* 74b7–c5," 198–99). Cf. Socrates' account of the monads under consideration in the arithmetic of the philosophers in contrast with the unequal units counted in the arithmetic of the many (*Philebus* 56d–e).

13 The formula suggests those "mathematicals" to which Plato, according to Aristotle, assigned an intermediary status: insofar as they are eternal and unchangeable, they are unlike the phenomena, but insofar as they are a plurality of many alike, they are unlike the *eidē* (see *Metaphysics* 987b14–18). Against this interpretation, J. M. Rist argues that *hē isotēs*, *auto to ison*, and *auta ta isa* are simply three phrases Plato uses to describe the form of equal because he felt no one of them to be entirely satisfactory ("Equals and Intermediaries in Plato," 31). To support this claim, Rist contends that *hē trias*, *hē idea tōn triōn*, and *ta tria* at *Phaedo* 104a–e are three different ways of referring to the form threeness (29). But three must be related to the triad just as whatever is to be two must participate in the dyad and whatever is to be one in the monad (101c). If the equals themselves "bring forward" the *idea* of equality to any equal phenomena, like the dyad that "brings forward" the *idea* of the even to any collection of two (105a), they would indeed seem to be intermediary between "opposites in nature" and the things characterized by them (cf. 102d–103b).

14 Self-predication would be entailed, then, as Rist observes (32), only by the equals themselves; cf. R. E. Allen, "Participation and Predication in Plato's Middle Dialogues," 150. It would be difficult to account for why Plato introduced these various terms if one were to argue, as Mills does, for example, that he failed to distinguish between them ("*Plato's Phaedo* 74b7–c6," 49).

15 Cf. Socrates' account in the *Cratylus* of the name-givers who, while whirling around and dizzy with confusion themselves, mistakenly projected their own state onto the phenomena and laid down names in accordance with their belief that all things are in motion (439c).

16 Yet, if knowledge of the equal itself implied knowledge of its opposite, why would it be necessary to have acquired knowledge before birth of the greater and smaller as well (see Gallop, 130)? And since one thing can certainly be greater or smaller than another, what would it mean to say that it falls short of the greater or the smaller (see John Burnet, *Plato's Phaedo*, 58)? Cf. Socrates' attempt, in the *Philebus*, to identify "the *genos* of the unlimited" by including within it "the things that appear to us to become more and less," in contrast to "the limit," to which the equal and equality belong (24e– 25b; but contrast 25d–e).

17 "The holy" takes the place here of health and strength in the list Socrates presented to Simmias in his initial defense to illustrate "the being, what each happens to be" (65d). Cf. Socrates' description in the myth of the fate after death of those found to have lived a holy life (113d, 114b). "The holy" appears only one more time in the dialogue, in conflict with the good: despite the fact that it may be better for the philosopher to be dead, it is not holy to benefit himself (62a).

18 On the metaphor of stamping with a seal, see *Philebus* 26d; *Statesman* 258c.

19 See, for example, *Crito* 50c; *Republic* 534d; *Protagoras* 329a; *Gorgias* 449b.

20 See, for example, *Euthyphro* 5d; *Charmides* 159a; *Laches* 190e; *Hippias Major* 286d; *Theaetetus* 146c; *Minos* 313a.

21 For if we already possessed the answer, why would we engage in inquiry at all (*Meno* 80e)? Socrates identifies the dialectician, in the *Cratylus*, as he who knows how to ask and answer (390c), but he suggests the etymological derivation of *hēros* not only from *erōs*, but also from *erōtan* ("questioning"), so that the heroes must have been rhetoricians and dialecticians who knew not how to answer, but only how to question (398d).

22 See, for example, *Meno* 97e–98a; *Gorgias* 465a; *Republic* 534b; *Theaetetus* 202c; *Statesman* 286a.

23 Cf. *Phaedrus* 249b–c.

24 See Aristotle *Posterior Analytics* 71b6–8, 99b26–34.

25 See ch. 3, n. 13.

26 Just as the first argument proves that the soul continues to exist after death in Hades but not that it is imperishable, Olympiodorus argues, the second argument proves that it exists for some time before birth but not that it is ungenerated (*Commentary on the Phaedo* 11.2).

27 Simmias' fear that when the soul is released from the body, it will suffer corruption (*diaphtheiresthai*, 77b) echoes Cebes' fear that when a man dies, his soul suffers corruption and is destroyed (*diaphtheirētai te kai apolluētai*, 70a); both interlocutors conclude their later objections to the argument by expressing their fear that, at death, the soul is destroyed (*apollusthai*, 86d; and *apolētai*, 88b).

28 See 71d10–13 and 72a4–6, in contrast with 70c8–9, d3–4, 71d14–15, 71e14–72a2, d1–3, d8–9.

29 On the various traditional enumerations and divisions of the arguments, see W. D. Geddes, *Phaedo of Plato*, xviii–xix. See also ch. 8, n. 1, below.

30 See Dorter's analysis of the relation between the first and second arguments, which show different sides of the separated soul as motive and wise; while the third argument makes this disparity explicit, Dorter finds its reconciliation in the final argument, which defines soul as the bearer of the form "life" to the body (*Plato's Phaedo*, 44–46). But to take this as a reconciliation neglects the radical consequences of the transition from the first to the second half of the dialogue: the relation of soul to life in the final argument in no way suggests the cognitive relation between the soul and the forms that is assumed in the first series of arguments.

Chapter Six

1 See ch. 3, n. 22.

2 Cf. *Charmides* 155e–157c, 175e–176b. Just before presenting a comic description of the reincarnation of the soul in other species, Socrates recommends that Cebes pay money to be enchanted by the Pythagoreans, perhaps, or the legendary Thracian orphics (see John Burnet, *Plato's Phaedo*, 64), as if they were sophists; Socrates certainly gives Cebes a double-edged message in advising him to be charmed by himself, if not by another, while simultaneously disenchanting him about enchantment.

3 Compare the final stage of the last argument, where Cebes agrees that the immortal must escape destruction, *if* anything can (106d).

4 To give a *logos* of the being of the *ousia* would be, Hans Wagner puts it, to seek a definition of a determination as such ("Die Eigenart der Ideenlehre," 13–14).

5 For an analysis of the monoeidetic form as the Platonic transformation of the conditions of Parmenidean being to each among a plurality of ideas, see Gerold Prauss, *Platon und der logische Eleatismus*, 36–40. This "early theory of ideas" becomes subject to criticism in the *Theaetetus* and *Sophist*, Prauss argues (174–83), whereas one, if not the, primary exposition of it is in the *Phaedo*, and particularly in this passage (36). But given the manner in which the account is introduced and employed here, one can hardly assume that it is meant to be uncritically accepted.

6 Socrates foreshadows the examples in his final argument, in which the even is opposed to the odd as well as to the uneven, the hot and cold opposed to each other as well as to the "unhot" and "uncoolable," on the basis of which the soul is said to be "not dead" (105d–e).

7 Cf. *Phaedo* 80d, 81a; *Cratylus* 403a; *Gorgias* 493b.

8 For the insides of the living body are as invisible, Socrates implies in his concluding myth, as the soul is said to be (see ch. 12).

9 The ancient commentators find it necessary to explain why Plato should call *phronēsis* a *pathēma* of the soul (see the *Commentary on the Phaedo* of Olympiodorus, 13.19, and of Damascius, 1.334, 2.39).

10 Damascius distinguishes the three parts of the argument as concerned with being as sensible and intelligible, with cognitive power and activity, and finally with practical power and activity (1.325).

11 The six terms seem to correspond in pairs to the three parts of the argument, beginning with the last. The center is marked by the reverse order, in which noetic and monoeidetic are opposed to polyeidetic and "anoetic." While *anoēton* could mean "incapable of thinking" (cf. 88b4, 95c4, d7; see also R. Hackforth, *Plato's Phaedo*, 64), its opposite, *noēton*, means "accessible to thought." The ancient commentators, however, attempt to assimilate the positive term to the negative, in order to deduce the characterization of soul as "capable of thought" (see Olympiodorus 13.2; Damascius 1.315).

12 The art of embalming is one sign of Egypt as *the* symbol of the fixed and permanent (cf. *Phaedrus* 274c–275b; *Timaeus* 21e–23c; *Laws* 656d–657b; Herodotus, *Histories*, Book 2).

13 It is precisely his bones and sinews that Socrates will describe in great detail as the mechanical cause of his sitting in prison—the necessary condition for, but not to be identified with, the intention that is truly a cause of his situation (98c–d). But Socrates' playful attribution of "deathlessness" to them points ahead to the connection he will bring to light between mechanism and teleology, body and soul: his bones and sinews, Socrates will admit, would have been carried off long ago by an opinion of the best, had he not considered it more just to remain behind (99a).

14 After he has seen a perfect likeness of the dead Patroclus, Achilles discovers, "So even in the house of Hades soul and image are, after all, something" (*Iliad* 23.103–4). Hades, Benardete comments, "is the locus of the reality of the image; it is the natural home of the poet" ("On Greek Tragedy," 135, 140).

15 Cf. *Apology* 41a–c; *Crito* 54b–c; *Gorgias* 523a–527a, *Republic* 363c–e; but contrast *Republic* 386a–387c.

16 Cf. *Cratylus* 403b–404b.

17 Cf. *Laws* 959b.

18 Cf. Socrates' etymology, for which he credits the Orphic poets, of the body (*sōma*) as the grave (*sēma*) of the soul (*Cratylus* 400c).

19 Cf. *Republic* 500d, 619c–d; *Protagoras* 323a–b; *Meno* 73a–c; *Gorgias* 504d–e, 507d–e.

20 See ch. 2, n. 35.

21 See *Republic* 514a–518b. See also Allan Bloom, *The Republic of Plato*, 404–5; Leo Strauss, "Plato," in *History of Political Philosophy*, 31.

22 See *Republic* 515c–e.

23 Compare *Republic* 517a with 521b and 540b.

24 Philosophy persuades the soul to "withdraw" (*anachōrein*) intact from the senses, just as an opposite or anything essentially characterized by an opposite must withdraw (*hupekchōrein*) from the approach of the other opposite, unless it is to be destroyed (cf. 102d, 103d, 104c, 106e).

25 Cf. *Timaeus* 73b–d, 91a–d.

26 This double motivation—refraining from bodily pleasures for the sake of (*toutōn heneka*, 82c) entering the *genos* of the gods and following the guidance of philosophy for the sake of (*toutōn toinun heneka*, 83e) communion with the divine and monoeidetic—is echoed in the double motivation Socrates affirms at the end of his myth: participating in virtue and *phronēsis* for the sake of (*toutōn dē heneka*, 114d) the rewards to come in the after-life and being confident about one's own soul, for the sake of (*toutōn dē heneka*, 114d) being prepared for the call of fate.

27 See Robert Loriaux, *Le Phédon de Platon: Commentaire et traduction*, 1:186–87.

28 Cf. Léon Robin, *Platon Phédon*, 4:35.

Chapter Seven

1 Socrates alone falls into silent reflection once more in the conversation, just after restating Cebes' objection to the argument (95e), which he subsequently interprets as a question about the cause of coming into being and passing away in general and offers his "intellectual autobiography" in response.

2 Cf. *Theaetetus* 189e and *Sophist* 263e.

3 See ch. 3, n. 22.

4 Cf. Paul Friedländer, *Platon*, 3:32–33. Given the controversy over the historical accuracy of the portrait of Socrates in the *Phaedo*, it is of interest to consider the description that the ancient "biographies" ascribe to Plato. He was an Apollonian man, according to certain dreams and his own words, for he called himself a "fellow servant of the swans." Socrates is said to have dreamed, before Plato became his pupil, that an unfledged swan sat in his lap, then grew wings and flew away with a cry that made all who heard it spellbound. And Plato is said to have dreamed, before he died, of a swan darting from tree to tree, unable to be caught by the fowlers; this dream, in the interpretation of Simmias the Socratic, meant that all men would try to grasp Plato's meaning but none would succeed, and each would understand him according to his own views. See L. G. Westerink, trans. and ed., *Anonymous Prolegomena to Platonic Philosophy*, 2; see also Diogenes Laertius, "Plato," *Lives of Eminent Philosophers* 3.5.

5 See *Apology* 20e–21a.

6 See *Apology* 29a.

7 See *Apology* 37c.

8 On the meaning of *harmonia* as attunement, and its relation to scale and octave, see W. K. C. Guthrie, *History of Greek Philosophy*, 1:223. When Simmias later refers to *harmonia* in the works of the craftsmen, he points to its original sense as a "fitting together," from the verb *harmottein* (see David Gallop, *Plato Phaedo*, 147).

9   On the Pythagorean conception of the heavens as *harmonia* and number, which may constitute the basis for this account of soul, see Aristotle *Metaphysics* 985b31–986a6; cf. *Timaeus* 37a. On the controversy over the Pythagorean origin of the doctrine, see John Burnet, *Plato's Phaedo*, 82; and F.M. Cornford, "Mysticism and Science in the Pythagorean Tradition," 137–50. On Philolaus as Simmias' authority for the notion of soul as *harmonia*, see Guthrie, 1:312–17.

10 Cf. the speech of the physician Eryximachus in the *Symposium* (187a–188b), where *harmonia* reveals the relation between music and medicine, for health is identified as the result of the opposites hot, cold, wet, and dry being brought together in ordered harmony through "heavenly Eros"; see also Alcmaeon DK 24B4. The understanding of harmony as a balance of contrary elements of the body is a more appropriate definition of health, Aristotle argues, than of the soul (*De Anima* 408a2–4). He raises the question of whether the supporters of the theory understand harmony as the *logos* of the combination or rather as the actual mixture of contraries and then argues that the soul can be neither (407b33–35).

11 Cf. *Timaeus* 36e–37c, 47d, 90d; *Protagoras* 326b; *Laws* 653c–654a, 664e–665a, 689d; *Republic* 430e, 591c–d; Aristotle *Politics* 1340b17–19.

12 Cf. *Republic* 530d–531c.

13 See Aristotle *Metaphysics* 1083b8–19, 1090a30–35.

14 Consider the use of *sumphōnein* in Socrates' account of his art of hypothetical reasoning (100a and 101d).

15 The last word of Simmias' speech is *apollusthai* (86d5), just as the last word of Cebes' speech is *apolētai* (88b10). See Konrad Gaiser, *Protreptik und Paränese bei Platon*, 151.

16 Cf. 60a, 63a, 116d, 117b. Burnet notes (84) that the verb *diablepō* occurs nowhere else before *On Dreams* (462a12), where Aristotle, explaining dream images as movements in the sense organs, refers to children who, staring with wide open eyes (*diablepousin*) in the dark, see multitudes of phantoms before them and cover their heads in terror.

17 While Simmias' persuasive image could easily be mistaken for the object it represents, Cebes' proposal could not fail to be recognized as an image. The conjunction recalls the two images of the soul that Socrates presents in the *Theaetetus*: in contrast with the laughable image of an aviary (197d–200c), the image of a wax block containing the impressions of memory (191c–e, 194c–195a) is so intuitively persuasive—as its predominance in the philosophic tradition might suggest—that it conceals its status as an image. See Seth Benardete's discussion in *Plato's Theaetetus*, 1:154–69.

18 On the notion of the soul wrapping itself in the garment of the body, see Empedocles DK 31B126.

19 This problem was introduced by Phaedo's original reference to the ship of Theseus (see ch. 1, n. 9) and was then implied by Socrates' image of Penelope's web (84a). Cf. Diotima's teaching on *erōs* as the principle through which the mortal participates in immortality, according to which not only the body but also the soul and even knowledge possess no permanent identity, but only a constant perishing and coming to be (*Symposium* 207d–208b).

20 By implicitly showing Socrates' acceptance of Cebes' challenge, Schleiermacher argues, Plato presents a critique of the Pythagoreans, who assume reincarnation to be a proof of immortality. See *Platons Werke*, 2(3), 12.

21 Cebes, like Simmias, believes he has proven the mortality of the soul against Socrates' attempt to deny it; but Socrates has announced twice, before and after his third argument, that the soul dies (77d, 84b).

Chapter Eight

1 Although Socrates' discussion with Phaedo on the subject of misology is the center of the dialogue both quantitatively and thematically, it is displaced from the center by the relation among the arguments, as the following outline of the structure of the dialogue shows:

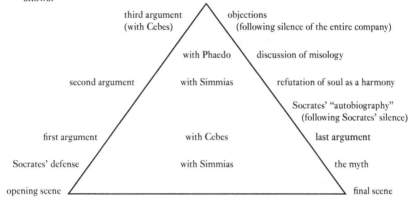

third argument (with Cebes)

objections (following silence of the entire company)

with Phaedo

discussion of misology

second argument

with Simmias

refutation of soul as a harmony

Socrates' "autobiography" (following Socrates' silence)

first argument

with Cebes

last argument

Socrates' defense

with Simmias

the myth

opening scene

final scene

2 This has been taken as evidence for the identification of Echecrates as a member of the Pythagorean community in Phlius (see Diogenes Laertius *Lives of Eminent Philosophers* 9.46). If Philolaus maintained the notion of the soul as a harmony of corporeal elements together with a belief in its immortality, Socrates' refutation of Simmias would indicate Plato's charge against the self-contradictory presuppositions of the Pythagorean teaching (see W.K.C. Guthrie, *History of Greek Philosophy*, 1:312–19).

3 Phaedo anticipates the metaphoric language through which Socrates will describe the war of opposites on the battlefield of the *pragmata* (cf. 102d–106e) when he compares Socrates to a general who calls his men back from flight. Socrates prepares for that image when he encourages his ally Phaedo, if the *logos* escapes him, to take an oath like the Argives not to let his hair grow until winning a victory over the Thebans (89c; see Herodotus *Histories* 1.82).

4 Whereas the first argument concluded with the claim that "there is really (*tō onti*) coming back to life" (*to anabiōskesthai*, 72d), Socrates marks the new direction of the discussion by expressing his hope only that the *logos* will be brought to life again (*anabiōsasthai*, 89b).

5 Cf. the use of this image in the *Euthydemus* (297c).

6 Cf. *Apology* 20e–22e.

7 The generation of opposite *pragmata* is exemplified in the first argument, therefore, by comparatives, the greater and the smaller (70e), whereas the mutual exclusion of opposites themselves is exemplified in the last argument by the great and the small, distinguished from the *pragma* that shares in both, being greater in one relation and smaller in another (102b–e).

8 When Glaucon describes the perfectly just and the perfectly unjust man, each of whom appears in perfect opposition to what he truly is, Socrates commends the way he polishes up his two statues (*Republic* 361d; cf. 540c).

9 See *Apology* 23a–b.

10 See Konrad Gaiser, *Protreptik und Paränese bei Platon*, 153–57.
11 The "beautiful persuasiveness" of the first series of arguments seems to have the same status as the "beautiful danger" of accepting Socrates' final myth as a magic charm (114d). When an interlocutor in a Platonic dialogue gives approval to an argument by responding "beautifully" (*kalōs*), Seth Benardete observes, it is often a sign that some difficulty has been avoided, thus allowing the argument to proceed ("The Right, the True, and the Beautiful," 94).
12 Cf. *Apology* 40c.
13 Although most editors follow Stephanus in reading *agnoia* (ignorance), Burnet notes (92) that the manuscript authority supports the reading *anoia* (folly).
14 But when Socrates likens himself before the Athenian jury to a gadfly stinging a sluggish horse, he defends this activity as a gift of the god to the city (*Apology* 30e–31a). Compare the warning, however, that Socrates issues to his interlocutors before entering into his radical proposals for the communization of the guardian class in his "best city in speech" (*Republic* 450d–451b).

Chapter Nine

1 The reason why Simmias and Cebes show such enthusiasm for the recollection argument may be that it seems to them a perfect combination of the Pythagorean belief in reincarnation and the Socratic method of inquiry (cf. John Burnet, *Plato's Phaedo*, 51–52). Yet they don't seem to be at all disturbed by the question of why Socratic inquiry is necessary if, according to the argument, recollection is awakened by perception alone.
2 Timaeus describes the cosmic soul as a harmony not of corporeal elements, but of mathematical ratios (*Timaeus* 35a–37d). Philolaus, according to one late report (Claudianus Mamertus), described the soul as "set in the body by means of number and an immortal and incorporeal harmony" (DK44B22); Cornford defends the authenticity of this ascription in "Science and Mysticism in the Pythagorean Tradition," 146. The way in which Plato has Simmias interpret his own image may constitute his criticism of the ambiguity of the Pythagorean doctrine, with its lack of separation between numbers, physical elements, and psychic qualities (W.K.C. Guthrie, *History of Greek Philosophy*, 1:312–17).
3 Socrates' use of the image might reflect the notion that rhythm and harmony not only affect, but may be construed as imitations of, the *pathē* of the human soul (see *Republic* 398e–399c, 401c–e; *Timaeus* 47d–e, 90d; *Laws* 812c–d, cf. 653d–654a, 665a, 672c–d; cf. also Aristotle *Poetics* 1448b20–24, together with 1449b27–28).
4 Consider Aristotle's remarks on the inseparability of the *pathē* of the soul from the body (*De Anima* 403a4–b19).
5 Simmias refers here to the procedures of the geometers, and thus points to the link between reliance on images and the use of hypotheses for deducing consistent consequences (cf. *Republic* 510b–511a; *Meno* 86e–87b).
6 For an analysis of the complex structure of the following section and its various interpretations, see W.F. Hicken, "*Phaedo* 93a11–94b3," 16–22. David Gallop (*Plato Phaedo*, 158–67) offers the following outline of the chiastic structure of the set of arguments: (a) premises for argument A (92e4–93a10); (b) premises for argument B (93a11–c10); (B) argument B (93d1–94b3); and (A) argument A (94b4–95a3).
7 Socrates recalls the original premise of his third argument (78c) and with it, the undefended assumption of the noncomposite nature of the soul.

8   Cf. Aristotle *On Interpretation* 16a10–18. The perplexities that result from not taking into account the distinctive status of a whole as a unity of its parts are exhibited in the final discussion of the *Theaetetus* (201e–206b; cf. *Sophist* 261d–263d; *Statesman* 278a–d). See also Gerold Prauss, *Platon und der logische Eleatismus*, 140–82.

9   "More and more fully," according to Damascius (*Commentary on the Phaedo* 1.368), means either in quantity (the intervals and their combination) or in degree (our perception of higher and lower pitches).

10 What, Damascius asks, does Socrates mean by saying that the harmony is itself harmonized? For what is really harmonized is the substratum, insofar as it is a harmony that has its cause elsewhere (1.381).

11 Socrates and Glaucon discuss the various harmonies, which have different effects on, because they are themselves imitations of, states of the soul, but they do not suggest that one is more or less of a harmony than another (see *Republic* 398e–399c). According, however, to Damascius' report on the view of the followers of Aristoxenus, shared by some Pythagoreans, the octave was called "the fullest," being most of all a harmony, the fourth considered least of all a harmony (1.368).

12 Cf. Aristotle *Categories* 3b33–4a9, together with *De Amina* 402a23–26.

13 Socrates attempts to establish, according to Hicken (16–21), only that the specific character of an attunement must reflect and be reflected by the character of the process of attunement with which it is associated; but this does not seem to account for Socrates' implicit distinction between the soul as a kind, which exists when the body as substratum is correctly attuned, and its qualification as more or less virtuous, insofar as the soul itself is the substratum correctly attuned or not.

14 Cf. Socrates' first oath by Zeus, which contrasts the philosopher with the lover of money or honor (82d). His oath, *pros Dios*, might be literally translated, "with regard to Zeus," that is, *the* standard for the soul with *nous* and *aretē* (cf. *Philebus* 30d; *Phaedrus* 252c).

15 On the controversial reading of this passage, see R. Hackforth, 115–16; see also Gallop, 162, 233.

16 Cf. ch. 5, n. 16. Socrates foreshadows here his account of the cause of anything coming to be what it is by "participating in the proper *ousia* of each in which it participates" (101c, cf. 100c).

17 Cf. *Republic* 439a–e; *Philebus* 34e–35d.

18 Homer *Odyssey* 20.17–18.

19 See *Republic* 439e–441c. But the interpretation through which Socrates is able to separate *thumos*, as a third part of the soul, between *epithumetikon* and *logistikon*, is problematic, as he himself admits (441c), for the intermediary always appears to join forces with one pole in opposition to the other. Leontius' desire to see corpses of enemies of the city would seem to represent *thumos* as much as it would desire, so that his self-reproach, like that of Odysseus, would exhibit an inseparable reason and anger against an inseparable anger and desire, or anger against itself.

20 This self-alienation suggests that *thumos*, unlike desire, has no natural object but can transfer itself from one object to another without awareness. See Seth Benardete, "On Plato's *Timaeus* and Timaeus' Science Fiction," 175. Describing topics useful for the rhetorician wishing to appease his audience, Aristotle notes that men cease to be angry with the dead (*Rhetoric* 1380b25–29); his quotation from Homer, however, describing Achilles' wrath against the dead Hector, in fact points to the nature of this easily misdirected passion: "For behold in his fury he doth despite to the senseless clay" (*Iliad* 24.54).

21 See *Republic* 436b–c, cf. 603c–d; *Gorgias* 482b–c. Cf. also Aristotle *Metaphysics* 1005b12–34.
22 The goddess Harmonia, according to Damascius (1.377), represents the noetic and separate harmony, and Socrates' "propitiation" is his detachment of that true harmony from its phantom. Cf. *Philebus* 22c.
23 See Pindar *Pythian* 3.88–99; cf. Pausanius *Description of Greece* 9.12.3.
24 Cf. Friedrich Schleiermacher, *Platons Werke*, 2(3), 12 and ch. 7, n. 20, above.

Chapter Ten

1 Contrast John Burnet's defense of the autobiography as a portrait of the historical Socrates (*Plato's Phaedo*, xxxviii–xlviii) with, for example, R. D. Archer-Hind's contention that "such inquiries must have always been alien to the strongly practical genius of Socrates" (*Phaedo of Plato*, 86). See also R. Hackforth's discussion (*Plato's Phaedo*, 127–31). But in accordance with the theme of the dialogue—and perhaps of every Platonic dialogue—the importance of Plato's presentation of Socrates' autobiography lies in the fact that it is, as Paul Friedländer puts it, "the way philosophy discovers itself " (*Platon*, 3:56). Cf. Introduction, n. 24 above.
2 Since the primary meaning of *aitia* is charge or accusation, based on the notion of human responsibility, it is hardly accidental that Socrates chooses his own condemnation and acceptance of it to illustrate what is "truly an *aitia*." Gregory Vlastos argues that, given the range covered by Socrates' use of the term, the proper translation of *aitia* would be "reason" (see "Reasons and Causes in the *Phaedo*"). If Socrates is concerned with an *aitia* useful for "conceptual clarification," and "cause" refers only to a temporal antecedent that is the sufficient condition for a subsequent event, then "cause" is indeed a misleading term for *aitia*. It is precisely by using the word *aitia*, however, that Socrates draws attention to the limitations, as well as the virtues, of his reconstruction of its meaning: the *eidē* cannot replace mechanistic or teleological causality, but they are the "causes" of the determinacy of the *pragmata*, hence of their intelligibility.
3 Whereas Socrates tossed himself *anō katō* investigating these questions, that is precisely how the disputatious describe the tide in the Euripus, as an image for the instability of *logos* and all the beings (90c).
4 On the hot and the cold, see Archelaos DK 60A17 and Empedocles DK 31B68; on the blood, see Empedocles DK 31B105; on air, see Anaximenes DK 13B2 and Diogenes of Apollonia DK 64B4, 5; on fire, see Heraclitus DK 22B64; on the brain, see Alcmaeon DK 24A5.
5 Michael Davis sees the questions about life and thinking as amounting to the Socratic question, "What is man?" ("Socrates' Pre-Socratism: Some Remarks on the Structure of Plato's *Phaedo*," 560).
6 See 82d, 93b; cf. ch. 2, n. 37, and ch. 13, n. 21.
7 Cf. *Parmenides* 143c–d; *Hippias Major* 302a–b.
8 Cf. *Hippias Major* 300a–303d.
9 See *Theaetetus* 155d; Aristotle *Metaphysics* 982b12–19; cf. *Phaedo* 60b, 62a.
10 See *Parmenides* 142d–e; *Sophist* 237d; Aristotle *Metaphysics* 1054a13–19.
11 Cf. Aristotle *Metaphysics* 984a18–21, b8–11.
12 Aeschylus *Prometheus Bound* 450. This allusion would be especially appropriate if, as Seth Benardete shows, Prometheus' gift of the arts would have been useless had he

not coupled it with "blind hopes" to replace the pre-Promethean situation of man, characterized by the constant awareness of death ("On Greek Tragedy," 115).

13 Socrates separates his report of Anaxagoras' claim that mind is the cause of all (see DK59B11, 13) from his own interpretation of it in terms of the good (cf. Aristotle *Metaphysics* 984b14–18, 985a18–21).

14 Cf. *Ion* 531d–532b; *Republic* 333e–334a. Socrates stresses that the *epistēmē* of what is best and what is worse is the same: if the good were known by nature rather than by "science," it might not entail knowledge of what is worse (cf. *Republic* 409a–e).

15 Timaeus delivers the same critique, reproaching those who mistake co-causes for the cause operating as far as possible in accordance with the idea of the best (*Timaeus* 46c–d). But he must make a new beginning in turning from the causality of mind to that of necessity as the "wandering cause," for mind could persuade necessity to bring only "the greater part" of the cosmos to perfection (47e–48a).

16 Consider Socrates' image for the problem of the good of his best city in speech: although it may be best for the eyes of a statue to be painted a brilliant purple, it may not be good for the whole statue, of which those eyes are only a part (*Republic* 420c–d).

17 Cf. *Republic* 505a–b; *Lysis* 219c–220b; cf. also Aristotle *Metaphysics* 994b9–16.

18 Aristotle considers Anaxagoras' *nous* a "deus ex machina" (*Metaphysics* 985a18–22).

19 Socrates recalls not only the action accompanying his opening remarks on pleasure and pain (60b), but also the conclusion of the third argument, with its detailed description of the preservation of the corpse and its characterization of the bones and sinews as "so to speak, deathless" (80d).

20 See *Apology* 30d.

21 By rejecting an earlier flight from the Athenian prison, Socrates can flee from the approach of the metaphoric "opposite" to his own essential determination, namely the command of the *dēmos* to cease the practice of philosophy: he thus exemplifies in his own conduct the battle of opposites he is about to analyze (cf. 104b–c).

22 Cf. *Timaeus* 46d–e; Aristotle *Physics* 199b34–200a5.

23 The vortex theory to which Socrates refers is ascribed by Aristotle to Empedocles (*De Caelo* 295a17–18), and the theory of the flat earth supported by a foundation of air to Anaximenes, Anaxagoras, and Democritus (*De Caelo* 294b14–15).

24 Socrates begins his concluding myth, however, with a hypothesis about the position of the earth that leads to consequences that seem to satisfy the principle of sufficient reason without depending on knowledge of the good (see 108e–109a and ch. 12, n. 15).

25 See *Cratylus* 418e–419b.

26 Socrates' image implies either the necessity of taking to the oars when the wind has failed (see Menander frag. 241) or, as the scholiast on this passage suggests, making a second, safer journey. The Socratic second sailing not only proves to be safer, but can also be understood as a laborious human effort that must be undertaken in the absence of a more direct route. Its apparent inferiority, in any case, must be put into question in light of the danger or unreliability of the first way. Compare the uses of the image in *Statesman* 300c; *Philebus* 19c; cf. Aristotle *Nicomachean Ethics* 1109a34–35; *Politics* 1284b19.

27 On Socrates' second sailing as a means of overcoming misology, see K. M. W. Shipton, "A good second-best: *Phaedo* 99bff." But the second way pursued by Socrates cannot be distinguished from the first as probability is to the ideal of certain knowledge, as Shipton argues, for Socrates' hypothesis of the causality of the ideas is intended to provide absolute certainty, at the price, of course, of abandoning probable knowledge of

coming to be. His *technē* of *logoi* would thus seem necessarily to alter the goal that he claimed to have sought in Anaxagorean teleology, rather than to be distinguished merely as a different means (see Shipton, 40; Kenneth Dorter, *Plato's Phaedo*, 120).

28 Socrates' specification of the sun being eclipsed cannot, therefore, be a "mere illustration" (Burnet, 108) or "mentioned merely as the occasion when people are most inclined to look at it" (Gallop, 177).

29 Consider Socrates' use of the verb *pragmateuomai*, "to be concerned with" (99d, 100b, cf. *diapragmateuomai*, 95e), or the noun *pragmateia*, "a matter of concern," or "occupation" (64e, 67b), or the expression *pragmata parechein tini*, "to cause someone trouble" (115a). Cf. Socrates' account of the first name-givers who, becoming dizzy in their search for the beings, did not "accuse" their own *pathos*, but believed that *auta ta pragmata* are by nature turning and always in motion (*Cratylus* 411b–e).

30 On the allusion to the divided line and the cave, see René Schaerer, "La Composition du Phédon," 38–40. For a discussion of dianoetic *eikasia*, through which an image fulfills its function as an image by pointing beyond itself, see Jacob Klein, *Commentary on Plato's Meno*, 112–25; on the divided line and cave in particular, 125.

31 On *erga* as the result of human action, in contrast with "mere speeches," see particularly *Apology* 32a–e. After reminding Glaucon that their purpose in constructing a model of the best city was not to demonstrate the possibility of bringing it into being, Socrates asks whether it is possible for anything to be realized in deed as it is in speech, or rather whether action is by nature less able to attain to truth that speech (*Republic* 473a). But contrast Xenophon *Memorabilia* 4.4.10.

32 Cf. *Republic* 507d–509b.

33 For a discussion of the difficulties involved in the meaning of *sumphōnein*, see Richard Robinson, *Plato's Earlier Dialectic*, 126–29. If it means "to be consistent with," that would seem to be an inadequate ground for positing as true whatever is consistent with the initial hypothesis, but if it means "to be deducible from" it would seem equally inadequate to posit as not true whatever cannot be deduced from the hypothesis. Robinson concludes that propositions deduced from the hypothesis are to be considered true, whereas those whose contradictory follows from the hypothesis are to be considered untrue; for a similar interpretation, see Hackforth, 139. It should be noted, however, that Socrates claims to posit not as false, but only as "not true" whatever does not harmonize with the hypothesis: he means, perhaps, only that it is impossible to establish, on the ground of a given hypothesis, the truth of something that cannot be deduced from it.

34 Among others, Robinson (143–44) and Norman Gulley (*Plato's Theory of Knowledge*, 40–41) argue that there is no necessary connection between the hypothetical method and the ideas as cause.

35 To create an image, for example, that represents the combination of the great and the beautiful would require the special art of "phantastics"—knowledge, that is, of how to adjust the proportions of the great in order for it to appear beautiful from the perspective of the perceiver; see *Sophist* 235d–236c and Seth Benardete's commentary in the chapter entitled "Appearing" (*Plato's Sophist*, 2:109–12).

36 That Socrates proceeds to illustrate his hypothesis with regard to the beautiful and the great but not the good indicates, Dorter argues, a deficiency Plato may have recognized in the "theory of forms," which must posit something it cannot clarify; it involves the circularity, he suggests, that knowledge of the forms both presupposes knowledge of the good and is presupposed by knowledge of the good (139).

37 The interlacing of words, in that case, is not merely "curious and characteristic" (Burnet, 110).

38 Consider the sequence of questions Socrates poses to Hippias—beginning with the agreement that all the beautiful are beautiful by the beautiful, then inferring that the beautiful is something, and finally asking what it is (*Hippias Major* 287c–d). While the *auto* points to the being in itself of the idea, its being is precisely for the other, as Nicolai Hartmann puts it, since it is the hypothesized ground through which anything in the world of becoming can and should be judged as being (*Platons Logik des Seins*, 244).

39 This allusion to the ritual address to the gods (see *Cratylus* 400d–e; cf. *Philebus* 12c; *Timaeus* 28b) depends on the reading *hopos prosagoreumenē*, "however it may be called," rather than *hopos prosgenomenē*, "however it is added to it" (see Burnet, 111; Gallop, 234–35). If the latter reading were correct, Socrates might be implying one more version of the problem of addition lurking behind the notion of "participation." On either reading, Socrates clarifies the grounds for the unwillingness he expressed to insist on his thoughts about the afterlife (63c) or the unwillingness he will express to insist on the truth of his concluding myth (114d).

40 See Aristotle's critique of Platonic "participation" (*Metaphysics* 987b10–14). Socrates' analysis in the *Phaedo*, according to Aristotle's interpretation, should be criticized for presenting the *eidē* as sufficient to account for *genesis*, as well as being (see *Metaphysics* 991b3–9; *On Generation and Corruption* 335b8–17).

41 Socrates says goodbye to these wise causes, while the soul of the philosopher, according to his earlier description, says goodbye to the body (65c) or those who care for their own soul say goodbye to those who live in service to their bodies (82d); cf. 63e, 116d.

42 Socrates takes up the question, What is the beautiful?, in the *Hippias Major*. Hippias, "the beautiful and wise," is confident about his first answer, that a beautiful maiden is beautiful. But as the examination of that opinion unfolds, it finds the evaluation of the beautiful always relative to a kind. It thus leads to the problem Socrates states with a citation from Heraclitus: "The most beautiful ape is ugly in comparison with the class of humans" (DK 82). And the most beautiful maiden, Socrates gets Hippias to agree, would appear ugly compared with the race of gods (*Hippias Major* 287e–289c). Cf. John Brentlinger on *pros ti* qualities, which require a qualification "in relation to something" ("Incomplete Predicates and the Two-World Theory of the *Phaedo*," 70–71.) On the wide range of such predications, see G. E. L. Owen, "A Proof in the '*Peri Ideon*,'" 306.

43 See ch. 3, n. 31.

44 In contrast with the answer, "By number," where the dative *plethei* is supplemented by the accusative *dia to plethos*, the answer "by magnitude" (*megethei*) is not supplemented by the neuter substantive; Socrates suggests perhaps, by this lack of parallel, the impossibility of reducing measure to number, pointing to the problem of incommensurability (see Klein, *Greek Mathematical Thought*, 67–68).

45 Reading *ephoito*, "would attack," rather than *echoito*, "would hold on to" (see Gallop, 235; Burnet, 113), although in either case Socrates' warning seems to be directed against a challenger who demands a defense of the hypothesis before examining its consequences. That "safety of the hypothesis" that Cebes is told to "hold on to" must be the causality of participation in the *eidē*, in accordance with which all further consequences are to be examined. Since Socrates now specifies the harmony or discord of the consequences with each other, *sumphōnein* would seem to mean here consistency; but the fact

that Socrates is considering the *hormēthenta* of the hypothesis—the things that follow from it—would seem to confirm the meaning of *sumphōnein* at 100a as entailment (see Kenneth Sayre, *Plato's Analytic Method*, 9–11).

46 The status of any particular hypothesis as a measure of the truth of its consistent consequences can itself be justified, Hans Wagner argues, only insofar as it is based on the safe hypothesis of the causality of the ideas (see "Platos Phaedo und der Beginn der Metaphysik als Wissenschaft," 367–71). That the "*logos* judged strongest" at 100a is not necessarily identical with the safe hypothesis of the causality of the ideas at 101d does not itself justify R. S. Bluck's identification of the former with Socratic definitions and the latter with Platonic separated *eidē* (see *Plato's Phaedo*, 160–65).

47 It has been suggested that, since no single proposition could logically entail contradictory consequences, some of the consequences of a given hypothesis may contradict other standing assumptions: Socrates refutes Simmias' image of the soul as a harmony by appealing to his acceptance of the premises of recollection. Another possibility is a hypothesis understood as a whole of parts, some of which might be latently inconsistent with each other. See the analysis by Robinson (131–33), who finds in this account the operation of the elenchic procedure, as a case in which a hypothesis may entail the contradiction of itself. Paul Plass proposes, in this context, the existence of the ideas as the fundamental hypothesis and the causality of participation in the ideas, in contrast with all other kinds of cause, as a concordant consequence ("Socrates' Method of Hypothesis in the *Phaedo*," 103–12). But is the hypothetical being of the ideas separable in this way from the causal role ascribed to them?

48 This procedure may explain the fact that ancient writers, including Proclus and Diogenes Laertius, credit Plato with the invention of the mathematical method of "analysis" (see Klein, *Greek Mathematical Thought*, 260; see also Sayre, 25). The mathematical analytic method, Klein explains, begins with the assumption of what is sought as if it were given, then proceeds through its consequences to a truth already granted (155, 260–61). If the analysis generates consequences convertible with the original hypothesis, that hypothesis can be proved through the method of "synthesis," by reversing the order of propositions arrived at during the analysis (see Sayre, 20–28). The difficulties that Sayre finds in applying this analogy (37–38) seem to be reflected in this fact: the analytic process as typically represented in the Platonic dialogues shows a given hypothesis to be refuted by leading to contradictory consequences rather than vindicated by leading to something incontrovertibly true (see Klein, *Commentary on Plato's Meno*, 83–84).

49 "The best among the higher hypotheses," Hartmann argues, cannot be one more hypothesis among others, and must therefore be the principle of hypothesizing itself (253); cf. Paul Natorp, *Platos Ideenlehre*, 155. But Socrates has never identified the hypothetical procedure of reasoning as itself a hypothesis, and it is not clear what it would mean to do so.

50 The Eleatic Stranger, remarking on the criteria for determining the fitting length of a discourse intended to make its hearers "more dialectical" (*Statesman* 286d–287a; cf. 302b), suggests the necessity of a compromise between the primary goal of discovering the beings and whatever discovery constitutes the ostensible goal of the discussion. See Benardete, "On Plato's *Timaeus* and Timaeus' Science Fiction," 170.

51 Cf. Aristotle *Nicomachean Ethics* 1095a30–35.

52 Cf. *Republic* 454a–b, or the Eleatic Stranger's classification of the sophist as *antilogikos*, where Socrates seems to show up in the money-wasting, private part of the class (*Sophist* 225c–e).

53 Cf. *Republic* 393b.

54 Cf. Socrates' warning to Theaetetus of an *antilogikos* attack against the "impurity" of their *dialegesthai* (*Theaetetus* 196d–197a), together with Socrates' admission on the following day of his fear of being "worthless in *logoi*," for which he suspects the Eleatic Stranger may have come to refute them (*Sophist* 216a–b).

Chapter Eleven

1 See Gerold Prauss's discussion of the contrast between the Platonic notion of the individual thing as a mere aggregate of *dunameis* and the Aristotelian notion of substance and attribute, in *Platon und der logische Eleatismus*, especially 99–101; cf. ch. 6, n. 5 above. Plato is committed to the view, as Hector-Neri Castañeda puts it, that ordinary individuals are bundles of microindividuals; at least what he says about the soul in the *Phaedo* suggests that Plato rejected the notion of an indeterminate, quality-less substrate as the core of ordinary individuals ("Leibniz and Plato's *Phaedo*: Theory of Relations and Predication," 132–33).

2 Simmias is just like the middle finger between a larger and smaller one, which Socrates chooses in order to illustrate the nature of those perceptions whose contradictory report awakens thought. When perception of the middle finger as at once great and small puts the soul into a state of perplexity, it summons *logismos* and *noēsis* to investigate whether these are one or two; whereas for sight great and small are simply mixed together, *noēsis* must clarify how each can be one and both together two; it is compelled, consequently, to see them as separated, and finally to raise the question, "Whatever is the great and again the small?" In this way, Socrates concludes, we are led to distinguish the noetic from the visible (see *Republic* 523b–524d). Cf. n. 19 below.

3 "The great and the small," Aristotle reports, as a replacement for the Pythagorean infinite, constitutes, together with "the one," the first principles of Platonic philosophy (*Physics* 187a17–19; *Metaphysics* 987b21–27). For an analysis of these principles, see Hans Joachim Krämer, *Arete bei Platon und Aristoteles*, especially 250–59; on the Aristotelian and doxographic sources, see Konrad Gaiser, *Platons ungeschriebene Lehre*, 522–33. On their role in the *Sophist*, *Parmenides*, and *Philebus*, see Jacob Klein, *Plato's Trilogy*, 61–63.

4 For an analysis of the similar use of this metaphor to account for the transformation of the elements of the cosmos (*Timaeus* 57a–c), see David O'Brien, "A Metaphor in Plato: 'Running Away' and 'Staying Behind' in the *Phaedo* and *Timaeus*," 297–99.

5 Cf. *Theaetetus* 159b–c.

6 See John Burnet, *Plato's Phaedo*, 116, 117, 119, 121.

7 No one present except Socrates, Hans-Georg Gadamer argues, could have raised this objection ("The Proofs of Immortality in Plato's *Phaedo*," in *Dialogue and Dialectic*, 35). Plato seems to offer a different clue, however, by connecting Phaedo's uncertain report of Plato's absence (59b) with his inability to name the challenger of Socrates' argument.

8 See especially *Statesman* 262d–e. Cf. Klein's analysis of these most comprehensive *eidē* of number, in *Greek Mathematical Thought and the Origin of Algebra*, 57.

9 Socrates refers to each number that is odd by nature as a singular entity (*hē trias, hē pemptas*), while he refers to each number in "the other (*heteros*) series" as a collection (*ta duo kai tettara*, 104b) and says nothing about their being even by nature. This is unlikely to reflect "no systematic distinction" (David Gallop, *Plato Phaedo*, 201); for

if evenness is defined as division into two equal parts, and oddness as division yielding a remainder of one indivisible unit, evenness would be common to numbers as well as to infinitely divisible magnitudes, while oddness would be characteristic only of discrete and indivisible units that can be counted (Klein, 57–58). The priority of the odd over the even is suggested as well by the Pythagorean identification of the even with the infinite and the odd with the limit (Aristotle *Physics* 203a10–15). Aristotle refers to the Platonic notion of the dyad as *hē hetera phusis* through which numbers other than "the first" can be generated as from a matrix (*Metaphysics* 987b33–988a1; cf. W. D. Ross, *Plato's Theory of Ideas*, 188–89). The Platonists claim, Aristotle reports, that there is no generation of odd numbers, implying that there is a generation of even ones; he proceeds with an analysis of the construction of the first even from the unequal, the great and small, when equalized (*Metaphysics* 1091a23–26).

10 Socrates introduces the word "*idea*" as a synonym, apparently, for "*eidos*"; but the *idea* is always spoken of here as being "in" something or excluded by something that has the opposite *idea* in it, although not every *idea* is an opposite. Each reference to "*idea*" in this argument is exemplified, furthermore, by mathematicals, either the odd or the even, or the *idea* of three (104b9, d2, d6, d9, e1, 105d13). But contrast the occurrences of "*idea*" in Socrates' myth (108d9, 109b5).

11 But cf. *Hippias Major* 302a–b.

12 On the distinction between mathematical number as a collection of "associable and undifferentiated" units and eidetic number as an indivisible unit or a set of "inassociable and differentiated" units, see especially *Metaphysics* 1080b11–14, 1080b37–1083a20, 1090b32–36. See the interpretation of eidetic number by Anders Wedberg, in *Plato's Philosophy of Mathematics*, 80–84, 116–22; cf. Klein, 79–99.

13 Along with other evidence that O'Brien offers to support the identity of *hē trias* with the *idea* of three is the fact that it seems to be parallel to *hē duas* and *hē monas*, in which anything that is to be two or one must participate (101c); see "The Last Argument of Plato's *Phaedo*.I," 216–19. He finds a problem, though, in the introduction of *hē trias* parallel to *ta duo kai tettara* (104b), but see n. 9 above.

14 On the controversial readings resulting from the complicated grammar of this passage, see Gallop, *Plato Phaedo*, 202–3, 235–36.

15 The term *morphē*, which is not used again in the dialogue, was introduced in a consistent way at 103c5 to describe the opposite *eidos* insofar as it represents the character of something that always possesses it—for example, the heat in fire or the cold in snow.

16 Unlike the triad, R. D. Archer-Hind asserts, "the soul which quickens the body is not the *idea* of soul, but a particular soul, just as the fever is a particular fever" (*Phaedo of Plato*, 115–16). The soul, Aristotle maintains (*De Anima* 403b14–19), or at least its *pathē* (cf. 431b25–33), being inseparable from the body, does not have the status of the mathematicals that are inseparable in being but separable in thought.

17 But Socrates has conspicuously omitted snow, which would seem incapable not only of defending itself against the approach of the hot, but also of approaching something else to impose on it its own character.

18 Just as five will not admit the *idea* of the even, Socrates adds, its double, ten—will not admit the *idea* of the odd. But in stressing the mathematical operation by which an even number is produced as the double of some odd number, Socrates suggests its simultaneous participation in the even and the odd. See the fragment assigned to Philolaus (DK 44B5), in which the even-odd appears as a third, derivative form of number. Cf. also *Parmenides* 143e–144a and the analysis by Wedberg, 140; on its re-

lation to Euclid's *Elements* (9.21–34), see Thomas Heath, *A History of Greek Mathematics*, 1:71–72, 292. The *idea* of the whole, Socrates continues, would not be admitted by the one-and-a-half and all such, or by the one-third and all such (105b). As a mixed fraction, however, the former would seem to be characterized, once again, by two opposites at once. Since, moreover, the opposite of the whole should be the part, it is not surprising that Socrates suddenly changes the pattern and does not add the complementary claim that no whole number could admit the *idea* of the part. If mathematical operations, as Socrates implies, present a threat to the principle of exclusion of opposites, only the eidetic number could guarantee the safety of *logos*.

19 Given this progression, it is not surprising to find a debate as to whether Plato recognized the distinctive character of relations. That this is the purpose of *Phaedo* 102b–d is the contention of Castañeda ("Plato's *Phaedo* Theory of Relations," 467–80). But to see genuine puzzles about relational facts in this passage, Castañeda asserts, it must be "understood from what it says" and "not interpreted in view of the final argument for immortality" ("Plato's Relations, Not Essences or Accidents, at *Phaedo* 102b2–d2," 52). It is the context of the final argument, Gallop maintains, that shows Plato's primary concern to be the contrast between essential and accidental attributes ("Castañeda on *Phaedo* 102b–d," 55). The question, as Christopher Kirwan understands it, is whether the exceptions Plato admits to the principle forbidding compresence of opposites include all nonessential contraries, all relative contraries, or as Kirwan argues, only comparative contraries: Simmias can be greater and smaller, but not simultaneously great and small ("Plato and Relativity," 123–27).

20 The monad could be the cause of anything being one or of any number being odd without itself being construed as a number: just before this Socrates listed the even numbers beginning with two and the odd with three (104a–b). Cf. *Republic* 524d, where Socrates asks about "number and the one" as if they were not the same. One is not itself a number, Aristotle argues, but a principle of numbers (*Metaphysics* 1087b34–1088a8).

21 Cf. Klein, *Commentary on Plato's Meno*, 142–44.

22 The Pythagoreans, according to Aristotle, identify one as both, insofar as it consists of the limit, which is odd, as well as the unlimited, which is even (*Metaphysics* 986a17–21). Since the fragment attributed to Philolaus refers to the even-odd in the singular (DK 4485), M. E. Hager argues that this characterizes only the one ("Philolaus on the Even–Odd," 1–2). For an analysis of how the monad could function as a cause of oddness in number without itself being odd, see Wedberg, 137–38; cf. Klein, *Commentary on Plato's Meno*, 142–44.

23 Cf. Nietzsche, *Die Fröhliche Wissenschaft*, Book 4, §340. See ch. 13, n. 32 below.

24 Socrates' list of refined causes, consequently, does not simply replace his original list of safe ones: he offers no noncontradictory cause of something being beautiful, greater or smaller, with which he began the analysis (100b–101b).

25 Socrates must now demonstrate, O'Brien argues, that soul excludes death in the new sense—that is, its own destruction (*olethros*)—whereas he has already demonstrated that it can survive the passage from life to death in the old sense—that is, separation from the body ("The Last Argument of Plato's *Phaedo*.II," 98). But the first part of the last argument has demonstrated that soul cannot admit death insofar as it is that which animates a living body; it has not and could not have shown, consequently, the ability of soul to exist apart from the body.

26 That Socrates' reference to "the unjust and unmusical" recalls the need to supplement "the greatest music" with "demotic music" is a suggestion, among many others, that I owe to Seth Benardete.

27 A dead living being, Strato objects, is as impossible as dead soul (see Damascius *Commentary on the Phaedo* 1.431). To overcome this objection, Damascius postulates a distinction between the life "brought forward," which is the opposite of death and exists in a substratum—that is, the body—and the life "bringing forward," which exists by itself and is identified with soul (1.458–460). But the distinction seems to be sufficiently accounted for by the difference between body as a neutral subject that can be bonded to either of two opposites and soul as a "refined cause" inseparably bonded to one opposite.

28 Socrates should not be accused of unjustifiably transferring the ascription of deathlessness from that which has soul to soul itself, as David Keyt argues ("The Fallacies in Plato's *Phaedo* 102a–107b," 171). For he can, on the basis of the preceding argument, ascribe deathlessness to that which is always the cause of life, even if it is itself not necessarily characterized as living.

29 Only in the case of soul, O'Brien argues, is it unnecessary to add the qualification "whenever it is," since in being always or essentially *athanatos*, soul cannot be or become dead ("Last Argument of Plato's *Phaedo*.I," 213). But the impossibility of soul remaining what it is and being dead is not identical with the impossibility of its ceasing to exist, hence the necessity of the supplementary argument to establish the premise that the immortal is imperishable (cf. Gallop, 216; Keyt, 171). Cebes' cursory agreement to that premise, O'Brien contends, is based on his assumption that *anōlethros* means "always *athanatos*" ("Last Argument of Plato's *Phaedo*.II," 103). But if he does make that assumption, he illustrates the error of ignoring the distinction between "what" something is and "that" it is.

30 Since the alternative now at stake is that of withdrawal or destruction, it is a demonstration of the indestructibility of soul that would seem to be required. The formulation of Socrates' question calls attention, therefore, to the first appearance in the argument of the term "*anōlethros*," which Cebes introduced with his demand for a demonstration that the soul is completely deathless and imperishable (88b; cf. 95b–c).

31 But the fact that the two cases are not formulated in precisely the same way—snow, for example, is unhot (*athermon*), but fire is uncoolable (*apsukton*), as Burnet remarks (123–24)—may be significant insofar as the pair constitute a model for the conclusion of the argument.

32 Cf. especially *Parmenides* 156a–b, where becoming (*gignesthai*) is defined as receiving an *ousia*, and being destroyed (*appolusthai*) as losing an *ousia*: in becoming one, being many is destroyed, and vice versa.

33 *To athanaton* must mean, O'Brien argues, that which is deathless, not deathlessness itself ("Last Argument of Plato's *Phaedo*.I," 207); for Socrates asks if it is *also* imperishable, although he did not establish the imperishability of the essential qualities in the previous examples. If, however, Socrates means that whatever is deathless is also imperishable, it is odd that he concludes not that the soul is imperishable, but rather that it cannot be destroyed.

34 The word "*aïdion*" has not been mentioned before and will not be mentioned again. Cf. *Timaeus* 29a, 37c–d, 40b; *Philebus* 66a; *Republic* 611b.

35 But Cebes gives no argument to defend the inference from the assumption that there must always be something existing to the required claim that there must be something that always exists (see Gallop, 219–20).

36 The argument would have to demonstrate that soul is essentially characterized by existence, so that it would necessarily exclude nonexistence. It would thus be shown to

be a necessary being, of the kind required as the object of the ontological argument for the existence of God (cf. O'Brien, "Last Argument of Plato's *Phaedo*.II," 103–6). That Socrates does not succeed in this demonstration seems to be Plato's indication of the impossibility of treating existence as a predicate that, if denied, would contradict the necessary characterization of a subject (cf. Kant's criticism of the ontological argument, *Critique of Pure Reason*, B621–29).

37 The model for this transformation is the problem of the cause of two:

38 On the expression "*tō onti*" in the dialogue as a whole, see ch. 4, n. 41 above.

39 Compare the claim defending skepticism about our knowledge of the gods attributed to Protagoras (DK 80B4).

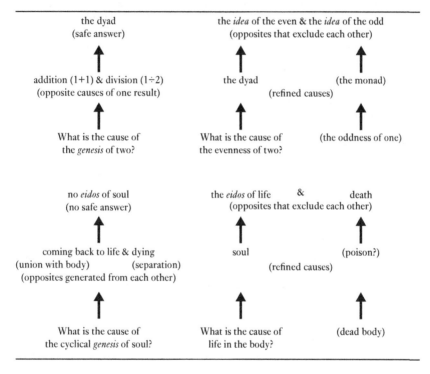

40 The final argument does not, therefore, reconcile the conflicting functions of soul in its relation to the body, on the one hand, and to the forms, on the other, as Kenneth Dorter contends (see ch. 5, n. 30, above). That there is no reference in the last argument to other forms besides life, Dorter argues, is simply because it would have complicated the argument without furthering it (*Plato's Phaedo*, 151). But this is one, if not the, crucial issue of the dialogue, and Plato has hardly refrained from complications in this final argument.

41 Apart from its appearances in the discussion of Anaxagoras (97c–d, 98a–c, 99a), all other occurrences of *nous* in the dialogue seem to be an informal usage: a man "with sense" (62e, 102a, 114d), a thought "in mind" (63c), "mindless" demotic virtues (82b), a "sensible" soul that is virtuous and good (93b).

218

Chapter Twelve

1 Cf. *Timaeus* 29c.

2 Socrates will use this address on one last occasion (115c), when it is least appropriate as a description but most necessary as an exhortation.

3 Cf. *Republic* 608c.

4 Cf. *Republic* 610d. See also Leo Strauss's analysis of the theme and tone of Moses Mendelssohn's *Phädon*, in contrast to the Platonic dialogue (Introduction to Mendelssohn, *Schriften zur Philosophie*, 3.1, xiii–xxxiii). When Socrates remarks that, if death were the end it would be a benefit to the wicked (*Phaedo* 107c), he does not imply that the belief in immortality is a prerequisite for being good. Mendelssohn's Socrates, on the other hand, is made to claim that, if the soul were mortal, it would make no difference whether my life has been a credit or a shame to creation (*Phädon* 79.30–31). Whereas the comforting character of the belief in immortality is grounds for suspicion in the eyes of the Platonic Socrates, for Mendelssohn's Socrates, it is grounds for accepting its truth or at least its high probability (88.16–25).

5 Cf. *Republic* 608e–611a.

6 Cf. *Republic* 423d–424a; *Laws* 874d.

7 Cf. *Republic* 617e.

8 See Damascius *Commentary on the Phaedo* 1.492.

9 Cf. *Gorgias* 524a. A tripartite path, Damascius suggests, could be inferred from the cult of Hecate, at places where three roads meet (1.495–96).

10 The Athenian Stranger distinguishes murders committed involuntarily, or in *thumos*, from those that are voluntary and unjust, resulting from submission to pleasure, lust, or envy (*Laws* 869e ff.). He leaves to the "Interpreters" the legal treatment of "one who slays the nearest and dearest"; but his prescription for the isolated tomb of the suicide (873c–d) sounds like the isolation Socrates describes here of the unpurified soul in Hades.

11 Cf. *Apology* 30d, 41d.

12 Of the earth's spherical shape, at least, Socrates may be persuaded by the Pythagorean Archytas (see Erich Frank, *Platon und die sogennanten Pythagoreer*, 185). On the influence of Democritus or Archelaos on Socrates' account of the hollows of the earth's surface, see Frank (189); cf. Paul Friedländer, *Platon*, 1:287.

13 See *Apology* 18b–c.

14 See Burnet, *Plato's Phaedo*, 150; cf. n. 17 below.

15 Aristotle criticizes the argument, which he attributes to Anaximander, that the earth must remain at rest in the center of the heavens, since it cannot move in opposite directions at once (*De Caelo* 295b11–25).

16 Cf. Socrates' construction of the best city in speech as a model writ large, in order to discover the nature of justice in the individual, or as it turns out, in the individual soul (*Republic* 368d–369a, 434e–435d).

17 Socrates' description of the true earth echoes the description he presents to Glaucon, at the conclusion of an argument on the immortality of the soul, of the sea god Glaucus (to whom he may allude at *Phaedo* 108d): the difficulty of apprehending the true nature of the sea god, concealed by the earthy accretions clinging to him, illustrates the difficulty of apprehending the true nature of soul itself, whether polyeidetic or monoeidetic or whatever it is like, as long as it is not cleansed of the earthy accretions clinging to it (*Republic* 611b–612a).

18 Cf. *Phaedrus* 248a–b.

19 Cf. *Republic* 514a–517b.
20 Socrates alludes, Burnet suggests (131), to the Pythagorean theory of the dodeca-hedron, with twelve sides, each of which is a regular pentagon. This seems to be the fifth regular solid, most nearly approaching the sphere to which Timaeus refers, as that which the demiurge used for the construction of the whole (*Timaeus* 55c).
21 Like the direct vision of the heavenly bodies and the gods, the precious metals require no *technē* to be brought into the open. Cf. Aeschylus *Prometheus Bound* 501–4 and the analysis by Seth Benardete, "The Crimes and Arts of Prometheus," 33–34.
22 Cf. *Apology* 41c.
23 Since Socrates has replaced the image of the cave representing the *polis* with his account of the hollows of the earth, one might speculate that the epistemological equivalent to this ratio of elements is the ratio represented by the "divided line" (see *Republic* 509d–511e). *Aither*, the highest element that is inaccessible to us, would fittingly correspond to *noēsis*, while earth would correspond to the domain of *pistis*; and just as *eikasia* and *dianoia*, the lower levels of each half of the divided line, are connected by virtue of the doubleness that allows for the recognition of an image as an image, our water, in which images are reflected, is said to be equiv-alent, as the lowest element here, to the air that is the lowest element in the region above.
24 See ch. 4, n. 41.
25 With their perfect sight of the heavenly bodies, the inhabitants of the true earth would have no impulse to ascend to the noetic science of astronomy, based not on vision but on calculation (cf. *Republic* 529a–530c).
26 Socrates' account of the true earth should be compared with Aetius' report (DK 44A20): "Some of the Pythagoreans, among whom is Philolaus, explain the earthlike appearance of the moon by saying that it is inhabited like our own, with living creatures and plants that are bigger and fairer than ours. Indeed, the animals on it are fifteen times as powerful and do not excrete, and the day is correspondingly long." (See W.K.C. Guthrie, *History of Greek Philosophy*, 1:285.)
27 Cf. *Timaeus* 73a, 78a–79a; Herodotus *Histories* 2.40, 86, 92.
28 The subterranean channels function like the channels cut through the body, as through a garden, so that it might be watered as if from a running stream (*Timaeus* 77c).
29 Cf. *Timaeus* 89a; *Laws* 789d.
30 See Homer *Iliad* 8.14; cf. Hesiod *Theogony* 720–26.
31 Cf. *Timaeus* 78e–79a.
32 See Aristotle's report and criticism of Socrates' "hydrography" (*Meteorology* 355b33–356a33). If the rivers are to flow downhill only, J. S. Morrison argues, the earth would have to be hemispherical ("The Shape of the Earth in Plato's *Phaedo*," 113–16). But Socrates' reference to the "so-called lower regions" would seem to confirm the spher-ical shape of the earth.
33 See *Timaeus* 51a–b.
34 See *Timaeus* 80e.
35 See *Timaeus* 73a.
36 For either side of the central point would be uphill to both the streams that flow in on the opposite side from where they flowed out and those that flow in on the same side (see Burnet, 136–38).
37 See *Timaeus* 70a–b.

38 Homer's list of the "great and terrible" rivers of the Underworld includes the Acheron, Pyriphlegethon, and Cocytus as a branch of the Styx (*Odyssey* 10.512–14, 11.157); cf. Hesiod *Theogony* 361, 775–806.

39 Homer's Okeanos, which encircles the earth's surface (*Odyssey* 10.508–11; cf. *Iliad* 18.607–8; Hesiod *Theogony* 133), Socrates adds to his own list of the rivers flowing in and out of Tartarus. Perhaps, since it plays no explicit role in his account of the souls of the dead carried through the rivers under the earth, it is meant to carry the purified souls to the surface of the true earth.

40 See Homer *Iliad* 2.753.

41 See Aeschylus *Agamemnon* 1160; Euripides *Alcestis* 458.

42 Cf. *Republic* 386b, 387b; *Laws* 904d.

43 On the Styx and Cocytus, see *Republic* 387b–c; the boiling of the Pyriphlegethon is like the boiling of *thumos* (cf. *Republic* 440c).

44 The souls do not appear here naked before naked judges, as they do in the underworld court of the *Gorgias* (523b–e).

45 On incurable evil, see *Protagoras* 325a; *Gorgias* 525c–e; *Republic* 410a, 615e; *Laws* 854d–e, 862d–e. On unjust homicide, see *Laws* 869e–873b, and n. 10 above.

46 Cf. Glenn Morrow, *Plato's Cretan City*, 466. The psychological understanding underlying such a provision is brought to light by the Athenian Stranger, who prefaces his laws dealing with pollution from involuntary murder with a prelude in the form of an ancient *mythos*: the soul of the man who has died by violence, even from an accidental act, is enraged with his slayer, particularly when he sees him inhabiting his old haunts, for the dead man in his anger has the slayer's memory as his ally and thus gives the guilty man no peace until he does·penance (*Laws* 865d–e).

47 It should be noted, given the context of the dialogue as a whole, that purification for pollution is the province of Apollo (cf. *Laws* 865b) and, in light of the dramatic conclusion of the dialogue, that pollution is thought to result primarily not only from bloodshed, but also from contact with a corpse (cf. *Laws* 947d; and Morrow, 415–51).

48 According to the legal code of the Athenian Stranger, the readmission after a period of exile of a man who committed involuntary homicide depends on pardon granted by the nearest of kin to the dead man (*Laws* 866a), while readmission of a man who committed murder in passion, either with or without deliberate intention, depends on a pardon granted by the team of twelve law wardens appointed as judges for such cases (867e). The absolution of a murderer on the basis of the forgiveness of the victim himself is indicated only in the case of a man who kills a parent in the madness of rage, or a slave who kills a free man in self-defense; in these situations, the voluntary forgiveness of the dying victim suffices to release the murderer, at least after he purifies himself in the same way as an involuntary murderer would (869a).

49 Cf. Damascius 1.550.

50 Cf. 116c; *Apology* 39c–d.

51 Cf. *Laws* 903d–904e.

52 The lover of the body has been distinguished only from the lover of wisdom and not from a "lover of soul," for *philopsychos* is the label for a coward who clings to life at all costs (see ch. 3, n. 28).

53 Cf. the double "for the sake of " at 82c and 83e, and ch. 6, n. 26.

54 See ch. 6, n. 26.

Chapter Thirteen

1   Socrates bathes himself in preparation for drinking the *pharmakon*. The best motion for *katharsis*, according to Timaeus, is gymnastics, through which the body moves itself, and then the *aiōra* of swaying vehicles, through which the body is moved as a whole by another, but purification by a *pharmakon* is useful for one compelled to rely on it (*Timaeus* 89a).

2   A Platonic commentary on the final scene of the *Phaedo* is provided in the division through which the Eleatic Stranger discovers "the sophist of noble descent" as the practitioner of an art of purification (*Sophist* 226c–231b). Having identified the latter as the diacritic art of separating better from worse, the Stranger asserts that the *logos* wants to separate out the purification of *dianoia* (227c; cf. *Phaedo* 67c); yet he accepts, for their present purposes, Theaetetus' agreement on the division between purification of bodies and of soul. After the purification of nonensouled bodies is separated from that of the bodies of living animals, the latter is in turn divided into that within the body, accomplished by gymnastics and medicine, and that outside the body, accomplished by bathing. But insofar as the *logos* wants to know what is akin, rather than what is better and worse, the Stranger insists, there would be no difference between this inner and outer. "The method of the *logos*" would never consider whether the benefit to be derived from a *pharmakon* is more or less than that to be derived from bathing, for it has no more interest in the one than the other (227a–b). Plato's Socrates, who looks very like the "noble sophist" discovered by the Stranger, enacts this double corporeal purification just before he is transformed from a living animal into a nonensouled body.

3   See *Crito* 45e–46a.

4   See *Crito* 45c–d.

5   See *Crito* 46b–e, 48b, 49a–b, e.

6   Cf. *Crito* 46b.

7   Cf. *Crito* 46e–47a, 54c–d.

8   See *Apology* 38b.

9   It was Simmias and Cebes, Crito informs Socrates, who offered to help pay for his escape from the Athenian prison (*Crito* 45b).

10   If Socrates' indifference to his burial were carried out in deed, it would violate a fundamental sacred law. Socrates thus appears as the Platonic alternative to the tragic Antigone, whose defiant burial of her brother at all costs allows, Seth Benardete observes, for "a blurring of the distinction between body and soul, Hades and the grave" ("A Reading of Sophocles' *Antigone*," 163).

11   The fatherless children Socrates leaves behind are like the "orphaned" written word that has no power to defend itself (*Theaetetus* 164e); to guard against such guilt, the philosopher eager to "withdraw" would have to leave behind a product of writing (*Statesman* 295c), able to defend itself and live independently of its father (*Phaedrus* 275e)—like the Platonic dialogue.

12   Cf. *Apology* 34d; *Crito* 45c–d, 54a.

13   Cf. *Phaedo* 84c, 95e. The *Phaedo* presents the rare, but not unique occasion on which the Platonic Socrates, typically presented in conversation with others, is reported to have been absorbed in thought alone (cf. *Symposium* 174d–175b, 220c–d).

14   The contrast between the jailer's initial reference to "the Eleven" and Phaedo's reference to their "servant" implicitly raises the question of responsibility, which the servant of the Eleven is about to make thematic.

15 For Socrates has not only been condemned to death but has had to await his execution for some length of time in the Athenian prison, and he regards it as an evil, as he acknowledged at his trial, to be compelled to live like a slave to those in authority (*Apology* 37b–c).

16 Cf. 60a, 63a, 86d, 117b. The expression "*anablepsas*," through which Phaedo describes Socrates' response to the servant of the Eleven, Socrates uses to describe the recovery of sight after blindness (*Phaedrus* 243b; *Republic* 621b), like that of the prisoner released from the cave who experiences great pain when he first lifts up his eyes to the light (*Republic* 515c; cf. 586a).

17 Socrates concludes his speech to Crito—"But come, be persuaded and don't do otherwise" (*Phaedo* 117a)—in the same words with which Crito concluded his exhortation to Socrates to escape from prison (*Crito* 46a).

18 Perhaps the dialogue suggests a situation corresponding to its mythical model: when the legendary ship returned from Crete to Athens, the great victory of Theseus over the Minotaur brought in its wake, by a mistaken signal, the death of his father, Aegeus (see Plutarch, "Theseus," *Lives*, ch. 22).

19 Cf. Cicero's report of Theramenes who, when ordered by the Thirty Tyrants to drink the hemlock, raised his cup to the health of the fair Critias (*Tusculan Disputations* 1.96).

20 Socrates wishes to pour a libation to the gods from the cup of poison after completing his speeches on philosophy as the practice of dying, just as the participants of Plato's *Symposium* pour a libation of wine to the gods before beginning their speeches on *erōs* (176a): *erōs* might be understood as an "antidote" to the practice of dying, just as wine is an antidote to hemlock (*Lysis* 219e).

21 Cf. *Charmides* 167a; *Republic* 583b; *Philebus* 66d; *Seventh Letter* 334d, 340a; and ch. 2, n. 37, above.

22 Socrates' prayer could not bring the danger of inadvertently asking for a curse rather than a blessing (cf. *Laws* 687c–688b, 801a–b).

23 Cf. *Phaedrus* 237a.

24 Socrates cites a Pythagorean maxim, according to Damascius (1.559), identifying death as good and sacred, while aiming to overcome disturbances diverting the "upward impulse." But Plato seems to indicate, with this formula, one more union of opposites, for he had Phaedo, at the very outset of the conversation, introduce Xanthippe's "womanly" lament by reporting that she *aneuphēmēse* (60a). (See Burnet's note on the term in *Plato's Phaedo*, 12–13.)

25 It is not easy to understand why Socrates allows the young men to be present and witness the process of dying, even feeling his body grow cold. They are not motivated, presumably, by the spirited desire to see justice done by gazing at the corpse of a criminal punished, as in the story Socrates tells of Leontius to illustrate the complexity of *thumos* (*Republic* 439e–440a, cf. ch. 9, n. 19 above).

26 Socrates finds in the hemlock just the drug useful to test and train for courage that the Athenian Stranger presents as a counterpart to his discovery of wine as a drug useful to test and train for shame (*Laws* 647e–650b). Socrates presides over his death scene, attempting to control the men overcome with fear, precisely like the sober commander required, according to the Stranger, to preside over a gathering of shameless drunkards (671d–672a).

27 If pleasure is not simply the absence of pain, then the condition of experiencing neither pleasure nor pain, Socrates argues with Protarchus, must be distinguished from each of the others (*Philebus* 43d–e); this state—which may, Socrates surmises, be most divine (33b)—would characterize the "chosen life" of purest thought (55a).

28 Cf. Aristotle *On the Generation of Animals* 741b15–24.

29 Socrates' life ends at dusk with his request to have a cock sacrificed to Asclepius; it is the crowing of the cocks at dawn that awakens Aristodemus, who reports to Apollodorus the conversation he narrates in the *Symposium*. This awakening enables us to hear the conclusion of Socrates' last speeches with Agathon and Aristophanes, compelling them to admit that the same man might be capable of writing by art both tragedy and comedy (223c–d). That the *Symposium* and the *Phaedo* together form one whole, like comedy and tragedy, does not, however, preclude the possibility that each is itself a whole, an inseparable union of comedy and tragedy.

30 Socrates' command to Crito—"But give back what is due and do not neglect it"— seems to echo his self-command in regard to the dream he believes he has neglected: Socrates thought he should "not disobey it but do it" (61a).

31 See *Republic* 407c–408c.

32 "Dieses lächerliche und furchtbare 'letzte Wort' heißt für den, der Ohren hat: 'O Kriton, das Leben ist eine Krankheit!' Ist es möglich! Ein Mann wie er, der heiter und vor aller Augen wie ein Soldat gelebt hat—war Pessimist!" (Nietzsche, *Die fröhliche Wissenschaft*, Book 4, §340. Cf. "Das Problem des Sokrates," §12, in *Götzen-Dämmerung*).

33 If Nietzsche misunderstood Socrates, he would have unwittingly revealed the truth of Socrates' last words in the speech Zarathustra wishes to address to death: "'War das—das Leben?', will ich zum Tode sprechen. 'Wohlan! Noch einmal!'" ("Das trunkene Lied," in *Also Sprach Zarathustra*).

34 Cf. *Phaedrus* 274e–275a and Introduction, n. 25 above.

35 Cf. Damascius' account of these death rites (1.552, 2.150).

36 Consider Socrates' allusion at *Euthyphro* 15d–16a to Homer *Odyssey* 4.455–79; cf. *Apology* 26b–27a and *Euthyphro* 3a–b.

Achillis Bocchii Bonon. Symbolicarum quaestionum de Universo genere quas serio ludebat. Menelaos binding Proteus to force him to reveal the future. Giulio Bonasone, copperplate (1555). Print, book-illustration, Bologna.

On Plato's *Euthyphro*

At the Stoa of the King (2a–5c)

In the year 399 BCE the philosopher Socrates was put on trial in Athens for not acknowledging the gods of the city and corrupting the young; he was convicted by a jury of his fellow citizens, imprisoned, and put to death. In Plato's dramatic universe, that series of events is set in motion on the day Socrates receives the indictment against him, when he encounters a young man, Euthyphro, who claims to have prophetic powers and special knowledge of the divine. The circumstances lead quite naturally to the question, What is the holy? In raising and addressing such a question, every Platonic dialogue represents an exchange of speeches embedded in the context of deeds; but in the *Euthyphro*, and the whole sequence of dialogues centering on Socrates' trial and death, Plato's ability to imbue the circumstances with philosophic significance is especially striking.

The setting of the *Euthyphro*, to begin with, reflects the inseparable connection of the theological issue at stake in the dialogue and its political framework: Socrates meets up with Euthyphro at the Stoa of the King, the vestigial royal title of the Athenian archon in charge of the city's ancestral sacrifices as well as impiety cases in the court.[1] Socrates' retrieval of the indictment at the Stoa of the King may be an historical fact;[2] it certainly serves Plato's purposes in the dialogue quite beautifully, with its startling reminder of the sophisticated democratic city of arts that engages in the public practice of sacrifice supervised by a "king." The inquiry Socrates is about to share with Euthyphro will conclude its attempt to define the holy with a consideration of that public practice of sacrifice. The action of the dialogue, at the same time, points to a further meaning of sacrifice, as it prepares for Socrates' trial and death on the horizon.

Euthyphro, we soon learn, has come to the Stoa of the King with a plan to initiate a legal proceeding against his own father, which he justifies with a claim to knowledge of the divine that is not accessible to ordinary human beings. On that basis, Euthyphro is confident about defying conventions, in particular, the custom of filial piety. He is in the process of enacting, unwittingly, an Oedipal plot that happens to have a perfect parallel in Socrates' description of his own situation: like a boy running to his mother to complain about his father, a zealous young man has run to the city to accuse Socrates of corrupting the youth (2c). Given the far greater power of the city than of a mother, the accusation that has brought Socrates to the Stoa of the King will culminate with his drinking hemlock in an Athenian prison.

The encounter of the philosopher with the seer in these highly fraught circumstances should be a matter of the utmost gravity, yet it becomes in Plato's representation a comic masterpiece treated with the lightest touch. In choosing the laughable boaster Euthyphro as Socrates' interlocutor, Plato seems to avoid providing an adequate test of the philosopher in the face of the true believer. The issues of great consequence to which the conversation points lie beneath the surface, as the very language of the work indicates: *The* dialogue on the holy speaks only of "gods"—in contrast with the other dialogues representing Socrates' trial, imprisonment, and death, which each refer at an important moment to "god" in the singular; it is equally silent about "*physis*," "*erōs*," or "*philosophia*," and perhaps most conspicuously, "*psychē.*"[3] Like the irony (*eironeia*) of an individual who makes himself appear less than he is,[4] the *Euthyphro*'s treatment of its important theme exhibits an ironic self-deprecation.

In their playful representation of the most serious matters, many of the Platonic dialogues betray the philosopher's debt to the comic poet, Aristophanes; but the *Euthyphro* proves to be a very particular Platonic response to Aristophanes' *Clouds*. In that work the comic poet puts Socrates on stage as the teacher of an art of speaking and an investigator of "things above the heavens and beneath the earth"—an image Socrates is still trying to combat in his trial, at the end of his life (*Apology* 18a–19c). Aristophanes' Socrates, a sophist and a naturalist, introduces new deities of a most fitting sort—the Clouds, natural goddesses of imitation—while revealing that Zeus does not exist. The potentially corrupting effect of his teaching lies at the heart of the drama. A profligate young man has been sent by his father to learn Socrates' art of speaking in order to acquire the skill to talk his way out of the debts he has incurred. Returning home after his lessons with Socrates, the young man finds himself in a disagreement with his father about the old poets and the new (exemplified by a Euripidean tale of incest)—a disagreement so virulent it ends with beating his father. Having himself sought out the Socratic education, the old man must accept his son's appeal to the Socratic principle that authority belongs, not to the paternal or the ancestral, but to the wise. When, however, his son threatens to turn against his mother, the father reaches a limit and the play comes to an ominous end with his setting Socrates' think-tank on fire. In the *Clouds*, Aristophanes thinks through the Socratic teaching to its furthest consequences—violation of the fundamental prohibitions of parricide and incest, implied in the play by their comic equivalents: the Socrates of the *Clouds* undermines the foundations of the family by putting into question their divine support.[5] The *Euthyphro*, as its dramatic action unfolds, offers Plato's response.

The profoundly meaningful intersection of philosopher and seer at the Stoa of the King is represented, in Plato's philosophic comedy, as a sheer coincidence. Euthyphro is certainly surprised to see Socrates; he knows enough about the philosopher to assume that he is not there to initiate a lawsuit against someone else. Socrates confirms that assumption. He has been summoned because of an allegation against him of corrupting the youth; and when Euthyphro questions, "By making what?," Socrates explains, "making new gods" (3b). Socrates, who in principle refrained his whole life from producing any writings, now faces an indictment—a *graphē*, literally a "writ"— as a maker (*poiētēs*) of gods. With this unique formulation of the charge against Socrates, the *Euthyphro* sets the question of the gods in the frame of "the ancient quarrel between poetry and philosophy."[6] If poetry, in contrast with philosophy, is essentially a matter of production (*poiēsis*), the charge against Socrates looks like a real misunderstanding. Of course, making new gods is a criminal offense because it entails, as Socrates adds, not believing (*nomizein*) in the old ones: the verb, from the word *nomos*, indicates how much impiety in the Greek *polis* consists, not in lacking faith, but in failing to respect the conventions of the city, which links its authority to the ancestral gods.[7]

As soon as he hears the accusation, Euthyphro expresses empathy with the philosopher: he himself is a constant victim of the Athenians' ridicule whenever he issues his prophesies in the assembly.[8] If only, Socrates wishes, he would incur the ridicule of his fellow citizens, rather than their lethal anger! That difference is illustrated in the cave image of the *Republic*: if someone who had ascended came back into the darkness still blinded by the light and tried to compete in making out the shadows on the wall, he would be laughed at mercilessly, but if he tried to free another from his chains, the prisoners would want to kill him.[9] In contrasting Euthyphro's complaints about being ridiculed with his own life-threatening situation, Socrates' apparently casual remark brings out a deep fissure in the city's self-understanding. The Athenians laugh at Euthyphro for taking literally the stories of the gods—they mock the seer for believing what they are supposed to hold sacred; yet they are ready to sentence the philosopher to death for not believing it. Theologically, the gods of the city are somehow recognized as figures produced by the poets; politically, the denial of these gods is a crime that can meet with capital punishment. Euthyphro's "fundamentalism" makes him a laughing stock in the enlightened city of arts; but the same city, whose darker side has its roots in the sacred, can execute the philosopher for putting into question the gods that give it its identity.[10]

Seeing Socrates as a mirror of himself, Euthyphro has his own interpretation of why the philosopher is so distrusted. He has heard of Socrates' famous *daimonion*, the semi-divine voice he claims to have within himself, which always holds him back from something that would endanger him. In Euthyphro's eyes, this prophetic *daimonion* puts Socrates, like himself, in a class of special individuals bound to arouse envy for their wisdom. Euthyphro ascribes to the Athenians the sort of envy Plato's Socrates analyzes in the complex psychology he develops of the comic poet, which applies most obviously to Aristophanes and his motivation in representing Socrates as a target of laughter.[11] If envy is indeed at work, as Euthyphro believes, why should it arouse in his case only the city's laughter, while it evokes such fear and anger when it comes to the philosopher? As Socrates explains, it is the belief that he can make others like himself that leads the city to feel threatened by him (3c). Euthyphro in that case must misunderstand the distrust of Socrates; it cannot be about the *daimonion*, insofar as this silent inner voice is the mark of Socrates' individuality and could never be reproduced in another.[12]

What then are the philosopher's "innovations concerning the divine things," as Euthyphro reformulates the charge and Socrates repeats it (3b, 5a)? We are given a clue when Socrates introduces the search for an *idea* of the holy—something that does not come to be or pass away, something that remains one and the same behind a manifold of changing appearances and can serve as a paradigm for all the particulars that imitate it or participate in it: the *idea* looks like the philosopher's replacement of the deathless gods, in particular, the poets' fabrication of gods like Nemesis and her siblings, Friendship and Strife, Fate and Death, Blame and Woe, among others.[13] Still, the philosopher, it seems, would not be a "*maker* of new gods" if the *idea* is not his product, but the truth he seeks to discover in his examination of opinion. Or is he indeed a kind of maker when he posits the unitary form as an independent being, which allows him to pose the question, What is it?[14] Euthyphro, in any case, will soon accept Socrates' question about the *idea* of the holy as if he has heard this kind of thing before; yet he never considers that it might illustrate the new conception of the highest beings by which Socratic philosophy has left its mark on others in the city, including himself.

Socrates, who is well aware of the effects his "divine innovations" have had, harbors no illusions about his situation. It would not be unpleasant, he reiterates, to pass the time in court with play and laughter—if only the trial were an Aristophanic comedy on stage! But if the city is serious, it would take a seer or prophet (*mantis*) like Euthyphro to know how things will turn out (3d–e). Perhaps Socrates' suit (*dikē*), Euthyphro assures him, may come to as satisfactory a conclusion as he expects of his own.[15] Socrates does not try to assess the seer's prophetic powers; he is apparently more interested now in the suit that has brought him to the Stoa of the King.

It is not a case of defense, Euthyphro explains, but prosecution, on the charge of murder, and it is against someone others think he is mad to prosecute—his own father. Socrates is shocked: by Heracles, only someone very far advanced in wisdom would proceed with such a plan! Surely the victim must have been a relative, perhaps his mother—that would have been the stuff of tragedy. Surprised at Socrates' conventional reaction, Euthyphro elaborates.

A laborer of his got drunk and in a fit of anger murdered one of the family's household servants; the murderer then died while being held in bonds by Euthyphro's father, who had sent for a religious official to learn what he should do. While his behavior sounds neglectful, Euthyphro's father was in fact simply waiting for advice from the interpreter (*exēgētēs*) of sacred customs and ancestral laws—waiting for a priestly communication of what the holy requires. If Euthyphro's intention is to prosecute his father for involuntary homicide, he is acting on behalf of the victim as if he were the next of kin: he adopts a familial relationship to his laborer that he denies in connection with his own father, just as he overlooks his laborer's act of murder while not hesitating to label his father a murderer. His father's deliberate action, meanwhile, in simply binding the man, happens to be precisely the deed of Zeus, to whom Euthyphro is about to appeal. Of course, what Euthyphro will refer to in his own defense is specifically Zeus' binding of his father for acting unjustly. This divine father-son drama has its human echo in the story of Oedipus, whose father sets out to do away with his son, in order to preempt a prophesy about being overthrown by him. Euthyphro steps into that plot as if he took his laborer to be a stand-in for himself, and his father's treatment of the man equivalent to the treatment of Oedipus by his father.

With no consideration of all the complexities of the case, Euthyphro is certain a crime has been committed that he must punish, and he cannot believe Socrates would care that the criminal happens to be his father. After all, knowingly associating with one who has shed blood, even, or especially, if he shares hearth and table, brings a state of pollution (*miasma*), unless purified by prosecuting him (4c). Euthyphro appeals to a procedure for dealing with the stain that defiles an involuntary slayer: if it remains un-purified, the contamination passes to the individual responsible for de-manding purification, which should be the victim's closest family member.[16] An archaic notion that concerns the sacred sphere of the family becomes, in Euthyphro's application, a universal standard of justice, to be carried out by anyone in the city, while in fact expressing quite specifically an angry desire to punish his father and assert his own independence.[17]

Feeling so misunderstood by the many, the enlightened seer expects the philosopher's approval, but Socrates portrays himself being as dis-turbed as Euthyphro's relations are about his lack of filial piety. Having described his own indictment as the product of a youthful zealot rebelling against paternal authority, Socrates has already put himself on the side of the fathers. Now, as Aristophanes recognized, that is hardly the role ex-pected of the philosopher, who is understandably suspected by the fathers of corrupting the young. Socrates' reaction to Euthyphro is called for, however, by the dangerous connection the seer has forged between the radical principle he will espouse in justification of his action and the con-tent he gives it, with his literal understanding of the traditional—puni-tive—gods.[18] Socrates' aim in the conversation is clearly to bring this young man back into the fold of generally accepted opinion. Of course, the dialogue also reveals how much Socratic philosophy is in the air, and hence perhaps a contributing factor, albeit unintentional, in the partial, and therefore dangerous, liberation that has led Euthyphro to his suppos-edly free-thinking plan.

His family's belief that it is unholy for a son to prosecute his own father fills Euthyphro with contempt for how little they know about "the divine, how it stands concerning the holy and the unholy" (4e). Euthyphro has stumbled unawares on a deep question: What exactly is "the divine" and how is it related to the holy? Socrates, who must have that question in mind, expresses his astonishment to the seer: By Zeus!, do you really believe you have such precise knowledge about the divine things that you are not afraid of doing something unholy?

The inquiry that opens up from here is divided in two halves. The first undertakes a search for the *idea* of the holy; it reaches its peak with the question whether a god would be subordinate to such an *idea* or rather the source of it, which ultimately points, if only implicitly, to the question, What is god? Euthyphro's failure to grasp the implications of that argument brings an end to the search for an *idea* of the holy and its replacement by something quite different—an examination of piety in the city and its relation to justice. The action of the dialogue, as it traverses these two halves, moves from a radical starting point, in which Euthyphro places himself on the level of the divine, to a conclusion affirming the most conventional understanding of piety, which assumes the complete subordination of humans to gods: in Socrates' strategic effort to deprive the seer of his pretentions to knowledge, the holy is dragged down from the heavens into the homes and cities.[19] That movement turns out to be, at the same time, a development in the philosopher's self-understanding.

What is the Holy? (5c–11b)

Socrates begins, not with the question of the divine in relation to the holy, but with the crime of impiety (*asebeia*), for which he will be put on trial: By Zeus, he implores Euthyphro, regarding murder or anything else, what sort of thing do you say the pious and the impious are (*to eusebes* and *to asesbes*, 5c)? Those terms, which concern human attitudes or practices, never recur in the first half of the dialogue. Indeed, Socrates drops his initial query even before giving Euthyphro a chance to respond, and immediately poses instead a more abstract and obscure question: Isn't the holy (*to hosion*) the same as itself in every action, and the unholy (*to anhosion*) completely the opposite, having some one *idea* (5d)? What, then, does Euthyphro say the holy and the unholy are?[20]

Undisturbed by the many puzzles in Socrates' question, or sequence of questions,[21] Euthyphro is ready to answer without hesitation: the holy is "the very thing I am now doing," that is, prosecuting the one who is acting unjustly (5d–e). What he is doing—literally, "making" (*poiein*)—is an act of punitive justice; but what makes it holy in Euthyphro's mind is its divine model, as he explains by reminding Socrates of the tales recounted by Hesiod.[22] Zeus, who is acknowledged to be the best and most just of the gods, put in bonds his father, Cronos, for acting unjustly.

Cronos had learned from his parents that he was destined to be overcome by his own son. He tried to prevent that destiny by devouring each of his children as they were born, but Zeus was rescued at birth, and a great stone given to Cronos to swallow in his place, leaving the young god behind to overturn his father's reign. Cronos had in turn acted even more terribly against his own father: Uranus, that is, Heaven, was so threatened by the birth of his children that he tried to shove each newborn back into their mother Earth, until she, scheming with her son Cronos, provided him with a sickle, with which he succeeded in castrating his father. The cosmological separation of Heaven from Earth is interpreted as a psychological account of a son violently separating his father from union with his mother in the Oedipal drama Hesiod stages among the first generations of the gods, which Euthyphro has adopted as his model.

It is Euthyphro's passionate devotion to justice—if specifically punitive justice, and more specifically, punishment of his father's injustice—that determines his conception of the holy, based on the paradigm of the highest god. Zeus reveals himself to Euthyphro through the poet's story, from which the seer derives a law—the word "*nomos*" appears here for the first and only time in the dialogue: anyone acting impiously must be punished, whoever he may be (5e).[23] The dramatic action of the *Euthyphro* takes place within the horizon of an all-encompassing law that is at once religious, civil, and moral;[24] yet the one mention of "*nomos*" in the speeches of the dialogue is focused exclusively on punishment. Euthyphro has, it seems, uncovered the special link between the gods of the poets and the law of the city. The poets depict not only gods who defend justice but also gods who embody the beautiful; it is divinities connected with punishment, however, not with the experience of eros, that are of use to the city, and a philosopher who questioned the legitimacy of punishment could not in principle accept them.[25] At his trial, Socrates does not even try to defend himself against the charge of not believing in the gods of the city. Instead, he brings to light the ignorance of his accuser, who does not know whether the philosopher's crime is not believing in the gods of the city, as the official charge runs, or not believing in gods at all. The accuser's seemingly accidental slip from the one formula to the other exhibits a deep confusion about the divine: is it subordinate to or does it transcend the political authority of the city?[26]

However the divine status of Zeus is to be understood, Euthyphro is enraged that people consider him the best and most just of the gods, yet they rebuke the seer for acting exactly the same way in proceeding against his father's injustice: by what right do they treat him so differently from the highest deity! Socrates does not question the principle Euthyphro is following, but only the content: Isn't it precisely because he cannot accept these stories of the gods that he is being dragged into court? Without waiting for an answer to the question he poses, Socrates reminds himself of his characteristic claim to know nothing of these matters, hence the great need, as it seems, to learn from the seer, who has such special knowledge.[27] By Philios!, Socrates swears (6b)—appealing, most inappropriately, to Zeus the god of friendship: Does Euthyphro really believe that a great war once took place between the Olympians and the Titans? Hesiod's story, which magnifies the family quarrel between Zeus and his father on a grand scale,[28] is represented, as Socrates notes, on the robe of Athena, used in the Great Panathenaea; it is transformed by the city into a public festival that brings all the citizens together, though none, presumably, believe as Euthyphro does in the reality of the celebrated events. The seer promises even more wondrous divine things he could recount: he must deem the philosopher worthy, at this point at least, of being initiated into the esoteric knowledge he possesses.

Now, the response one might have expected from the philosopher is indicated in the second book of the *Republic*, where Socrates discusses the need for censorship of poetry as if he had precisely the situation of Euthyphro in mind: the poet's tale of Zeus attacking his father Cronos, and Cronos in turn attacking Uranus, might lead young men to believe that in punishing their fathers' acts of injustice, they would only be doing what the greatest of the gods are said to do.[29] And yet, Socrates acknowledges on that occasion, there may be some underlying meaning (*hyponoia*) that would make the poet's work a possible source of illumination. Hesiod's tale about the first generations of the gods sheds light on the need for the fundamental prohibitions, in particular, of incest and parricide; the poem reveals something about the human passions that the law covers over precisely while it forbids the actions motivated by them. A consideration of the poet's *hyponoia* might have led Socrates to propose to Euthyphro that Hesiod's Zeus, who puts his father in bonds, is not a model to be imitated, but a portrait from which he could learn something about the antagonism between sons and fathers. Socrates seems to realize from the outset that this is just the opposite of the strategy he should follow. Euthyphro is not a candidate for self-knowledge, and he must be pulled down from his Olympian heights in some other way. Socrates finds the proper means in the *idea* of the holy, which in subordinating the gods might set constraints on Euthyphro with them.

Whatever wondrous divine things the seer may know, Socrates is interested in something else—the form itself (*auto to eidos*) by which all the holy things are holy (6d). He is seeking an *idea*, Socrates explains, that would serve as a model for any action that can count as holy. In fact, Euthyphro has furnished just such a paradigm. Had he understood the significance of his initial response—he is doing what the greatest god did—he would have recognized the form it instantiates: the holy is imitation of god.[30] If there are, ultimately, two possible relations to the divine, the one—*imitatio dei*—denies an unbridgeable gap between human being and god, the other—obedience to divine command—insists on it. The seer assumes that the philosopher belongs with him in shunning the subservience of obedience to divine command, aiming instead to express his special status through some kind of assimilation to god. Now, Socrates does describe the philosopher, in Book VI of the *Republic*, contemplating the divine and orderly and likening himself to it as far as possible (500b–d); but "the divine and orderly" is not necessarily an individual, living god.[31] The principle of imitation of god presupposes an answer to the question, What is god? But for the philosopher this is a—possibly *the*—question that generates and confirms his knowledge of ignorance. One thing at least is certain: if there were any god a philosopher could consider worthy of emulation, it would look nothing like the punishing god Euthyphro is imitating.

Socrates does not take up the principle of the holy implied by Euthyphro's first answer and inquire whether it means there is no higher standard beyond the god one imitates. He points to that question, however, when he proceeds to criticize the seer on formal grounds, for failing to provide an *idea* by which all holy actions could be included in one class and all that are not would be excluded. Euthyphro now responds "altogether beautifully," in Socrates' words of praise, though whether his proposal is true remains to be seen: what is dear to the gods is holy and what is not is unholy (7a). Everything, according to the seer's formula, must be either holy or unholy: all things are determined by the attitude of the gods. Socrates' supposed repetition—the thing, or person, dear-to-god is holy, while one hated-by-god is unholy (7a)—is in fact a revision: while introducing a compound term (*theophiles*) that could refer to a single deity, it carves out a neutral territory, neither loved nor hated, that is of no concern to god or gods.

The immediate issue, however, concerns anything that does fall within the restricted sphere, as long as it is subject to gods who dispute its status. Now, when disputes are about matters like the dimensions of an object or its weight, one can take out a ruler or a scale and settle the issue; it is when there no agreed-upon measure that real enmity is aroused. And that would be the case above all for disputes concerning the just and unjust, the beautiful and ugly, or the good and bad. The gods, Socrates reasons—in a casual remark that proves to be a key to the argument—would love whatever they take to be beautiful or just or good, while hating the opposite. Warring gods, however, like those who have revealed themselves to Euthyphro through the poets' stories, would fight amongst themselves over their judgments of the beautiful, the just, and the good in the same way that humans do, hence they could furnish no standard for us (7d–e). The action Euthyphro is contemplating against his father would undoubtedly be dear to Zeus, but it would be hateful to Cronos, and thus turn out to be holy and not holy at once. The criterion of being dear-to-the-gods would only issue in self-contradiction.

The problem at this point is presumably the polytheism of the poets, where conflicting attitudes among a plurality of gods preclude the possibility of an authoritative standard. This would be solved by monotheism—at least a single god with no internal dissonance. But perhaps the problem is a benefit, a very great benefit, in disguise: would not quarreling gods be a liberating condition for human beings who think for themselves? Indeed, what could more inspire our reflection than the divine contradictions, if we were aware of them! Surely the just, the beautiful, and the good are complex and many-sided. If the various gods dogmatically insisted on their conflicting opinions generated by those complexities, they would mirror the human situation in the city; if they were engaged in debating those complexities in search of the truth, they would be a projected image of the philosophers. Or would the philosophers' gods, if they are beings of a supposedly superior rank, have to be, not lovers of wisdom, but the wise? They would be, in that case, not seekers of knowledge of the just, the beautiful, and the good, but possessors of it, and that would guaranty the unanimity of a plurality of knowers—or the self-consistency of one. It would represent the goal for human lovers of wisdom and the standard they hold up for any being that is divine.

Confronted with the demand for a unified divine measure, however, Euthyphro appeals, not to wisdom, but to a very different ground of concurrence: no god would disagree with the claim that one who kills unjustly must be punished. Socrates appears to concede the point when he admits that what the gods dispute, just as human beings do, is whether a particular action is just or unjust. "Certainly, wondrous one," he addresses Euthyphro, "no one either among gods or humans dares to say that someone doing injustice ought not be punished" (8d–e). But there is in fact one very important disputant of this principle, and that is Socrates himself. If, according to the philosopher's standard argument, all human beings desire the good, or the fulfillment of their own self-interest, and acting unjustly is ultimately not in one's true interest, any wrongdoer necessarily acts out of ignorance; but if ignorance is not willed, while voluntary action is a prerequisite for legitimate punishment, the ignorant wrongdoer could not justifiably be punished.[32]

Having allowed, for a moment, that it is not the legitimacy of punishment in principle but only the injustice of a particular case that could be disputed, Socrates recalls the challenge Euthyphro faces: if he can demonstrate that all the gods support his plan, Socrates would never cease praising his wisdom (9a–b). This reminder of the action of the dialogue comes at the quantitative center of the work as a whole.[33] Euthyphro admits that the task Socrates assigns him is no small thing: is it not simply impossible? How could he go about obtaining a proof of the gods' unanimity? It would not, in any case, solve the problem of defining the holy, as Socrates notes; hence he is ready to grant that all the gods think the death of the murdering laborer a product of injustice—he says nothing about Euthyphro's prosecution of his father.

With this concession, they can get on to an examination of the revised definition the philosopher now proposes: the holy is what *all* the gods love, the unholy what they *all* hate, while those matters that some love and some hate would be neither, or both together (9d).[34] The self-contradictory case is now as irrelevant as one that lies outside the jurisdiction of the gods altogether. The distinctive problem of polytheism has been left behind, since the unity of all the gods would be equivalent to one. But the revised formula opens up a more fundamental question, which applies to divine authority in any form: Is something holy *because* it is loved by the gods or, rather, is it loved by the gods *because* it is in itself holy (10a)?

This question lies at the heart of the relation between philosophy and revelation. On the first option Socrates poses, the gods provide our only guidance. We would have to learn what they approve or disapprove of by relying on a divine communication, if not in a direct encounter, then through a mediating prophet, a hallowed tradition, or a sacred text; of course, we would have to interpret that divine communication, but with no independent standard to determine its author's intention. Only the second alternative Socrates offers enables, or compels us to try to figure out for ourselves what by its own nature would merit divine approval. The

Bible points to the difference between these possibilities by juxtaposing two radically different portraits of the first patriarch. In one, Abraham negotiates with God about His plan to destroy Sodom and Gomorrah—a dialogue for which the biblical author prepares by presenting God debating within Himself about whether to share with Abraham what He intends to do (Gen. 18:17–33). In this situation Abraham holds up a humanly comprehensible, independent standard of what he takes to be just and rational, and he urges God to live up to it, if He is to be a divinity worthy of human respect. *That* Abraham stands at the furthest extreme from the man who receives God's command to sacrifice his dearly beloved son, the son born miraculously in accordance with God's promise (Gen. 22). Faced with this incomprehensible demand, Abraham raises no question about its justice or rationality; he accepts it in silence as the will of God and becomes *the* model of obedient faith.[35]

Given the two logical alternatives Socrates has posed, we might expect Euthyphro to insist that the holy is simply the product of the gods' approval. That choice would support his proposed definition and possibly seal it off from any further Socratic interrogation. It would, moreover, make him indispensable—the seer who has special access to the mysterious will of the gods. The philosopher, on the other hand, might be assumed to acknowledge only a god who discerns and approves of what is in itself holy. But Socrates does not voice any opinion of his own; instead, he manipulates a sequence of questions in order to elicit a particular result, and it is only by seeing where objections could have been raised that the meaning of the argument comes to light.

With a set of examples that practically hypnotize Euthyphro, Socrates reaches the conclusion that something is a loved thing only because it is loved by someone, or as he first puts it, by "the loving thing" (10a); it is not loved because it is something intrinsically lovable.[36] When Socrates returns, however, to the proposed definition of the holy, he asks only whether something is loved by the gods because it is holy, or for some other reason, to which Euthyphro understandably replies: "Because of this" (10d). He thinks he is saying that something holy is loved by the gods because it is holy; but his words more naturally refer to the last thing said—"some other reason" why the gods love what is holy. The ambiguity of his reply, however unintended, proves to be more significant than it may look. Euthyphro has granted, at any rate, that there must be *some* reason for the gods' approval or disapproval—he seems to have simply forgotten the option that the holy might be nothing but the product of the gods' will.[37] He has been led to this point, admittedly, by Socrates' ma-neuvering, though perhaps that would not have succeeded if it had not tapped into an essential need of a believer who claims to possess *knowledge* of the divine and the holy.

The seer has now set his own trap. On the general model he accepted, something is loved only because someone loves it and no question is raised about an intrinsic property that might motivate that love. But in the spe-cific case of the gods, the only question was whether they love something because of its being holy, or some other property; and despite the exact words he uttered, Euthyphro has no other property in mind, so being holy must seem the obvious ground for eliciting the gods' approval. He does not see that their approval, in that case, would not be the *cause* of some-thing being holy, and as a result, his definition stands refuted. Socrates has accomplished something crucial for his strategy with the seer—the will of god or gods is now constrained by an *idea* of the holy; yet with no account of what determines it, that *idea* is left completely empty.

Euthyphro accepts one of two supposedly exclusive and exhaustive al-ternatives. But the way Socrates split those options in his sequence of questions leaves something conspicuously missing, and that is the possi-bility of a dynamic movement—from the intrinsic property of an object to a response, which would in turn confer a further property on the object. That dynamic is paradigmatically illustrated by the Platonic account of the experience of eros: the lover perceives and responds to something in the beloved, but his love in turn magnifies or enhances the one he loves in such a way that the beloved becomes more than what he was in himself.[38] On this model, nothing would be holy apart from the gods' approval, or unholy apart from their disapproval; but those responses would be the re-sult of the gods' discernment of an intrinsic property in the things they love or hate. And Socrates had already indicated what those intrinsic prop-erties are when he noted in passing that the gods would love what they find to be just, beautiful, or good and hate the opposites (7e).

This dynamic account would confirm the definition of the holy as that which is dear to all the gods, but without sacrificing the possibility of ra-tional grounds for their response, that is, their understanding of an *idea* like the beautiful, the just, and the good. That divine understanding would be indirectly communicated to human beings through whatever bears the imprimatur of the holy, although, with this derivative status, the holy itself no longer looks like an *idea*. If Plato intended to communicate this account to his reader, why, one might ask, does Socrates not convey it to Euthyphro?

Instead, he leaves him with an indeterminate *idea* of the holy that does nothing but set limits to the will of the gods. In fact, however, that is just what is required if the seer is to be brought—in the second half of the conversation—to take his bearings from the practices of piety in the city.

Had Socrates developed the premise that the gods love what they take to be intrinsically just, beautiful, or good, he would have opened up this question: if the holy status conferred by the gods is nothing but an indirect way to the just, the beautiful, and the good, why not bypass that mediation? The philosopher, in any case, could not be what he is if he did not pursue the just, the beautiful, and the good as *problems*; any authoritative claim about them would necessarily be transformed into the questions that articulate his quest for knowledge. At his trial, Socrates does trace that quest in his own life to a witness the jury deems worthy, the god at Delphi (*Apology* 20a). Of course, Socrates must have been involved in his characteristic activity already, without any divine sanction, when one of his companions decided to consult the oracle with the question whether anyone is wiser than Socrates. The answer he brought back—No one is wiser—was altogether perplexing to Socrates, who was aware of his own lack of knowledge. Yet he did not ignore the word of the god, but on the assumption that it could not simply be false, he set out to make sense of it. By examining, and refuting, the opinions of all who claimed to know, he came to the conclusion that wisdom belongs only to the god. If "Socrates is wisest"— his own reformulation of the oracle's claim—it must mean that "human wisdom" consists in knowing what one does not know.[39] Socrates arrived at an interpretation that confirmed the truth of the divine word by questioning it and making it conform to his own reasoning and his own unquestionable understanding of himself. Is this "philosophic piety" or radical impiety?[40] It is certainly not obedience to the command of a higher authority; but neither is it exactly imitation of a divine paradigm. It does postulate a god-like wisdom, but only in order to inspire the effort to construct the most adequate understanding of it. Socrates' interpretation of the Delphic oracle looks like the implicit model Plato holds up for the active reader of his own works.

Socratic philosophy, on this account, recognizes human limits in light of a divine standard, just as ordinary piety does. But a profound gap separates the two. The limits that the philosopher faces as challenges are for ordinary piety prohibitions by god or gods against human overreaching.[41] The philosopher's awareness of falling short in light of the divine standard he posits consists in knowledge of ignorance; its counterpart in ordinary piety consists in the experiences of shame and fear. Those experiences become central when the *Euthyphro* turns, in the second half of the inquiry, to the practices of piety in the city and their relation to justice.

Piety in the City (11b–16a)

Spurred on by the very problems they have uncovered, Socrates is ready to return to the question, What is the holy? Euthyphro, in contrast, has nothing further to say, after seeing everything they put forward fail to remain fixed. In the image Socrates offers, their speeches are like the statues of Daedalus, said to be so lifelike they would get up and run away (11c–d).[42] The statues of Daedalus exhibit self-moving motion—that is, soul—not, however, in a living body but in a work of art: this can only be Plato's image for the argument of the dialogue. That, of course, is something Euthyphro cannot recognize; in his eyes, it must be Socrates who is responsible for his words not sticking. Socrates, in turn, is amazed at his own artistry if, surpassing the skill of Daedalus, it can move the works of others, and do so, indeed, against his will, for he too wishes the speeches would remain at rest. Of course, the fixity Euthyphro wants to preserve is the dogmatism of opinion, while Socrates is looking to an unachieved end—knowledge of the *idea*—which arouses the desire that keeps the speeches alive. That this is not the desire moving Euthyphro Socrates must have realized all along; but it is only now, at the end of the first half of the inquiry, that the seer has reached the point where he is receptive to other passions—fear of the punishing gods he wants to imitate and shame in the face of the human conventions they sanctify.

Those passions enter the argument through Socrates' allusion to a poet's verses about a god—literally, "the maker (*poiētēs*) who made Zeus..." With this one reminder of the charge against Socrates, the dialogue identifies the poet, more specifically, as the maker of a god of whom human beings are unwilling to speak, for "where fear is, there too is shame" (12a).[43] The poet's verse strikes a chord with the Book of Genesis, where the first human beings, after their transgression of the primordial divine command, react with shame before each other and fear before God (3:7–10). To be unwilling to speak the name of a god is a sign of shame or awe before a mysterious higher being, not subject to our knowledge. The poet gives a genetic account of that experience: such shame or awe is a product of fear, evoked by a god who is thought to punish the overstepping of limits. Socrates does not pursue the question whether that view is essential to poetry in its quarrel with philosophy. He cites the verse only to insist upon the opposite—"where shame is, there is fear"—not as a rival to the poet's genetic account, but as a replacement of it with a class analysis: there are many things that are feared—disease or poverty, for instance—which are not objects of shame or awe, but shame is itself a kind of fear, of a wicked reputation.

Socrates introduces this relation of classes in order to provide a model for the holy things as a subset of just things. That subordination would spell out the consequences of the theological reform the philosopher suggested by the end of the first half of the dialogue, when he implied that the holy is a product of the gods' approval, but that approval is itself elicited by the gods' recognition of an intrinsic property, more specifically, the just.[44] The account of the holy and the just things would be settled, then, if Socrates let it rest on the model of shame as a kind of fear. Instead, he complicates matters by adding another, seemingly unnecessary example: the odd as a kind of number (12e). If the holy and the just were like odd and even number, they would be two mutually exclusive species of some comprehensive genus, and no single action could be both holy and just. Abraham negotiating with God about the fate of Sodom and Gomorrah might illustrate a holy action as a kind of justice, like shame as a kind of fear; but Abraham's sacrifice of his son appears to be a holy action in opposition to a just one, like odd as opposed to even number. Euthyphro conflates the two models. Thinking of shame as a species of fear, he retains "the just" as the name for the comprehensive genus; but on the model of number divided into even and odd, he distinguishes care of the gods, which is pious and holy (*eusebes* and *hosion*), from care of humans, which must be just in the strict sense (12e). The genus, in that case, would be care (*therapeia*), and a particular action—like Euthyphro's prosecution of his father—could be either care for the gods or for humans, but not both.

The incorporation of the holy things as a species of the just, analogous to shame as a kind of fear, would seem to be a model desirable in practice: it should have the moderating effect of requiring that any action undertaken in the name of the gods conform to justice as a standard independently determined. Yet on the same basis, it would allow the fanatic to claim divine sanction for his pursuit of justice, and that is perhaps the potential danger that makes Socrates lead the seer away from this model. Turning instead to the genus *therapeia*, which allows the species of the holy to be decoupled from the just, Socrates finds only "one small problem": Is the *therapeia* that defines piety, which we practice on the gods, the kind of artful care that experts perform for the needy, like the care oxherders practice on oxen (13b–c)? Are the gods defective and in need of our art of improvement? Actually, Socrates has been engaged in just such an activity of *therapeia*, albeit on the fictional gods of the poets, whom he transformed into a standard for the philosophers in their search for knowledge of the just, the beautiful, and the good.[45] But Euthyphro, who still has punitive gods in mind, is suddenly ashamed or frightened by the implications of his proposed definition. By Zeus!, he certainly did not intend *therapeia* of the gods to mean an art of the superior caring for the inferior; on the contrary, what he humbly intended is the kind of care slaves pay to their masters (13c–d). Socrates, who will tell the Athenian jury of his own "service (*hyperesia*) to the god" (*Apology* 30a), offers Euthyphro the designation "artful service" (*hyperetikē*)—a grammatical form that implies a claim to expertise.

If piety, however, belongs to the division of arts in the city, there must be a particular function or work (*ergon*) it accomplishes. Socrates' initial illustration—artful service to doctors produces health (13d)—seems to refer to a subsidiary role, like that of the nurse, who ministers to the master artisan, not for his benefit, but for the good of the patient whose malady needs treatment. The subsidiary practice by which we serve the gods, accordingly, would be undertaken with a view to human needs, but to what end in particular? Euthyphro can identify the specific end in the two further examples Socrates introduces—service to shipbuilders or service to housebuilders—but all he can say about the gods' use of us as servants is that it produces "many beautiful things." So do generals and farmers, Socrates adds, yet each accomplishes a very particular end. This seemingly unnecessary pair of examples provides a clue to the direction of the argument.

Why should there be an appeal to god or gods in prayer or sacrifice, or some ritual equivalent, before planting crops, or especially before going into battle, but not before building a ship or a house? If all the arts had as much control as carpentry does over its material and none were as vulnerable to chance as agriculture or military strategy, the city of arts would be, or perceive itself to be, self-sufficient; in its mastery of nature it would need no supplement of pious practices that acknowledge dependence on the divine. As it is, that acknowledgment addresses a twofold need. On the one hand, it encourages confidence in the face of uncertainty and counteracts a passivity that might otherwise prevail when we realize the limits of our control; at the same time, in reminding us of those limits, it puts a check on the exercise of the arts, in which we might forge ahead without sufficient regard for their unintended consequences. Philosophy, out of knowledge of ignorance and the desire to know, has its own intrinsic source of moderation and courage; for the arts in the city, piety serves that purpose.

Having grown tired of trying to enlighten the philosopher about the many beautiful things the gods accomplish, the seer is finally ready to give a simple answer:[46] knowing how to say and to do what is gratifying to the gods, in praying and sacrificing, these are the holy things (*ta hosia*), which save private families and the city in common, while the things contrary to the gratifying, which are impious (*asebē*), overturn and destroy everything (14b). Socrates is about to criticize Euthyphro for failing to answer the question about the function of piety, but of course he has done just that in passing: the holy things save families and the city—mentioned here together for the first and only time—while the impious things destroy them. The holy, most generally, establishes limits: it applies the principle that not everything human beings are capable of doing is permissible to do. In particular, the holy things preserve the family, and with that the city, by protecting the boundary between them. This function is expressed most fundamentally in the prohibitions of incest and parricide. Violations of those prohibitions are the impious things—represented by the tragic poets—which destroy the sphere of the family, and with that the city.

The action of the dialogue, concerned with Euthyphro's comic equivalent of such a violation, highlights this function of piety. But the speeches must follow, Socrates now claims, wherever the one questioned leads, and from that he derives a final proposal for a definition: holiness is a "science of sacrificing and praying" (14c). This, of course, is exactly where Socrates has been driving the conversation all along, to the ritual practices in the city—the most conventional understanding of piety, albeit offered to Euthyphro under the title of a "science" (*epistēmē*). Prayer and sacrifice presuppose, however unwittingly, some implicit assumption about god or gods: if the fundamental prohibitions of incest and parricide express the holy, prayer and sacrifice express our awareness of the divine. There must, it would seem, be some relation between them, but it is perhaps always indirect and obscure.[47] Socrates leaves that problem shrouded in darkness when he turns away from the issue lurking in the action of the dialogue and claims to follow Euthyphro's speeches.

Prayer, Socrates reasons, is a matter of asking from the gods and sacrifice of giving to them; so holiness is really an art of barter (14c–d). Holiness as an economic exchange between humans and gods is not exactly an awe-inspiring conception; at best, it replaces Euthyphro's punitive justice by commercial justice, though giving to the gods, in the hopes of gaining their favors, looks hard to distinguish from bribery.[48] The gods certainly must be foolish partners in the deal if there is nothing they can get from it for themselves, and what, indeed, could such superior beings get from those who are inferior? Our gifts to the gods, Euthyphro presumes, could only be honor, praise, and gratitude. But honor from an inferior is hardly a source of satisfaction: a god would be in an even more impossible situation than Aristotle's great-souled man.[49] Socrates wonders, in any event, how piety could be gratifying to the gods but not advantageous or dear to them; and when Euthyphro grants that it is certainly dear to them, Socrates quickly jumps on it to blame *him* for being more artful than Daedalus and making the speeches go round, right back to the impasse they reached at the center of the inquiry.

Perhaps they did not agree beautifully before, Socrates concedes, or else they are now positing something incorrect. Euthyphro can only respond, "It seems so" (15c); in fact he should have protested the conclusion drawn at both points: being dear to the gods was originally rejected—on a very questionable basis—as the *cause* of anything being holy, whereas now it is only an *attribute* of something holy, which should be perfectly acceptable. Euthyphro's misunderstanding of the argument, nevertheless, has a positive practical result: whatever knowledge he may still believe he has, he must at least realize now he does not have the ability to convey it to someone as unenlightened as his partner in this conversation, or perhaps the jury he would have to convince of his case. Socrates, meanwhile, who must have achieved a more articulate knowledge of ignorance in the course of the conversation, is prepared to begin again and inquire, What is the holy (15c)? At this late point he entreats Euthyphro to tell him the truth and not withhold what he surely must know, otherwise the thought of prosecuting his father would fill him with fear before angry gods and shame before disapproving humans. Euthyphro is suddenly in a hurry to leave.[50]

The argument may not have gone in a circle, as Socrates claims, but it has been in motion—from the holy as imitation of god to prayer and sacrifice. While apparently gaining no self-knowledge in the process, Euthyphro has been moved from his boastful identification with a punishing god to acceptance of the public practices that foster in the family and the city recognition of limits, sanctioned by higher powers. At the same time, in leading the seer through this movement Socrates has been applying it to himself, as he indicates by the Homeric allusion that brings the dialogue to a close.

Socrates likens his encounter with the seer to Menelaus wrestling with the prophetic sea-god Proteus, in his slippery transformation from one shape into another. The reference is to the account Menelaus gives Telemachus of his thwarted return home at the end of the Trojan War (*Odyssey* IV.351–485). Unaware of a sacrifice he owed to the gods, Menelaus was held back in Egypt, until one of the higher beings, the goddess Eidotheia, took pity on him and informed him how he could wrest from her father Proteus the secret of the sacrifice required. What Menelaus learned from Proteus led him back to the river Egyptus to offer holy hecatombs, which made possible the continuation of his way homeward. What the gods want from us, Homer implies—the sacrifice they demand—is ultimately mysterious and we have no direct access to it. There is some guidance to be found in "the first things" (that is, Proteus in Greek), but only if one can arrest the unintelligible flux and get hold of some stable nature, which requires the mediation of "divine form" (*Eidotheia*).

Casting himself in the role of Menelaus, Socrates interprets his indictment as an impediment of divine provenance blocking his way home. With the accusation against him for impiety and corruption, he cannot simply go on practicing philosophy in Athens. At the Stoa of the King, supervisor of the ancestral sacrifices, he has been hoping to discover what is required of him by trying to get hold of a seer in all his Protean flux. This is in fact a twofold task, which is split between the action of the dialogue and its speeches. The aim of the speeches, to pin down a stable *idea* of the holy, has apparently not been achieved, but the action has come to a conclusion with Euthyphro's hasty departure, under the shadow of fear and shame.[51] Socrates, at the same time, seems to have arrived at a decision about his own course: he will go on to face the trial, rather than flee from the city,[52] and when he does, he will try to persuade the jury that his practice of philosophy is a service to the god and his activity of examination the god's great gift to the city. If and only if he fails in that effort, the sacrifice called for will be his life.[53]

Socrates has come to this crisis because of the threat he is thought to present by his practice of "making new gods" and leading others along the same path. A twofold interpretation is suggested, once again, by the speeches and the action of the *Euthyphro*. The philosopher's new conception of the highest kind of being shows up, in the speeches of the dialogue, as the *idea*. The simple *idea* of the holy posited at the outset of this conversation enabled Socrates to explore the question, What is it?, and in doing so, to uncover and articulate the problem of the holy, in all its complexity. The action of the dialogue represents Socrates, at the same time, putting that *idea* to work in his task of imposing limits on Euthyphro. This representation turns the most unique and incomparable individual into *the* paradigm of the philosopher and his distinctive way of life.[54] Perhaps Euthyphro was not altogether wrong, then, in thinking of the idiosyncratic *daimonion* in connection with the charge against Socrates. If the *idea* takes the place of an abstract god like Hesiod's Nemesis, there is a different stand-in for the poets' Olympians, individual characters who exemplify the highest human types: that is the figure of Socrates and "the maker of new gods," Plato.[55]

In the conversation that takes place on the morning after the *Euthyphro*, according to Plato's dramatic chronology, Socrates meets up with a Stranger, introduced as a "very philosophic man," and wonders if he might not be a god in disguise, since the philosopher, he warns, is as hard to recognize behind his changing appearances as Homer's gods.[56] Socrates is about to go on trial, perceived by the city through the lens of the image first put forward by Aristophanes' comedy. In the *Euthyphro*, Plato presents a defense of Socrates in advance, through the appearance he takes on in his playful encounter with a seer. At his trial Socrates will fail to convince a majority of his fellow citizens that his practice of philosophy is the god's greatest gift to the city; Plato imagines, before that momentous occasion, a Socrates who comes forward as the defender of the fathers and the practices of piety in the city, precisely while developing his own understanding of the divine and the holy. But Plato's philosophic comedy is more than a defensive response to Aristophanes' accusatory comedy: through its representation of Socrates' activity as a model of what makes a human life worth living, it carries on the philosopher's endeavor of finding others like or potentially like himself.

---

1   In Plato's *Statesman*, which is dramatically set on the day after the *Euthyphro*, Socrates listens to an Eleatic Stranger reflect on this office: "In Egypt it is not even possible for a king to rule without a hieratic (art)... And, further, in many places among the Greeks one would find that the greatest kinds of sacrifices that deal with matters of this sort are enjoined upon the greatest offices of rule to perform, and in particular here among you it's not least of all plain what I mean, for they say whoever gets to be king here by lot has been assigned the most august and particularly ancestral (native) of the ancient sacrifices" (290d–e, translated by Seth Benardete).

2   See Aristotle *Athenian Constitution* 57. Fustel de Coulanges, describing the ancient city where "the state and religion were so completely confounded that it was impossible even to distinguish the one from the other," refers to the annual magistrate called

"king," whose sacred title recalls the ancient priest of the public hearth. See *The Ancient City: A Study on the Religion, Laws, and Institutions of Greece and Rome*, 174, 180.

3   On the references to "the god" in the *Apology*, *Crito*, and *Phaedo*, see n. 12 below. On the *Euthyphro*'s silence about the soul, see n. 36 below. Hannes Kerber has observed another conspicuous absence in the dialogue: *aretē* is never mentioned, thus piety is not identified as a virtue.

4   This is the definition Aristotle offers, with Socrates as the exemplar (*Nicomachean Ethics* 1127b22–26).

5   See Leo Strauss's reading of the play in *Socrates and Aristophanes*, especially pp. 41–46; cf. pp. 311–14. Strauss's study as a whole points, as Heinrich Meier explains, to the unspoken question that is central to Aristophanes, in an appropriate comic form: *quid sit deus?* See *Leo Strauss and the Theologico-Political Problem*, 27, cf. 91–95.

6   See *Republic* 607b. According to Herodotus, the most primitive roots of the Greek gods can be traced to Egypt, but it is Homer and Hesiod "who created for the Greeks their theogony" and "who gave to the gods the special names for their descent from their ancestors and divided among them their honors, their arts, and their shapes." See *The History* 2.50 and 2.53, trans. David Grene (Chicago: University of Chicago Press, 1987).

7   In Plato's dramatization of Socrates' trial, the formal charge is "not believing in (*nomizein*) the gods of the city" (*Apology of Socrates* 24b). The meaning of this verb is suggested by Socrates' image of the chained prisoners in the cave who see only images on the wall in front of them and believe (*nomizein*) they are the beings (*Republic* 515b).

8   In the *Theaetetus*, the conversation dramatically set just before the *Euthyphro*, Socrates encounters the same character type in the mathematician Theodorus, the theoretical man who thinks that the greatest evil is to be ridiculed by the many (see 174a–175b).

9   See *Republic* 516e–517a. Whether the *Republic*'s philosopher-king is an object of laughter or lethal anger is an issue that runs through the whole discussion, beginning with 473c–e.

10 "The holy city in contradistinction to the natural city," Strauss observes, is brought out more clearly by Thucydides—in describing phenomena like the city's responses to oracles, earthquakes, or eclipses—than by the classical philosophers, for whom "the concern with the divine has become identical with philosophy" (*The City and Man*, 240–41).

11 On this account, which Socrates offers in Plato's *Philebus* (48a–50d), Aristophanes experiences a painful envy of some superiority he recognizes in Socrates; but he finds relief from that pain in the pleasure of laughing at the philosopher's weakness, more specifically, his insufficient self-knowledge. See Strauss, *Socrates and Aristophanes*, 5–6 and Benardete, *The Tragedy and Comedy of Life: Plato's Philebus*, 201–8.

12 Describing the conditions that might account for a saved remnant of philosophic natures not corrupted by the city, Socrates makes light of his own case, since he credits the *daimonion*, which is such a rare, or rather unique phenomenon (*Republic* 496c). In Plato's representation, the *daimonion* plays a crucial role in the individual decisions that bring Socrates' life to an end. The *Apology* concludes with Socrates comforting those who acquitted him by assuring them that "the sign" did not come to hold him back that day, and he departs from the jury shortly afterward with the words that they go to live and he to die, but the better course is known only to "the god." Socrates seems to have the *daimonion* in mind again when he exhorts Crito, at the end of their conversation, to accept the sentence of death since it is the way "the god" leads (*Crito* 54e) and once more when he acknowledges on the day of his death that one must not take his own life, unless a god sends some necessity (*Phaedo* 62c).

13 See Hesiod *Theogony* 211–25 and Strauss, "On Plato's *Euthyphro*" (2023), 88–90. In a letter to Benardete, Strauss expresses his observation of how the doctrine of ideas is prefigured in particular by gods like Nike (reprinted in Meier, *Leo Strauss and the Theologico-Political Problem*, 27).

14 In his analysis of mimetic poetry in Book X of the *Republic*, Socrates first speaks of the *idea* made by a god, which the poet imitates at a third degree removed (597a–e); but he soon revises that analysis and replaces the maker-god by "the user," who knows the function to which any maker would look for his production (601c–602b).

15 In referring to both their cases as a *dikē* (3e), Euthyphro forgets or ignores Socrates' earlier correction that the indictment against him is a *graphē* (2a). Stuart Warner suggests how this seemingly small error encapsulates Euthyphro's basic confusion about family and city. As the newer form of a public suit that could be initiated by any citizen, the *graphē* stands in contrast with the older *dikē*, in the form of a private suit brought by the injured party or his representative, typically a family relation. Euthyphro prosecutes a *dikē* on behalf of his "dependant" (*pelatēs*, 4c—a word that appears in no other Platonic dialogue).

16 This is the provision laid down in the penal code of Plato's *Laws* (866a–b, cf. 871a–c).

17 The family members are united, as Fustel de Coulanges describes it, "by something more powerful than birth, affection, or physical strength"—by "the religion of the sacred fire, and of dead ancestors" (*The Ancient City*, 42). It is only by extension that the city could be understood as "the collective group of those who had the same protecting deities, and who performed the religious ceremony at the same altar" (146).

18 Euthyphro looks like a member of the class Maimonides describes, including the soothsayer or augur, in whom the "intellectual overflow" reaches only the imaginative and not the rational faculty: "They bring great confusion into speculative matters of great import, true notions being strangely mixed up in their minds with imaginary ones" (*Guide of the Perplexed* 2.37, 374).

19 In Cicero's well known description, Socrates "first called philosophy down from heaven, and gave it a place in the cities, and introduced it even into men's homes, and forced it to make inquiry into life, and morals, and things good and evil" (*Tusculan Disputations* 5.4.10–11).

20 All references to the *idea* or *eidos* occur here, at the beginning of the inquiry (5d, 6d, 6e), in connection with *to hosion and to anhosion*, while they are absent from the second half of the dialogue, when *asebeia* and *eusebeia* come back. Thomas and Grace West translate *hosion* as "pious," which is the same term they use for *eusebes* although, as they explain, the latter notion "emphasizes the reverence and respect, even fear, which one feels or ought to feel toward the gods" (*Four Texts on Socrates*, 46 n. 18; cf. 45 n. 17). In the striking statement of Isocrates: "To change nothing of what our forefathers have left behind—this is *eusebeia*" (*Speeches* 7.30). Cited in *Greek Religion*, by Walter Burkert, trans. John Raffan (Cambridge: Cambridge University Press, 1985), 273.

21 After dropping his question about the pious and impious, Socrates asks, more precisely: Isn't the holy itself the same as itself in every action, and the unholy again completely the opposite of the holy, itself like itself, all having some one *idea*, whatever is to be unholy (5d)? If the holy is one and the same class characteristic in every instance, why is the unholy only *like* itself? And why, then, is there is an *idea* only, as Socrates seems to say, for that which is unholy? Is the implication that the holy is always primarily a matter of prohibition, hence we take our bearings from the negative? In fact, when Socrates returns to the question moments later, Euthyphro "remembers" that he said "somehow by one *idea* the unholy things are unholy and the holy things holy" (6d). In that case, as

Euthyphro's proposed definition indicates, everything that is not holy is necessarily unholy and there is no neutral territory (see 6e and Socrates' revision at 7a).

22 See *Theogony* 154–210 and 453–506.

23 Actually, Zeus punished his father, just as Euthyphro wants to punish his father, for
acting *unjustly* (5d, 6a), and Euthyphro later appeals to the agreement of all gods about
the need to punish one who kills *unjustly* (8b). In formulating the *nomos* that demands
punishment of anyone acting *impiously*, the seer takes for granted what Socrates will
find it necessary to examine at length—that all impious action is unjust.

In the Platonic dialogue where holiness (*hosiotēs*) makes a rare appearance as a virtue,
the Sophist Protagoras ends his tale of the origin of the city by speaking in the voice of
Zeus, as he lays down the law (*nomos*) imposing the punishment of death on anyone incapable of partaking of shame and justice (*Protagoras* 322d).

24 This horizon reflects the notion of divine law, in which Strauss finds "the common
ground between the Bible and Greek philosophy." More precisely, that common ground
is the *problem* of divine law, which the two traditions solve "in a diametrically opposed
manner" ("Progress or Return?," 248). Cf. Remi Brague's discussion in *La Loi de Dieu*,
especially 31. However divine law may be understood in historical Athens, its significance in Plato's *Laws* is indicated by Avicenna's remark, which Strauss uses as the epigraph for his study of the dialogue: "...the treatment of prophecy and the Divine law
is contained in...the *Laws*" (*The Argument and the Action of Plato's Laws*, 1). On the
importance of Strauss's discovery of this line, **see** Meier, *Leo Strauss and the Theologico-Political Problem*, 12–13.

25 Consider Socrates' argument in the *Crito* (see n. 32 below). Maimonides distinguishes
between the correct opinions that the Law communicates, like the belief in the unity
and eternity and non-corporeality of the deity, and those beliefs that are "necessary for
the sake of political welfare," such as the "belief that He, may He be exalted, is violently
angry with those who disobey Him and that it is therefore necessary to fear Him and to
dread Him and to take care not to disobey" (*Guide of the Perplexed* III.28, 514).

26 See *Apology* 24b, 26b–27a. Varro's *theologia tripertita*, preserved in Augustine's critical
discussion (*The City of God* VI.5), famously distinguishes three categories: the gods of
the poets, the gods of the philosophers, and the gods of the city. In the gods of the poets,
Varro found "many falsehoods contrary to the dignity and nature of immortal beings";
by the gods of the philosophers, he understood the natural principles—like Heraclitean
fire, Pythagorean numbers, or Epicurean atoms—which belong inside the walls of a
school, not in the forum; it is the gods of the city—those worshipped in public rites and
sacrifices—that are the concern of the citizens as well as the priests.

27 In the *Kuzari* Yehuda Halevi presents Socrates' apparently moderate declaration:
"O my people, I do not deny your knowledge of the gods, but I confess that I do not understand it. As for me, I am only wise in human matters" (IV.13, 272). Commenting on
this passage, Strauss raises the question whether such a "merely defensive attitude on
the part of the philosopher" is really a possibility ("The Law of Reason in the *Kuzari*,"
105–7, see especially n. 33.)

28 See *Theogony* 621–819.

29 See *Republic* 377e–378e. Aristophanes' Unjust Speech taunts Just Speech, who claims
that justice exists at least among the gods: Why, then, didn't Zeus perish when he bound
his father? (*Clouds* 903–5).

30 The definition implied by Euthyphro's original response stands in contrast, Strauss observes, to the orthodox view, that piety is doing what the gods tell us to do, which consists

in worshipping the ancestral gods according to ancestral custom ("On Plato's *Euthyphro*," 85–86). Commenting on the analysis of poetic imitation in *Republic* X, Benardete discerns these two principles of piety in the double function of poetry: "It supports the law through its gods who urge mortals to think mortal thoughts; and it subverts the law through its gods whom it serves up as beings to be emulated" (*Socrates' Second Sailing: On Plato's Republic*, 218). David Daube makes the perhaps surprising observation that in the Pentateuch there is "no single express instance" of God as a model to be followed. "You shall be holy for I the Lord am holy" does not mean "You shall be holy like me" (*Law and Wisdom in the Bible*, 144).

31 On one occasion—in fact, the conversation Socrates holds just before this meeting with Euthyphro—he recommends "likening oneself to god as far as possible" (*Theaetetus* 176b); when he characterizes it, however, as the only escape from the necessary evils hovering around "mortal nature and this place," he must be thinking, not of his lifelong practice of philosophy, but of his imminent trial and the withdrawal from life it may require.

32 See, for example, *Apology* 25c–26a. Socrates leads Crito to grant that it is always wrong, not only to requite injustice by acting unjustly, but to defend ourselves when suffering bad by doing bad in return; in fact, that principle is so basic that there can never be a conversation between those who disagree on it (*Crito* 49d), that is, between Socrates and the city that punishes him. See Robert Berman, "The Socratic Principle and the Problem of Punishment," 130–31.

33 Once the inquiry into the holy begins, on the other hand, the center comes with the failure of the search for an *idea*, at 11c, marked by the image of the statues of Daedalus. With this twofold center, Plato distinguishes the speeches from the action of the dialogue.

34 What the gods "love," more precisely, is what they "find dear" (*philein*): this is the verb throughout the argument, not *eraō*, which would imply some neediness in the lover to be fulfilled by the object of his love.

35 See especially Kierkegaard's *Fear and Trembling*.

36 Reflecting on the complicated grammatical basis of this argument, Michael Davis shows how the dialogue that never mentions "soul" presents us instead with its characteristic motion and suggests why that makes Socrates, finally, the example of "the living soul at work" ("The Grammar of the Soul: On Plato's *Euthyphro*," *The Soul of the Greeks*, 214–16, 220–21). In Socrates' reference to "the loving thing," and his silence about the lovable, Jan Blits finds a sign of the disregard of the soul, which "goes to the heart of the dialogue and underlies its apparent failure" ("The Holy and the Human: An Interpretation of Plato's *Euthyphro*," 19, 29–30).

Strauss concludes his reading of the *Euthyphro* with a reflection on the "half-truth" it conveys through its emphasis on the ideas and correlative silence about the soul, which precludes any argument for the existence of gods. If the partial truth is the primacy of the ideas, it is only a "half-truth" because we know, Strauss asserts, by demonstration from the phenomenon of self-moving motion, that the gods exist—not the gods of the city, but "the living gods" ("On Plato's *Euthyphro*," 93; cf. 75). Strauss presumably has in mind *Laws* X, where the Athenian Stranger constructs an argument for the priority of soul as self-moving motion, which is supposed to demonstrate the existence of the gods (893b–899d). Whatever problems that entails, the closest anything in the *Euthyphro* comes to the primordial self-moving motion of soul is an image Socrates offers: responding to Euthyphro's complaint about the way his proposals never stay put, Socrates likens their "deeds in speeches" to the self-moving statues of his ancestor Daedalus (11b–d). If this means the unending motion of thinking, would Strauss's "living gods" be the philosophers?

37 The option Euthyphro chooses, Christopher Bruell observes, is already implicit in the notion of piety that leads him to prosecute his father—the notion that what the gods demand of us is to punish the unjust; for knowledge of what piety is thus depends on independent knowledge of what justice is, which does not in turn depend on a prior knowledge of the divine (*On the Socratic Education*, 126–27). Or, does Euthyphro derive his understanding of justice from his belief in the model of Zeus, as presented in particular by Hesiod?

38 See *Phaedrus* 251a–253c. "The beloved," as Benardete puts it, "appears as an Olympian god in conformity with the nature of the soul of the lover"; but the lover in turn "fashions the beloved into a statue of his own soul and worships it as if it were a god" ("Socrates and Plato: The Dialectics of Eros," 77).

39 See *Apology* 20e–21b, cf. 23a–b.

40 Both Plato and Aristotle speak, not of piety, but of the holy (*to hosion*) in connection with the philosopher—only, however, to characterize his devotion to truth. Hesitant to criticize Homer, Socrates acknowledges the power of the poet's magic while admitting the need for examination, since "it would not be holy to betray what seems to be true" (*Republic* 607c). When Aristotle introduces his reluctant critique of the Platonic "*idea* of the good" with an echo of that statement (*Nicomachean Ethics* 1096a14–17), he in fact expresses beautifully his debt to Plato modeled on Plato's expression of his debt to Homer. Cf. Burger, *Aristotle's Dialogue with Socrates*, 24–25, 159–60.

41 Aristotle distinguishes the poets' conception of jealous gods, who impose prohibitions on the human quest for knowledge, from the limits set by human nature (*Metaphysics* 982b29–983a11).

42 The same image, in the *Meno*, illustrates the instability of true opinion that has not been transformed into knowledge (97d–98a).

43 In the translation of Thomas and Grace West: "I am saying the opposite of what the poet composed who said: / Zeus, the one who enclosed and planted all these things, / You are not willing to speak of; for where dread is, there too is awe" (12a).

44 In Socrates' turn to a relation of classification, Bruell sees his rejection of the unstated causal relation according to which a concern for justice gives rise to piety (*On the Socratic Education*, 132). Yet while Socrates has abandoned the causal analysis of the last argument, its implications seem to be guiding the class analysis that replaces it: if the just is an intrinsic property of something that leads the gods to approve of it, while that approval in turn makes something holy, the holy things would be a subset of the just, as shame is of fear.

45 This characterization of Socrates' "philosophic *therapeia*" is suggested by Robert Berman.

46 Socrates originally asked Euthyphro: What does *our artful service to the gods* accomplish (13e)? After reminding the seer of his claim to know more beautifully than other human beings about the divine things, he restated the question: What is that all-beautiful function that *the gods accomplish using us as servants*? Finally, after offering examples of other particular arts, Socrates asks simply: What is the chief thing among the many beautiful ones *the gods accomplish*? Euthyphro must be thinking in the end of a benefit bestowed by active gods in reward for pious practices; but Socrates' original formulation made human beings the agents, whose activity construed as service to higher beings might produce a benefit whether or not those beings exist, or have any concern with human affairs.

47 The separation of the holy and the divine is reflected in Plato's *Laws* by the problematic relation between the penal code of Book IX and the theology of Book X. Explaining the

deeper effect of the holy in contrast with beliefs about the divine, Benardete compares the crime of incest, on the one hand, with atheism, on the other (*Discovery of Being*, 256).

48 Cephalus, in Book I of the *Republic*, looks like the representative of this piety. What he stands for reappears in Book II, when Adeimantus challenges Socrates to provide an adequate defense of justice in contrast with the poets, who present the gods moved by prayers and sacrifices to overlook injustice (364d–e, 365d–e). The belief that gods can be easily persuaded by prayers and sacrifice is the last of the three forms of impiety the Athenian Stranger confronts in Book X of Plato's *Laws* (885b).

49 The great-souled man claims and is worthy of the greatest things, which should be that which we offer to the gods, and such a thing is honor (*Nicomachean Ethics* 1123b16–20); but honor is rejected as a candidate for the human good on the grounds that it makes one dependent on those who bestow it (1095b24–26).

50 Diogenes Laertius chooses this example, as Hannes Kerber reminds me, to illustrate Socrates' ability at dissuading no less than persuading: "After conversing with Theaetetus about knowledge, he sent him away, as Plato says, fired with a divine impulse; but when Euthyphro had indicted his father for manslaughter, Socrates, after some conversation with him upon piety, diverted him from his purpose" (*Lives of Eminent Philosophers* II.29).

51 The sequence of seven dialogues that ends with the *Apology*, *Crito*, and *Phaedo* begins with the *Theaetetus*, the first work in a trilogy completed by the *Sophist* and *Statesman*. That progression is interrupted, however, by the *Euthyphro*, though the action of the dialogue should place it in a final quartet, introducing Socrates' trial, imprisonment, and death. Plato's choice to insert it instead into the "theoretical" trilogy must be due, then, to the speeches of the dialogue, and the question of the holy they address.

52 When Crito comes to the Athenian prison to exhort Socrates to save his life, he reproaches him not only for refusing the opportunity to escape, but for having conducted the trial as he did and allowing it to come to court in the first place (*Crito* 45e–46a). Socrates' conversation with Theaetetus had already motivated him to come to the Stoa of the King and receive the indictment against him; his conversation with Euthyphro drives him on to the trial.

53 See *Apology* 23b, 30a, 30d–31a. The divine sign Socrates credits with guiding him is the silence of the *daimonion*, which has ceased to intervene and preserve his life in the city (see n.12 above). If, like Menelaus, Socrates can now proceed on his homeward journey, it is not to the marketplace of Athens, but to Hades, "the invisible place" (*aidēs*) that is the natural home of the philosopher (*Phaedo* 80d).

54 Alcibiades declares Socrates so absolutely unique that he can be compared to no other, ancient or contemporary—unless, perhaps, the Silenuses and Satyrs, which furnish such a vivid image (*Symposium* 221c–d).

55 See n.13 above. Reflecting on the destruction of Dionysian tragedy by Euripides, Nietzsche remarks that the poet was, in a certain sense, just a mask through whom a divinity speaks—"not Dionysus, nor Apollo, but a completely newborn daemon, called Socrates" (*Birth of Tragedy* section 12). The dying Socrates may have become "the new ideal, never seen before, of the noble Greek youth," which in particular inspired the young Plato (13); but if Socrates is the "turning point and vortex of so-called world history" (15), that is the result of the image constructed by Plato.

56 See *Sophist* 216a–d. More specifically, Socrates observes that the philosophers appear sometimes as sophists and sometimes as statesmen, thus setting up the particular questions for the pair of dialogues that follow, which ultimately ask, What is the philosopher?

Bibliography

Editions and Translations

Archer-Hind, R.D., ed. *The Phaedo of Plato*. Edited with Introduction, Notes and Appendices. 2nd ed. London: Macmillan, 1894.

Bluck, R.S., ed. *Plato's Phaedo: A Translation of Plato's Phaedo with Introduction, Notes and Appendices*. London: Routledge & Kegan Paul, 1955.

Brann, Eva, with Peter Kalkavage, and Eric Salem, eds. *Plato's Phaedo: Translation, Introduction and Glossary*. Newburyport, MA: Focus and R. Pullins, 1998.

Burnet, John, ed. *Plato's Phaedo*. Edited with Introduction and Notes. Oxford: Clarendon Press, 1911.

Fowler, Harold North, ed. and trans. *Phaedo*. In *Plato*. Vol. 1. Loeb Classical Library. 1914; Cambridge, MA: Harvard University Press, 1999.

Gallop, David, ed. *Plato Phaedo*. Translated with Notes. Oxford: Clarendon Press, 1975.

Geddes, W.D., ed. *The Phaedo of Plato*. Edited with Introduction and Notes. 2nd ed. London: Macmillan, 1885.

Grewal, Gwenda-lin, trans. *Plato's Phaedo*. Center for Hellenic Studies, Harvard University. Online, 2018.

Hackforth, R., ed. *Plato's Phaedo*. Translation with Introduction and Commentary. Cambridge: Cambridge University Press, 1972.

Loriaux, Robert, S.J., ed. *Le Phédon de Platon: Commentaire et traduction*. 2 vols. Namur: Secrétariat des publications, Facultés universitaires, 1969.

Robin, Léon, ed. *Œuvres complètes*. Vol. 4, Part 1. *Phédon*. Text prepared and translated by Paul Vicaire. Collection Budé. Paris: Collections des Universités de France Série Grecque, 1926.

Primary Sources

I have used the Loeb Classical Library editions of the following Greek and Latin texts, sometimes adapting the translations: Aristophanes, *Clouds*; Aristotle, *Athenian Constitution, De Anima, Metaphysics, Nicomachean Ethics, On Generation and Corruption, Physics, Politics, Rhetoric*; Aulus Gellius, *Attic Nights*; Cicero, *De Finibus, Tusculan Disputations*; Diogenes Laertius, *Lives of Eminent Philosophers*; Herodotus, *Histories*; Hesiod, *Theogony*; Homer, *Iliad, Odyssey*; Plato, *Apology, Crito, Euthydemus, Euthyphro, Gorgias, Hippias Major, Lysis, Meno, Parmenides, Phaedo, Philebus, Protagoras, Republic, Sophist, Statesman, Symposium, Theaetetus, Timaeus*; Plutarch, *Lives*; Xenophon, *Apology of Socrates, Memorabilia*.

Alfarabi. *The Attainment of Happiness, Philosophy of Plato and Philosophy of Aristotle*. Translated by Muhsin Mahdi. 1962; Ithaca: Cornell University Press, 1969.
———. *The Political Writings*. Vol. 2. *Political Regime and Plato's Laws*. Translated, annotated, and with Introductions by Charles Butterworth. Ithaca: Cornell University Press, 2015.
Aristophanes. *Clouds*. In *Four Texts on Socrates*, translated with notes by Thomas G. West and Grace Starry West. Introduction by Thomas G. West. Ithaca: Cornell University Press, 1984.
Aristotle. *Aristotle's Nicomachean Ethics*. Translated, with an interpretive essay, notes, and glossary by Robert C. Bartlett and Susan D. Collins. Chicago: University of Chicago Press, 2011.
Diels, Hermann, ed. [DK.] *Die Fragmente der Vorsokratiker*. Revised edition by Walther Kranz. 6th ed. 3 vols. Berlin: Weidmann, 1951–1952.
Fustel de Coulanges, Numa Denis. *The Ancient City: A Study on the Religion, Laws, and Institutions of Greece and Rome*. Translated by Willard Small. Boston: Lee and Shepard, 1874.
Halevi, Judah. *The Kuzari: An Argument for the Faith of Israel*. Translated by Hartwig Hirschfeld. New York: Schocken Books, 1964.
Hegel, Georg. *Vorlesungen über die Geschichte der Philosophie: Erster Teil*. In *Theorie Werkausgabe*. Vol. 19. Frankfurt: Suhrkamp, 1971.
Maimonides. *Eight Chapters*. In *Ethical Writings of Maimonides*, edited and translated by Raymond Weiss and Charles Butterworth. 1975; New York: Dover, 1983.
———. *The Guide of the Perplexed*. Translated by Shlomo Pines. Chicago: University of Chicago Press, 1963.

Mendelssohn, Moses. *Phädon, Oder über die Unsterblichkeit der Seele, in drey Gesprächen*. In *Gesammelte Schriften: Jubiläumsausgabe; Schriften zur Philosophie*, Vol. 3.1. Edited by Fritz Bamberger and Leo Strauss, with Introduction to *Phädon* by Strauss. Berlin: Frommann-Holzboog, 1972 (1932).

Nietzsche, Friedrich. *The Birth of Tragedy*. Translated by Walter Kaufman. New York: Random House, 1967.

_____. *Werke in Drei Bänden*. Edited by Karl Schlechta. Munich: Karl Hanser, 1966.

Plato. *Euthyphro, Apology, and Crito*. In *Four Texts on Socrates*, translated with notes by Thomas G. West and Grace Starry West. Introduction by Thomas G. West. Ithaca: Cornell University Press, 1984.

_____. *Laws*. Translated with notes and interpretive essay by Thomas Pangle. Ithaca: Cornell University Press, 1987.

_____. *Philebus*. In *The Tragedy and Comedy of Life: Plato's Philebus*. Translation and commentary by Seth Benardete. Chicago: University of Chicago Press, 1993.

_____. *The Republic of Plato*. Translated with an interpretive essay by Allan Bloom. New York: Basic Books, 1979.

_____. *Theaetetus, Sophist, and Statesman*. In *The Being of the Beautiful*. Parts I, II, and III. Translation and commentary by Seth Benardete. Chicago: University of Chicago Press, 1984.

Schleiermacher, Friedrich. *Platons Werke*. Berlin: Georg Reimer, 1861.

Westerink, L.G., ed. and trans. *Anonymous Prolegomena to Platonic Philosophy*. Amsterdam: North-Holland, 1962.

_____. *The Greek Commentators on Plato's Phaedo*. Vol. 1, *Olympiodorus*; vol. 2, *Damascius*. Amsterdam: North-Holland, 1976, 1977.

Secondary Sources—Books

Ahrensdorf, Peter. *The Death of Socrates and the Life of Philosophy: An Interpretation of Plato's Phaedo*. Albany: SUNY Press, 1995.

Bailey, Jesse I. *Logos and Psyche in the Phaedo*. Lanham, MD: Rowman & Littlefield, 2018.

Benardete, Seth. *The Being of the Beautiful*. Part I: *Plato's Theaetetus*; Part II: *Plato's Sophist*; Part III: *Plato's Statesman*. (See Primary Sources.)

_____. *Herodotean Inquiries*. The Hague: Martinus Nijhoff, 1969.

_____. *Plato's Laws: The Discovery of Being*. Chicago: University of Chicago Press, 2001.

_____. *Sacred Transgressions: A Reading of Sophocles' Antigone*. South Bend: St. Augustine's Press, 1999. Originally published in three parts in *Interpretation*, 1975.

_____. *Socrates' Second Sailing: On Plato's Republic*. Chicago: University of Chicago Press, 1989.

Bloom, Allan. *The Republic of Plato*. Translation with notes and interpretative essay. New York: Basic Books, 1968.

Brague, Remi. *La Loi de Dieu: Histoire philosophique d'une alliance*. Paris: Gallimard, 2005.

Bröcker, Walter. *Platos Gespräche*. Frankfurt: Klostermann, 1964.

Bruell, Christopher. *On the Socratic Education*. Lanham, MD: Rowman & Littlefield Press, 1999.

Burger, Ronna. *Aristotle's Dialogue with Socrates: On the Nicomachean Ethics*. Chicago: University of Chicago Press, 2008.

_____. *Plato's Phaedrus: A Defense of a Philosophic Art of Writing*. Tuscaloosa: University of Alabama Press, 1980.

Cornford, Francis M. *The Republic of Plato*. London: Oxford University Press, 1941.

Daube, David. *Law and Wisdom in the Bible*. Edited and compiled by Calum Carmichael. *David Daube's Gifford Lectures*. Vol. 2. West Conshohocken, PA: Templeton Press, 2010.

Davis, Michael. *The Soul of the Greeks: An Inquiry*. Chicago: University of Chicago Press, 2011.

Dorter, Kenneth. *Plato's Phaedo: An Interpretation*. Toronto: University of Toronto Press, 1982.

Eckstein, Jerome. *The Deathday of Socrates: Living, Dying, and Immortality — The Theater of Ideas in Plato's Phaedo*. Frenchtown, NJ: Columbia, 1981.

Frank, Erich. *Plato und die sogennanten Pythagoreer*. 2nd ed. Tübingen: Niemeyer, 1962.

Friedländer, Paul. *Platon*. 3 vols. Berlin: Walter de Gruyter, 1928.

Gadamer, Hans-Georg. *Dialogue and Dialectic: Eight Hermeneutical Studies on Plato*. Translated by Christopher Smith. New Haven: Yale University Press, 1980.

Gaiser, Konrad, ed. *Das Platonbild: Zehn Beiträge zum Platonverständnis*. Hildesheim: Georg Olms, 1969.

_____. *Platons ungeschriebene Lehre*. Stuttgart: Ernst Klett, 1962.

_____. *Protreptik und Paränese bei Platon*. Stuttgart: Kohlhammer, 1959.

Grewal, Gwenda-lin. *Thinking of Death in Plato's Euthydemus*. Oxford: Oxford University Press, 2022.

Grube, G. M. A. *Plato's Thought*. Boston: Beacon Press, 1958.

Gulley, Norman. *Plato's Theory of Knowledge*. London: Methuen, 1962.

Guthrie, W. K. C. *A History of Greek Philosophy*. Vol. 1. Cambridge: Cambridge University Press, 1957.

Hartmann, Nicolai. *Platons Logik des Seins*. Gießen: Alfred Töpelmann, 1909.

Heath, Thomas. *A History of Greek Mathematics*. Oxford: Clarendon Press, 1921.

Howland, Jacob. *The Paradox of Political Philosophy*. Lanham, MD: Rowman & Littlefield, 1997.

Kerber, Hannes, and Svetozar Minkov, eds. *Leo Strauss on Plato's Euthyphro. With Translation of the Euthyphro by Seth Benardete*. University Park: Pennsylvania State University Press, 2023.

Klein, Jacob. *A Commentary on Plato's Meno*. Chapel Hill: University of North Carolina Press, 1965.

_____. *Greek Mathematical Thought and the Origin of Algebra*. Translated by Eva Brann. Cambridge, MA: MIT Press, 1968.

_____. *Plato's Trilogy*. Chicago: University of Chicago Press, 1977.

Krämer, Hans Joachim. *Arete bei Platon und Aristoteles: Zum Wesen und zur Geschichte der platonischen Ontologie*. Heidelberg: Carl Winter Universitätsverlag, 1959.

Lampert, Laurence. *How Socrates Became Socrates: A Study of Plato's Phaedo, Parmenides, and Symposium*. Chicago: University of Chicago Press, 2021.

Meier, Heinrich. *Leo Strauss and the Theological-Political Problem*. Translated by Marcus Brainard. Cambridge: Cambridge University Press, 2006.

Morrow, Glenn. *Plato's Cretan City: A Historical Interpretation of the Laws*. Princeton: Princeton University Press, 1960.

Natorp, Paul. *Platos Ideenlehre*. Leipzig: Felix Meiner, 1921.

Nichols, Mary. *Socrates on Friendship and Community: Reflections on Plato's Symposium, Phaedrus, and Lysis*. Cambridge: Cambridge University Press, 2009.

Prauss, Gerold. *Platon und der logische Eleatismus*. Berlin: Walter de Gruyter, 1966.

Priou, Alex. *Becoming Socrates: Political Philosophy in Plato's Parmenides*. Rochester: University of Rochester Press, 2018.

_____. *Defending Socrates: Political Philosophy Before the Tribunal of Science*. Macon: Mercer University Press, 2023.

Robinson, Richard. *Plato's Earlier Dialectic*. Oxford: Clarendon Press, 1953.

Romero, M. Ross, S.J. *Without the Least Tremor: The Sacrifice of Socrates in Plato's Phaedo.* Albany: SUNY Press, 2016.

Rosen, Stanley. *Plato's Symposium.* New Haven: Yale University Press, 1968.

Ross, W. D. *Plato's Theory of Ideas.* Oxford: Clarendon Press, 1961.

Sayre, Kenneth. *Plato's Analytic Method.* Chicago: University of Chicago Press, 1969.

Sebell, Dustin. *The Socratic Turn: Knowledge of Good and Evil in an Age of Science.* Philadelphia: University of Pennsylvania Press, 2015.

Stern, Paul. *Socratic Rationalism and Political Philosophy: An Interpretation of Plato's Phaedo.* Albany: SUNY Press, 1993.

Strauss, Leo. *The Argument and the Action of Plato's Laws.* Chicago: University of Chicago Press, 1975.

_____. *The City and Man.* Chicago: University of Chicago Press, 1964.

_____. *Socrates and Aristophanes.* New York: Basic Books, 1966.

Taylor, A. E. *Plato: The Man and His Work.* London: Methuen, 1926.

Wedberg, Anders. *Plato's Philosophy of Mathematics.* Stockholm: Almquist and Wiksell, 1955.

Wippern, Jürgen, ed. *Das Problem der ungeschriebenen Lehre Platons.* Darmstadt: Wissenschaftliche Buchgesellschaft, 1972.

Zuckert, Catherine. *Plato's Philosophers: The Coherence of the Dialogues.* Chicago: University of Chicago Press, 2009.

Secondary Sources—Articles

Ackrill, J. L. "Anamnesis in the *Phaedo*: Remarks on 73c–75c." In *Exegesis and Argument, Phronesis* Supplementary Vol. 1 (1973): 175–95.

Allen, R. E. "Participation and Predication in Plato's Middle Dialogues." *Philosophical Review* 69/2 (1960): 147–64.

Appelbaum, Seth. "The World-to-Come in Maimonides' Introduction to Pereq Helcq." In *Nature, Law, and the Sacred*, edited by Evanthia Speliotis. Macon: Mercer University Press, 2019.

Benardete, Seth. "The Crimes and Arts of Prometheus." 1964. In *The Archaeology of the Soul: Platonic Readings of Ancient Poetry and Philosophy*, edited by Ronna Burger and Michael Davis, 30–40. South Bend: St. Augustine's Press, 2012.

_____. "On Greek Tragedy." 1980. In *The Argument of the Action: Essays on Greek Poetry and Philosophy*, edited by Ronna Burger and Michael Davis, 99–145. Chicago: University of Chicago Press, 2000.

_____. "On Plato's *Phaedo*." 1980. In *The Argument of the Action*, 277–96.

_____. "On Plato's *Symposium*." 1994. In *The Argument of the Action*, 167–85.

_____. "On Plato's *Timaeus* and Timaeus' Science Fiction." 1971. In *The Archaeology of the Soul*, 141–82.

_____. "Plato's *Parmenides*: A Sketch." 2001. In *The Archaeology of the Soul*, 229–43.

_____. "Plato's *Theaetetus*: On the Way of the *Logos*." 1997. In *The Argument of the Action*, 297–322.

_____. "Socrates and Plato: The Dialectics of *Eros*." 2000. In *The Archaeology of the Soul*, 244–60.

Berman, Robert. "The Socratic Principle and the Problem of Punishment." In *The Eccentric Core: The Thought of Seth Benardete*, edited by Ronna Burger and Patrick Goodin, 125–42. South Bend: St. Augustine's Press, 2018.

_____. "Ways of Being Singular: The Logic of Individuality." *Cardozo Public Law, Policy, and Ethics Journal* 2/1 (2004). Reprinted in *Hegel's Theory of the Subject*, edited by D. G. Carlson. London: Palgrave Macmillan, 2005.

Blits, Jan. "The Holy and the Human: An Interpretation of Plato's *Euthyphro*." *Apeiron* 14/1 (1980): 19–40.

Brentlinger, John. "Incomplete Predicates and the Two-World Theory of the *Phaedo*." *Phronesis* 17/1 (1972): 61–79.

Bolotin, David. "The Life of Philosophy and the Immortality of the Soul: An Introduction to Plato's *Phaedo*." *Ancient Philosophy* 7 (1987): 39–56.

Bruell, Christopher. "Der Tod aus der Sicht der Philosophie." In *Der Tod im Leben, Ein Symposion*, edited by Friedrich Wilhelm Graf and Heinrich Meier. Munich: Piper Verlag, 2004.

Burger, Ronna. "Eros and Mind: Aristotle on Philosophic Friendship and the Cosmos of Life." *Epoché* 23/2 (2019): 365–80.

_____. "The Thumotic Soul." *Epoché* 7/2 (2003): 151–68.

Castañeda, Hector-Neri. "Plato's Relations, Not Essences or Accidents, at *Phaedo* 102b2–d2." *Canadian Journal of Philosophy* 8/1 (1978): 39–53.

Cornford, F. M. "Mysticism and Science in the Pythagorean Tradition." *Classical Quarterly* 16, no. 3/4 (1922): 137–50.

Davis, Michael. "Philosophy and the Question of Being in Aristotle's *Metaphysics A*." In *The Autobiography of Philosophy*. Lanham, MD: Rowman & Littlefield, 1999.

_____. "Plato and Nietzsche on Death: An Introduction to Plato's *Phaedo*." *Ancient Philosophy* 1 (1980): 69–80.

_____. "Socrates' Pre-Socratism: Some Remarks on the Structure of Plato's *Phaedo*." *Review of Metaphysics* 33/3 (1980): 559–77.

Derrida, Jacques. "La Pharmacie de Plato." In *La Dissémination*. Paris: Éditions du Seuil, 1972.

Duplessie, Derek. "Socrates' Analysis of Comedy in Plato's *Philebus*." *Review of Metaphysics* 74/1 (2020): 3–20.

Gallop, David. "Castañeda on *Phaedo* 102b–d." *Canadian Journal of Philosophy* 8/1 (1978): 55–57.

Gooch, P. D. "Plato's Antapodosis Argument for the Soul's Immortality: *Phaedo* 70–72." *Proceedings of the Seventh Inter-Amerian Congress of Philosophy*, 2:239–44. Québec: Les Presses de L'Université Laval, 1968.

Hager, M. E. "Philolaus and the Even-Odd." *Classical Review* 12/1 (1962): 1–2.

Haynes, Richard P. "The form equality, as a set of equals: *Phaedo* 74b–c." *Phronesis* 9/1 (1964): 17–26.

Hicken, W. F. "*Phaedo* 93a11–94b3." *Classical Quarterly* 4, no. 1/2 (1954): 16–22.

Keyt, David. "The Fallacies in Plato's *Phaedo* 102a–107b." *Phronesis* 8/2 (1963): 167–72.

Kirwan, Christopher. "Plato and Relativity." *Phronesis* 19/2 (1974): 123–27.

Klein, Jacob. "Plato's *Phaedo*." *Journal of St. John's College* (January 1975): 1–10.

Meier, Heinrich. "Why Leo Strauss? Four Answers and One Consideration Concerning the Uses and Disadvantages of the School for the Philosophical Life." *American Dialectic* 1/1 (2011): 192–205.

Mills, K. W. "Plato's *Phaedo* 74b7–c6." *Phronesis* 2/2 (1957): 128–47, 3/1 (1958): 40–58.

Morrison, J. S. "The Shape of the Earth in Plato's *Phaedo*." *Phronesis* 4/2 (1959): 101–19.

O'Brien, David. "The Last Argument of Plato's *Phaedo*. I." *Classical Quarterly* 17 (1967): 198–231. And "The Last Argument of Plato's *Phaedo*. II." *Classical Quarterly* 18 (1968): 95–106.

_____. "A Metaphor in Plato: 'Running Away' and 'Staying Behind' in the *Phaedo* and *Timaeus*." *Classical Quarterly* 27 (1977): 297–99.

Owen, G. E. L. "A Proof in the 'Peri Ideon'." In *Studies in Plato's Metaphysics*, edited by R. E. Allen. London: Routledge & Kegan Paul, 1965.

Plass, Paul. "Socrates' Method of Hypothesis in the *Phaedo*." *Phronesis* 5/2 (1960): 103–15.

Reynen, Hans. "Phaidon Interpretationen: zu Plat. *Phaed.* 62a und 69a–b." *Hermes* 96/1 (1968): 41–60.

Rist, J. M. "Equals and Intermediaries in Plato." *Phronesis* 9/1 (1964): 27–37.

Rosen, Stanley. "Socrates' Hypothesis." In *The Question of Being.* New Haven: Yale University Press, 1993.

_____. "Thought and Touch: A Note on Aristotle's *De Anima.*" *Phronesis* 6/2 (1961): 127–37.

Schaerer, René. "La Composition du *Phédon.*" *Revue des Études Grècques* 53/249 (1940): 1–50.

Shipton, K. M. W. "A good second-best: *Phaedo* 99b ff." *Phronesis* 24/1 (1979): 33–53.

Speliotis, Evanthia. "Enlightened Piety in Sophocles' *Antigone.*" In *Nature, Law, and the Sacred,* edited by Evanthia Speliotis. Macon: Mercer University Press, 2019.

Strauss, Leo. "Farabi's Plato." In *Louis Ginzberg Jubilee Volume,* 357-93. New York: American Academy for Jewish Research, 1945.

_____. "The Law of Reason in the *Kuzari.*" In *Persecution and the Art of Writing.* Glencoe, IL: Free Press, 1952.

_____. "Maimonides' Statement on Political Science." In *What is Political Philosophy? and Other Studies.* Westport, CT: Greenwood Press, 1959.

_____. "The Origins of Political Science and the Problem of Socrates." Edited by David Bolotin, Christopher Bruell, and Thomas Pangle. *Interpretation* 23/2 (Winter 1996): 127–208.

_____. "On Plato's *Apology of Socrates* and *Crito.*" In *Studies in Platonic Political Philosophy.* With an introduction by Thomas Pangle. Chicago: University of Chicago Press, 1963.

_____. "On Plato's *Euthyphro.*" In *Leo Strauss on Plato's Euthyphro: The 1948 Notebook.* Edited with an introduction by Hannes Kerber and Svetozar Minkov; and with a translation of the *Euthyphro* by Seth Benardete. University Park: Pennsylvania State University Press, 2023. Previously published as "An Untitled Lecture on Plato's *Euthyphro*" (1952 Strauss lecture), edited by David Bolotin, Christopher Bruell, and Thomas Pangle. *Interpretation* 24/1 (1996): 5–23.

_____. "Progress or Return?" In *The Rebirth of Classical Political Rationalism.* Selected and introduced by Thomas Pangle. Chicago: University of Chicago Press, 1989.

_____. "Restatement on Xenophon's *Hiero.*" In *What is Political Philosophy? and Other Studies.*

Taylor, A. E. "The Words *Eidos, Idea* in pre-Platonic Literature." *Varia Socratica*. 1st ser. Oxford: James Parker, 1911.

Velkley, Richard. "On Possessed Individualism: Hegel, Socrates' *Daimon*, and the Modern State." *Review of Metaphysics* 59/3 (2006): 577–99.

Vlastos, Gregory. "Reasons and Causes in the *Phaedo*." *Philosophical Review* 78/3 (1969): 291–325.

Wagner, Hans. "Die Eigenart der Ideenlehre in Platons *Phaedo*." *Kant-Studien* 57/1–4 (1966): 5–16.

_____. "Platos *Phaedo* und der Beginn der Metaphysik als Wissenschaft." In *Kritik und Metaphysik: Studien*, edited by Friedrich Kaulbach and Joachim Ritter. Berlin: Walter de Gruyter, 1966.

Wedin, Michael. "*Auta ta Isa* and the Argument at *Phaedo* 74b7–c5." *Phronesis* 22, no. 3 (1977): 191–205.

Wolfe, Julian. "Plato's Cyclical Argument for Immortality." *Proceedings of the Seventh Inter-American Congress of Philosophy*, 2:251–54. Québec: Les Presses de L'Université Laval, 1968.

Name Index

Subject Index

78, 157, 162, 169, 189n21; as
measure of true virtue, 41–42,
112, 131, 174–75; as thoughtfulness in action, xxxii–xxxi-
iin16, 189n21, 193n29. *See also
under* Eros; Imprudence: of
Socrates
Piety. *See under* Holy (the);
Justice; Philosophy
Plato, works of: *Apology*, xxiii,
xxvi, xxixn2, xxxiin15,
xxxviin31, xxxviiin36, 46,
190nn4, 14, 191n1, 194nn3, 6,
195n25, 196n32, 197nn5, 6,
198n22, 207n14, 223n15, 228,
241, 244, 249nn7, 12, 254n53;
Cratylus, xxixn2, 193nn24, 27,
194n11, 201n15, 202n21,
203n18, 211n29, 212n39; *Crito*,
xii, xxix, xxixn2, xxxiin15,
xxxviiin36, xlin49, 7, 23,
191nn24, 1, 222n9, 223n17,
249n12, 252n32, 254n52;
Euthydemus, xxixn2, xlin47,
190n12, 195n15; *Euthyphro*,
xxixn2, 224n36, 227–48,
254nn50, 51, 52; *Gorgias*,
189n23, 193n27, 194n3, 197n4,
221nn44, 45; *Hippias Major*,
xxxin9, 197n14, 212nn38, 42;
Laws, xlin48–49, 191n18,
195n15, 199n39, 221n45,
221nn46, 47, 48, 223nn22, 26,
250n16, 251n24, 252n36, 253–
54n47, 254n48; *Lysis*, xlin48,
190n12, 223n20; *Meno*, 192n17,
197n4, 200n3, 207n5, 253n42;
Parmenides, xxiv–xxv, xxixn3,
xxxvin30, xxxvi–xxxviin31,

189n1, 215–16n18, 217n32;
Phaedrus, xxxin7, xxxiin12,
xxxvn27, xlin48, 190n15,
197nn3, 8, 199n39, 203n12,
222n11, 223n16, 253n38;
Philebus, xxxin7, xxxin10,
xxxiin13, xxxvn24, xxxviiin33,
xlin48, 192nn7, 10, 195n22,
196n29, 200n8, 201n12,
209n22, 210n26, 223n27,
249n11; *Protagoras*, 196n30,
197n4, 221n45, 251n23; *Republic*, xxxiiinn19–20, xxxvn24,
xlin48, 192n10, 192n17,
195n18, 195n25, 196nn39, 1,
200n5, 206nn8, 14, 207nn3, 5,
208nn11, 19, 210nn14, 16,
211n31, 214n2, 216n20,
219n16, 219n17, 220nn23, 25,
221n45, 223nn16, 25, 229, 235,
249nn6, 7, 9, 249n12, 250n14,
250n14, 253n40, 254n48;
Sophist, xxvii, xxixn2, xxxn5,
xxxvin29, xxxviin31, xxxviii35,
xln42, xlin48, 195n15, 197n3,
211n35, 213n52, 214n54,
222n2, 254n51, 254n56; *Statesman*, xxixn2, xxxiiin18,
xxxviin31, xxxviii35, 196n35,
210n26, 213n50, 222n11;
248n1, 254n51; *Symposium*,
xxiv, xxixn3, xxxviinn30–31,
xxxviii–xxxixn37, xlin48, 189–
90n1, 192n17, 198n20, 205n10,
205n19, 222n13, 223n20,
224n29, 254n54; *Theaetetus*, xii,
xxiv, xxv–xxviii, xxixn2, xxix–
xxxn3, xxxvin29, xxxviiin35,
xxxixn41, xlin48, 189–90n1,